ASIAN HISTORICAL DICTIONARIES
Edited by Jon Woronoff

1. *Vietnam,* by William J. Duiker. 1989
2. *Bangladesh,* by Craig Baxter and Syedur Rahman. 1989
3. *Pakistan,* by Shahid Javed Burki. 1991
4. *Jordan,* by Peter Gubser. 1991
5. *Afghanistan,* by Ludwig W. Adamec. 1991
6. *Laos,* by Martin Stuart-Fox and Mary Kooyman. 1992
7. *Singapore,* by K. Mulliner and Lian The-Mulliner. 1991
8. *Israel,* by Bernard Reich. 1992
9. *Indonesia,* by Robert Cribb. 1992
10. *Hong Kong and Macau,* by Elfed Vaughan Roberts, Sum Ngai Ling, and Peter Bradshaw. 1992
11. *Korea,* by Andrew C. Nahm. 1993
12. *Taiwan,* by John F. Copper. 1993
13. *Malaysia,* by Amarjit Kaur. 1993
14. *Saudi Arabia,* by J. E. Peterson. 1993
15. *Myanmar,* by Jan Bečka. 1995
16. *Iran,* by John H. Lorentz. 1995
17. *Yemen,* by Robert D. Burrowes. 1995

UNION OF MYANMAR — STATES AND DIVISIONS

Map Labels

- INDIA
- BANGLADESH
- CHINA
- LAOS
- THAILAND
- KACHIN STATE — Myitkyina
- SAGAING DIVISION — Sagaing
- CHIN STATE — Haka
- MANDALAY DIVISION — Mandalay
- SHAN STATE — Taunggyi
- RAKHINE STATE — Sittwe
- MAGWAY DIVISION — Magway
- KAYAH STATE — Loikaw
- BAGO DIVISION — Bago
- KAYIN STATE — Hpa-An
- AYEYARWADY DIVISION — Pathein
- YANGON DIVISION — YANGON
- MON STATE — Mawlamyine
- TANINTHARYI DIVISION — Dawei
- BAY OF BENGAL
- ANDAMAN SEA
- GULF OF MARTABAN
- GULF OF THAILAND

Legend

- —·—·— international boundary
- ------ state or division boundary
- ◉ Capital of Country
- • Capital of State or Division

Scale: 0, 100, 200, 300 km / 0, 50, 100, 150, 200 miles

N ↑

HISTORICAL DICTIONARY OF MYANMAR

by
Jan Bečka

Asian Historical Dictionaries, No. 15

The Scarecrow Press, Inc.
Lanham, Md., & London
1995

British Library Cataloguing-in-Publication data available

Library of Congress Cataloging-in-Publication Data

Bečka, Jan.
    Historical dictionary of Myanmar / by Jan Bečka.
      p.   cm. — (Asian historical dictionaries : no. 15)
    Includes bibliographical references.
    ISBN 0-8108-2840-5 (acid-free paper)
    1. Burma—History—Dictionaries.   I. Title.   II. Series.
DS528.34.B43   1995
959.1'003—dc20   93-48303

Copyright © 1995 by Jan Bečka
Manufactured in the United States of America

Printed on acid-free paper

CONTENTS

Union of Myanmar — States and Divisions	
Editor's Foreword (Jon Woronoff)	iv
Acknowledgments	vi
Note on Romanization and Terms	vii
Guide to Former and Current Names	ix
Abbreviations and Acronyms	xi
Chronology of Myanmar History	xiv
Map of Union of Myanmar	xxii
Introduction	1
THE DICTIONARY	9
Bibliography	222
About the Author	328

EDITOR'S FOREWORD

To those who have visited even briefly, Myanmar—still remembered as Burma—is one of the most attractive and intriguing places in Asia. It has vast potential for economic growth thanks to its natural resources. And its human resources are equally promising. Indeed, it was expected that after independence the country would do as well as most and better than those less endowed. Yet, several decades later, it has failed to make much progress economically and has, if anything, slipped back politically.

The not very comforting story of postwar Myanmar is elucidated in this historical dictionary. True to its name, it also reaches much further back, shedding light on earlier periods, whether the British colonial era, the age of the three empires, or even what preceded that. Going beyond history, politics and economics, there are many interesting entries on Myanmar's culture and religion. This is rounded out by an extensive chronology and comprehensive bibliography. All of this material is useful for those who want to know more. But the most important sections remain those dealing with contemporary Myanmar. For this country, once known for its hospitality, has closed itself to the world to such an extent that it is often easier to find information on the past than the present.

Fortunately, the *Historical Dictionary of Myanmar* was written by a specialist with several decades of experience. Jan Bečka studied at the University of Rangoon, in what was then Burma, in 1958–1960. Ever since, he has followed events there and returned for periodic visits.

Over the years, he has written broadly on Myanmar, with some emphasis on the national liberation movement, military rule, foreign policy, ideology and religion. Dr. Bečka, who has long been a researcher (and then senior researcher) at the Oriental Institute in Prague, is now also Head of the Department of South Asia.

Jon Woronoff
Series Editor

ACKNOWLEDGMENTS

Mrs. Anna J. Allott, Lecturer in Burmese of the School of Oriental and African Studies (SOAS) at the University of London, introduced me to the project of historical dictionaries and recommended me as author of the Myanmar (Burma) volume to the editor of the series. During the preparation of this volume, I have received help directly or indirectly from several people. Professor R. H. Taylor, Pro-Director of SOAS, offered a great deal of assistance by providing me with some recent publications and materials on Myanmar. Professor John W. Okell of SOAS gave me his suggestions on the romanization of Myanmar names and terms. I also received advice on the usage of geographic terms relating to Myanmar in the United States from the United States Board on Geographic Names. My great thanks are due to Daw May Kyi Win, Curator, Southeast Asian Collection, Founder Memorial Library, Northern Illinois University, DeKalb, who kindly contributed to updating the bibliography part of the dictionary and offered other useful information. The author wishes to thank his wife, Stanislava, and his son, Jan, who assisted in various ways in compiling the volume. The previous works of numerous scholars and their publications have been important to me, particularly Joel M. Maring and Ester G. Maring, *Historical and Cultural Dictionary of Burma*, published by Scarecrow Press.

NOTE ON ROMANIZATION AND TERMS

Although there have been various attempts at rendering the Myanmar script in the Roman alphabet, there still exists no standard, generally accepted and scientific system of romanization. The author of this dictionary therefore decided (despite its drawbacks and inconsistencies) to employ, more or less, the traditional romanization of Myanmar names and expressions which has been used in historical writings on Myanmar in the English language.

On 18 June 1989, the present military government of Myanmar, the State Law and Order Restoration Council (SLORC), issued a ruling whereby the official name of the country in English—Burma—was altered to Myanmar, which is the transcription of the official name of the country in the Myanmar language used since independence in 1948. The traditional English spelling of many towns, divisions, states, rivers as well as ethnic groups had been changed earlier, such as Rangoon to Yangon, Arakan to Rakhine, Irrawaddy to Ayeyarwady, etc. These new official terms are used in the dictionary, except in referring to specific institutions, organizations or events. For the convenience of readers, reference is provided from old terms to new ones throughout the volume. There is also a partial list of former and current names on page ix.

As a rule, the Myanmars do not use Christian names. There are also no family names (surnames) in the Western sense of this term. Each Myanmar surname is separate and independent. Men and women, parents and children, married couples and young people cannot be differentiated by their names. Myanmar women keep their maiden name after marriage and a child's name is not related to the parents' name. A Myanmar personal name consists of one or more syllables. It is usually chosen according to the day when a person was born. Certain letters of the alphabet are ascribed to each day and the naming ceremony takes place shortly after the child's birth. The titles are prefixed to personal names, to denote sex, age and social status. *Maung* (originally meaning "younger brother") is generally used toward persons who are younger or of an inferior status. *Ko* (meaning "elder brother") is usually used among persons of the same age and status when addressing one another. *U* (derived from *ulei,* meaning "uncle") is reserved for persons of superior age or social position. When referring to himself, a person usually drops affixes, or addresses himself as *Maung,* out of modesty. For women, the titles are *Ma* and *Daw,* the former denoting a younger woman and the latter an older or married woman. Aside from these honorific prefixes, others, such as military, political or academic titles, may be prefixed to a name. As a result, a person whose name is *Nu* may be referred to, in different contexts, as *Maung Nu, Ko Nu, Thakin Nu, U Nu,* etc.

In this dictionary, Myanmar personal names are entered in direct order; all titles, including honorifics (such as *U, Daw*), are listed after personal names, divided from them by a comma. In the text of the dictionary, however, personal Myanmar names are occasionally quoted without any honorifics, with no discourtesy intended.

GUIDE TO FORMER AND CURRENT NAMES

FORMER NAME	CURRENT NAME
Akyab	Sittwe
Arakan State	Rakhine State
Arakan Yoma	Rakhine Yoma
Ava	Inwa
Bassein (town)	Pathein (town)
Bassein River	Pathein River
Burma	Myanmar
Chindwin River	Chindwinn River
Irrawaddy Delta	Ayeyarwady Delta
Division	Division
River	River
Karen State	Kayin State
Kyaukpyu	Kyaukphyu
Magwe (town)	Magway (town)
Magwe Division	Magway Division
Maymyo	Pyin-Oo-Lwin
Mergui	Beik
Moulmein	Mawlamyine
Pa-an	Hpa-an
Pagan	Bagan
Pegu (town)	Bago (town)
Pegu Division	Bago Division
Pegu River	Bago River
Pegu Yoma	Bago Yoma
Prome	Pyay
Rangoon (city)	Yangon (city)
Rangoon Division	Yangon Division
Rangoon River	Yangon River
Salween River	Thanlwin River

Guide to Former and Current Names

Sittang River	Sittoung River
Syriam	Thanlyin
Tavoy	Dawei
Tenasserim Division	Tanintharyi Division
Union of Burma	Union of Myanmar; Myanma(r) Naing Ngan; Myanmar Naingngandaw

ABBREVIATIONS AND ACRONYMS

ABFSU	All Burma Federation of Students Union
ABPO	All Burma Peasants' Organization
ABSDF	All Burma Students' Democratic Front
ABSU	All Burma Students' Union
ABTUC	All Burma Trade Union Congress
ABYL	All Burma Youth League
AFO	Anti-Fascist Organization
AFPFL	Anti-Fascist People's Freedom League
AIO	Arakan Independence Organization
aka	also known as
ALP	Arakan Liberation Party
ANC	Arakan National Congress
ANLP	Arakan National Liberation Party
ANUO	Arakan (Arakanese) National United Organization
ASEAN	Association of Southeast Asian Nations
BDA	Burma Defence Army
BIA	Burma Independence Army
BNA	Burma National Army
BNDAA	Burma National Democratic Alliance Army
BOC	Burmah Oil Company
BPCC	Burma Provincial Congress Committee
BSPP	Burma Socialist Programme Party
BTUC	Burma Trade Union Congress
BWPP	Burma Workers' and Peasants' Party
CAS(B)	Civil Affairs Service (Burma)
CC	Central Committee
CNA	Chin National Army
CNF	Chin National Front
CPA	Communist Party of Arakan
CPB	Communist Party of Burma
CP (RF)	Communist Party (Red Flag)

xii/ Abbreviations and Acronyms

DAB	Democratic Alliance of Burma
DPNS	Democratic Party for New Society
DSI	Defence Services Institute
EC	European Community
EC	Executive Committee/Council
FNDF	Federal National Democratic Front
FRG	Federal Republic of Germany
GCBA	General Council of Burmese Associations
GCSS	General Council of Sangha Sammeggi
GDP	Gross Domestic Product
K	*kyat*
KCO	Karen Central Organization
KIO/KIA	Kachin Independence Organization/Army
KMT	Kuomintang
KNA	Karen National Association
KNDO	Karen National Defence Organization
KNLA	Karen National Liberation Army
KNLC	Karen National Liberation Council
KNLP	Kayan/Karen New Land Party
KNPP	Karenni National Progressive Party
KNU	Karen National Union
KNUF	Karen National United Front
KNUP	Karen National United Party
KPLA	Kawthoolei People's Liberation Army
KRC	Karen/Kawthoolei Revolutionary Council
KSNLF	Karenni State Nationalities Liberation Front
KYO	Karen Youth Organization
LNO	Lahu National Organization
LNUP	Lahu National United Party
MNDO	Mon National Defence Organization
NAM	News Agency of Myanmar
NDF	National Democratic Front
NDUF	National Democratic United Front
NKA	National Karen Association
NLD	National League for Democracy
NMSP	New Mon State Party
NNC	Naga National Council
NUF	National Unity (United) Front
NUFA	National Unity Front of Arakan
NULF	National United Liberation Front

Abbreviations and Acronyms /xiii

NUP	National Unity Party
PBF	Patriotic Burmese Forces
PCP	People's Comrade Party
PDF	People's Democratic Front
PDP	Parliamentary Democracy Party
PLA	Patriotic (People's) Liberation Army
PLAB	People's Liberation Army of Burma
PNDP	Pawngyawng National Defence Force
PNO	Pao National Organization
PPP	People's Patriotic Party
PRC	People's Republic of China
PRP	People's Revolutionary Party
PVO	People's Volunteer Organization
RBA	Revolutionary Burma Army
RC	Revolutionary Council
RUSU	Rangoon University Students' Union
SLORC	State Law and Order Restoration Council
SNUF	Shan National United Front
SRUB	Socialist Republic of the Union of Burma
SSA	Shan State Army
SSIA	Shan State Independence Army
SSNLO	Shan State Nationalities Liberation Organization
SSPP	Shan State Progress Party
SUA	Shan United Army
SURA	Shan United Revolutionary Army
TRC	Tai Revolutionary Council
TUC(B)	Trade Union Congress (Burma)
UKL	Union Karen League
UKO	Union Karen Organization
ULO	Union Labour Organization
UN	United Nations
UNDP	United Nationals Democracy Party
UNDP	United Nations Development Program
UNESCO	United Nations Educational, Scientific and Cultural Organization
UWSA	United Wa State Army
VOPB	Voice of the People of Burma
WNA	Wa National Army
YMBA	Young Men's Buddhist Association
ZNF	Zomi National Front

CHRONOLOGY OF MYANMAR HISTORY

5,000–3,000 B.C.	Anyathian culture flourishes in northern Myanmar.
c. 500 B.C.	Pyus enter the upper part of Ayeyarwady valley.
3rd Cent. B.C.	Mons settle in the Sittoung valley.
c. A.D. 0000	Pyu state of Sri Ksetra founded.
832	Conquest of Pyu capital of Halin by Tai-Shans of Nan-Chao.
9th Cent.	Bamars arrive in Dry Zone of northern Myanmar.
1057	Anawrahta conquers Thaton and founds First Myanmar Empire at Bagan.
1287	Mongol invasion of Bagan leads to fall of First Myanmar Empire.
1287	Mons establish state at Martaban.
1364	Inwa founded as capital of a Shan-Bamar dynasty in northern Myanmar.
1369	Mon capital transferred to Bago.
1385–1425	War between Inwa and Bago.
1519	Portuguese establish trading station at Martaban.
1527	Inwa sacked by the Maw Shans.
1531	Second Myanmar Empire established under Toungoo Dynasty (1531–1752).
1600–1613	Portuguese de Brito rules at Thanlyin.
1635	Myanmar capital is moved to Inwa.
17th Cent.	British, French and Dutch develop trade with Myanmar.
1752	Mons conquer Inwa, ending Second Myanmar Empire.
1755	Alaungpaya founds new dynasty and Third Myanmar Empire at Shwebo.

Chronology of Myanmar History / xv

1767	Myanmars conquer Thai capital of Ayutthaya.
1785	Rakhine is conquered by King Bodawpaya.
1824–1826	First Anglo-Myanmar war; under Treaty of Yandabo, Britain gains Rakhine and Tanintharyi.
1852	Second Anglo-Myanmar war; Britain annexes southern Myanmar.
1885	Third Anglo-Myanmar war; Britain annexes all Myanmar.
January 1, 1886	Myanmar declared part of British India.
1886–1895	Myanmars wage guerilla warfare against British in northern Myanmar.
1906	Young Men's Buddhist Association founded in Yangon.
September 1920	General Council of Burmese Associations established.
December 1920	First strike at University of Yangon.
January 1923	"Dyarchy" constitution introduced in Myanmar.
1930	*Do Bama Asi Ayon* founded in Yangon.
1930–1931	Saya San Rebellion.
1937	Myanmar is separated from India.
1938	Oil-field workers' strike.
August 15, 1939	Communist Party of Burma (CPB) founded.
October 1939	Freedom Bloc formed.
November 1940	Aung San arrives secretly in Japan.
1941	"Thirty Comrades" given military training by the Japanese at Hainan.
December 28, 1941	Burma Independence Army formed in Bangkok.
December 1941-May 1942	Japanese military campaign in Myanmar.
1942–1945	Myanmar under Japanese occupation.
August 1, 1943	Declaration of Myanmar's independence under the Japanese military.
August 1944	Anti-Fascist People's Freedom League (AFPFL) established.

March 27, 1945	Burma National Army starts anti-Japanese uprising.
May 1945	Allies reconquer most of Myanmar.
October 4, 1946	New Executive Council of British Governor, with Aung San as Deputy Chairman, is formed.
October 1946	CPB is expelled from AFPFL.
January 27, 1947	Aung San-Attlee agreement signed.
February 12, 1947	Panglong agreement signed.
April 1947	Constituent Assembly elections.
July 19, 1947	Aung San and six other members of Interim Government assassinated.
September 24, 1947	Constituent Assembly adopts new Myanmar constitution.
October 17, 1947	Nu-Attlee agreement concluded.
January 4, 1948	Myanmar regains independence (as Union of Burma) and leaves Commonwealth.
March 27, 1948	CPB goes underground and civil war begins.
1949	Kayin rebellion breaks out.
December 1949	Kuomintang troops invade Shan State.
1951	First parliamentary elections in post-independence Myanmar are held.
August 1952	*Pyidawtha* Eight-Year Plan adopted.
1956	Second parliamentary elections.
May 1958	Ruling AFPFL splits into two factions.
October 1958	Caretaker Government, headed by General Ne Win, assumes office.
January 28, 1960	Border agreement and treaty of friendship and non-aggression concluded between Myanmar and People's Republic of China (PRC)
February 1960	U Nu's *Pyidaungsu* Party wins in parliamentary elections.
August 1961	Union Parliament makes Buddhism the state religion.
March 2, 1962	Military coup brings to power the Revolutionary Council (RC) of General Ne Win.

April 30, 1962	Declaration of "Burmese Way to Socialism."
July 4, 1962	Burma Socialist Programme Party (BSPP) founded.
February 1963	Nationalization of banks and timber trade.
June-November 1963	Peace talks between RC and various rebel organizations and groups are held in Yangon.
March 28, 1964	All legal political parties and organizations except BSPP are banned.
April 1964	Nationalization of all export trade and commodity distribution.
June 1967	Anti-Chinese riots in Yangon.
August 1969	Former Prime Minister U Nu founds Parliamentary Democracy Party to fight RC from abroad.
June 28–July 11, 1971	First BSPP Congress is held and Twenty-Year Plan (1974–1994) announced.
August 1971	General Ne Win's state visit to PRC marks normalization of official relations between the two countries.
January 3, 1974	New constitution, creating "Socialist Republic of the Union of Burma," becomes effective.
March 2, 1974	RC transfers power to *Pyithu Hluttaw* (People's Assembly).
May-June 1974	Strikes by workers because of food shortages.
December 1974	Student and Buddhist monks demonstrate over former UN Secretary-General U Thant's burial site issue.
September 7, 1979	Myanmar withdraws from Non-Aligned Movement.
May 24–26, 1980	Congregation of Buddhist monks convened in Yangon to set out measures to "purify, disseminate and perpetuate" Buddhist teaching.
May 28, 1980	General amnesty granted to insurgents by State Council.

August 1980	U Ne Win announces his retirement from presidency.
November 1980	U San Yu elected new President of the State.
October 1982	*Pyithu Hluttaw* passes new Burma Citizenship Law.
September 1, 1987	Government decontrols domestic trade in rice, maize, pulses and beans.
September 5, 1987	Demonetization of 23, 35 and 75 *kyat* banknotes.
December 11, 1987	UN General Assembly approves of "Least Developed Nation Status" for Myanmar.
March 13–18, 1988	Major demonstrations at Yangon University campuses.
June 1988	Protest demonstrations resumed; unrest spreads to Bago, Mawlamyine and other places. All schools are closed indefinitely.
July 23, 1988	U Nu and U San Yu resign from their party and state posts at BSPP emergency congress.
July 26–27, 1988	Brigadier-General Sein Lwin eleted as both BSPP's new Chairman and Chairman of State Council (President of the State).
August 3, 1988	Martial law declared in Yangon.
August 8, 1988	General strike and demonstrations in Yangon, army opens fire on demonstrators and kills many of them.
August 12, 1988	Sein Lwin resigns and is replaced by Dr. Maung Maung.
August 24, 1988	Thus far largest demonstration in Yangon; martial law is lifted there; Dr. Maung Maung announces holding of extraordinary BSPP Congress.
August 28, 1988	All Burma Federation of Students Union (ABSU) formed. U Nu sets up League for Democracy and Peace.
September 9, 1988	U Nu proclaims "parallel government" with himself as Prime Minister.

Chronology of Myanmar History / xix

September 18, 1988	Military takes power in a coup. State Law and Order Restoration Council (SLORC), headed by General Saw Maung, is formed.
September 24, 1988	Aung Gyi, Tin U and Daw Aung San Suu Kyi found National League for Democracy (NLD).
September 26, 1988	BSPP becomes National Unity Party (NUP).
October 26, 1988	Political Parties Registration Law enacted allowing civilian parties to register with the military authorities.
October 1988	Daw Aung San Suu Kyi on tour around Myanmar, holding mass rallies.
November 5, 1988	All Burma Students' Democratic Front (ABSDF) founded in Myanmar-Thai border area.
November 18, 1988	Democratic Alliance of Burma (DAB), an umbrella rebel organization, is formed in Myanmar-Thai border area.
April 17, 1989	Rebellious Wa troops capture CPB's headquarters at Panghsang, ending 41-year-long Communist insurgency in Myanmar.
May 27, 1989	English name of country becomes Myanmar.
July 20, 1989	Daw Aung San Suu Kyi and U Tin U placed under house arrest. The latter is sentenced to three years in jail at hard labor on 22 December.
December 29, 1989	U Nu and 12 of his associates placed under house arrest.
May 27, 1990	"Multi-party democracy" general elections held throughout Myanmar. NLD gains over 80 percent of seats in the Assembly.
September 1990	United States, Canada, Australia, Japan, New Zealand, Sweden and 12 EC countries issue cordinated statements urging SLORC to respect NLD's electoral victory and release political prisoners.

December 8, 1990	Eight MP's, elected for NLD, declare formation of "National Coalition Government of the Union of Burma" (headed by Dr. Sein Win as Premier) at DAB's headquarters at Manerplaw, near Myanmar-Thai border.
September 1991	SLORC decides to extend Daw Aung San Suu Kyi's arrest term by another three years.
October 14, 1991	Daw Aung San Suu Kyi is awarded Nobel Peace Prize for 1991.
February 21, 1992	U Tin U sentenced to another seven years of jail term.
March 5, 1992	UN Human Rights Commission unanimously condemns Myanmar for serious rights violations.
April 23, 1992	General Saw Maung resigns and is succeeded by General Than Shwe (Vice-Chairman of SLORC) who becomes new Prime Minister of Union of Myanmar.
April 24, 1992	SLORC offers dialogue with leaders of opposition parties and holding of a national convention to draft a new constitution of Myanmar.
April 28, 1992	Agreement reached between Bangladeshi and Myanmar Foreign Ministers on repatriation of about 265,000 Rohingya Muslim refugees from Bangladesh to Myanmar.
June 23, 1992	First coordination meeting for convening of National Convention held in Yangon.
July 1, 1992	Up to that day, 277 political prisoners have been released from custody.
August 24, 1992	Universities, degree colleges and institutes of higher learning reopen (following earlier reopening of primary and middle schools).

September 1, 1992	Myanmar is readmitted to Non-Aligned Movement.
September 6, 1992.	Curfew, in effect since September 1988, is abolished.
September 26, 1992	Last two decrees of martial law, including the military tribunals, are abolished.
January 9, 1993	National Convention, to prepare new Myanmar constitution, convened in Yangon.
February 16–21, 1993	Group of Nobel laureates assembles in Bangkok, asking SLORC to release Daw Aung San Suu Kyi and other political prisoners in Myanmar.
March 3, 1993	Total of 16 chapters, including a preamble, proposed at National Convention to draft new constitution, held in Yangon.
September 1993	SLORC approves the "basic principles" of the new constitution as drawn up by the National Convention.
October 1993	Myanmar's biggest ethnic rebel group, the Kachin Independence Army (KIA), makes peace with SLORC.

xxii / Chronology of Myanmar History

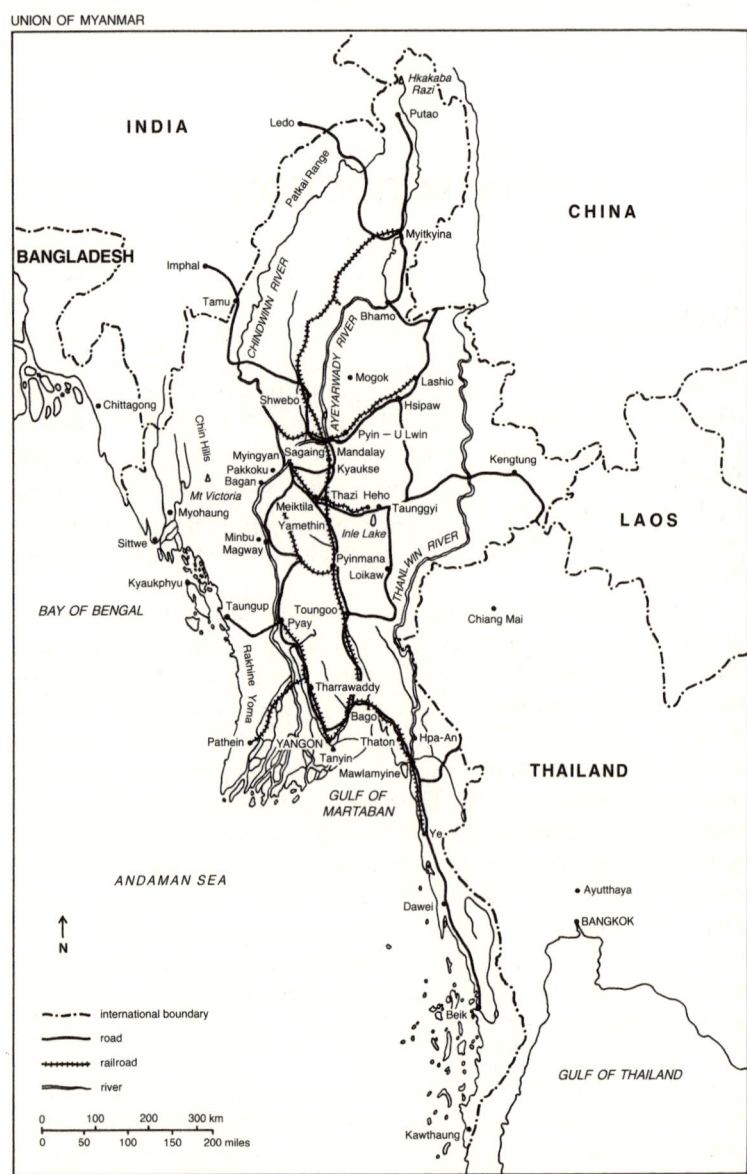

Author's Note: "Pakkoku" should read "Pakokku," "Pyin U Lwin" should read "Pyia-Oo-Lwin," and "Tanyin" should read "Thanlyin."

INTRODUCTION

Background

Myanmar lies on the western edge of the Indochina peninsula. This diamond-shaped country of some 676,570 square kilometers (261,228 square miles), with a narrow coastal strip extending from the main area further south to the peninsula, is surrounded by Bangladesh, India, China, Laos and Thailand, and a coastline which borders the Indian Ocean from the Bay of Bengal to the Andaman Sea.

There are four main geographic zones in the country: the northern mountains, the western mountains, the central lowlands and the Shan Plateau in the east. The hills, serving as natural barriers, mostly run from north to south, as well as the valleys of the main rivers, Ayeyarwady, Chindwinn, Sittoung and Thanlwin. Climatic conditions vary from place to place, although generally a tropical monsoon climate prevails. The rains, carried mainly by the southwest monsoon from the Bay of Bengal, are not distributed evenly in the country. Thus, coastal regions of Rakhine and Tanintharyi receive up to 5,100 millimeters (200 inches) per year, while the Dry Zone which lies further in the interior gets only 500 to 600 millimeters (20 to 25 inches). Temperatures are also affected by topographical positions, though most parts of the country have an annual temperature ranging between 21° and 27° C (71° and 82° F).

There is a variety of vegetation types, influenced by difference in climate, especially regional rainfall. In Rakhine, Tanintharyi and Ayeyarwady Delta, tropical evergreen forest growth, such as mango, palms and mangrove swamps, are typical. On the eastern slopes of Rakhine Yoma, in Bago Yoma as well as in the higher parts of the Shan Plateau, the monsoon forests, comprising teak and other kinds of precious hardwood, predominate. In the Dry Zone, cacti and acacia trees are common; in many other areas of

Myanmar, savanna vegetation predominates. Myanmar's fauna is extremely rich and varied. There are more than 1,000 kinds of birds, numerous mammals such as monkeys, leopards, tigers and elephants, and many reptiles, including poisonous snakes.

Administratively, the country is divided into seven states (Chin State, Kachin State, Kayah State, Kayin State, Mon State, Shan State and Rakhine State) and seven divisions (Ayeyarwady, Bago, Magway, Mandalay, Sagain, Tanintharyi and Yangon). The states, inhabited mainly by ethnic minorities, and the divisions have equal status. Minor administrative units are townships.

The population of 44.5 million persons (1993 estimate) lives mainly in rural areas. About 38 percent of the population are less than 15 years old. The population is increasing at about 2 percent per year. Only about 25 percent of the people are city dwellers. The major urban centers are Yangon and Mandalay; smaller cities include Bago, Mawlamyine and Pathein. About 60 percent of the workforce is in agriculture, animal husbandry and fishery.

Myanmar is a multi-ethnic country, with the number of ethnic groups estimated to be between 50 and 140. Aside from Bamars, or Myanmars, who make up around 69 percent of the total population, Shan, Kayin, Rakhine, Mon, Chin and Kachin are ethnic groups of major importance. Foreigners (Indians, Chinese, Eurasians) make up about 5.3 percent of the population. Buddhists constitute the largest religious group (89.4 percent); the remainder are Christians, Muslims, animists and Hindu.

HISTORY

The discovery of Paleolithic and Proto-Neolithic settlements in the middle portion of the Ayeyarwady valley and in northern Shan State suggest the existence of a civilization (known as Anyathian culture) in Myanmar at least 5,000 years ago.

About 500 B.C., the Tibeto-Burman people known as the Pyus reached the upper Ayeyarwady valley. Moving gradually southwards, they gained control over the entire valley as far as Pyay in the south, establishing several city-states: Beikthano, Sri Ksetra and Halin. The Pyus reached a high level of economic and cultural development, but did not establish a unified kingdom. Their last capital, Halin, was overrun by the Tai-Shans of the Nan-Chao kingdom in southern China in the 9th century A.D.

Around the 3rd century B.C., the Mons, who belong to the Austro-Asiatic people, moved along the Mekong and settled in the Sittoung valley in southern Myanmar, making their capital at Thaton. The Mon culture was, to quite an extent, shaped under the influence of India, from where the Mons took their script and also their religion—Theravada Buddhism. The Mons developed a temple architecture and a more advanced political and social organization, with the king at its top. By the 9th century A.D., they had become the dominant force in the Ayeyarwady Delta and built their center at Bago.

About the 9th century A.D., the Bamars, migrating from the northeast, moved into the Dry Zone of northern Myanmar. In 849 A.D., they fortified the city of Bagan and made it their capital. King Anawrahta of the Bagan Dynasty (1044–1077) brought much of the country, including the Mon capital of Thaton (1057), under his rule. He founded the First Myanmar Empire which lasted until the 13th century when the Mongol invasion of 1287 led to its decline.

For over 200 years after the fall of Bagan, the country was divided into a number of petty, ethnically diverse states with at least four major ethnic groups (Bamars, Mons, Shans and Rakhines) involved in an internal power struggle for hegemony.

Reunification of Myanmar was achieved in the 16th century, under the founder of the Toungoo Dynasty, King Tabinswehti, and his successor, King Bayinnaung. However, the unity of the Second Myanmar Empire was shattered by continuous Myanmar warfare with Thai Ayutthaya, as well as Manipuri and Mon revolts. Under the Restored Toungoo Dynasty (1597–1752), the policy of military conquests was discontinued and the administration was reformed, to strengthen central control. Still, in the late 17th century, the empire began to disintegrate. In 1752, the Mons revolted, took the capital Inwa and brought the Second Myanmar Empire to an end.

In 1752, in opposition to Mon rule, Alaungpaya rallied the Bamars, founded the Konbaung Dynasty and established the foundations of the Third Myanmar Empire which lasted until 1885. This empire reached its zenith under King Bodawpaya who annexed Rakhine (1785) and Assam (1812). However, this brought the Myanmar Empire closer to British power in India. The clash of interests led to three Anglo-Myanmar wars (1824–1826;

1851–1852; 1885), as a result of which the whole of Myanmar was annexed by the British in three stages. In 1885, the last Myanmar king Thibaw was deposed and exiled to India.

Under British rule, Myanmar became known as Burma and was made a province of British India. It was first administered by a Chief Commissioner, from 1897 by a Lieutenant Governor, and in 1923 it became a full Governor's Province. Under the Government of Burma Act of 1935, effective since April 1937, Myanmar was separated from India. The Act brought some constitutional advance, including a new bicameral legislature (parliament) which was partly responsible for the administration of the portion of the country known as Burma proper (Ministerial Burma). However, the areas inhabited by ethnic minority groups, and known as "Excluded" or "Scheduled" Areas, were kept apart, under a British Governor, and administered indirectly, through local hereditary or tribal chiefs.

The imposition of British rule largely disrupted Buddhist monastic order, the *sangha*, and religious values and institutions on which the traditional political and social system of Myanmar was based. The British impact on Myanmar's economy was ambivalent. The British promoted a rapid expansion of rice cultivation in southern Myanmar as well as the extraction of timber and minerals, mainly for export. However, the economic growth was one-sided. It brought substantial benefits to a handful of British companies, to Indian moneylenders (*Chettiars*) as well as Chinese merchants who acted as British middlemen. On the other hand, the conditions of the Myanmar peasantry, forming the bulk of the population, became unbearable, mainly as a result of land alienation.

The response to the British annexation of Myanmar in 1885 was a patriotic armed resistance by Bamars, Chins, Kachins, Shans and other ethnic groups which was crushed only around 1895. These struggles, as well as later uprisings, such as the Saya San Rebellion (1930–1931) demonstrated that the people of the country could not be reconciled to alien rule.

Modern Myanmar nationalism began as a movement for the defense of Buddhism as a national religion. In 1906, the Young Men's Buddhist Association (YMBA) was founded in Yangon. It was reorganized as the General Council of Burmese Associations (GCBA) in 1920. The GCBA leaders cooperated with publicly active Buddhist monks, the "political" *pongyis*, who had a popular base of support in rural areas, and their coalition dominated Myanmar nationalist politics up to the 1930s. Following World War I, university students' strikes (in 1920, 1936, 1938) also occurred and became an important tool of nationalist agitation against British rule. With the constitutional reforms of 1923 and 1936, many nationalist leaders joined the legislature and became involved in official politics.

During the 1930s, the *Thakins* of the *Do Bama Asi Ayon* (We Burmans Association), whose main goal was Myanmar's independence, came to the foreground of the independence movement. In the wake of the oil-field workers' strike in 1938, the radical *Thakin* leaders founded the clandestine Communist Party of Burma (CPB) in 1939 and also organized the first nationwide trade unions. Between 1940 and 1942, most of the *Thakins* and other nationalist leaders were arrested by the British or forced into hiding. An underground section of the independence movement, the People's Revolutionary Party (PRP), initiated secret cooperation with Japanese agents. The major result of this cooperation was the smuggling out of the country of Aung San and other young Bamars (known subsequently as the "Thirty Comrades") who received Japanese military training at Hainan and formed the Burma Independence Army (BIA) in December 1941. The BIA participated in the Japanese campaign in Myanmar (December 1941–May 1942).

From 1942 to 1945, Myanmar was under Japanese occupation. In August 1943, Myanmar's nominal independence was proclaimed, but by now Myanmar public opinion had turned against the Japanese. The main forces of the anti-fascist resistance, the CPB, the PRP and the national army, agreed on establishing a common front, the Anti-Fascist People's Freedom League (AFPFL) in August 1944. In March 1945, the army and the AFPFL launched an anti-Japanese uprising, greatly assisting the Allied reconquest of Myanmar.

In August 1945, the AFPFL was constituted as a national front which became a leading political force of the postwar independence movement. The AFPFL leaders, including its President, Major-General Aung San, were made an offer of positions on the British Governor's Executive Council in September 1946. In January 1947, Aung San, as Deputy Chairman of the Executive

Council, signed an agreement with the British on the terms of transfer of power to Myanmar. Under the Panglong Agreement of 12 February 1947, an understanding was reached between Bamars and most of the ethnic minority leaders on establishing one common state—the Union of Burma. In July 1947, Aung San and several other leaders of the Interim Government (formerly Executive Council) were assassinated by their political opponents. But Aung San was succeeded in his post by his close AFPFL associate, Thakin (U) Nu. The Constitution of the Union of Burma was drafted by the Constituent Assembly and adopted in September 1947. Under the treaty which U Nu and British Prime Minister Clement Attlee signed in October 1947, Myanmar declared its independence on 4 January 1948.

Between 1948 and 1962, Myanmar (known then officially as the Union of Burma) was a parliamentary democracy which followed a foreign policy of neutralism and non-alignment. However, at least until 1951, the authority of the Union government, headed by U Nu as Prime Minister, was seriously challenged by Communist and ethnic, mainly Kayin, rebellions.

Myanmar's major task during the parliamentary era was to bring unity to the diverse peoples of the Union. However, the goal was not achieved, as ever growing numbers of ethnic minorities leaders voiced their dissatisfaction with the federal system, as instituted by the 1947 Constitution, which turned out to be largely nominal. Also the attempts to recover and diversify Myanmar's economy brought only modest results and economic and social progress was only sluggish.

In 1958, the AFPFL split into two rival factions. In September 1958, the mounting political crisis forced Prime Minister U Nu to resign and to ask General Ne Win, Commander-in-Chief of the armed forces, to set up a caretaker government. The elections held in February 1960 brought back to power U Nu's *Pyidaungsu* Party, but after 1960, political, religious and ethnic tensions in Myanmar again increased.

The danger of disintegration of the Union of Burma was the main pretext of the military coup on 2 March 1962, which brought to power the Revolutionary Council (RC) led by General Ne Win and composed of high-ranking army officers. The RC strove to replace the system of parliamentary democracy with a new arrangement based on the military leadership of the nation, the program of the "Burmese Way to Socialism" and the existence (from March 1964) of the Burma Socialist Programme Party (BSPP) as the only legal and governing political party of the country. In January 1974, the Constitution of the Socialist Republic of the Union of Burma came into force. After the elections to the *Pyithu Hluttaw* (People's Assembly) and other organs of state power and administration, military rule was formally terminated on 2 March 1974. But even thereafter the military and political (BSPP) elite remained largely in power.

Myanmar's military leaders carried out an extensive nationalization of the economy in the 1960s. Agricultural land remained private, but farmers were required to deliver agricultural products to the state at fixed prices. The cumulative effect of these economic policies proved largely disruptive in the lives of the people. Production rapidly declined, commodity distribution faltered and the "black market" thrived. Although the government made attempts at improving the situation from the late 1970s on, economic growth was hindered by huge trade deficits and external debt payments. Students' and workers' riots occurred (in 1974 and 1976) while many political and ethnic rebellions continued despite the 1980 amnesty. By the late 1980s, Myanmar had turned into one of the poorest countries in the world. In December 1987, acting on previous Myanmar government's requests, the United Nations approved "Least Developed Nation" status for Myanmar.

The demonetization by the government in September 1987 of several higher *kyat* banknotes, cancelling without compensation almost 80 percent of the country's currency, provoked student protests and gave an impetus to the events finally leading to a mass pro-democracy movement in summer 1988. On 23 July 1988, U Ne Win resigned from his post as Chairman of the BSPP, but neither of his two successors, General Sein Lwin or the more moderate Dr. Maung Maung, who proposed a peaceful transition to the reforms asked for by the people, was able to stop the movement.

Using the deterioration of law and order in the country as the main pretext, on 18 September 1988, the army, headed by General Saw Maung, seized power in a coup. It established the State Law and Order Restoration Council (SLORC) and placed most of the country under martial law. The SLORC ultimately suppressed the pro-democracy movement, although it allowed for registration of political parties for multi-party general elections. The elections, held in May 1990, brought a decisive victory to the National League for Democracy (NLD), the major opposition party, despite the fact that the NLD's principal leaders, Daw Aung San Suu Kyi (the daughter of the late Major-General Aung San) and U Tin U had been detained since July 1989. However, the SLORC has failed to honor the outcome of the elections. Late 1990 and 1991 saw a major SLORC crackdown against NLD activists and other opposition leaders, including students.

In August 1991, the SLORC proposed a new constitutional program, indicating that an assembly representing all the political parties which contested the 1990 elections, representatives of the ethnic groups of the country and some other persons should meet to draw up guidelines for a new constitutional law.

The SLORC has become more pragmatic since Senior General Than Shwe took over as Chairman in April 1992. During 1992, several hundred political prisoners (excluding high-ranking NLD leaders) were released from custody. The martial law decrees were lifted and the universities and colleges were reopened. In January 1993, the National Convention to prepare the new constitution was convened in Yangon.

Since 1989, Myanmar's military rulers have also made successful unilateral approaches and struck separate cease-fire deals with ten ethnic rebel groups. Several other ethnic guerillas were about to discuss peace with the SLORC in late 1993. There is, of course, the question if the cease-fire deals, which do not address major political issues, will guarantee a lasting peace and stability in Myanmar. Some other problems, such as violation of human rights and personal freedoms, also persist. Many observers are inclined to believe that the present constitutional process will not bring democracy to Myanmar, but, rather, it will ensure the leading role of the military in national politics.

THE DICTIONARY

ABHIRAJA. Also Abhiyaza. According to Myanmar chronicles, the founder of the first Myanmar dynasty at Tagaung (q.v.), who is popularly regarded as the first king in the history of Myanmar.

ADIPADI. A Pali (q.v.) term meaning a person of the highest rank or authority. Used as a title by Dr. Ba Maw (q.v.) in his capacity as the Head of State of "independent" Myanmar from August 1943 to 1945.

ADMINISTRATION OF MYANMAR, BRITISH COLONIAL ERA. After the Third Anglo-Myanmar war (1885), the hitherto independent kingdom in northern Myanmar was annexed to British territories in southern Myanmar. In the British colonial era, Burma (q.v.) became the name of the country. In January 1886, the Province of Burma, as part of British India, was created. It was placed under a Chief Commissioner who was responsible to the Governor-General in India. The Province was organized into eight divisions, four in Lower Burma and four in Upper Burma (qq.v.), and these were further divided into 37 districts. The administrative services were divided into three classes, of which class I was until 1923 composed entirely of British officers of the Indian Civil Service. The Provincial Civil Service (Class II), known as Burma Service, was predominantly Myanmar and Eurasian (qq.v.).

In 1897, the Chief Commissioner was elevated to the rank of Lieutenant-Governor. The Legislative Council was also formed and subsequently enlarged from nine to 17 members in 1909. Under the Montagu-Chelmsford reforms, the dyarchy (q.v.) system was extended to Myanmar which became a full Governor's Province in January 1923. Under the Government of Burma Act of 1935 (q.v.), which became effective on 1 April 1937, Myanmar was separated from India and placed under a Governor who was responsible to the Government of the United Kingdom. This administrative system remained in force until the Japanese occupation of Myanmar (1942–1945) (q.v.).

Although the administrative reforms of 1923 and 1935 brought some constitutional advance to Myanmar, the ultimate power remained in the hands of the British Governor. The Governor alone was also primarily responsible for the parts of the country known as "Excluded" or "Scheduled" (later "Frontier") Areas (qq.v.). These areas comprised the Shan States (q.v.), the Kachin and Chin Hill Tracts and Karenni State (q.v.), nominally an independent state under British protection. As a result of this arrangement, the governance of Burma proper (q.v.) was based on the administrative principle, while in the remaining areas of the country, the British retained, to quite an extent, the traditional political and social system of control. (*See also* Colonial Education; Economy, British Colonial Era; Plural Society.)

ADMINISTRATION OF MYANMAR, PRECOLONIAL ERA. The king was the apex of the system of governance and administration of precolonial Myanmar. The concept of kingship (q.v.), derived to a large extent from Theravada Buddhism (q.v.), enhanced the status of the monarchy, and the king himself, although his theoretically unlimited claims to power were circumscribed by customs and etiquette as well as the ability to enforce his authority. There was also the Buddhist order, the *sangha* (q.v.), usually subordinated to secular power, but nonetheless quite influential and even aggressive when the monarchy was weak.

Despite the reforms under the Toungoo and Konbaung Dynasties (qq.v.) which aimed at consolidating central power, the royal administration was only loosely integrated. Next to the king stood the princes of blood who frequently became rivals on his demise. There were principles of succession, but these were often challenged by the sons, uncles and brothers of the king. The king provided for their income through the assignment of an appanage (q.v.). Below the royal princes, in the political and social hierarchy, stood the royal officials. All were selected on a personal basis and no appointment was permanent.

The affairs of the state were divided into two different administrative units, the court's administration, which was under the king's Privy Council, *byedaik* (q.v.), and public affairs of the state, which was the responsibility of the Council of Ministers, the *hluttaw* (q.v.).

The territorial organization, as it developed during the Toungoo and Konbaung Dynasties, was based on the existence of three main zones, the nucleus, dependent and tributary zones. In the nucleus of the state, comprising the central plains of Myanmar, the king recruited the bulk of his officials, provisioned his most concentrated military power, and ruled directly through his ministers. Apart from the officials appointed by the crown, there were also officials holding their office by hereditary succession, such as *thugyi* (q.v.). The dependent zones came under supervision of the royal administration, while in the tributary zones, mainly periphery non-Bamar (q.v.) areas, the immediate authority was exercised by local hereditary rulers, such as Kachin *Duwas* or Shan *Sawbwas* (qq.v.).

The population which was obliged to serve the state was divided into two different categories, royal service people, *ahmudan*, and free service people, *athi* (qq.v.). There were also slaves and debt bondsmen whose labor was the resource of their lay or monastic masters.

AGRICULTURE. Agriculture is the basis of Myanmar's economy. In 1991, the agricultural sector accounted for about 65 percent of total employment and it contributed some 40 percent of GDP. Agricultural products accounted for 27 percent of the total exports of the country in the same year.

Until the mid-1970s, the growth in agricultural production was achieved mainly through a gradual increase in the area under cultivation. Since then greater emphasis has been given to raising productivity through the use of improved seeds and modern imputs. A high yield variety paddy project was launched in 1975 with state aid and extended to 19 other crops from 1980. Other methods used were the expansion of state agricultural loans and the subsidized use of fertilizers. There has been an extension of irrigation (q.v.) works, although about 85 percent of the net cultivated area still has to rely on rain water. The use of modern machines and implements, such as tractors and water pumps, is rather modest and limited to state cooperative farms. These are, however, of marginal importance, as over 90 percent of total agricultural output is in private ownership.

In 1991, the total crop area was about 10,117,250 hectares (25,100,000 acres). It represents only about 12 percent of the land area and less than 50 percent of the land available for cultivation. The increase in area under cultivation has not been constant during recent decades and has not kept pace with population (q.v.) growth. The modernization of agricultural production is hampered by the extensive fragmentation of land ownership. In 1991, more than 60 percent of the peasant families in Myanmar possessed farms of less than 2,023 hectares (5 acres), a size which is not considered sufficient to allow a cultivator to rise above the poverty line.

There are three main regions of agricultural production in Myanmar: the valleys and deltas of the main rivers in southern Myanmar; the Dry Zone (q.v.) in central Myanmar; and the hill areas. In southern Myanmar, as well as in most irrigated land of the Dry Zone, rice (q.v.) is the major crop. There is also substantial production of groundnuts, maize (q.v.), pulses and beans (q.v.) and sesame. Other food crops cultivated in Myanmar are cereals and fruits and vegetables of all kinds. Industrial crops, such as cotton, jute, sugarcane, tobacco and rubber (qq.v.) are cultivated mainly for domestic use. Swidden agriculture, practised in some hill areas, produces dry rice, sugarcane and several other products.

AHMUDAN. A term for crown service people. The *ahmudan* group provided the crown with regular military service or labor on a fixed rotational basis. It was also required to provide *corvée* labor on demand. The *ahmudan* people usually lived nearest to the capital and received grants of land and village sites from the state. They were generally administered by departmental agencies, beneath the *hluttaw* (q.v.), regardless of their place of residence.

AIR TRANSPORT. The national carrier is Myanmar Airways, formerly Burma Airways Corporation, founded in 1948 as the Union of Burma Airways. Myanmar Airways operates internal routes and external services to several Asian capitals. More recently, air traffic has been adversely affected by a shortage of foreign currency to buy air fuel and spare parts and has been on the decline since the 1980s. In 1991, Myanmar Airways carried 406,000 passengers and 3,880,000 tons of freight, mainly on internal routes. There are 37 airfields in Myanmar, but only one international airport at Mingaladon near Yangon. (q.v.).

Airlines operating regular flights in and out of Yangon include Biman, CAAC, Thai International and Tradewinds. There are direct links from Yangon to Bangkok, Beijing, Dhaka, Hong Kong, Kumming, Moscow, Singapore and Vientiane. (*See also* Railroads; Roads; Water Transport.)

AKYAB *see* SITTWE.

ALAUNGPAYA. First king of the Alaungpaya or Konbaung Dynasty (1752–1760) (q.v.). His original name was Aung Zeiya and he was a chieftain at Moksobo in northern Myanmar. He came into prominence as a Myanmar leader against the Mons (q.v.). He made Moksobo, subsequently renamed Shwebo (q.v.), the center of Myanmar resistance against Mon rule. By 1757, Alaungpaya had conquered the larger part of the Mon country in southern Myanmar, making Dagon, which he renamed Yangon (q.v.), his principal port. In the years 1755 and 1758 he raided Manipur and, in 1760, he seized Tanintharyi (q.v.) and marched on to Thailand. He was wounded while besieging the Thai capital, Ayutthaya, and died en route back to Myanmar in 1760. Although Alaungpaya reigned only eight years, he reunified the country and founded the Third Myanmar Empire (q.v.) which lasted until 1885.

ALAUNGPAYA DYNASTY *see* KONBAUNG DYNASTY.

ALAUNGSITHU. Fourth king of the Bagan Dynasty (1111–1167) (q.v.). He spent the earlier years of his reign supressing rebellions and restoring to the throne in Rakhine (q.v.) the son of a rightful heir. In Myanmar chronicles Alaungsithu is noted as a builder of works of religious merit, such as the Thatbinnyu Temple in Bagan (q.v.). In his old age, Alaungsithu fell a victim to court intrigue. He was murdered by one of his three sons, Narathu, who then seized the throne.

ALL BURMA FEDERATION OF STUDENTS UNION (ABFSU). An organization which emerged and was active in the pro-democracy movement of 1988 (q.v.). Set up in August 1988 in Yangon and led by Min Ko Naing (qq.v.), the ABFSU claimed membership of over 50,000 students. After the military coup of 1988 (q.v.), many ABFSU leaders, including Min Ko Naing, were forced into hiding or went underground.

ALL BURMA MUSLIM CONGRESS. Founded in 1945, it was one of the more important mass organizations affiliated with the postwar Anti-Fascist People's Freedom League (AFPFL) (q.v.). After independence in 1948, the Congress leaders sought to be recognized and accepted by Myanmar Buddhists. However, in 1956, the Congress was refused continued affiliation with the AFPFL as a communal political group.

ALL BURMA PEASANTS' ORGANIZATION (ABPO). This organization was founded in January 1939. It was presided over by Thakin Mya (q.v.) and associated with the *Do Bama Asi Ayon* (q.v.). The ABPO's declared aims were to fight for Myanmar independence and for the establishment of Myanmar as a socialist state. In 1945, the ABPO was reconstituted by the Socialist Party of Burma (q.v.). Between the years 1945 and 1948, the ABPO came under strong influence of the Communist Party of Burma (q.v.). After independence in 1948, the ABPO's Communist leadership was removed. In the parliamentary era (q.v.), the ABPO became a Socialist-controlled mass organization. The main aim of the ABPO was to mobilize the peasants to give support to the Socialist

Party leaders. The ABPO was also instrumental in directing the land nationalization committees, distributing state loans to peasants and similar activities; the ABPO had its own "army" known as the "Peace Guerillas." The ABPO ceased to exist in March 1964, when the Revolutionary Council of General Ne Win (qq.v.) banned all legal political parties and mass organizations, except the ruling Burma Socialist Programme Party (q.v.).

ALL BURMA STUDENTS' DEMOCRATIC FRONT (ABSDF). The umbrella organization of Myanmar students who went underground after the military coup of 1988 (q.v.). The ABSDF was formed in November 1988 at the Karen National Union's (KNU) (q.v.) base of Kawmoorah, on the Myanmar-Thai border, with U Tun Aung Gyaw (q.v.) as its Chairman. The ABSDF is affiliated with the Democratic Alliance of Burma (q.v.). A few hundred ABSDF members have undergone military training in the areas controlled by the KNU and other rebel organizations.

ALL BURMA STUDENTS' UNION (ABSU). Formed in 1936, the ABSU brought together student unions at secondary schools throughout the country and a few at the University of Yangon (q.v.). Several leading nationalist politicians of the 1940s, including Aung San and Ba Hein (qq.v.), started their public careers as ABSU leaders. In October 1939, the ABSU was one of the founding members of the Freedom Bloc (q.v.). After independence in 1948, the ABSU resumed its former place in student politics and remained an important symbol of student traditions even after its suppression following the military coup of 1962 (q.v.). More recently, the ABSU was a general form of reference to various students' groups active in the pro-democracy movement of 1988 (q.v.).

ALL BURMA TRADE UNION CONGRESS (ABTUC). The trade union established in 1940 by leftist leaders of the *Do Bama Asi Ayon* (q.v.). In July 1945, it was reestablished with Ba Hein (q.v.) as Chairman. Later, it was led by Than Tun, Chairman of the Communist Party of Burma (CPB) (qq.v.). Altogether 14 trade unions in Myanmar were affiliated with the ABTUC. Many ABTUC leaders joined the CPB when it went underground in March 1948.

ALL BURMA WOMEN'S FREEDOM LEAGUE. Also known as the Women's Freedom League, it became one of the most important non-political organizations which were affiliated with the Anti-Fascist People's Freedom League (AFPFL) (q.v.) in 1945. Its main aim was to work for an improvement in women's conditions in Myanmar and to draw support for the AFPFL.

ALL BURMA YOUTH LEAGUE (ABYL). A youth organization started in 1930 (or in 1931) by *Thakins* to expand the activities of the *Do Bama Asi Ayon* (qq.v.) among young Myanmars.

Also the term used in 1944 to refer to the wartime youth organization known hitherto as the East Asia Youth League (q.v.). Led by U Ba Gyan (q.v.), the ABYL became a constituent member of the Anti-Fascist People's Freedom League (q.v.) and remained an active element until 1948. It then disintegrated, mainly as a result of the civil war (q.v.). In 1950, the ABYL was reorganized under the leadership of Justice U Thein Maung. It continued as a non-political, youth-training organization during the parliamentary era (q.v.).

AMARAPURA. "The City of the Immortals," the former Myanmar capital, situated on the bank of the Ayeyarwady River, about 11 kilometers (7 miles) south of Mandalay (qq.v.). It was founded as the capital in 1783 by King Bodawpaya (q.v.). In 1822, King Bagyidaw moved the capital back to Inwa (qq.v.). In 1841, Amarapura again became the capital city and remained so until 1860, when the capital was moved to Mandalay (q.v.). Little remains of ancient Amarapura now. The modern town of Amarapura, known as Taungmyo (Southern Town), is an important center of the traditional silk-weaving industry.

AMERICAN BAPTIST FOREIGN MISSIONARY SOCIETY *see* CHRISTIANITY.

AMERICAN BAPTIST INTERMEDIATE COLLEGE *see* JUDSON COLLEGE.

ANA. Also *ah-nah, an-ah, arna or arnar*. A term which means "authority, power."

ANANDA TEMPLE. Built in 1090 A.D. by King Kyanzittha (q.v.), it is one of the finest and most venerated temples in Bagan (q.v.). The temple symbolized in its name one of the attributes of the Buddha, his endless wisdom, or *anandapinnya* in Myanmar. The grand plan of the temple is in the shape of a perfect Greek cross. Inside the temple, there are colossal statues of Buddhas of the present world as well as two life-size figures of Kyanzittha and his teacher, Shin Arahan (q.v.). Another interesting feature of the temple are 1,500 terra cotta glazed tiles, ornamenting the base and receding terraces, which illustrate the *jataka* (q.v.) tales. (*See also* Architecture; First Myanmar Empire.)

ANAUKPETLUN. King of the Toungoo Dynasty (1606–1628) (q.v.). Trying to restore the Second Myanmar Empire (q.v.), Anaukpetlun brought under his rule the greater part of northern Myanmar as well as coastal regions in the south. His southern campaign culminated in 1613 in a long and successful siege of Thanlyin (q.v.), which had been usurped by a Portuguese mercenary Felipe de Brito. Anaukpetlun is also remembered for his economic initiatives and reforms of provincial administration. (*See also* Portuguese and Myanmar.)

ANAWRAHTA. Also Aniruddha. King of the Bagan Dynasty (1044–1077), founder of the First Myanmar Empire (qq.v.). Starting his reign in 1044 A.D. as ruler of the small state centered on Bagan (q.v.), located in the middle portion of the Ayeyarwady River (q.v.), by 1077 he had brought under his control the greater part of Myanmar, including the northern Rakhine (q.v.), the northern Tanintharyi (q.v.) and part of the present Shan State (q.v.).

Anawrahta imposed his administration by reinforcing his forts north of the capital, repairing or building new irrigation (q.v.) works in the heartland of his state, and leaving garrisons and appointing governors in the conquered territories. Most important was his annexation of the Mon (q.v.) country in the south of Myanmar. The conquest of the Mon capital at Thaton (q.v.) in 1057 brought Anawrahta much needed skilled labor to build up his own state at Bagan, as he took all of Thaton's 30,000 inhabitants, including King Manuha (q.v.) and his family, with him back to Bagan. The conquest of the Mon country brought the Bamars into direct contact with Indian civilizing influences and the Mon culture. It also opened a way to the seacoast, and intercourse with the neighboring countries, namely India and Sri Lanka.

Although Anawrahta's wars of unification were dictated mainly by strategic political and economic considerations, in traditional accounts of his reign, such as those given in the *Hmannan Yazawin* (q.v.), they are justified mainly on religious grounds. Thus, Anawrahta's conquest of Thaton is explained as his attempt to purify Buddhism (q.v.) and religious practices prevailing in Bagan with a set of sacred scriptures, the *Tipitaka* (q.v.), which were also the most celebrated spoils of his southern campaign. Anawrahta is known to have created new relations with the Buddhist *sangha* (q.v.), increasing royal patronage to it. Still, Theravada Buddhism was not the prevalent faith in early Bagan. Rather, it had a syncretic religion, including also elements of Mahayana, Brahmanism and indigenous *nat* (q.v.) worship. Anawrahta built Buddhist pagodas, but not great temples which were only started by his successors.

ANGLO-BURMAN *see* EURASIAN.

ANGLO-BURMESE WARS *see* ANGLO-MYANMAR WAR, FIRST; ANGLO-MYANMAR WAR, SECOND; ANGLO-MYANMAR WAR, THIRD.

ANGLO-INDIAN *see* EURASIAN.

ANGLO-MYANMAR WAR, FIRST (1824–1826). The first war, which the Myanmar fought against the British East India Company in the reign of King Bagyidaw (q.v.), was inspired by the conflict of British and Myanmar imperial interests. The war grew out of minor incidents and border clashes in Rakhine (q.v.) which, in fact, dated back to 1785 when Myanmar's conquest of that country brought it face to face with British power in India. A similar situation also arose in Assam and Manipur, where the Myanmar court often intervened on behalf of its nominees or interests.

Scattered clashes between British and Myanmar troops across the Naaf River in Rakhine began in September 1823 and in Manipur in January 1824. In the same month, General Maha Bandula (q.v.) began to prepare for the campaign in Rakhine. The East India Company formally declared war on 5 March 1824. Treating Rakhine as of lesser strategic importance, it concentrated on a seaborne invasion of southern Myanmar. The surprise British capture of Yangon (q.v.) on 10 May 1824 led the king to recall Maha Bandula to southern Myanmar. However, the attacks which the Myanmar army delivered under his command were repulsed by the British, and Maha Bandula was killed in action in April 1825 at Danubyu, halfway between Yangon and Pyay (q.v.). By that time, the Myanmar troops had been driven from Assam, Manipur and Rakhine, and the British expeditionary force, under Sir Archibald Campbell, advanced into the interior of the country. A peace treaty was finally signed at Yandabo, only 64 kilometers from Inwa (q.v.), on 24 February 1826.

The Myanmars, despite their fighting ability, lacked modern arms and were no match for the British army which lost 15,000 men (out of a force of 40,000), but mostly through disease and insufficient logistic supplies. The Treaty of Yandabo (q.v.), among other things, involved for the Myanmar king the loss of Rakhine and Tanintharyi which came under direct control of British Governor-General in India. (*See also* European Colonial Expansion.)

ANGLO-MYANMAR WAR, SECOND (1852). The Second Anglo-Myanmar war was to some extent the result of the negative foreign policy of Inwa (q.v.) towards the British. On the other side, the British, namely Lord Dalhousie, as Governor-General of British India, pursued an expansionist policy and his handling of matters relating to Myanmar also contributed greatly to the outbreak of war.

The war developed out of a series of petty causes and incidents, thereafter rationalized as a protection of British mercantile interests. One of these was a dispute which arose in connection with the fines imposed on two British sea captains by the Myanmar governor of Yangon (q.v.). Commodore Lambert, who was sent to Myanmar by Lord Dalhousie to demand satisfaction, decided to force the issue instead of seeking a peaceful solution. Before he returned to Calcutta, he had declared a blockade of several ports in southern Myanmar and destroyed many Myanmar ships.

On 1 April 1852, Dalhousie sent an ultimatum and, as he received no answer from the court of Inwa, the British troops moved in. The British advance met with only feeble and unorganized Myanmar resistance. The British could have marched on the capital, but Lord Dalhousie decided that the annexation of the province of Bago (q.v.) and the principal sea ports of Martaban, Pathein (qq.v.) and Yangon were sufficient. On 20 December 1852, the Viceroy of India was informed that the British Province of Pegu was established.

The war ended with no peace treaty, as King Mindon (q.v.), who came to the throne in 1852, was not willing to cede Myanmar territory to a foreign power, though he was keen to develop good relations with the British. The Second Anglo-Myanmar war marked the beginning of the end for the Myanmar kingdom, as much of its natural wealth and all its sea ports were lost to the British. In 1682, the province of British Burma was formed by the amalgamation of Bago with Rakhine and Tanintharyi, gained in the First Anglo-Myanmar war. (*See also* Anglo-Myanmar War, First.)

ANGLO-MYANMAR WAR, THIRD (1885). The immediate cause of the Third Anglo-Myanmar War was the decision of the court of Mandalay (q.v.) to impose a fine on the Bombay Burmah Trading Corporation (q.v.) for the illegal extraction of teak (q.v..) from the royal preserves. Another important factor which drove the British to act was King Thibaw's (q.v.) attempt to counterbalance the British imperial advance by developing friendly relations with other European powers, namely France.

On 22 October 1885, the British Government of India sent an ultimatum to the Myanmar king which called for a settlement of the dispute with the Bombay Burmah Trading Corporation by negotiation. It also included a demand that the British diplomatic agent (who had been virtually recalled by British authorities) should be allowed to reside in Mandalay. The ultimatum also asked the court to provide facilities for opening up British trade with China and required the Myanmar court to regulate its external relations in accordance with the advice of the Government of India.

A reply to the British ultimatum was demanded by 10 November. The Myanmar reply which came on 9 November, although leaving some room for further negotiations, was read by the British as an "unconditional refusal." On 14 November, General Prendergast, the commander in chief of the British forces, was ordered to march northward. King Thibaw issued a call to the people to take up arms and fight the invader. However, there was a little resistance and, after an almost bloodless campaign, the British forces took Mandalay on 28 November 1885. King Thibaw surrendered to General Prendergast and was subsequently sent, with his family and some followers, into exile in India. On 1 January 1886, Lord Dufferin proclaimed the annexation of the Myanmar kingdom and all Myanmar, called Burma by the British, was incorporated into the British Empire as a province of British India. (*See also* Pacification of Burma.)

ANIMISM. The belief in and worship of various spirits which still prevails among certain people of Myanmar and elements of which have also been incorporated into Buddhism (q.v.) as professed in the country. According to the 1983 census, animists make up about 1.1 percent of the total population of the Union of Myanmar. (*See also* Nat.)

ANTI-FASCIST ORGANIZATION (AFO). The British term of reference to the Anti-Fascist People's Freedom League (AFPFL) (q.v.) during World War II (q.v.). The term AFO is also used by some historians to refer to the initial period of the AFPFL, from August 1944 to May 1945. Other references to the AFPFL are the Anti-Fascist League (wartime American usage) or People's Freedom League, the denotation of the early postwar Myanmar resistance forces. (*See also* Anti-Fascist Resistance.)

ANTI-FASCIST PEOPLE'S FREEDOM LEAGUE (AFPFL).
Major organization of the independence movement (q.v.) in Myanmar and the ruling political party in the postindependence parliamentary era (q.v.). It was founded in August 1944 as a coalition of three major resistance forces, the Communist Party of Burma (CPB) (q.v.), the People's Revolutionary Party (q.v.) and the army resistance groups. The AFPFL's original leadership consisted of Aung San (q.v.) as the League's President, Than Tun (q.v.) as Secretary General, and Thakin Soe (q.v.) as a political leader. The two main and twin objectives of the AFPFL, as embodied in the Manifesto of 8 August 1944, were to expel the Japanese occupiers of Myanmar and to gain genuine independence for the country. The AFPFL led the successful anti-Japanese uprising which started on 27 March 1945 and greatly helped the Allied troops to clear Myanmar of the Japanese.

After the war, other political parties, such as the *Maha Bama, Do Bama Asi Ayon*, and Fabian Party (qq.v.), as well as non-political, professional, mass and ethnic organizations joined the AFPFL, making it a broad national front. The Supreme Council and other leading bodies were established to form a nationwide political representation.

The landmarks of the postwar AFPFL's struggle for Myanmar's independence, from 1945 to 1947, were: the AFPFL First National Congress in January 1946 which rejected the British plan for Myanmar's self-government with a status of dominion and which reiterated the AFPFL's demand for Myanmar's full independence; the inclusion of Aung San and several other AFPFL representatives as members of the Executive Council of the British Governor in September 1946; the talks of an Aung San-headed delegation with the British Labour Government in London in January 1947 on the terms of transfer of power; the holding of the conference at Panglong and the signing of the Panglong Agreement (q.v.) in February 1947 which laid the foundation of the Union of Burma (q.v.); the elections to the Constituent Assembly (q.v.) in April 1947 which brought a decisive victory to the AFPFL candidates; the framing of the Constitution of the Union of Burma (q.v.) in September 1947. On the negative side, the postwar decolonization process in Myanmar was accompanied by a growing rivalry between the non-Communist elements of the League and the CPB, which was finally expelled from the AFPFL in October 1946. Another tragic event was the assassination of Aung San and several other national leaders by their political rivals, represented by U Saw (q.v.) in July 1947. After Aung San's death, U Nu (q.v.) assumed the leadership of the AFPFL. In October 1947, he signed a treaty with British Premier Clement Attlee whereby the United Kingdom recognized the Republic of the Union of Burma as an independent and sovereign state.

After independence, declared on 4 January 1948, the AFPFL formed the first government with U Nu as Prime Minister. Due to the ensuing civil war (q.v.), the AFPFL lost its original structure of a national front. Of its founding members, only the Socialist Party (q.v.) (formerly People's Revolutionary Party) and Socialist-controlled labor unions, such as the All Burma Peasants' Organization and Trade Union Congress (Burma) (qq.v.), remained in the League, in an alliance with non-party organizations and individual members. According to the rules, the executive power in the AFPFL between the sessions of the National Conference was lodged with the Supreme Council and its Executive Committee. As the Supreme Council was enlarged to 36 members, and the National Conference was convened only once (in 1958), the policy decisions of the AFPFL were in fact formulated by its Executive Committee, composed mainly of Socialist Party members. The post of AFPFL Chairman (between 1947 and 1958) was held by U Nu who formally did not belong to any political party.

The primary political aim which the AFPFL officially pursued was building a welfare, *pyidawtha* (q.v.), state in Myanmar. In the 1950s, most AFPFL leaders were committed to a kind of socialist ideology. The late 1950s saw growing dissension within the AFPFL, largely as result of personal rivalries and power struggles. In June 1958, the AFPFL split into two independent and rival factions: the Clean AFPFL, led by U Nu, Thakin Tin, Kyaw Dun and others, and the Stable AFPFL, headed by U Kyaw Nyein and U Ba Swe (qq.v.). In the tense political situation, U Nu, as Prime Minister of the Union government, was forced to transfer state power to the Caretaker Government of General Ne Win (q.v.) which administered Myanmar from 1958 to 1960. The 1960 elections returned U Nu and his *Pyidaungsu* Party (q.v.) to power. However, the military coup of 1962 deposed U Nu's government and many leading politicians of both factions of the AFPFL were imprisoned. The AFPFL was disbanded in March 1964, as a result of the Revolutionary Council's (q.v.) ban on legal political parties and mass organizations of the parliamentary era (q.v.). (*See also* Anti-Fascist Resistance; Aung San-Attlee Agreement; Interim Government; Nu-Attlee Agreement; White Paper on Burma.)

ANTI-FASCIST RESISTANCE (1942–1945). The anti-fascist (essentially anti-Japanese) resistance in Myanmar between 1942 and 1945 centered on three main groups: the Communist Party of Burma (CPB), the People's Revolutionary Party (PRP) (qq.v.) and the army. Aside from this resistance movement, which was based from August 1944 on the Anti-Fascist People's Freedom League (q.v.), there were several resistance groups or forces of Myanmar's minority ethnic groups, namely Kachins and Kayins (qq.v.) which were formed or directed by Allied (British or American) officers.

Of the three main and essentially Bamar (q.v.) resistance partners, the CPB had the longest record of involvement in the anti-fascist struggle dating back to early 1943 when the first underground groups were organized by Thakin Soe in the Ayeyarwady Delta (qq.v.) region. The CPB was also responsible for drawing into the resistance movement the members of various mass organizations of the Japanese occupation period, such as the *Do Bama Sinyetha Asi Ayon* and the East Asia Youth League (qq.v.). Than Tun, a minister in Dr. Ba Maw's government (qq.v.) was a well-placed and capable organizer who considerably helped the underground CPB's organizations. As compared with the CPB, the PRP viewed the resistance rather as an activity centered on the army. The PRP leaders, Ba Se, Kyaw Nyein (qq.v.) and Chit, were in contact with junior army officers, some of whom, known as the Army Young Resistance Group, were organizing secret networks in various army units from late 1942. The senior army officers and commanders, including Aung San and Ne Win (qq.v.), also made their resistance preparations.

In early 1945, the resistance was ready, both militarily and politically, to fight the Japanese. On 27 March 1945, the day commemorated now as Resistance Day (q.v.) or Armed Forces Day, the Burma National Army (BNA) (q.v.) launched an armed uprising. Assisted by guerillas, the BNA engaged the Japanese troops in ten resistance zones covering most of southern and central Myanmar. The most intensive fighting with the Japanese took place between March and June 1945 when the army, assisted by civilian resistance organizations, liberated many rural areas of the country as well as some major towns, including Yangon (q.v.). Thereafter, until Japan's formal surrender to the Allies in Myanmar on 12 August 1945, the army was involved in the campaigns in the Sittoung (q.v.) valley.

A significant aspect of the anti-fascist resistance was that it gave its leaders legitimacy not only in Myanmar, but also in British eyes. The British military, namely Force 136, maintained contacts with the Myanmar resistance mainly through Thein Pe Myint (q.v.) who had escaped to India in 1942 where he acted since as liaison between the British and Myanmar resistance forces, later represented by the AFPFL. The Supreme Allied Commander, Admiral Louis Mountbatten (q.v.), who regarded the AFPFL as a viable military ally, was instrumental in promoting the accommodation and reconciliation with its leaders. On 30 March 1945, the British Government approved the policy of supporting the anti-Japanese uprising by the BNA. Following talks on 16 May 1945 between Aung San and Lt. General W. Slim, a representative of the British command in Myanmar, the BNA acquired the status of a temporary British ally, under the name of Patriotic Burmese Forces.

Through the formation of the AFPFL in April 1944, as well as by including the national army within the AFPFL, the anti-fascist resistance created conditions which proved essential for the success of the postwar independence movement (q.v.) in Myanmar.

ANTI-SEPARATIONIST LEAGUE. Also known as Anti-Separation League. This organization was formed in July 1932 to bring together political groups and individuals opposed to the separation of Myanmar from India (q.v.). Basically, the League consisted of two main factions: one, headed by U Chit Hlaing (q.v.), favored Myanmar federation with India; the other, represented by Dr. Ba Maw (q.v.), proposed federation only as a temporary measure to advance the Myanmar independence cause. The Anti-Separationist League won a decisive victory in the elections to the Legislative Council which were held in November 1931. (*See also* Government of Burma Act; Indians; Indian National Congress; Separation League.)

APHWE. Also *ahpwe* or *apwe*. The Myanmar word meaning "association, body, organization."

APPANAGE. The system existing in precolonial Myanmar under which the king provided for the support of his royal relatives through the assignment of an appanage, usually based on a provincial town, the *myo* (q.v.). The holder of such an appanage was known as a *myoza*, the term meaning literally "eater of the town." The *myoza* usually assigned agents to collect the fiefs on his behalf. Even after the replacement of princely provincial governors, the *bayins*, with centrally appointed officials, *myowuns*, representing the king in provincial capitals, the monarch continued to assign appanages to the royalty to ensure their political support. However, the appanage system was not allowed to develop into a feudal system of European type. No proprietary rights were assigned with the grant, no military service was necessarily required and no grant was made in perpetuity. (*See also* Administration of Myanmar, Precolonial Era.)

ARAKAN. The former name of a region and state in the western part of Myanmar, presently known as Rakhine (q.v.). (*See also* Rakhine State.)

ARAKAN LEAGUE FOR DEMOCRACY. The Rakhine (q.v.) political party founded by U Tha Tun and Dr. Saw Mra Aung in the wake of the pro-democracy movement of 1988 (q.v.) in Myanmar. The party won the majority of votes in Rakhine constituencies in the May 1990 elections to the Constituent Assembly. (*See also* Political Organizations.)

ARAKAN NATIONAL CONGRESS (ANC). The organization founded in 1938 through amalgamation of several Rakhine (q.v.) nationalist associations. In 1945, the ANC, led by U Aung Zan Wai, joined the Anti-Fascist People's Freedom League (q.v.) and was formally merged into it in 1947.

ARAKAN NATIONAL LIBERATION PARTY (ANLP). The Rakhine (q.v.) rebel organization. Formed in 1960, it joined the National Unity Front of Arakan (q.v.) in 1989. The ANLP was active mainly in northern Rakhine.

ARAKAN NATIONAL UNITED ORGANIZATION (ANUO). Rakhine (q.v.) political party which grew out of the Independent Arakanese Parliamentary Group established in 1951, in opposition to the Anti-Fascist People's Freedom League government (q.v.) and with a demand of creating a separate Rakhine State in Myanmar. The ANUO was allied, for a time, with the National Unity Front (q.v.) and gained five seats in the 1956 elections to the Union parliament. (*See also* Parliamentary Era.)

ARAKAN YOMA *see* **RAKHINE YOMA.**

ARAKANESE *see* **RAKHINE.**

ARCHITECTURE. Myanmar classical architecture is best symbolized by religious monuments, such as Buddhist pagodas, temples and monasteries.

The term pagoda comes from the Sanskrit term *dhātu garbha*, meaning a shrine for relics. The Myanmar term applied to such structures is *zedi*. It has the same meaning but is derived from Pali (q.v.) *cetiya*. The *zedi* are further classified into those which enshrine relics, implements or garments of the Buddha and sacred books. Pagodas are mostly brickworks covered with stucco and whitewashed; some are made of stones. The tumulus in the shape of an inverted alms bowl, *thabeik*, with a staff, *hti* (q.v.) upon it, projected the main architectural concept of the pagoda which is further embellished by various elements evidently derived from Buddhist cosmology.

The temple (*stupa*) is formed of a square hollow structure, rising up in gradually diminishing terraces and a pyramidal roof, and crowned by a finial. The primary purpose of the temple is to enshrine the Buddha image. Temples, such as those found in Bagan (q.v.), witness Indian and Mon (q.v.) cultural influences, but the peculiar Myanmar style and form, symbolized by huge, high constructions, also evolved.

Apart from pagodas and temples, there are also Buddhist monasteries built of wood, some of them beautifully carved and adorned with gilding and glass mosaics. However, only very few ancient monasteries of this type, such as Shwenandaw Kyaung in Mandalay (q.v.), have been preserved. (*See also* Ananda; Shwedagon.)

ARI. A term of reference to the sects of monks who seemed to have enjoyed considerable wealth and power in the early Bagan (q.v.) period. Although often associated with *naga* (q.v.) worship and Mahayanist (Tantric) practices, the Aris were rather dwellers in jungle monasteries. Their power was broken by King Anawrahta (q.v.), but the sect was never suppressed, continuing its existence over the post-Bagan period until today. (*See also* Buddhism.)

ARMED FORCES. The armed forces at Myanmar's independence in 1948 originated from the Burma Army which incorporated some servicemen of the Patriotic Burmese Forces (q.v.). Due to its origin in the independence movement (q.v.), the Myanmar army has played a key role in the governance and politics of independent Myanmar, particularly following the military coup of 1962 (q.v.).

In 1989, the total strength of Myanmar's armed forces was estimated to be 200,000; there were 182,000 army, 9,000 navy and 9,000 air force personnel. Since then the total number of active duty personnel is reported to have increased and be close to 300,000. The armed forces are controlled by the Ministry of Defense which also functions as a military headquarters. Military service is voluntary, except for the conscriptions of medical doctors. Since 1955, the military has maintained the Defense Services Academy at Pyin-Oo-Lwin (formerly Maymyo) (qq.v.).

In 1991, Myanmar's defense expenditures were estimated to be about 30 percent of total government expenditures. In addition to the direct defense budget, a large percentage of the health budget went to providing medical services to the armed forces.

ARMED FORCES DAY *see* RESISTANCE DAY.

ARTISANAL INDUSTRIES. These consist of major activities dealing with arts and crafts work. Centers of artisanal industry exist in various parts of the country, but they are particularly significant in certain areas of central and southern Myanmar.

Myanmar craftsmen excelled in making fine objects of ivory, bronze, silver and stone for religious purposes, such as Buddha statues, as well as for popular use. A notable and still flourishing ancient craft is the manufacture of gold leaf, which is then pasted on Buddha images and pagodas, concentrated in Mandalay (q.v.). A distinctive handicraft of Myanmar is lacquerware, with principal centers at Nyaung-U by Bagan and at Pyay (qq.v.). Woodcarving, one of the oldest Myanmar crafts, is becoming rather rare now. Another of the ancient Myanmar crafts, the weaving of silk and cotton, still continues to some extent, but only in certain places, like Amarapura (q.v.) and villages at Inle Lake (q.v.). Myanmar is also noted for its ceramics (pottery) and parasols, centered in Pathein (q.v.) in southern Myanmar.

ASI AYON. Also *asi-ayon, asiayon, asi ayone* or *asiayone*. Myanmar term which means "association, organization."

ASOYA. a Myanmar term for "government."

ASSOCIATION OF SOUTHEAST ASIAN NATIONS (ASEAN) (RELATIONS WITH). Although several offers have been made to Myanmar to become a member of ASEAN since the inception of this organization in 1967, successive Myanmar governments have shown as yet no explicit desire to join it. One of the reasons seems to be that Myanmar has deemed it more productive to stress bilateralism in regional relations. During recent years, Myanmar has developed dynamic relations with several ASEAN states, namely with Thailand (q.v.) and Singapore.

Following the military coup of 1988 (q.v.), ASEAN has resisted several attempts by the United States, the EC countries and United Nations to force it to adopt a more resolute stand on human rights abuses by the State Law and Order Restoration Council (SLORC) (q.v.). Considering the SLORC (q.v.) as Myanmar's legitimate government, ASEAN has instead offered a policy of "constructive engagement" which it regards as more effective to bring about political change in the country. Within the framework of business-like relations some ASEAN countries, such as Thailand and Singapore, even signaled outright support to the SLORC. It was only in connection with the Rohingya (q.v.) issue that the attitude of at least some ASEAN countries, like Indonesia and Malaysia, toward the SLORC became more critical. (*See also* Foreign Policy.)

ATHI. "Free service" people in precolonial Myanmar. Unlike the *ahmudan* (q.v.) group, the *athi* population was mostly found in more distant provinces of the state. The *athi* were exempted from regular military service, but in time of need were required to serve as military auxiliaries. They were also subject to higher taxation. (*See also* Administration of Myanmar, Precolonial Era.)

AUNG, BOHMU (aka SAW HLAING, THAKIN) (1910–   ). One of the "Thirty Comrades," he served in the national army during the period of the Japanese occupation of Myanmar (1942–1945) (qq.v.). He was Deputy Commander of the People's Volunteer Organization (1946) and Vice-President of the Anti-Fascist People's Freedom League (1947) (qq.v.). After independence, he served as Deputy Prime Minister (1958) and Minister of Defense (1961). One of the main leaders of the *Pyidaungsu* Party (q.v.), he was twice arrested after the military coup of 1962 (q.v.). In 1968, he was appointed a member of the Internal Unity Advisory Board. In 1972, he fled to Thailand where he joined the U Nu-led Parliamentary Democracy Party (qq.v.). In 1980, he returned to Myanmar in the amnesty. Currently he is Chairman of the League for Democracy and Peace. (*See also* Political Organizations.)

AUNG GYI, BRIGADIER GENERAL (1919–   ). A leading army dissident in 1988, Aung Gyi started his career in the Burma National Army (q.v.). He was one of the leading military administrators in the Caretaker Government of General Ne Win (1958–1960), Ne Win's Deputy and co-conspirator of the military coup of 1962 (qq.v.). He emerged as spokesman of the Revolutionary Council (q.v.), but was dismissed in February 1962, presumably for advocating a more liberal economic policy. After a long retirement from public life, he reemerged in early 1988 as the author of public letters highly critical of the ruling Burma Socialist Programme Party (q.v.). Aung Gyi gained prominence in the pro-democracy movement of 1988 (q.v.). In September 1988, he was elected Chairman of the National League for Democracy (q.v.), but he split from it in early 1989 and founded the Union Nationals Democracy Party. Since then Aung Gyi is supposed to have reverted to support of the ruling State Law and Order Restoration Council (q.v.). His party scored only poor results in the 1990 elections to the Constituent Assembly. (*See also* Political Organizations.)

AUNG SAN, U (1915–1947). Principal leader of the Myanmar independence movement from 1935 to 1947, widely recognized as the architect of the Union of Burma (q.v.) and national hero. Known also under the name Bo Tc Za and under the titles Bogyoke and Thakin (qq.v.). Born on 13 February 1915 in Natmauk, Magway Division (q.v.), he completed his secondary education at Yenangyaung (q.v.) and entered the University of Yangon (q.v.) in 1935. He first became involved in politics as a leader of the students' strike in 1936 when he was elected President of the All Burma Students' Union (q.v.) for the years 1936 to 1938. In 1938, Aung San joined the *Do Bama Asi Ayon* (q.v.) and was its Secretary General until 1940. In the years 1939 to 1940, he was also Secretary General of the Communist Party of Burma (q.v.) and of the Freedom Bloc (q.v.).

In 1940, Aung San left Myanmar to avoid arrest and to seek foreign assistance to fight the British. He was the leader of the "Thirty Comrades" (q.v.) trained by the Japanese in the years 1940 to 1941. From 1941 to 1942 he commanded the Burma Independence Army (q.v.) and, from 1943 to 1945, he was Minister of Defense in Dr. Ba Maw's (q.v.) government. He was also one of the main leaders of the anti-fascist resistance (1942–1945) (q.v.); from 1945 to 1947 he served as President of the Anti-Fascist People's Freedom League (q.v.). In October 1946, he became Deputy Chairman of the British Governor's Executive Council, the Interim Government (q.v.). In January 1947, he negotiated an agreement with the British government in London laying down the terms of Myanmar's independence, known as the Aung San-Attlee Agreement (q.v.). In February 1947, he took part in signing the Panglong Agreement (q.v.) with the ethnic minorities' leaders. He was assassinated at the instigation of his political rival, U Saw (q.v.), along with five other members of the Interim Government on 19 July 1947.

AUNG SAN-ATTLEE AGREEMENT. An agreement which was signed on 27 January 1947 in London, at the conclusion of talks between the Myanmar delegation led by the President of the Anti-Fascist People's Freedom League, Aung San (qq.v.), and British Prime Minister Clement Attlee. This agreement replaced the White Paper on Burma (1945) (q.v.). Myanmar gained the right to hold elections to a Constituent Assembly (q.v.), which was to draw up the constitution of an independent Myanmar and to decide whether Myanmar was to remain within the British Commonwealth or not. The early unification of the whole country, Ministerial Burma and the Frontier Areas (qq.v.), with the free consent of the inhabitants of the latter regions, was also an agreed objective. The British Government recognized the Executive Council of the British Governor in Myanmar as the "Interim Government" (q.v.), agreed to Myanmar's establishment of direct diplomatic relations with foreign countries and promised also to facilitate Myanmar's admission to the United Nations. (*See also* Nu-Attlee Agreement.)

AUNG SAN SUU KYI, DAW (1945–   ). Daughter of Myanmar's national hero, U Aung San (q.v.), she became the main leader and symbol of the pro-democracy movement in Myanmar in 1988 (q.v.). Born on 19 June 1945, she was educated at Yangon (q.v.), New Delhi and Oxford. She then held several posts at the UN Secretariat in New York and in Bhutan. In 1972, she married a British Tibetologist, Dr. Michael Aris, and the next 16 years were spent occupied with her family and academic interests. She returned to Myanmar in early 1988 to take care of her dying mother, Daw Khin Kyi (q.v.), and became involved in the great mass upsurge. On 24 September 1988, a few days after the military coup (q.v.) which brought to power the State Law and Order Restoration Council (q.v.), she was elected Secretary General of the newly formed National League for Democracy (NLD) (q.v.). In early 1989, Daw Aung San Suu Kyi travelled widely across the country and was instrumental in transforming the people's upsurge into an organized movement, based on the principle of non-violence. Nonetheless, she was threatened by the military authorities and put under house arrest in July 1989. She has not been released since then and remains in isolation from the outside world. Her campaigns brought her wide popularity and were among the factors resulting in the NLD's landslide victory in the 1990 elections (q.v.). Daw Aung San Suu Kyi is widely known and respected abroad. In 1990, she was awarded the Thorolf Rafto Prize for Human Rights in Norway and the Sakharov Prize for Freedom of Thought by the European Parliament. In 1991, on nomination by the Czechoslovak President Václav Havel, she was awarded the Nobel Peace Prize.

AVA *see* INWA.

AYEYARWADY DELTA. A fertile area of some 33,670 square kilometers (13,000 square miles) in southern Myanmar. It consists of the Ayeyarwady River (q.v.) and its tributaries and is covered by a network of canals and some four million hectares (nine million acres) of irrigated rice (q.v.) lands. The Delta, originally a tall jungle of grass and swamps, was opened up for rice cultivation and colonization after the British annexation of southern Myanmar in the Second Anglo-Myanmar war in 1852. (*See also* Agriculture; Economy, British Colonial Era; Migration; Population.)

AYEYARWADY DIVISION. It has an area of 35,138 square kilometers (13,567 square miles) and includes almost the whole of the Ayeyarwady Delta (q.v.). The region is the southernmost part of the Central Basin (q.v.) and it is almost flat. The Ayeyarwady Division consists of 2,129 wards and village tracts and 26 townships. Its (1983 census) population was 4,994,061. The majority people are Bamars (q.v.), but there is also a considerable number of Kayins (q.v.). The capital city is Pathein (q.v.). Other important towns are Hinthata, Pyapon and Yandoon. Ayeyarwady Division is the main producer of rice (q.v.) in Myanmar and is known as the "granary" or the "rice bowl" of the country. It is also noted for production of jute (q.v.). Other crops include groundnuts, maize (q.v.), pulses (q.v.), sesame and tobacco (q.v.). The Division is criss-crossed with rivers and lakes, and it is also a major producer of fish, fish paste, fish sauce and dried prawns which are important items in the Myanmar diet. The manufacturing industry is based on agriculture (q.v.); the majority of factories are rice mills.

AYEYARWADY RIVER. Principal river of Myanmar. The Ayeyarwady River is of primary importance as a source of irrigation (q.v.) as well as the main communication line of Myanmar, as several important towns are situated on its banks. Its headwaters are formed by the confluence of the Nmai Kha and Mali Kha in Kachin State, north of Myitkyina (qq.v.). Near Bhamo (q.v.), the Ayeyarwady River becomes broader and it is navigable from this point to the mouth, for about 1,448 km (900 miles). It receives its main tributary, the Chindwinn River (q.v.), below Mandalay (q.v.) and begins to widen into the delta north of Hinthata. The main stream of the river continues towards the Andaman Sea where it empties into dense mangrove swamps. It is linked to Yangon (q.v.) by the Twante Canal, an important navigation channel about 35 kilometers (22 miles) long, which was built in 1883.

AZANI. Also *arzani*. A Myanmar term for "hero." The expression *Azani Ne* ("Heroes' Day") is the name in Myanmar language of a public holiday known in English as Martyrs' Day (q.v.).

-B-

BA CHOE, U (1893–1947). A Myanmar journalist and politician of the preindependence period. As of 1925, he edited the *Deedok* literary magazine; in 1936, he founded the Fabian Party (q.v.). He was a member of the Privy Council during the Japanese occupation of Myanmar (1942–1945) (q.v.). From 1946, he served on the Governor's Executive Council, subsequently the Interim Government, and was assassinated with Aung San (qq.v.) on 19 July 1947. (*See also* Socialism.)

BA GYAN, U. Born in 1909, he was the founder and first President of the East Asia Youth League (q.v.) in 1942. He was also Minister of Education, Health and Municipal Affairs in Dr. Ba Maw's (q.v.) government. From 1945, he served as President of the All Burma Youth League (q.v.) and as a member of the Supreme and Executive Councils of the Anti-Fascist People's Freedom League (q.v.). At independence, in 1948, he became Minister of Judicial Affairs.

BA HEIN, THAKIN (1913–1946). Myanmar journalist, poet, writer and politician of the preindependence period. He first became involved in politics as a leader of the students' strike at Mandalay College in 1936. In 1938, he became Chairman of the All Burma Students' Union (q.v.) and one of the student activists who helped the cause of the oil-field workers' strike (q.v.). In 1939, Ba Hein joined the *Do Bama Asi Ayon* and was a co-founder of the Communist Party of Burma (qq.v.). In 1941, he became Chairman of the *Do Bama Asi Ayon* and was also active in the People's Revolutionary

Party (q.v.). Imprisoned by the British from 1941 to 1942, he joined Dr. Ba Maw's government during the Japanese occupation of Myanmar (1942–1945) (qq.v.). In early 1945, he went underground and acted as political adviser to Aung San (q.v.). He became a member of the Central Committee of the CPB in July 1945. From 1945 to 1946, he was President of the All Burma Trade Union Congress (q.v.). His writings also include translations of Marxist literature and some original political tracts. (*See also* Nagani Book Club; Socialism.)

BA KHAING, MAHN. Also Ba Khin(e), Mahng. A Kayin (q.v.) politician of the preindependence period who advocated the unity of Bamars (q.v.) and Kayins and their existence in a common state. He organized the Karen Youth Organization which became affiliated with the Anti-Fascist People's Freedom League (qq.v.) in 1945. He was a member of the Governor's Executive Council, subsequently the Interim Government (q.v.). He was assassinated with Aung San (q.v.) on 19 July 1947.

BA MAW, DR. (1893–1977). A leading figure in Myanmar politics from the early 1930s to 1945, Ba Maw was educated at Rangoon College, Calcutta University, Cambridge University and University of Bordeaux where he received a Ph.D. in 1924. He set up a legal practice in Yangon and became a defense lawyer for Saya San (qq.v.). He led a faction of the Anti-Separationist League (q.v.). In 1936, he founded and led the *Sinyetha Party* (q.v.), was elected to parliament and became the first Myanmar Prime Minister (1937–1939). When his government fell in February 1939, he joined the opposition. In October 1939, he allied his party with the *Do Bama Asi Ayon* and some other parties to form the Freedom Bloc (qq.v.). From 1940 to 1942, he was imprisoned by the British. Upon the Japanese occupation of Myanmar in 1942, he first became Head of the Burmese Provisional Administrative Committee and then, from 1 August 1943 to 1945, he was Head of State of a nominally independent Myanmar. In 1944, he founded the *Maha Bama Asi Ayon* (q.v.). In 1945, he fled to Japan where he surrendered to the Allied authorities who tried and imprisoned him in Tokyo (1945–1946). On his return to Myanmar in 1946 he reestablished the *Maha Bama* as a political party but failed to gain mass support. In 1957, he retired from active politics and returned to legal practice. In 1966, he was imprisoned and interned for some time by the Revolutionary Council (q.v.).

BA NYEIN, U (1914–   ). One of the leaders of the Burma Workers' and Peasants' Party and member of the presidium of the National United Front (qq.v.). In 1956, Ba Nyein was elected to the Union Parliament. After the military coup of 1962 (q.v.), he was appointed a member of the Revolutionary Council (q.v.) and also served as a financial adviser to General Ne Win's (q.v.) government. Ba Nyein is considered to be one of the authors of the "Burmese Way to Socialism" (q.v.) program in 1962. (*See also* Burma Socialist Programme Party; Socialism.)

BA PE, U. One of the founders of the Young Men's Buddhist Association (q.v.) in 1906, Ba Pe also started the oldest Myanmar-language newspaper, the *Thuriya* ("The Sun") in 1911. He gained prominence as a leading figure in Myanmar politics in the 1920s and the 1930s. After the split in the General Council of Burmese Associations (q.v.) in 1922, he joined the group of nationalist politicians who subsequently founded the Nationalist Party (q.v.). From 1923, he served in the Legislative Council (q.v.) and later was Cabinet Minister (1930–1932; 1934–1936; 1939–1940). During the period of the Japanese occupation of Myanmar (q.v.), he stayed out of politics. After the war, he was appointed as a representative of the Anti-Fascist People's Freedom League (q.v.) in the Governor's Executive Council. In 1947, he founded his own political party. In 1949, he was tried on the charge of high treason and, from 1954 to 1958, he was imprisoned. After 1958, he retired from active politics.

BA SEIN, THAKIN (1910–1964). Myanmar politician of the preindependence and postindependence period. From 1930 to 1931, he was President of the Rangoon University Students' Union and, from 1935 to 1936, Chairman of the *Do*

Bama Asi Ayon (qq.v.). In 1938, along with Thakin Tun Ok (q.v.), he led a splinter fraction from the *Do Bama Asi Ayon*, known also as Ba Sein-Tun Ok *Do Bama*. In 1940, he was arrested by the British (1940–1942). During the Japanese occupation of Myanmar (1942–1945) (q.v.), he served in various administrative capacities. In 1943, he was a minister in Dr. Ba Maw's (q.v.) government, but became involved in political intrigues and was sent by the Japanese to Java for the duration of war. On his return to Myanmar in 1946, he became a councillor in the Governor's Executive Council. In January 1947, he accompanied Aung San (q.v.) to London, but refused to sign the Aung San-Attlee Agreement (q.v.). From 1947 to 1948, he was imprisoned in connection with the assassination of Aung San (q.v.) and his colleagues. In 1947, he reorganized the *Do Bama Asi Ayon* into the Burma Democratic Party. In 1962, he retired from active politics.

BA SWE, U (1915–1987). One of the leading figures of Myanmar politics and of the Socialist Party (q.v.) from the early 1940s. Born in Dawei District on 7 October 1915, Ba Swe was educated at the University of Yangon (q.v.). He was Secretary of the All Burma Students' Union (q.v.) from 1938 to 1939. He joined the *Do Bama Asi Ayon* (q.v.) and was one of the founders and leaders of the People's Revolutionary Party (q.v.) in 1939. During the Japanese occupation of Myanmar (q.v.), he served as Chief of the *Keibotai* (q.v.) or Civil Defense in Yangon, utilizing the organization as one of the channels for drawing young Bamars into the anti-fascist resistance (q.v.). In September 1945, Ba Swe became President of the Socialist Party and, from 1947 to 1952, he served as Secretary General of the Anti-Fascist People's Freedom League (AFPFL) (q.v.). In 1952, he became a Member of Parliament; in 1953, he joined the cabinet as Minister of Defense. He then served as Prime Minister of the Union of Burma (q.v.) (1956–1957) and as Deputy Prime Minister (1957–1958). On the AFPFL's split in June 1958, he and U Kyaw Nyein (q.v.) became the main leaders of the Stable AFPFL. After the military coup of 1962 (q.v.), Ba Swe was detained for some time by the military authorities.

U Ba Swe was regarded as the main ideologue of the Socialist Party and a political leader with an international reputation. In 1953, he was elected President of the Asian Socialist International.

BA THEIN TIN, THAKIN (1914–). One of the principal leaders of the Communist Party of Burma (q.v.) in the postindependence period. He became a member of the Central Committee of the CPB in July 1945. In 1948, he went underground, in 1950, he was elected Vice-Chairman and, in March 1975, Chairman of the CPB. He was reelected Chairman in 1985. He held the post until April 1989 when the CPB disintegrated and he was forced, with other veteran party leaders, to flee from the CPB's headquarters at Panghsang in Shan State to the People's Republic of China (qq.v.).

BA U GYI, SAW. A Kayin (q.v.) leader who became a member of Governor's Executive Council in 1946. He resigned, organized the Karen National Union (q.v.) and, in February 1949, joined the Kayin (q.v.) revolt. He was killed in a battle in August 1950. (*See also* Civil War.)

BA ZAN, MAHN. The first commander of the Karen National Defence Organization (q.v.) in 1949, and one of the main leaders of the Kayin (q.v.) revolt. For a time, he advocated a leftist political line, serving as Chairman of the Karen National United Party (KNUP) (q.v.). But, in 1966, he split from the KNUP and joined the Karen National Liberation Council led by Bo Mya (qq.v.). In 1968, together with Bo Mya, he formed the Karen National United Front, as a successor organization to the KLNC. He was the KLNC's Chairman until May 1976 when he was replaced by Bo Mya. He died in 1981.

BAGAN. The ancient, now ruined capital located on the eastern bank of the Ayeyarwady River (q.v.), about 193 kilometers (120 miles) south of Mandalay (q.v.). Bagan is one of the richest archaeological sites in Asia, an impressive repository of ancient Myanmar architecture (q.v.). The ruins of the city, consisting of some 5,000 pagodas, temples and other religious edifices, cover an area of some 40 square kilometers (16 square miles). Bagan's classical name is Arimaddana, this term meaning "crushing of the enemies." The name Bagan (Pagan) is said to have been derived from the word "Pyugama," a Pyu (q.v.) village. The area of present Bagan was settled in the early 2nd century A.D., probably by the Pyus, whose king, Thammudarit, is regarded by Myanmar chronicles to be the founder of Bagan. The city walls were erected in the 9th century by King Pinbya of the first Bagan dynasty. It was, however, only with King Anawrahta (q.v.) and his successors that Bagan attained its importance as the capital of the First Myanmar Empire (q.v.) as well as the center of Buddhist culture and learning.

The majority of Bagan's great temples, including Ananda (q.v.), were built during the "golden age of Bagan," between the 11th and the 13th centuries, before Bagan was overrun by the Mongols in 1287. In 1975, Bagan was hit by a powerful earthquake which shattered many of its buildings, though only few important temples were irreparably damaged. Reconstruction, aided by UNESCO, and carried out by the Myanmar government, started almost immediately and major reconstruction work has been completed. (*See also* Bagan Dynasty.)

BAGAN DYNASTY. Known also as the Dynasty of the Temple Builders, it ruled Myanmar from 1044 A.D. to 1287 A.D. Its kings were: Anawrahta (1044–1077) (q.v.), Sawlu (1077–1084), Kyanzittha (1084–1111) (q.v.), Alaungsithu (1111–1167) (q.v.), Narathu (1167–1170), Naratheinkha (1170–1173), Narapatisithu (1173–1210) (q.v.), Nadaungmya (1210–1234), Kyazwa (1234–1249), Uzana (1249–1254), and Narathihapati (1254–1287) (q.v.). Kyawzwa (1287–1300) and Sawhnit (1300–1312) were puppet kings who ruled after the fall of Bagan when the real power rested with the Three Shan Brothers (q.v.). With Kyawzwa and Sawhnit, the Bagan Dynasty died, although Bagan (q.v.) still remained an important Myanmar center. (*See also* First Myanmar Empire.)

BAGO. The capital of Bago Division (q.v.), with a (1983 census) population of 150,528. The city lies on the banks of the Bago

River (q.v.), about 80 kilometers (50 miles) northeast of Yangon (q.v.). It is a major road and railroad junction and a collecting center for agriculture (q.v.) and forest products, namely bamboo, rice and teak (qq.v.). Founded about 850 A.D., Bago was the capital of the Mon (q.v.) kingdom in southern Myanmar and of the Second Myanmar Empire (q.v.), between 1539 and 1634. During the 16th and 17th centuries, Bago was Myanmar's greatest sea port. Completely destroyed by King Alaungpaya (q.v.) in 1757, it was partially rebuilt by King Bodawpaya (q.v.). However, it did not regain its former significance and splendor, as the Bago River changed its course and Bago was cut off from the sea. Bago is noted for several famous pagodas, temples and religious buildings.

BAGO DIVISION. It covers an area of 39,404 square kilometers (15,214 square miles). It is located between Mandalay and Magway Divisions (qq.v.) on the north, Rakhine State and Ayeyarwady Division (qq.v.) on the south, and Kayin State and Shan State (qq.v.) on the east. It occupies the southern part of the Central Basin (q.v.), being a low-lying region, with the exception of its center, where the Bago Yoma (q.v.) extends. Bago Division is drained by the Ayeyarwady River (q.v.) and its tributaries. It consists of 28 townships and 1,624 wards and village tracts. Its (1983 census) population was 3,799,791, mostly Bamars, Kayins and Mons (qq.v.). The capital city is Bago (q.v.); other important towns include Pyay (q.v.), Toungoo (q.v.) and Tharrawaddy. Bago Division is the second major rice (q.v.) producing region of Myanmar, after the Ayeyarwady Division (q.v.). Other major crops are groundnuts, jute (q.v.), pulses (q.v.), sesame, sugarcane (q.v.), and tobacco (q.v.). The forests of the division offer valuable woods, such as *ingyin*, *pyinkado* and teak (q.v.). Industries are mostly based on agriculture and forestry (qq.v.) products; rice and saw mills prevail. With a broad network of roads and railroads, Bago Division is an important communications center of the country.

BAGO RIVER. A river about 240 kilometers (150 miles) long in Bago Division (q.v.). It rises in the Bago Yoma (q.v.), then flows southwest, passing through Bago (q.v.) and joins the Hlaing River at Thanlyin near Yangon (q.v.).

BAGO YOMA. A mountain range which is a continuation of the Minwun range of the Kachin Hills. It extends from Mount Popa (q.v.) near Myingyan in the north in a southward direction to Yangon (q.v.). One of its last spurs is Pagoda Hill on which Shwedagon Pagoda (q.v.) in Yangon stands. (*See also* Yoma.)

BAGYIDAW. King of the Konbaung Dynasty (1819–1837) (q.v.). In 1822, he moved the capital from Amarapura back to Inwa (qq.v.). Soon after he ascended the throne, he overran Assam and Manipur. These raids, as well as incidents on the Rakhine (q.v.) border with the British territory of Bengal, were among the factors leading to the First Anglo-Myanmar war in 1824. Despite losing about two-fifths of his empire in the war, Bagyidaw retained the throne. Shortly after the war he ordered a census. In 1829, he established the committee to compile the *Hmannan Yazawin* (q.v.), the standard chronicle down to 1752. From 1831, he became uncommunicative and finally went insane. In 1837, he was deposed by his brother, Prince Tharrawaddy (q.v.), who seized the throne. He died in 1846. (*See also* Burney, Henry; Treaty of Yandabo.)

BAMAR. The term now used in Myanmar to denote the majority ethnic group, previously referred to as Burman or Burmese (qq.v.). The "Adaptation of Expressions Law," promulgated by the State Law and Order Restoration Council (q.v.) on 18 June 1989, decreed that the expressions Burman and Burmese should be replaced by the term Myanmar (q.v.). As the latter term is also used to denote all indigenous citizens of the country (as well as the country as such), the term Bamar is employed when referring to ethnic Myanmars as opposed to other ethnic groups, such as Kachins, Kayins, Mons, Shans, etc. (qq.v.).

Bamars belong to a Tibeto-Burman ethnolinguistic group of Mongoloid racial origin, making up 69 percent of the total population of the Union of Myanmar (q.v.). They are settled in the valleys of the Ayeyarwady, Chindwinn and Sittoung Rivers (qq.v.) and in the delta plain to the south. They also live along the coast of Rakhine and Tanintharyi (qq.v.). The Rakhines, living in Rakhine State (q.v.), are an ethnic group akin to the Bamars; their language, however, has regional variations. In the Central Basin (q.v.) and in Tanintharyi there are large ethnic groups of Kayins and Mons, while in the northern part of the Central Basin the Bamars share their settlement with the Shans. The Bamars were known as people who rarely left their homeland for good; more recently, however, there have been Bamar migrations to other parts of Myanmar as well as abroad, mostly for economic and political reasons. According to the 1983 census, there were 23,532,433 Bamars out of the total 35,307,913 inhabitants of the Union of Myanmar.

Traditionally, Bamars are agrarian people. Most of them live in compact villages comprising the areas devoted to their houses, fields, the land of the monastery, waste land and the cemetery. There is usually a Buddhist pagoda and a rest house in every village. The rural Bamars make their living as wet-agriculturalists, with a variety of rice (q.v.) and other crops grown. The most common domestic animals, used for draft, are buffalo and cattle. The village, or a group of villages, is the basic unit of traditional Bamar socio-political organization.

After the British annexation of Myanmar in the 19th century, Bamar-inhabited areas of the country, which came under direct rule, felt the greatest impact of Western culture. Urbanization took place, though on a much more modest scale than in some other Southeast Asian countries. The English language and Western education have since become important tools of upward social mobility. Still, many Bamars, particularly in the rural areas, are tradition-bound due to the strong impact on their lives of Buddhism (q.v.) and religious values.

BAMBOO. A widely distributed and much used forest product throughout Myanmar. Bamboo is most plentiful in tropical evergreen forests. It provides household and farm utensils, such as beams, piles and supports in construction of houses. Furniture, such as boxes and containers, baskets, parts of clothing, and woven mats, are also made of bamboo. Bamboo is used as a material for constructing bridges, surfacing roads, making rafts and water conduits. It is fabricated into various utensils and artifacts and provides raw material for pulp and paper. Tender bamboo shoots and sprouts are utilized as food.

BANDULA, MAHA. Myanmar general, whose full name was Thado Mingyi Maha Bandula. He served under King Bodawpaya and his successor King Bagyidaw (qq.v.). In 1819, Maha Bandula was appointed Governor of Assam by King Bagyidaw. He commanded the Myanmar troops in the First Anglo-Myanmar war and was killed in action at the battle of Danubyu on 1 April 1825. (*See also* Anglo-Myanmar War, First.)

BANGLADESH (RELATIONS WITH). Myanmar was among the first Asian countries to recognize the new state of Bangladesh in 1971. However, relations between the two countries have not been entirely smooth. Problems arose primarily in connection with illegal immigrants from Bangladesh to Myanmar, the smuggling of goods across the border and the existence of the Rohingya (q.v.) Muslim community in the border areas of Rakhine State (q.v.). In 1978, some 300,000 Rohingya Muslims temporarily fled from Rakhine to Bangladesh when the Myanmar army conducted citizenship checks in the Rakhine border areas. In July 1979, the two countries signed an agreement which provided for the repatriation of most Muslim refugees to Myanmar. In 1982, an agreement on the demarcation line along the 142-kilometer-long frontier was signed and the boundary was formally agreed in 1985. Nonetheless, the crisis flared up again in 1991, as a result of renewed Myanmar army operations against the Rohingyas in northern Rakhine, with an estimated 280,000 Rohingyas again seeking refuge in Bangladesh. According to the agreement reached between the two countries in April 1992, the refugees are to be taken back to Myanmar, but the repatriation process only proceeds slowly. The Rohingya issue is likely to remain a strain on bilateral relations as well as the support the Muslim separatist organizations operating in Rakhine allegedly receive from abroad through Bangladesh.

BANKING *see* FINANCE.

BASSEIN *see* PATHEIN.

BASSEIN RIVER *see* PATHEIN RIVER.

BAWDWIN-NAMTU MINES. Mines situated near Lashio in northern Shan State (qq.v.). They are supposed to be among the richest lead and silver (qq.v.) mines in the world, their products including also zinc (q.v.) and copper. Worked from the 16th century on by the Chinese (q.v.), the mining and processing of minerals in Bawdwin-Namtu was considerably expanded during the British colonial era, when the mines belonged to the Burma Corporation (q.v.). By the 1920s, Bawdwin had become the most important lead mine in the world and a chief source of silver. The annual export was 75,000 tons of lead and 60,000 tons of zinc concentrates. In 1951, the Burma Corporation became a joint venture with the Myanmar government and, in 1965, the concern was nationalized. Due to the civil war (q.v.) and lack of funds and machinery, the postindependence output of the Bawdwin-Namtu mines fell considerably below prewar levels. (*See also* Minerals.)

BAYINGYI. A Myanmar term for referring to Portuguese and Eurasians, especially those who were resettled in the regions near Shwebo (q.v.) following the seizure of Felipe de Brito's capital of Thanlyin (q.v.) by Myanmar troops in 1612. (*See also* Feringhi; Portuguese and Myanmar; Second Myanmar Empire.)

BAYINNAUNG (r. 1551–1581). Myanmar's most celebrated king-warrior. In a series of campaigns conducted between 1555 and 1559, Bayinnaung brought under his rule northern Myanmar, including the present Shan State (q.v.), Manipur, Chiengmai and Vientiane. Continuing his conquests he subdued neighboring Ayutthaya, turning it into a vassal state of Myanmar between 1568 and 1569. He ruled from Bago (q.v.) and he treated Mons (q.v.) with respect. He forbade animal sacrifices and introduced prohibition. He also adopted a unified code of laws and tried to standardize weights and measures. He failed, however, to create an effective administration and the stability of his empire rested solely on military strength and allegiance to his person. The incessant military campaigns exhausted the country's human and material resources. On Bayinnaung's death, the people who were subjugated to his rule reasserted their independence. (*See also* Second Myanmar Empire; Toungoo Dynasty.)

BEIK. A town in Tanintharyi Division (q.v.) situated at the mouth of the Tanintharyi and the Kyaukpya rivers on the Andaman sea. Its port was crucial in coastal trade for export of fish products, rubber (q.v.), tin and tungsten. Beik was also an early British settlement in Myanmar and an outpost of the British East India Company from 1695.

BEIKTHANO. Also *Peikthano* or Vishnu City. An old, now ruined Pyu (q.v.) site near Taungdwingyi in Magway Division (q.v.). Excavations in Beikthano revealed an early Pyu culture, probably flourishing between the 1st and 5th centuries A.D. The finds include a gateway of the city wall, residential buildings and religious structures as well as burial urns and pottery. The city was evidently destroyed by fire. (*See also* Halin; Sri Ksetra.)

BHAMO. A town in Kachin State (q.v.) on the upper Ayeyarwady River (q.v.). Located on an ancient route to Myitkyina (q.v.) and through it into Yunnan, Bhamo was an important center of overland trade with China.

BO. A Myanmar term for commander, leader of a force, or military officer. More specifically, a term denoting the rank of lieutenant in the armed forces (q.v.). Also a term for referring (in the 1950s) to a local strongman or political boss as well as an archaic designation for Europeans in Myanmar. (*See also* Bogyoke.)

BODAWPAYA. Also Bodawhpaya. A king of the Konbaung Dynasty (1782–1819) (q.v.). In 1783, he moved the capital from Inwa to Amarapura (qq.v.). He was inclined towards religious bigotry, decreed the death penalty for taking intoxicants and conscripted forced labor for construction of religious buildings. His conquest of Rakhine (q.v.) in 1785 turned this hitherto independent kingdom into a province of Myanmar. Bodawpaya's expansion eastward to Ayutthaya was checked by the Thais. The king received British embassies, but refused to have diplomatic relations with the British East India Company. He is considered to have been a very powerful king of Myanmar, second only to Bayinnaung (q.v.). (*See also* Third Myanmar Empire.)

BOGYOKE. A Myanmar term meaning "general, senior commander." In modern usage, Major-General. The rank of Aung San and Ne Win (qq.v.).

BOMBAY BURMAH TRADING CORPORATION. The British trade corporation, founded in Bombay in 1863, which became directly involved in the events leading up to the Third Anglo-Myanmar war in 1885 and the annexation of the rest of Myanmar by the British. Most historians now agree that the cause of the Bombay Burmah Trading Corporation was only a contributing factor in the war.

During the period of British colonial rule in Myanmar, the Bombay Burmah Trading Corporation became the largest exporter of Myanmar teak (q.v.). It was nationalized by the government of the Union of Burma (q.v.) in June 1984. (*See also* Anglo-Myanmar War, Third; Economy, British Colonial Era.)

BRANG SENG, MARANG. A top-ranking Kachin (q.v.) rebel leader. In 1964, he joined the Kachin Independence Army (q.v.) and became its Chief Commander in 1975. He also became Chairman of the Kachin Independence Organization (q.v.) and of the Kachin Independence Council. In November 1988, he was appointed Vice-Chairman of the newly formed Democratic Alliance of Burma (q.v.). (*See also* Civil War.)

BRITISH BURMA, PROVINCE OF see ADMINISTRATION OF MYANMAR, BRITISH COLONIAL ERA.

BRITO, FELIPE DE see PORTUGUESE AND MYANMAR.

BUDDHISM. Almost 90 percent of the people of Myanmar, namely the Bamars, Mons and Shans (qq.v.), profess Buddhism as their religion. The Buddhism which prevails in Myanmar is Theravada Buddhism, known also as Hinayana, or the Lesser Vehicle.

It is assumed that Buddhism reached Myanmar from India in the first millennium A.D. The famous Indian monk Buddhagosa is believed to have carried the scriptures of the Pali Buddhist Canon, the *Tipitaka* (q.v.), to the Mon (q.v.) capital Thaton (q.v.) in 403 A.D. According to Myanmar chronicles, King Anawrahta (q.v.) obtained Pali scriptures on his conquest of Thaton in 1057 and introduced Buddhism to Bagan (q.v.). This process evidently involved the adoption into Buddhism of some elements of the indigenous animism (q.v.) and of Mahayana Buddhism, while breaking the power of the Ari (q.v.) priests.

The material manifestations of Theravada Buddhism in Myanmar include the *Tipitaka* and their commentaries, the Buddhist monastic order, the *sangha* (q.v.), and the architecture (q.v.) of a religious nature, such as pagodas, temples and monasteries.

The pure form of Buddhism has largely been confined to the monks, the *pongyis* (q.v.). Ordinary believers, the majority of whom are peasants, forming the bulk of the population, profess a syncretic religion, including basic Buddhist tenets, as well as many elements of animism coupled with cosmological beliefs of Hindu-Buddhist origin. The peasants' knowledge of doctrinal Buddhism is limited to the practical code of morality, embedded in a few verses and in the Five Precepts (q.v.); these may be enhanced by the stricter Eight or Ten Precepts on Buddhist sabbath days. Another kind of necessary knowledge of an ordinary believer is that of the tales of the lives of the Buddha, the *Jataka* (q.v.) tales. There is no true form of worship in Myanmar Buddhism. The only ritual is the *awgatha*, the standard thrice-daily recitation of the *tiyatana* (q.v.), or the Three Jewels. Another form of devotion is *bhavana* meditation, that is telling 108 rosary beads while concentrating one's mind on the virtues and glories of the Buddha, the *dhamma* (q.v.), or the law, and the *sangha*.

According to Buddhist doctrine, all living things are included in the endless, perpetual cycle of rebirth and suffering, or the *samsara* (q.v.), which can only be escaped by following the path leading to *nirvana* (q.v.). Most ordinary believers are, however, not as interested in pursuing the goal of *nirvana*, as in achieving a better rebirth in their next life. This philosophy is based on the idea of one's destiny, or *kan* (q.v.), and good merit, or *kutho* (q.v.), which can influence it in a positive way. *Kutho*, merit-making, is one of the basic concerns of ordinary Myanmar Buddhists.

Over the centuries, Buddhism has exerted considerable influence on Myanmar social life. Traditionally, the principles of social relations were based on Buddhist ethics which called for a high degree of respect for the *pongyi* as well as for elders. Although this traditional structure has undergone considerable change due to modernization, it is still preserved in the rural countryside. Elsewhere, religious holidays and festivals (q.v.) remain dominant in Myanmar family and social life. Buddhism has also determined the culture and traditions of the Myanmar people. It has become one of the most important and universally accepted symbols upon which the Bamars' sense of national identity is still based and which shapes their political thought.

BUDDHIST COUNCILS *see* FIFTH GREAT BUDDHIST COUNCIL; SIXTH GREAT BUDDHIST COUNCIL.

BUDDHIST LAW *see* DHAMMATHAT.

BUDDHIST MONASTIC ORDER *see* SANGHA.

BUDDHIST MONK *see* PONGYI.

BURMA. A still widely used term for referring to the country which is now officially known as *Myanmar, Myanma(r)*

Naingngandaw, Naing Ngan, or the Union of Myanmar (qq.v.). More specifically, the term Burma, or also Burma proper (q.v.), was used to denote that part of the Union of Myanmar inhabited mainly by the Bamars (q.v.). (*See also* Socialist Republic of the Union of Burma; Union of Burma.)

BURMA ARMY. The term designating the army of the British colonial era. Prior to 1945, the army was recruited mainly among the Indians and some minority ethnic groups such as Chins, Kachins and Kayins (qq.v.). In 1945, the Burma Army was reorganized to include a number of servicemen from Myanmar wartime military organizations, the Burma Independence Army (q.v.) and its successors. After some further expansion which took place between 1945 and 1947, and which also involved the development of the Burma Navy and Burma Air Force, the Burma Army subsequently became the nucleus of the armed forces of the Union of Burma (qq.v.) in 1948.

BURMA BAPTIST CONVENTION *see* CHRISTIANITY.

BURMA CITIZENSHIP LAW (1982) *see* NATIONALITY.

BURMA COMMUNIST PARTY *see* COMMUNIST PARTY OF BURMA.

BURMA CORPORATION. The British company which operated the Bawdwin-Namtu mines in Shan State (qq.v.) from the beginning of the 20th century. On 16 October 1951, the Burma Corporation was transformed into the Burma Corporation (Ltd) with about 50 percent of its shares held by the government of the Union of Burma (q.v.). The concern was nationalized on 18 January 1965. (*See also* Minerals.)

BURMA DEFENCE ARMY (BDA). A Myanmar wartime military organization which succeeded the Burma Independence Army (BIA) (q.v.) in August 1942. Compared with the BIA, the BDA was greatly reduced in numbers, totaling some 4,000 men, mostly former BIA servicemen. But the continuity of command was preserved with Aung San (q.v.) remaining Commander in Chief of the BDA and some of the "Thirty Comrades" (q.v.) serving on the army's general staff. It was conceived as a frontier guard and a force entrusted with the task of defending Burma. (*See also* Burma Independence Army; Burma National Army; Japanese Occupation of Myanmar.)

BURMA INDEPENDENCE ARMY (BIA). The first Myanmar nationalist military organization. The BIA was formally inaugurated at a ceremony held on 28 December 1941 in Bangkok by young Myanmar volunteers, previously trained by the Japanese and known as "Thirty Comrades," and some Japanese members of the *Minami Kikan* (qq.v.). The BIA joined the Japanese army in the campaign against the British in Myanmar from December 1941 to May 1942. BIA operations covered the whole of Myanmar, except the Shan States, the Chin Hills and the Rakhine Yoma (qq.v.). The army fought one major battle with the retreating British army at Shwedaung, a small town about 12 kilometers (9 miles) south of Pyay (q.v.). The BIA's ranks were vastly expanded to include more than 20,000 young Myanmars, mostly Bamars (q.v.) from southern Myanmar. With the fall of Yangon (q.v.) on 8 March 1942, Aung San replaced Keiji Suzuki (qq.v.) as Commander in Chief of the BIA and Bo Let Ya (q.v.) was named Chief of Staff. During the campaign, the BIA, assisted by the *Thakins* of the *Do Bama Asi Ayon* (qq.v.), set up local administrative committees in the areas of the country under their control. These committees were supervised by the *Bama Naingngan Okkyoke Baho Htanagyoke*, also known as the *Bama Naingngan Baho Asoya*, organs referred to in English as the Burma Administrative Headquarters and the Burma Central Government respectively, which were set up in Yangon on 7 April 1942 by the Japanese and headed by Thakin Tun Ok (q.v.).

However, these developments were not without problems. Clashes occurred between some BIA troops and the Kayins (q.v.) in the delta districts of southern Myanmar. They started in March 1942, largely as a result of the BIA's attempts to disarm the Kayin ex-servicemen of the Burma Army (q.v.). Rapid, largely unrestrained growth of the BIA resulted in a lack of effective central control of the troops and many cases of abuse of power by BIA servicemen. There were also conflicts with the Japanese due to a growing disappointment of BIA officers and other nationalists with Japan's failure to proclaim Myanmar independence.

In June 1942, the BIA local administrative committees and Burma Administrative Headquarters were dissolved. On 24 July, the BIA was disbanded and replaced by the Burma Defence Army (q.v.). (*See also* Burma Defence Army; Japanese Occupation of Myanmar.)

BURMA NATIONAL ARMY (BNA). A Myanmar wartime military organization which was created on 26 August 1943 by reorganizing and renaming the Burma Defence Army (q.v.). As former head of the army, Aung San (q.v.) became Minister of Defense in Dr Ba Maw's (q.v.) government; the post of Commander in Chief of the BNA went to Colonel Ne Win (q.v.). As of late 1944, the BNA's strength was about 15,000 men. The BNA played a major role in the final phase of the anti-fascist resistance (q.v.), by launching an armed uprising against the Japanese on 27 March 1945, now commemorated as Armed Forces Day (q.v.). (*See also* Japanese Occupation of Myanmar; Patriotic Burmese Forces.)

BURMA PROPER. The name used during the British colonial era for that part of Myanmar including the valleys of the Ayeyarwady and Chindwinn Rivers (qq.v.) and the delta plain to the south of this area which is inhabited mainly by the Bamars (q.v.). Under the Constitution of the Union of Burma (1947) (q.v.), the term Burma proper referred to the administrative divisions of Ayeyarwady, Bago, Magway, Mandalay, Sagaing, Rakhine, Tanintharyi and Yangon (qq.v.). Of these, Rakhine became a state under the Constitution of the Socialist Republic of the Union of Burma (q.v.) in 1974. (*See also* Lower Burma; Upper Burma.)

BURMA RESEARCH SOCIETY. A learned society initiated by J. S. Furnivall (q.v.) and founded on 29 March 1910 in Yangon (q.v.). Among its main objectives were to promote cultural and scientific studies and research on Myanmar and the neighboring countries. The Society attracted a number of outstanding scholars such as C. O. Bladgen, C. Duroiselle, D. G. E. Hall (q.v.) and G. H. Luce (q.v.) and, more recently, Myanmar scholars such as U Pe Maung Tin (q.v.). The Society organized regular sessions and conferences; it also published manuscripts and texts relating to Myanmar culture and history. *The Journal of the Burma Research Society* was started in 1911 by J. S. Furnivall and U May Oung (q.v.) and was published twice a year, in English and Myanmar. In 1980, on the government's order, the Society was closed down and its journal ceased to be published.

BURMA ROAD. Also known as the Lashio-Kunming Highway. The road, about 1120 kilometers (700 miles) long, extended from the Lashio (q.v.) railhead, through Muse and on to Kunming in China. Constructed largely through Chinese efforts, it was opened to traffic in late 1938. For three years the Burma Road carried to Nationalist China the war supplies which were first landed at Yangon (q.v.) and then shipped by railroad to Lashio. During the latter phase of World War II (q.v.), the Burma Road was joined by the Ledo Road (q.v.) and both played an important role as supply links to the Allied forces operating in the China-Burma-India theater of war. (*See also* Roads.)

BURMA SOCIALIST PROGRAMME PARTY (BSPP). Also referred to as the *Lanzin* Party. The political party formed in July 1962 by the Revolutionary Council (RC) (q.v.). Between March 1964 and September 1988, the BSPP was the only legal and also the ruling political party in Myanmar.

The party's ideology was based on the RC's policy declaration of the "Burmese Way to Socialism" of 30 April 1962, which rejected the parliamentary system and confirmed the commitment of Myanmar's military rulers to the goal of building in the country "a socialist society" based on "socialist democracy." The BSPP's philosophy was outlined in the document entitled "System of Correlation of Man and His Environment." Published in 1963, this document drew from various sources, but its main terms were Theravada Buddhist concepts. In 1964, another basic document, the "Specific Characteristics of the Burma Socialist Programme Party," was published and set forth the differences in the BSPP platform as compared to Communist and Social Democratic parties.

The BSPP was conceived as a small, "cadre" party and its transformation into a mass political party only began in 1971. Although the number of both full and candidate members rose rapidly during the 1970s and the early 1980s, until recently the majority of party members were drawn from the armed forces (q.v.) and the police. Senior military officers held almost all posts of importance in the leading organs of the BSPP. Between 1971 and 1988, several regular and extraordinary BSPP congresses were held which reflected the growing economic, social, organizational and political problems which the party leadership had to tackle while trying to implement its program goals. On 10 September 1988, the BSPP convened its last (emergency) congress which proposed to hold general elections in Myanmar under a multi-party system. The party's integrity was largely shattered as a result of the pro-democracy movement of 1988 (q.v.). On 26 September 1988, the BSPP was formally reorganized as the National Unity Party (q.v.). (*See also* Burma Socialist Programme Party Era; State Law and Order Restoration Council.)

BURMA SOCIALIST PROGRAMME PARTY (BSPP) ERA. Referred to by various terms, the BSPP era is considered here as the era which, unlike the preceding parliamentary era (1948–1962) (q.v.), was characterized by the existence of one legal and ruling party, the BSPP. It covers 26 years, from July 1962, when the BSPP was formed to ultimately become the only legally permitted party in March 1964, and it lasted until September 1988, when the transfer to a multi-party political system was sanctioned by the State Law and Order Restoration Council (q.v.).

The BSPP era may be divided into two successive sub-periods: military rule (1962–1974) and socialist constitutional rule (1974–1988) (qq.v.).

BURMA TRADE UNION CONGRESS *see* TRADE UNION CONGRESS (BURMA).

BURMA TRANSLATION SOCIETY *see* SARPAY BEIKMAN.

BURMA WORKERS' AND PEASANTS' PARTY (BWPP). The party formed in December 1950 by a splinter group of 42 leftist leaders of the Socialist Party of Burma (q.v.) including Thakin Chit Maung (q.v.), Thakin Hla Kywe, Thakin Lwin and U Ba Nyein (q.v.). The BWPP based its ideology on Marxism Leninism, favored closer Myanmar ties with the Soviet Union and other socialist countries and strove to end the civil war (q.v.) by political means. The BWPP formed the core of the National Unity Front (q.v.) formed in 1956. In January 1958, the party changed its name to Burma Workers' Party. In December 1962, it merged with the People's Comrades Party. The party was one of those banned by the decree of the Revolutionary Council (q.v.) in March 1964.

BURMAH OIL COMPANY (BOC). A Scottish firm, founded in 1886 in Edinburgh, the BOC became the most successful of the mineral and mining enterprises in Myanmar during the British colonial era prior to World War II (q.v.). The BOC developed oil fields at Chauk and Yenangyaung (qq.v.) in central Myanmar and laid a pipeline from there to a refinery at Thanlyin (q.v.) in 1908. During the Japanese occupation of Myanmar (1942–1945) (q.v.), the petroleum industry was almost completely paralyzed and, after the war, the BOC restored only some operations. In October 1954, the BOC was transformed into a joint venture with the Myanmar government. This was nationalized on 1 January 1963. (*See also* Minerals; Petroleum.)

BURMAN AND BURMESE. These terms are confusing and for quite a long time were used interchangeably in the English-language literature on Myanmar. But generally, there was a tendency to employ the term Burmese in a political sense, incorporating all of the indigenous nationalities of the country, while the term Burman was reserved to identify the majority ethnic group. The language of the Burmans, however, was called Burmese.

From 1989, Burman is officially referred to as "Bamar" (q.v.) while "Myanmar" (q.v.) is the word which covers both terms, Burman and Burmese.

BURMESE ERA *see* **MYANMAR ERA.**

BURMESE LANGUAGE *see* **MYANMAR LANGUAGE.**

BURMESE WAY TO SOCIALISM *see* **BURMA SOCIALIST PROGRAMME PARTY.**

BURNEY, HENRY (1792–1845). The British East India Company servant and resident in Inwa (q.v.), as successor to John Crawfurd (q.v.), from 1830. Burney was an Oriental scholar and experienced diplomat who won the confidence of King Bagyidaw (q.v.) by helping him to successfully negotiate with the British the rectification of the Manipur-Myanmar border and returning to Myanmar the disputed Kabaw Valley. In 1837, while mediating between the two rival royal factions at the court, Burney got involved in court politics. His relations with new king Tharrawaddy (q.v.) became strained and in 1837 Burney left Inwa.

BUTTERFLY SPIRIT. An English equivalent for the Myanmar term *leikpya*, also translated as "soul," which, Myanmars believe, is attached to a person from birth. The *leikpya* may be temporarily separated from the human body, such as in sleep, without entailing death. However, its permanent departure from the body is the ultimate cause of death, and its reembodiment in a new form is the basis for rebirth. The concept of *leikpya*, now incorporated into Buddhism (q.v.), is of animist origin. (*See also* Nat; Samsara.)

BYEDAIK. Also *byetaik*. King's Privy Council which was the focus of the court's administration in precolonial Myanmar.

The *byedaik* was supervised by four privy councillors, the *atwinwuns*. They had ready access to the monarch and exercised great influence through their close proximity to royal power. (*See also* Administration of Myanmar, Precolonial Era; Hluttaw.)

-C-

CAESAR, FREDERICK. A Venetian trader and one of the early European visitors of Myanmar. He wrote one of the best accounts of ports and trade in southern Myanmar of the 16th century. (*See also* Second Myanmar Empire.)

CARETAKER GOVERNMENT OF GENERAL NE WIN (1958–1960). The government, headed by General Ne Win (q.v.), which was formed in October 1958, following the split of the ruling Anti-Fascist People's Freedom League (AFPFL) (q.v.) and the ensuing political confusion which forced then Prime Minister U Nu (q.v.) to ask General Ne Win, commander in chief of the armed forces (q.v.), to take control of the government of the country. The original tenure of the Caretaker Government of six months was subsequently prolonged by the Parliament for a total of 18 months.

The leaders of the Caretaker Government promised to maintain law and order, to establish conditions for free and fair elections and to continue Myanmar's non-aligned foreign policy (q.v.). The government was composed mainly of civil service officials, but key administrative posts were filled by senior military officers. The formal institutions of the parliamentary era (q.v.) were retained, but the armed forces were the primary decision-makers.

In the economic sphere, the Caretaker Government attempted to reduce inefficient state enterprises while encouraging the growth of joint ventures between the Myanmar government and foreign firms. It also expanded the business activities of the Defence Services Institute (q.v.). Trying to win popular support, the military paved new ways in the political sphere, including a countrywide movement to create a National Solidarity Association. In its effort to deal more effectively with the insurgency and lawlessness, the Caretaker Government formed Security and Administrative Committees (q.v.), composed of administrative, army and police personnel. In 1959, the Caretaker Government amended the Constitution of the Union of Burma (q.v.), after reaching agreement with Kayar and Shan (qq.v.) chiefs, the *Sawbwas* (q.v.), that they would surrender their hereditary rights in favor of elected representatives and for financial compensation.

Although there was almost universal agreement as to the efficiency of the military authorities and some of their campaigns, such as cleaning up Yangon (q.v.) and other towns, their methods of rule, direct and often harsh, were greatly resented by most people. In the parliamentary elections, ultimately held in February 1960, U Nu's Clean AFPFL, renamed the *Pyidaungsu* Party (q.v.), won an overwhelming victory and formed a new cabinet, again headed by U Nu as Prime Minister. (*See also* Military Coup.)

CENTRAL BASIN. The central part of Myanmar, occupied by a vast plain watered by the Ayeyarwady and Sittoung (qq.v.) Rivers and their tributaries. It is also referred to as Central Myanmar.

CHANG CHI-FU *see* KHUN SA.

CHAUK. A town located on the bank of the Ayeyarwady River, north of Yenangyaung, in Magway Division (qq.v.). Chauk is an important petroleum production center; crude oil from Yenangyaung is piped and processed in the local refinery. Natural gas (q.v.) is also produced there. (*See also* Burmah Oil Company; Petroleum.)

CHETTIAR. Also *Chettyar*. South Indian caste from Chettinand whose main occupation is commerce and moneylending. The *Chettiars* migrated in great numbers to colonial Myanmar after 1880, playing a major role in transforming the peasant subsistence economy and connecting it with the export producing sector. By providing mortgage loans to Myanmar peasants, at 12 percent a month interest, they came to possess, through foreclosures, about 25 percent of the agricultural land in 13 main rice (q.v.)-growing regions of southern Myanmar by 1936. The *Chettiar* was seen by the Myanmar farmer as his main enemy. Indebtedness due to *Chettiar* moneylenders was one of the causes of peasant unrest and of the Saya San rebellion (q.v.) in 1930. The *Chettiars* were also engaged in extending credits to traders and urban landowners. Shortly before the Japanese occupation of Myanmar (1942–1945) (q.v.), total *Chettiar* investment in Myanmar was estimated at 56 million pounds sterling, the largest foreign investment in the country. From 1942 to 1945 most *Chettiars* resident in Myanmar left for India. After the war, they attempted a comeback, but without much success. (*See also* Economy, British Colonial Era; Indians.)

CHIN. A Tibeto-Burman ethnolinguistic group. While most Chins live in India and Bangladesh, those residing in the Union of Myanmar numbered 745,463, making up about 2 percent of the total population of the country, according to the 1983 census. Of these, more than 60 percent are settled in Chin State (q.v.); the rest are scattered in the Rakhine Yoma and in Magway Division (qq.v.).

The English term Chin is derived from Myanmar Chin; it is applied to the Chin people resident in Myanmar. Synonyms for Chins are *Cuci, Khyang, Khyeng, Kookie*, and *Kuki*. Myanmar's Chins are subdivided into two main groups: Northern Chins and Southern Chins. Together they speak some 44 mutually unintelligible dialects. Northern Chins comprise nearly all of the Chins of the Haka (q.v.), Falam and Tiddim areas. Southern Chins are generally the Chins settled in the plains outside the territory of Chin State.

The Chins are swidden agriculturalists. They build their settlements at an average elevation of 1,200–1,500 meters (4,000–5,000 feet). Northern Chin villages are sedentary and their homes are constructed of wooden planks. Maize (q.v.) is a major crop among Northern Chins. Southern Chins, who move frequently, build their houses of bamboo (q.v.) and rattan. Their major crop is rice (q.v.).

Most Chin marriages are monogamous. Polygyny is permitted but practiced only by aristocrats. Descent is patrilineal in all the Chin groups. For centuries prior to the British annexation of Myanmar in the 19th century, the Chins lived in relative isolation from the rest of Myanmar. They did not develop a state organization. Traditional Chin society was stratified into aristocrats, wealthy commoners, bondsmen and slaves. The last two groups were abolished by the British, who established their control over the Chin Hills (q.v.) only by 1918. The Chins won a reputation as excellent soldiers and were among the "martial races" from which the soldiers of the Burma Army (q.v.) were recruited. Social organization among the Northern and Southern Chins is rather different. While Northern Chins have an elaborate social hierarchy, the clan system of the Southern Chins is less rigid. The Chins in Myanmar are basically animists; about one-fifth of them are Christians.

CHIN HILLS. Part of the western mountain range in Myanmar and an extension of the Naga Hills (q.v.), they extend over much of Magway Division (q.v.). They are about 2,439 meters (8,000 feet) high, rising to a maximum elevation of 3,053 meters (10,016 feet) in Mount Victoria. These hills are interspersed with gorges and ravines through which the Kaladan River flows into the Bay of Bengal.

CHIN NATIONAL FRONT (CNF). Chin (q.v.) rebel organization which was set up in 1985. In 1988, the CNF formed its military wing, known as the Chin National Army (CNA), the first armed force of this kind in Chin State (q.v.). In 1989, the CNF joined the National Democratic Front (q.v.).

CHIN STATE. It covers an area of 36,019 square kilometers (13,907 square miles). It is bounded on the north and east by Sagaing Division, on the south by Magway Division and Rakhine State (qq.v.) and on the west by Bangladesh and India. The state is hilly, with very few plains or plateaux. It comprises 9 townships and 476 village tracts. Its (1983 census) population was 368,949. The capital city is Haka (q.v.); other important towns include Falam (the former capital), Paletwa and Tiddim. Chin State is inhabited by the Chins, Nagas, Rakhines and Bamars (qq.v.). The chief occupation is agriculture; swidden cultivation still prevails. Chin State is hardly accessible due to the lack of communications, such as railroads and roads. At the time of Myanmar's independence in 1948, it was known as Chin Special Division. On 3 January 1974, Chin Special Division became Chin State.

CHINA *see* PEOPLE'S REPUBLIC OF CHINA (RELATIONS WITH).

CHINDWIN *see* CHINDWINN.

CHINDWINN. A river about 800 kilometers (500 miles) long, the most important tributary of the Ayeyarwady (q.v.). The Chindwinn takes its source in the Kuman range in northern Myanmar and it then flows southward through the Hukawng Valley and the Naga Hills (q.v.). It empties into the Ayeyarwady River near Pakokku. The Chindwinn is navigable during the monsoon rainy season, but only through its lower part.

CHINESE (IN MYANMAR). Along with the Indians (q.v.), the largest, non-indigenous ethnic group of Myanmar's population. Their number is estimated at 250,000.

Many Chinese had settled in Myanmar, particularly in the north of the country and in Shan State (q.v.), prior to the British annexation of Myanmar in the 19th century, earning their living in mining and forest works. The British annexation of Myanmar witnessed a new, sizable Chinese immigration by sea, mainly from Fujian and Guangdong provinces. The Chinese immigrants settled in Yangon (q.v.) and other towns as well as in rural areas. Most of them were artisans and traders who gained a position of middlemen in Myanmar colonial society. Culturally and linguistically more akin to Myanmars (q.v.) than the Indians, the Chinese were more easily integrated in the general population, tending, nonetheless, to retain their separate national identity. After independence in 1948, the Chinese community in Myanmar remained strong, although after the military coup of 1962 (q.v.) many Chinese enterprises were nationalized. Since the anti-

Chinese riots in Yangon in 1967, Chinese residents in Myanmar have tried to adapt more strictly to local customs and rules. (*See also* Economy, British Colonial Era; People's Republic of China.)

CHINTHE. Term for a mythological lion, a guardian of Buddhist pagodas and temples in Myanmar, usually located at their entrances in pairs. (*See also* Architecture.)

CHIT HLAING, U (1879–1952). One of the early Myanmar nationalist politicians in the preindependence period. Born in Mawlamyine (q.v.), U Chit Hlaing received his education in England. He was one of the leaders of the Young Men's Buddhist Association and President of the General Council of Burmese Associations (qq.v.) from 1922. He opposed the dyarchy (q.v.) reform of 1923 and separation of Burma from India (q.v.). He was a delegate to the Burma Round Table Conference in London (1931–1932), President of the Legislative Council (1932–1935) and Speaker of the House of Representatives (1937). During the Japanese occupation of Myanmar (1942–1945) (q.v.), from 1943 to 1945, he served as Privy Councillor. After the war, in 1951, he organized the Union of Burma League.

CHIT MAUNG, THAKIN (1915–   ). Important Myanmar politician. Born in Hinthata (q.v.), he joined the *Do Bama Asi Ayon* (q.v.) in 1937. In 1945, he was elected member of the Constituent Assembly as the candidate of the Anti-Fascist People's Freedom League (q.v.). He became Secretary General of the All Burma Peasants' Organization (q.v.) and joined the Socialist Party of Burma (q.v.). After the split in the party, he became one of the founding members (later Secretary General) of the Burma Workers' and Peasants' Party (q.v.). He was also a member of the Presidium of the National Unity Front (q.v.) in the 1950s. He returned to active politics in the pro-democracy movement of 1988 (q.v.) as a leftist leader. Currently, he is Chairman of the Democratic Front for National Reconstruction.

CHRISTIANITY. Christianity in Myanmar dates back to the arrival of Roman Catholic missionaries who accompanied the Portuguese adventurers, first coming into the country in the 16th century. They were followed by Italian and French Catholic missions. Later, Protestant missions, namely the English Baptist Missionary Society and the American Baptist Mission came into the country. Protestant missionary activities largely developed after the British annexation of Myanmar in the 19th century.

American and European missionaries were spreading Christianity quite successfully, mainly among certain ethnic minority groups, such as the Chins, Kachins, Kayins and Kayahs (qq.v.). The Kayins—formerly animists—were a particularly fertile ground for missionary efforts, forming the largest single Christian group in Myanmar.

Missionary activities yielded some positive results, such as opening new schools and other institutions of Western knowledge and learning. The languages of several ethnic groups, including Kachin, were reduced into writing through missionary effort and books were published in these languages. On the reverse side, the missionaries, in general, tended to create psychological barriers between the Christianized minorities and the predominantly Buddhist Bamars (q.v.).

Of the 4.9 percent of Christians in Myanmar (as recorded in 1983 census), 3.2 percent were Baptists, 1 percent were Roman Catholics, and 0.6 percent belonged to the Church of England, while the remainder professed other denominations. The Myanmar Baptist Convention, established in 1865 as the Burma Baptist Missionary Convention, had about 452,364 members in 1987. The adherents of the Roman Catholic Church amounted to an estimated 456,520 (in 1989), while the Church of England numbered some 45,000 (in 1985), mainly Europeans and Eurasians (q.v.). (*See also* Colonial Education; Judson, Adoniram; Portuguese and Myanmar.)

CHRONICLES *see* HMANNAN YAZAWIN; KULA, U; LITERATURE.

CIVIL AFFAIRS SERVICE (BURMA) (CAS(B)). The British

military authority for the administration of Myanmar territory reconquered by the Allied troops from 1944 to 1945. Established in January 1944, the CAS(B), under Lord Louis Mountbatten (q.v.), was responsible for the most immediate tasks facing the British on their return to Myanmar, namely the rehabilitation of the economy and transportation and the restoration of law and order. It was headed by Major General C.F.B. Pearce who was succeeded by General Hubert Rance (q.v.) on 10 June 1945. The CAS(B) was terminated on 16 October 1945, when Governor Dorman-Smith (q.v.) assumed his post and reestablished civilian rule. By that time, at least in the view of many British military officers, the rehabilitation of Myanmar had just began and the transfer to civilian rule was premature. Although most of the CAS(B) staff were ex-civil servants and business people resident in prewar Myanmar, with no sympathy for Myanmar political aspirations, Sir Hubert Rance, who later succeeded Sir Dorman-Smith in his post, was able to come to terms with the strongest rival of British colonial rule, the Anti-Fascist People's Freedom League (q.v.). (*See also* White Paper on Burma.)

CIVIL WAR. From its inception in January 1948, the government of independent Myanmar was confronted with serious challenges to its authority which soon developed into the civil war, as several opposition groups resorted to arms to gain their political objectives.

The year 1948 began with two government rivals, the Communist Party (Red Flag) and the Mujahids from Rakhine (qq.v.) in the underground. On 27 March 1948, the Communist Party of Burma headed by Thakin Than Tun (qq.v.) started an armed uprising in several areas of central Myanmar. Between June and August 1948, mutineers in the armed forces (q.v.) and some units of the Union Military Police and a large part of the People's Volunteer Organization (q.v.) rose against the government. In early 1949, the Karen National Defence Organization (KNDO) rebelled and encouraged a large number of Kayin (qq.v.) soldiers in the armed forces to desert.

The KNDO was followed by the Mon National Defence

Organization (q.v.). During 1949, the rebels, representing at least eight groups with about 20,000 men in arms, controlled some 30 towns and most rural areas in central and southern Myanmar, while the government's authority was limited to Yangon (q.v.). But the insurgents were split into rival, and often hostile camps, while the government could rally the support of Chin, Kachin and Shan (qq.v.) leaders and also obtain military assistance from abroad. As a result of all these factors, the years 1950 to 1951 brought a reverse development and a gradual recovery of governmental authority and control over Myanmar. During the 1950s, the insurgency tended to fade into dacoity and banditry.

The civil war exacted a heavy toll in human and material resources and impeded the economic development of the country. The period after the military coup of 1962 (q.v.) saw a resurgence of the underground movement by Bamar (q.v.) dissident groups and, particularly, by many ethnic minority groups. Until quite recently, several border and peripheral areas of the Union of Myanmar were under the control of various ethnic rebel organizations and their forces.

CLEAN ANTI-FASCIST PEOPLE'S FREEDOM LEAGUE *see* ANTI-FASCIST PEOPLE'S FREEDOM LEAGUE; PYI-DAUNGSU PARTY.

COLONIAL EDUCATION. Western education, implanted in Myanmar after the British annexation of the country in the 19th century, posed a serious challenge to the traditional educational system based on monastic schools, the *pongyi kyanungs* (q.v.), of which the Buddhist *sangha* (q.v.) was the main agency. Unlike the Myanmar Buddhist tradition of learning as a means of pursuit of religious deliverance, the European-type schools which opened in towns and urban areas concentrated on training pupils for a future career as clerks or for commercial employment.

The colonial system of education, prior to World War II (q.v.), was based on the division of schools according to the age and the language of instruction. Another classification was of government schools and aided schools (private or missionary) which received some government support but charged tuition. Private schools, namely mission schools, taught only in English and afforded the easiest entrance to college. There were three main types of institutions of higher learning during the British colonial era: liberal arts/colleges, teachers' training schools and technical schools. Myanmar had only one university, The University of Yangon (q.v.), founded in 1920.

The structure of education as built up by the British was severely criticized for its emphasis on arts subjects and for providing higher education only to the privileged few from wealthy families. During the nationalist agitation in the 1920s, it was denounced by the Myanmars as "slave education." In protest against it, the national school movement (q.v.) was launched in the wake of the strike at Yangon University. (*See also* Christianity; Education; Student Strikes, British Colonial Era; Universities and Colleges.)

COMMUNICATION MEDIA *see* PRESS; RADIO; TELEVISION.

COMMUNISM *see* COMMUNIST PARTY OF ARAKAN; COMMUNIST PARTY OF BURMA; COMMUNIST PARTY (RED FLAG).

COMMUNIST PARTY OF ARAKAN (CPA). A breakaway organization from the Communist Party (Red Flag) (q.v.). Formed in 1962, the CPA claimed to represent local interests and it supported the creation of a separate Rakhine State. In 1973, the CPA split into two factions, one of which surrendered to the government in the 1980 amnesty. (*See also* Civil War.)

COMMUNIST PARTY OF BURMA (CPB). Also referred to as the Burma Communist Party. The major underground organization of independent Myanmar from 1948 to 1989.

The CPB was secretly founded on 15 August 1939 in Yangon (q.v.) by several Myanmar and Indian leftist and radical politicians, including Thakin Soe, Thakin Than Tun, A. N. Goshal, Thakin Hla Pe (Bo Let Ya) (qq.v.), and Dr. Naag. The CPB gained prominence as one of the leading organizations of the antifascist resistance during the period of the

Japanese occupation of Myanmar (1942–1945) and a founding member of the Anti-Fascist People's Freedom League (AFPFL) (qq.v.) in August 1944.

After the war, the CPB confirmed its status as a legal and open political party. At the second party congress held in July 1945, Than Tun was elected Chairman and Thein Pe Myint (q.v.), who became associated with the party during the war, Secretary General. The party developed a proper structure and gained important positions in the AFPFL as well as in several mass organizations, such as the All Burma Peasants' Organization (ABPO) and the All Burma Trade Union Congress (ABTUC), with many sympathizers in the Patriotic Burmese Forces (PBF) and the People's Volunteer Organization (PVO) (qq.v.). This development was, however, not without problems. Disputes arose in the party leadership over the CPB's future strategy and policy. The rejection by Thakin Soe and his followers of the party's line of "peaceful development" of Myanmar towards independence as "Browderism" resulted in a split in February 1946 and the formation of a splinter Communist Party known as "Red Flag" (q.v.) led by Thakin Soe. The main CPB, led by Than Tun, remained in the AFPFL initially. As result of its criticism of Thakin Aung San and some other AFPFL leaders, however, it was expelled from the AFPFL in October 1946. The CPB denounced the "Nu-Attlee Agreement" (q.v.) of October 1947. Following independence in 1948, the CPB was the first major organization to go underground and start the civil war (q.v.) on 27 March 1948, although it was only declared illegal in 1953.

Between the years 1948 and 1950, the CPB posed a major threat to U Nu's (q.v.) government. The CPB created its own force, the People's Liberation Army of Burma (PLAB), and, in March 1949, it initiated a broader front of underground leftist groups known as the National Democratic United Front (NDUF) (q.v.). After 1951, the CPB lost its military supremacy, though it remained in control of many rural areas of Myanmar up to 1955. In 1955, the CPB leadership adopted a new policy line which proclaimed "peace and unity" as its main objectives. However, the peace talks with U Nu government were not held.

Following the military coup of 1962 (q.v.), the party remained in the underground, though it took part in the (abortive) 1963 peace talks with the Revolutionary Council (q.v.). During the 1960s, the CPB sided with the Communist Party of China and Chinese influence over the Myanmar communist movement (enhanced by financial and military assistance to the CPB) increased greatly. Bloody purges of "revisionists" (including some veteran CPB leaders) by party radicals, inspired by the Chinese "Cultural Revolution," as well as stepped-up government military operations, largely disrupted the CPB's potential as a military and political force. Expelled from its traditional areas of operation in central Myanmar, namely the Bago Yoma (q.v.), in 1971 the CPB established its new bases in the northeastern part of Shan State (q.v.), along the China-Myanmar border. The CPB gradually expanded its zone of activity east of the Thanlwin River (q.v.). By 1986, the CPB controlled a territory extending along the Chinese border in northeastern Shan and Kachin States (q.v.), with headquarters at Panghsang.

From the late 1960s, the CPB was faced with problems resulting from its reconstitution in ethnic minority areas and from the conflict of interest with drug (q.v.) traffickers who had been incorporated into the CPB. Another major setback was the change in the official stance of the People's Republic of China which was steadily becoming more favorable toward the Burma Socialist Programme Party (BSPP) (q.v.) ruling regime, while cutting off its assistance to the CPB. In the meantime, growing dissatisfaction in the CPB's rank and file with the essentially Bamar (q.v.) leadership led to the rebellion of several ethnic organizations within the party in April 1989. This mutiny, in fact, put an end to the CPB as a viable force. The former party leadership, with Thakin Ba Thein Tin (q.v.) as Chairman, was sent into exile in China.

After the 1989 mutiny, at least five splinter organizations of former CPB were set up. However, none of them are based on communist ideology, but, rather on ethnic identities.

COMMUNIST PARTY (RED FLAG) (CP(RF)). Also known as Red Flag, or the Communist Party (Burma), it originated in

February 1946 as a splinter group of Thakin Soe (q.v.) and seven other members of the Central Committee of the Communist Party of Burma (CPB) (q.v.) who were convinced that the armed struggle was the only way of achieving Myanmar's independence. The CP(RF) went underground prior to Myanmar independence in January 1948 and was declared as illegal by the British colonial authorities; the ban on the CP(RF) was lifted for a while in October 1946, but reimposed later.

The CP(RF) always remained a minor organization with its area of activity restricted mainly to Minbu and Pakokku, lower Chin State (q.v.), and the Rakhine Yoma (q.v.). Led for over two decades by Thakin Soe, misleadingly labelled as "Trotskyist," the party earned a bad reputation for its ruthless, extremist policy, including such measures as enforcing land collectivization, making people join people's militia and oppressing Buddhist *pongyis* (q.v.). These policies, combined with the formation of other underground Marxist movements, such as the Communist Party of Arakan and the Arakan National Liberation Party (qq.v.), brought about the demise of the CP(RF) in the 1960s. The party became defunct in 1970 when Thakin Soe surrendered to government troops.

CONSTITUTION (1935) *see* GOVERNMENT OF BURMA ACT (1935).

CONSTITUTION OF THE SOCIALIST REPUBLIC OF THE UNION OF BURMA. The second basic law of the state which became effective on 3 January 1974 and remained in force until the military coup of 1988 (q.v.). Under the 1974 constitution, Myanmar was a state with a one-party (Burma Socialist Programme Party, q.v.) system. The People's Assembly, *Pyithu Hluttaw* (q.v.), a unicameral legislature, was the highest organ of state power. It elected from among its members a State Council vested with executive power and headed by a Chairman, who concurrently held the post of President of the Union. The Council of Ministers, elected by the People's Assembly, was the highest organ of public administration. Other high state organs were the Council of People's Justices, the Council of People's Attorneys, and the

Council of People's Inspectors. Local administration was the responsibility of People's Councils. All organs of state power and administration were elected for a period of four years.

On 18 September 1988, the State Law and Order Restoration Council, which came to power through a military coup (qq.v.), abolished all previous state organs as well as the one-party political system. The 1974 Constitution was not suspended or repealed *de jure*, but, in fact, is not operative.

CONSTITUTION OF THE UNION OF BURMA (1947). The first basic law of the Union of Burma (q.v.) which came into force on Independence Day (q.v.), 4 January 1948. The 1947 Constitution embodied the principles of parliamentary democracy, as the country's political system, and of the Union (consisting of Burma proper, four Union States and the Special Division of the Chins) as the state form. The Head of the Union of Burma was President. He was elected by the Union Parliament consisting of a Chamber of Deputies and a Chamber of Nationalities; the Union Parliament was vested with the supreme legislative power. The executive power was vested in the Union Government, composed of the Prime Minister and his cabinet. The Constitution laid down the rights and responsibilities of the various administrative organs in the Union states and their relation to the Union administration.

The first Constitution was operative from January 1948 to March 1962. The Revolutionary Council (q.v.), which came to power through the military coup of 1962 (q.v.), neither suspended nor repealed the first basic law *de jure*. However, in practice, it operated only in the areas where the new government did not take any specific action. On 3 January 1974, the first basic law was replaced by the Constitution of the Socialist Republic of the Union of Burma (q.v.).

CONTI, NICOLO DI. A Venetian merchant and traveller, the first known European to have come to Myanmar (in 1435). He visited and described Ava, Bago and Rakhine (qq.v.).

COPPER. One of the minerals (q.v.) found and exploited in the

Bawdwin-Namtu mines in Shan State (qq.v.). In 1983, a new copper plant was completed at Monywa near Mandalay (q.v.), with a production of some 32,000 tons a year of copper concentrates.

COTTON. One of the "industrial crops" whose cultivation is encouraged by the government. Over recent years, there has been an increase in cotton production, but domestic consumption also rose. In 1991, the production of cotton totalled 21,000 tons. In the same year, an additional 4,350 tons had to be imported to cover Myanmar's needs. (*See also* Agriculture.)

COX, HIRAM (1760–1799). Cox came to Myanmar in October 1796 as British Resident. His Residency was not successful. A harsh critic of the Myanmar people, their customs and manners, and disliked for his insolent behavior, Cox was recalled in 1798. His *Journal of a Residence in the Burmah Empire and More Particularly at the Court of Amarapoorah* was edited and prepared for publication in 1821 by his son. (*See also* Inwa; Symes, Michael.)

CRADDOCK, SIR REGINALD. The British Governor of Myanmar from 1918 to 1923. He was authorized by the Government of India to formulate a tentative scheme of reforms for Myanmar. His plan, known as the "Craddock Scheme," published in December 1918, however, aroused strong resentment among Myanmar nationalists. (*See also* Dyarchy; General Council of Burmese Associations; Independence Movement.)

CRAWFURD, JOHN (1783–1868). An Oriental scholar and physician of Scottish origin, Crawfurd was appointed British Resident at Inwa (q.v.) under the provisions of the Treaty of Yandabo (q.v.). His *Journal of an Embassy from the Governor General of India to the Court of Ava in the Year 1827*, a narrative of his mission in Myanmar (from September 1826 to February 1827), ranks among the best contemporary accounts of the Myanmar kingdom in the English language.

CURRENCY *see* FINANCE; KYAT.

-D-

DAGON *see* YANGON.

DAH. A Myanmar term for a hewing knife or sword.

DAWEI. The capital of Tanintharyi Division (q.v.) on the eastern bank of the Dawei River. A seaport and trade center of the Tanintharyi coast.

DEFENCE SERVICES ACADEMY. An independent college under the Ministry of Defence. Founded in 1955 and presently situated at Pyin-Oo-Lwin (Maymyo) (q.v.), the Academy offers degree courses for cadet training of regular commissioned officers in all three services of the armed forces (q.v.): the air force, the army and the navy. (*See also* Universities and Colleges.)

DEFENCE SERVICES INSTITUTE (DSI). Established in 1951, to provide the armed forces (q.v.) with consumer goods at reasonable prices, the DSI enlarged its scope of activities into various areas of commerce and the economy. During the tenure of the Caretaker Government of General Ne Win (1958–1960) (q.v.), the DSI became the major commercial institution in Myanmar which controlled 14 enterprises involved in shipping, banking, construction, transport, hotels and other services. The DSI was nationalized in 1963.

DEMOCRATIC ALLIANCE OF BURMA (DAB). An alliance formed in November 1988 at Klerday, in the territory controlled by the Karen National Union (q.v.) at the Myanmar-Thai border. The DAB consists of the National Democratic Front, the umbrella insurgent front, the All Burma Students' Democratic Front (qq.v.) and several other organizations, including the Committee for Restoration of Democracy in Burma, the US-based organization of Myanmar exiles. The main DAB objectives, at its inception, included to overturn the State Law and Order Restoration Council (q.v.), to set up an interim government before holding general elections, to restore democracy in Myanmar and to establish a federation of Myanmar states.

DEMOCRATIC PARTY FOR NEW SOCIETY (DPNS). The student-backed party which emerged in the wake of the pro-democracy movement of 1988 (q.v.). It was founded by Moe Thi Zon (aka Myo Than Htut) and several other student leaders who decided to continue legal political activities after the military coup of 1988 (q.v.). The DPNS was officially registered with the military authorities in October 1988. It built up a considerable following in Yangon (q.v.) and organized several peaceful, anti-government demonstrations. However, most of its leaders were arrested in July 1989.

DEPARTMENT OF ARCHAEOLOGY. Founded in 1902 and revived in 1946, the Department is presently under the Ministry of Planning and Finance in Yangon (q.v.). The Department is responsible for the maintenance of existing ancient monuments in Myanmar and, more recently, also for the exploration and excavation of Pyu (q.v.) sites. The important part of the Department is the epigraphical section which has continued to collect, decipher, transliterate and publish the facsimiles of lithic Myanmar inscriptions. Presently, there is no systematic academic training in archaeology in Myanmar. Previously, the subject was partly taught at the University of Yangon (q.v.), but most of Myanmar's senior archaeologists have received their education abroad. (*See also* Universities and Colleges.)

DHAMMA. A Pali (q.v.) form of the Sanskrit *dharma* which denotes a cosmic law, moral law or code of morality. In Buddhism (q.v.) the usage of the term is that of a doctrine or teaching, as embodied in the *Tipitaka* (q.v.).

DHAMMATHAT. The Myanmar term for the Sanskrit *dharmashastra* or "treatise on law." In precolonial Myanmar, the *dhammathats* were the principal source of Myanmar law. The arrangement of earlier *dhammathats* was borrowed from Sanskrit jurists, but the substance was probably the common law of present-day Southeast Asia.

The important Myanmar *dhammathats* were 36 in number, the earliest dating from the 11th century A.D. In 1752, in the reign of King Alaungpaya (q.v.), one of his ministers compiled the *Manu Kyay* which was the summary of the previous *dhammathats*. These were compiled by Myanmar jurists in the form of chronicles or textbooks. They were not codes or digests of law but rather records of manners and customs, decisions on disputed points and rulings preserved in former judgements. The entire body of law was generally divided in the *dhammathats* under 18 sections which covered five main categories: 1. Marriage, divorce, adoption and guardianship; 2. Property; 3. Inheritance; 4. Contracts; 5. Tort.

After the British annexation of Upper Burma (q.v.) in 1885, the law was administered as elsewhere in British India. The statutory laws which were designed on the British Common Law in India, the portion of law introduced into British India without legislation, and the rules of law resting upon the authority of the courts were also made applicable to Myanmar, except for the "Excluded Areas" (q.v.). The British courts gave Hindus and Muslims (q.v.) the benefit of their personal law in religious and family matters and applied Myanmar law to Buddhists in the same field. After independence in 1948, Myanmar Buddhist Law remained primarily applicable to family matters and inheritance of the Myanmar Buddhist community in the country. (*See also* Administration of Myanmar, British Colonial Era; Administration of Myanmar, Precolonial Era.)

DHAMMAZEDI (r. 1472–1492). Originally one of the two Buddhist *pongyis* (q.v.) who had helped Queen Shinsawbu (q.v.) to flee from the court of Inwa (q.v.), and who was then appointed by her as a successor to the throne in the Mon (q.v.) kingdom in southern Myanmar. Dhammazedi is remembered as one of the greatest rulers of the Wareru (q.v.) dynasty whose rule brought prosperity to the Mons. In 1745, he sent a mission of 22 *pongyis* to obtain valid ordination from the clergy of Mahavira monastery in Ceylon (Sri Lanka). He also compiled a collection of rulings, known after him as the Dhammazedi *pyatthats*.

DISEASE. The most serious disease threats to the population of Myanmar have been pneumonia, heart disease, various diarrheal diseases, tuberculosis, cancer, cerebrovascular disease and malaria. Respiratory diseases, cholera, amebic and bacillary dysentery, leprosy and trachoma are still common. More recently, problems arose in connection with the increasing number of drug addicts and persons who were HIV positive.

Despite the increase in health care and social services after independence in 1948, some serious problems persist. These include the small number of qualified medical personnel, doctors and nurses, in relation to the rapidly increasing population, the shortage or lack of modern medical facilities and medicines in many places and a general condition of poor sanitation. (*See also* Drug Abuse.)

DO BAMA ASI AYON. Major organization of the independence movement (q.v.) in Myanmar in the late 1930s. The English name of the organization is "We Burmans" or "Our Burma" Association/Party.

The *Do Bama Asi Ayon* was established in 1930 in Yangon by Ba Thaung and several other young Bamars, including some graduates of the University of Yangon (qq.v.). The members of the organization addressed each other as *thakin* (q.v.), the Myanmar word for "master." Their ultimate objective was Myanmar's independence. They found inspiration in various sources, including the writers of the Irish Sinn Fein Movement, Garibaldi, Mazzini, Sun-Yat Sen, Jawaharlal Nehru, Nietzsche, and in what they considered as achievements of totalitarian regimes of such countries as Germany, Italy and the Soviet Union. In the late 1930s, the ideology and program of the *Do Bama Asi Ayon* was influenced, to quite an extent, by socialism (q.v.).

The *Do Bama Asi Ayon's* first public appeals exhorted Bamars to completely change and modernize their society. In 1930/1931, it launched the All Burma Youth League and, later, it also established links with the Rangoon University Students' Union (qq.v.). In 1938, a fraction of conservative *Thakins,* headed by Ba Sein and Tun Ok (qq.v.) split from the main *Do Bama Asi Ayon* which was, for a while, headed by Thakin Kodaw Hmaing (q.v.). In the same year, important posts in the main *Do Bama Asi Ayon* went to former student leaders such as Aung San, Ba Swe, Kyaw Nyein, Nu and Raschid (qq.v.).

The *Do Bama Asi Ayon* played a crucial role in the oil-field workers' strike of 1983 (q.v.). Radical, leftist *Thakins* were also instrumental in forming the first nationwide trade unions. These were the All Burma Peasants' Organization (1939) and the All Burma Trade Union Congress (1940) (qq.v.). In October 1939, the *Do Bama Asi Ayon* intensified its public anti-colonial campaigns and joined a coalitional Freedom Bloc (q.v.). Between 1940 and 1942, many *Thakin* leaders were imprisoned by the British. Some, like Aung San, went abroad secretly to seek military assistance for Myanmar's independence struggle, while others worked underground, mainly in the People's Revolutionary Party (q.v.). During the Japanese occupation of Myanmar (1942–1945) (q.v.), the *Do Bama* ceased to play its former leading role in the independence movement. In August 1942, it was merged with Dr. Ba Maw's *Sinyetha* Party into the *Do Bama Sinyetha Asi Ayon* (qq.v.).

In 1946, Thakin Ba Sein attempted to reconstitute the *Do Bama Asi Ayon* as a political party but it did not draw much popular support. (*See also* Do Bama Song.)

DO BAMA SINYETHA ASI AYON. The political coalition formed in August 1942 by merging the *Do Bama Asi Ayon* and the *Sinyetha* Party, the two main organizations of then defunct Freedom Bloc (qq.v.). Dr. Ba Maw became President and Thakin Nu (qq.v.) Secretary General of the *Do Bama Sinyetha Asi Ayon*, which was the only legal political party in the period of the Japanese occupation of Myanmar (1942–1945) (q.v.). In late 1944, Dr. Ba Maw reorganized it as the *Maha Bama Asi Ayon* (q.v.)

DO BAMA SONG. The song composed in the early 1930s for the *Do Bama Asi Ayon* (q.v.) by Saya Tin. The song evokes the feelings of pride in Myanmar's past and it urges the Bamars (q.v.) to be courageous and to strive for the well-being of their motherland. In 1947, the *Do Bama* Song, with slight modifications, was chosen to become the national anthem of the Union of Burma (q.v.).

DORMAN-SMITH, SIR REGINALD. British Governor of Myanmar from 1941 to 1946. During the Japanese occupation of Myanmar (1942–1945) (q.v.), he headed the Government of Burma in exile at Simla, which included several

Myanmar senior civil officers and politicians, including former Prime Minister Sir Paw Tun, U Tin Tut (qq.v.) and U Htoon Aung Gyaw. Dorman-Smith returned to Myanmar and resumed his office on termination of the British military administration of the country, known as the Civil Affairs Service (Burma) (q.v.), on 16 October 1945. His postwar governorship was not successful because of his strained relations with the Anti-Fascist People's Freedom League (q.v.). In August 1946, he was succeeded in this post by Sir Hubert Rance (q.v.).

DRUG ABUSE. Myanmar is severely affected by the ready availability of narcotics, namely heroin and opium. Officially, the Union of Myanmar has only about 30,000 registered addicts, but unofficial estimates put the figure much higher. The addicts are found particularly among some insurgent rebel forces operating in the regions of the country where the opium is grown, such as the Golden Triangle (q.v.). But more recently youths in central Myanmar are also becoming addicted in increasing numbers.

The Revolutionary Council (q.v.) promulgated the 1974 Narcotics and Dangerous Drugs Law and started campaigns against the dangers of drug abuse, also involving activities for crop substitution, for treatment and rehabilitation of drug addicts as well as confiscated drug-burning ceremonies. The successive Myanmar governments' attempts to persuade the world community that they were trying to cope with the problem of drug abuse have remained, however, largely unconvincing. The increase in the area under poppy cultivation, of heroin refineries in the border areas of Shan State (q.v.) and cross-frontier narcotics trade are given as evidence that the military authorities, including the State Law and Order Restoration Council (q.v.), may be working in conjunction with certain insurgent organizations and opium warlords as one of the means of holding on to political power in Myanmar.

DRY ZONE. Also known as Dry Belt. Region in central Myanmar, situated in the middle Ayeyarwady (q.v.) basin, bounded by Shwebo (q.v.) and Ye U in the north, Thayek and Yamethin in the south and the hills in the east and west. The region, densely populated, was the center of Myanmar civilization; several former capitals, such as Bagan, Amarapura, Inwa and Mandalay (qq.v) fall within it. The region has a very low annual rainfall and agriculture (q.v.) is carried on by irrigation (q.v.) and other methods of dry farming. The most important crop is rice (q.v.); other crops include groundnuts, cotton (q.v.), maize (q.v.), sugarcane, fruits and vegetables.

DUWA. The Kachin (q.v.) village chief or tribal leader. Under British rule, the customary law of the tribes and the rule of the *Duwas* were retained in the Kachin mountains tracts. The size of groups and territories under the control of the *Duwa* varied from a few villages to as many as a hundred. The status of the chief was usually hereditary in the male line from father to youngest son. The *Duwa* exercised his power in consultation with a council of elders. After the creation of Kachin State, as part of the Union of Burma (qq.v), the *Duwa* continued to exercise his authority among the people loyal to the government as well as among the rebels, despite efforts of successive Myanmar governments to displace traditional leaders with other forms of administrative and political control.

DYARCHY. The term referring to the Montagu-Chelmsford reforms which were extended to Myanmar in January 1923. Under the dyarchy, or "dual government" reform, the Legislative Council, formed in 1897 to assist the British Lieutenant-Governor in discharging his duties, was increased to 103 members, of whom 79 elected in communal, general and special constituencies. The Legislative Council functioned until the implementation of the Government of Burma Act of 1935 (q.v.). The government was entrusted in the Governor and the newly formed Executive Council. This consisted of two members in charge of Reserved Subjects and two ministers responsible to the Legislative Council in charge of Transferred Subjects. The Reserved Subjects comprised vital subjects of the government, such as defense, law and order, finance and revenue. The Transferred Subjects included education, public health, forests and excise. (*See also* Administration of Myanmar, British Colonial Era.)

-E-

EAST ASIA YOUTH LEAGUE. The mass social welfare organization in the period of the Japanese occupation of Myanmar (1942–1945) (q.v.). Formed in June 1942 by the Japanese military administration to mobilize Myanmar youth, it claimed some 60,000 members in 1944. While U Ba Gyan (q.v.) and some other leaders stressed its apolitical character, the League became one of the most important channels for drawing young Myanmars into the anti-fascist resistance (q.v.). In 1944, the name of the organization was changed to All Burma Youth League (q.v.)

ECONOMY *see* AGRICULTURE; EXPORT PRODUCTS; FINANCE; FOREIGN TRADE; INDUSTRY; INTERNAL TRADE; LIVESTOCK AND FISHERIES; MINERALS.

ECONOMY, BRITISH COLONIAL ERA. With the introduction of British rule in Myanmar in the 19th century, production, not only for home consumption but also for export, increased. New, modern machinery and technology were introduced to some extent and public transport, such as roads and railroads (qq.v.), expanded. The economic development which affected the lives of the Myanmar people most profoundly was the rapid spread of rice (q.v.) cultivation in southern Myanmar. There was also an increase in the extraction and export of timber and minerals (qq.v.), such as teak, (q.v.), lead (q.v.), tin, tungsten and zinc (q.v.). However, the economic growth was mainly to the advantage of the British who controlled the larger part of Myanmar's rice trade, river transport, timber and mineral production. Foreign immigrants, Indian *Chettiars* (qq.v.) and Chinese (q.v.) merchants secured even greater control over Myanmar farmers who formed the bulk of the population. A gradual concentration of agricultural land in the hands of large landowners, many of them non-agriculturalists, a process followed by a parallel breakdown of peasant proprietorship, made conditions for the Myanmar peasantry unbearable. This situation, further aggravated by the World Depression of the early 1930s, contributed much to the spread of anti-colonial agitation in the rural areas, provoking the Saya San rebellion (q.v.).

EDUCATION. The main objective of the successive governments of independent Myanmar was to fashion a uniform, centrally-controlled system of education, providing the benefits of education to broader strata of the population while placing more emphasis on the teaching of science. More schools and colleges were opened in the post-independence era, such as the University of Mandalay (q.v.), the Engineering College and the Polytechnic in Yangon (q.v.). Education was made free in all state schools and colleges. This measure brought definite advantages, but also caused additional problems, as neither the facilities nor the teachers were enough to cope with the ever increasing numbers of pupils and students. In 1964, the Revolutionary Council (q.v.) introduced a new system of education for basic and higher standards, while universities and colleges (q.v.) came under direct control of the government. By 1966, almost all private schools were closed. Political indoctrination, with an emphasis on the Burmese Way to Socialism (q.v.) doctrine, became a part of all school curricula. Meanwhile, Myanmar was made the only language of instruction, with the exception of some minority languages in the early grades. In 1981, the teaching of English was restored to its previous position in all types of schools, starting from kindergarten.

In 1991, the expenditure on education was estimated at Kyats 3,864,000. In the same year, there were 36,449 state primary schools with 198,909 teachers and 4,670,000 pupils; 2,062 middle schools with 49,122 teachers and 930,207 pupils; and 858 high schools with 18,381 teachers and 331,849 students. The total number of students attending the 31 universities and colleges in 1991 was estimated at 218,848 and the number of teachers was 5,974.

Despite a system of compulsory basic education (for pupils between five and nine years of age) from 1975 on and efforts to ensure education for all, there are still areas in the country with no state schools, where the local Buddhist monastery, the *pongyi kyaung* (q.v.), takes care of the children's elementary education; as a rule it is open only to Buddhist boys, as it is not customary for a girl to enter the monastery. (*See also* Colonial Education; Literacy.)

ENERGY *see* NATURAL GAS; PETROLEUM; POWER, ELECTRIC.

EURASIAN. The term used to describe persons of mixed European and Asian parentage or their descendants in the census records of 1891 and 1901. From then until 1935, the term "Anglo-Indian" was employed for people of "mixed" race, even for those without any trace of Indian (q.v.) connections. Thereafter, the term "Anglo-Burman" came into use. Many Eurasians rose to a place of prominence and importance in public life in the colonial era prior to the Japanese occupation of Myanmar (1942–1945) (q.v.), often finding employment in government service. After independence in 1948, both main groups of Eurasians, the Anglo-Indians and the Anglo-Burmans, lost much of their former position. In the 1970s, the number of Eurasians living in Myanmar was estimated at 20,000.

EUROPEAN COLONIAL EXPANSION. European expansion in Myanmar was motivated mainly by commercial and political interests. The first Europeans to make their mark, as early as the 16th century, were the Portuguese. The more lasting impact of European activity came with the advent of Dutch, British and French commercial ventures in the 17th century. The Dutch East India Company opened several trading establishments in Rakhine (q.v.) and in Thanlyin (q.v.), gaining important positions in trade with Myanmar between 1627 and 1677. From the mid-17th century on, the British began to compete with the Dutch and, in 1686, they occupied Negrais (Hainggyi Island) at the mouth of the Pathein River (q.v.). The French were also taking an interest in Myanmar and soon became Britain's main rivals in the country. The British-French rivalry became apparent with Alaungpaya's (q.v.) conquest of the Mon (q.v.) kingdom in southern Myanmar. While the British tried to remain neutral, the French were allied with the Mons. With Alaungpaya's conquest of Thanlyin, the main French base in Mon territory, the French residents found there were killed, deported or made captives and forced to serve in the royal army. Alaungpaya succeeded in getting arms from the British and, in return, granted the East India Company the right to trade from Negrais, under the treaty signed in 1757. However, in 1759, the British traders and their Indian subordinates in Negrais were unexpectedly ambushed and massacred by the Myanmar army on suspicion of aiding the Mons. After Alaungpaya's death, the

British were allowed to operate in southern Myanmar, but on less favorable terms.

The Europeans were attracted by Myanmar's wealth of teak and minerals (qq.v.), but Myanmar kings were reluctant to release their monopoly on these items. Another area of European interest was to obtain commercial access to China through Myanmar trade routes leading to Yunnan.

The annexation of Rakhine by Bodawpaya (q.v.) in 1785 projected Myanmar into diplomatic, and ultimately military, confrontation with British power in neighboring India. After the First and Second Anglo-Myanmar wars (qq.v.), the British gained a dominant position in Myanmar. Although the French presence was still felt in the country, the efforts by the last Konbaung dynasty kings, Mindon and Thibaw (qq.v.), to counterbalance British domination by cultivating relations with France, and possibly other European countries (such as Germany and Italy), came too late to stop the British annexation of the whole of Myanmar in 1886. (*See also* Anglo-Myanmar War, First; Anglo-Myanmar War, Second; Anglo-Myanmar War, Third; Portuguese and Myanmar.)

EXCLUDED AREAS. One of the terms referring to those parts of Myanmar, inhabited mainly by minority ethnic groups, which were administered separately from Burma proper (q.v.) under British rule. (*See also* Administration of Myanmar, British Colonial Era.)

EXPORT PRODUCTS. Of Myanmar's export (in 1989), about 43 percent were forest products, 32 percent were agricultural products, 11 percent were minerals and gems (qq.v.) and some 5 percent were animal and marine products. (*See also* Agriculture; Foreign Trade; Forestry.)

-F-

FABIAN PARTY. The party formed in 1936 by Ba Choe (q.v.), Ba Kine and Nu (q.v.) to propagate Fabian socialism and social reforms. The party contested the 1936 elections to the legislature and won one seat in the House of Representatives. (*See also* Socialism.)

FEDERAL REPUBLIC OF GERMANY (RELATIONS WITH). Although there was no historical legacy of Myanmar relations with Germany, the cooperation between Myanmar and the Federal Republic of Germany (FRG) has developed continually since diplomatic relations were established in 1954. Over the years, the FRG has become the second major aid donor to Myanmar after Japan (q.v.). Prior to 1988, the FRG gave Myanmar about US$ 5 million a year in technical grants and capital goods investments. The visit of German President Richard von Weizcäker to Myanmar in 1986 was followed by a return visit of U Ne Win and U San Yu (qq.v.) in 1987.

Following the military coup of 1988 (q.v.), the FRG, following other major Western democracies, suspended economic aid to Myanmar pending an improvement in Myanmar's human rights record. (*See also* Foreign Policy.)

FEDERALISM. The Constitution of the Union of Burma (1947) (q.v.) contained no explicit definition of federalism, although it conformed with the federal concept by providing for a separate system of government in each Union state. In practice, however, the federal structure of the Union was more nominal than real, as decisive power remained with the central (Union) government. As a result of this development, secessionist movements among the Shans (q.v.) and some other minority groups became active in the early 1960s, providing a major pretext for the military coup of 1962 (q.v.).

After 1962, the Revolutionary Council (q.v.) attempted to bring the Union States under more effective central control. The Constitution of the Socialist Republic of the Union of Burma (q.v.), adopted in 1974 and valid until the military coup of 1988 (q.v.), created a unified state in Myanmar, removing the specific federal arrangements of the first basic law. Although the new constitution is only in the preparatory stage, there are indications that the present military regime, the State Law and Order Restoration Council (q.v.), would prefer a solution that would put an end to the federal system (wanted by many minority groups) as well as the unitary system as embodied in the 1974 constitution. (*See also* National Unity.)

FERINGHI. The Indian term for Europeans, namely the Portuguese. (*See also* Bayingyi.)

FESTIVALS. Festivals, most of them linked to animism or Buddhism (qq.v.), form the core of Myanmar social life. The main festivals are: *Thingyan*, the Water Festival, celebrated in the Myanmar month of *Tagu* (March-April), to mark the Myanmar New Year; *Kazon*, or Buddha's Day Festival, held on the full moon day of *Kazon* (April-May); *Waso*, the festival held on the full moon day of *Waso* (June-July), marking the beginning of the Buddhist Lent (*Wa*); *Thadingyut,* the Festival of Lights, held in *Thadingyut* (September-October), marking the end of the Buddhist Lent; and *Tazaundaing*, held on the full moon day of *Tazaungmon* (mid-November), combined with competitions of speed-weaving of the robes for the images of the Buddha.

Apart from above national festivals, there are also those held for each particular local pagoda. Similar in appearance to pagoda festivals are cremation ceremonies for venerable *sayadaws* (q.v.), abbots of monasteries.

FIFTH GREAT BUDDHIST COUNCIL. The Council convened in 1871 at Mandalay (q.v.). Presided over by King Mindon (q.v.), and composed of over 2,000 Buddhist monks, the Council produced an authoritative text of the Buddhist canon, the *Tipitaka* (q.v.). In 1872, the corrected text of the *Tipitaka* was inscribed on 729 marble slabs which were posted within the enclosure of the Kuthodaw pagoda. (*See also* Sixth Great Buddhist Council.)

FILM INDUSTRY. The film industry is of recent origin in Myanmar. The first Myanmar silent film was produced in 1920, the first sound film in 1932. Prior to World War II (q.v.), there were about 40 Myanmar film companies, but only two or three, including the Burma Film Company, had sufficient funds and modern technical equipment to operate with some success.

The lack of funds and equipment forced the producers to return to silent films at the war's end. Only from 1957 have sound films been produced again, but they cannot compete with foreign films, either in technical standards or in script and stories. Following the military coup of 1962 (q.v.), the Film Censor Board was entrusted with the task of implementing the policy of banning from the stage and screen any foreign and Myanmar films based on ideas not appropriate to the Burmese Way to Socialism (q.v.) ideology or alien to the national culture. The production and showing of ghost and witch films, in great popular demand, was discouraged. The private producers, who dominate the national film industry in numbers, found it difficult to comply with the demands placed on them by the state cultural policy and to make their films a commercial success. Most current Myanmar movies are action films, comedies and romances.

FINANCE. Myanmar has its own currency since 1952 when the Indian rupee was replaced by the *kyat* (q.v.) as the new monetary unit of the country. Up to 1967, Myanmar's currency had the full backing of the pound sterling. In 1971, the *kyat* was linked to US dollar, with a rate of about five *kyats* to one US dollar. From 1974, the fixed rate was replaced by a floating one. Although the official rates of the *kyat* to foreign currencies are not realistic, the ruling State Law and Order Restoration Council (q.v.) refused to devaluate the *kyat* on the grounds that the measure would fuel inflation and increase Myanmar's foreign debt. Still, in 1991, average prices increased about 60 percent, while real wages deteriorated, and the currency in circulation greatly increased, too.

The state budget estimates for 1992 were K 9,098 million on the receipt side, with current expenditures evaluated at K 12,022 million, the result being a deficit of K 2,923 million. Defense expenditures were officially put at 32 percent (unofficial estimates at closer to 50 percent) of total expenditures.

Most of the foreign aid, in the form of bilateral and multilateral loans, which Myanmar was receiving from the late 1970s was suspended after the military coup of 1988 (q.v.). Myanmar's present external debt is estimated to be US $ 4.8 billion.

There is one state-owned banking system in the Union of Myanmar. All banks were nationalized in 1963 to form the People's Bank of Burma. In 1972, it was renamed the Union of Burma Bank; in 1976 it reconstituted as the central bank. In 1989, it was renamed the Union of Myanmar Bank and, in 1990, transformed into the Central Bank of Myanmar. The state banking system also includes the Myanmar Agricultural Bank, Myanmar Economic Bank, Myanmar Foreign Trade Bank and Myanmar Investment and Commercial Bank. (*See also* Foreign Trade; Internal Trade.)

FIRST MYANMAR EMPIRE. The Bagan (q.v.) empire founded by King Anawrahta (q.v.) in 1057 A.D. and maintained until 1287 when, under the rule of King Narathihapati (q.v.), it was overrun by the Mongols.

The rule of the empire builders, Anawratha (1044–1077) and Kyanzittha (1084–1111) (q.v.), was characterized by the efforts for the unification of the country's human and material resources and by a syncretism of the cultures and traditions of the diverse people of Bagan—the Bamars, Mons and Pyus (qq.v.). In the reign of Alaungsithu (1113–1169), the trend was towards the institutionalization of the prevalent Theravada Buddhism (q.v.). The "golden age" of the First Myanmar Empire refers principally to the reigns of Narapatisithu (1173–1210) (q.v.) and Nadaungmya (1210–1234). During this period, the empire expanded considerably, the basis of a firm administrative, economic and political system of Myanmar society was laid and most of Bagan's famous religious monuments were also built. The main reason for the decline of the First Myanmar empire, which became noticeable from the middle of the 13th century, was internal. It was attributable to the strain which the state began to feel as a result of the growing expenses of religion, mainly for temple-building. Unable to effectively check this trend, the empire finally crumbled under the attacks of the Mongol armies of Kublai Khan and their conquest of the capital Bagan in 1287.

FOREIGN POLICY. Myanmar's foreign policy has been based on the same general principles since independence in 1948, though there were variations in their application in the policies of the successive Myanmar governments. In 1948, neutralism was favored as a policy which would ensure Myanmar's sovereignty and territorial integrity and also preclude the possibility of the country's involvement in the "Cold War." From the outset, Myanmar's understanding of neutralism was not neutrality in the purely legal sense of the word, but rather a policy allowing its proponents to weigh all international issues on "their merits," with regard to the nation's own interests.

In the mid-1950s, Myanmar's foreign policy assumed a more dynamic form of "positive" neutralism, emphasizing five principles of peaceful co-existence advocating anti-colonialism and linked with Myanmar's strong support for the United Nations. This also became the basis of Myanmar's understanding and application of the policy of non-alignment. Myanmar joined the non-alignment movement in 1961, but withdrew from it in 1979. It reapplied and was readmitted to the movement in 1992.

The Revolutionary Council (q.v.) in 1962 interpreted Myanmar's foreign policy as "strict neutralism," which in fact largely contributed to Myanmar's isolationism in international and regional affairs. More recently, Myanmar's foreign policy was defined as an "independent and active" one, with a special emphasis on relations with neighboring countries.

FOREIGN TRADE. Historically, Myanmar has been dependent on foreign trade as a major source of foreign currency and as a means of satisfying the country's needs. Generally, until World War II (q.v.), exports exceeded imports. After the war and independence in 1948, there was a steady decline in domestic production, and consequently exports, which contributed only about 5 percent of GDP in 1974. Since the late 1970s, export volumes have increased considerably, mainly as a result of the revival in rice (q.v.) cultivation, more effective exploitation of forest products, such as teak (q.v.), and adding some new crops, such as maize (q.v.), to its export products (q.v.). However, the growth in export revenue has been rather slow and evidently lower than the growth in imports in recent years. The bulk of Myanmar's exports went to markets in Southeast Asia, China, India, Japan and Africa.

The composition of Myanmar's imports underwent a major change after the advent of the Revolutionary Council (q.v.) in 1962, with the import of consumer goods drastically cut in favor of importing more capital goods and raw materials. This trend has continued until recently, though import volumes rose rapidly. Imports come mainly from Japan and the EC countries, primarily Germany. The present government, the State Law and Order Restoration Council (q.v.), has introduced new measures to encourage exports, but these efforts are hampered by an unfavorable exchange rate of the Myanmar *kyat* (q.v.).

Due to specific conditions prevailing in the country, a substantial share of its foreign trade occurs through illegal transactions. There is considerable smuggling of gems, rice, teak (qq.v.) and other products abroad, and illegal import of a wide range of consumer goods, particularly from neighboring countries, to supply the local "black market" which flourishes in certain towns and urban centers. More recently, some of these illegal transactions have been curbed and changed into regular, government-controlled border trade, namely with the People's Republic of China (q.v.). (*See also* Finance; Internal Trade.)

FREEDOM BLOC. Known in Myanmar as *Htwet Yat Gaing*, literally "The Association of the Way Out," this nationalist alliance was formed in October 1939, bringing together the *Do Bama Asi Ayon*, the *Sinyetha* Party and the All Burma Students' Union (qq.v.). Led by Dr. Ba Maw as its President, or *Anashin* (q.v.), and Thakin Aung San (q.v.) as Secretary General, the Bloc organized public rallies in Yangon, Mandalay (qq.v.) and other places in support of its demands, the basic one being British recognition of Myanmar's right to freedom. By 1941, most Freedom Bloc leaders had been arrested by the colonial authorities, or gone into hiding, and its public activity virtually ceased. (*See also* Independence Movement; People's Revolutionary Party.)

FRONTIER AREAS. One of the terms referring to those parts of Myanmar, inhabited mainly by minority ethnic groups, which were administered separately from Burma proper (q.v.) under British rule. (*See also* Administration of Myanmar, British Colonial Era.)

FURNIVALL, JOHN SYDENHAM (1878–1960). British scholar-official who lived and worked in Myanmar during the latter years of British rule there. He came to the country as an Indian Civil Service official in 1902. He retired in 1931, but returned to Myanmar several times. From 1948 to 1960, he served as an adviser to the government of the Union of Burma (q.v.). Furnivall is regarded as the founder of modern Myanmar economic and social studies. In 1910, he initiated the Burma Research Society (q.v.). He also founded the Burma Book Club and Burma Education Extension Association in 1928.

-G-

GAING. A Myanmar term for a "religious sect," a "group of followers."

GALON. A Myanmar term for mythological bird, also known as the *garuda*, considered to be the mortal enemy of the *naga* (q.v.), a mythological serpent. *Galon* was also the name of the Saya San (q.v.) followers in the peasants' rebellion of 1930.

GAUNG. A Myanmar term meaning "head" or "head person." Used for a village constable and assistant tax collector, subordinate to the village headman, or *thugyi* (q.v.), during the British colonial era. (*See also* Administration of Myanmar, British Colonial Era.)

GEMS. Myanmar is the chief source of the only true jade known as jadeite. It is mined in Mogaung, near Myitkyina (q.v.). In 1982, the world's largest piece of jade, weighing 33 tons, was discovered in this area. Also famous are the Myanmar ruby and sapphire, mined mostly in Mogok (q.v.). Since 1962, the gem trade is controlled by the state, under the Myanmar Gem Corporation. However, a large part of mining activity is private, and there is a lot of smuggling of gems abroad. (*See also* Minerals.)

GENERAL COUNCIL OF BURMESE ASSOCIATIONS (GCBA). A major nationalist organization in Myanmar in the 1920s. It grew out of the Young Men's Buddhist Association (YMBA) (q.v.) in 1920, as an alliance of local *wunthanu* (q.v.) associations. The GCBA leadership, less Westernized than the YMBA leaders, cooperated with the "political" monks, *pongyis* (q.v.), rallied in the General Council of Sangha Sammeggi (GCSS) (q.v.).

The GCBA-GCSS coalition dominated Myanmar nationalist politics up to the early 1930s. Both in political program and tactics, the GCBA was influenced to some extent by the Indian National Congress (q.v.). The GCBA's quest for Bamar (q.v.) national identity, primarily based on factors of "race and religion," was also characterized by a growing recognition of the instrumentalities and values of the modern colonial state. More and more GCBA leaders gradually abandoned the initial "boycott" of the dyarchy (q.v.) reform of 1923, frustrated by the overwhelming grip on the independence movement (q.v.) of the "political" *pongyis*. Parallel to this development, there was an increasing fragmentation of what used to be a united nationalist front, with U Chit Hlaing (q.v.) as the GCBA's Permanent President. The splinter groups from the original GCBA included the Nationalist Party (q.v.) in 1923, the Home Rule Party (q.v.) in 1926, "Soe Thein GCBA" and "Su GCBA," of which only the "Soe Thein" group backed the Saya San Rebellion (q.v.).

GENERAL COUNCIL OF SANGHA SAMMEGGI (GCSS). Also known as the All Burma Buddhist Sasana Sangha Sammeggi *Aphwegyok*, this organization was founded in 1921 to bring together radical Buddhist monks, subsequently known as "political" *pongyis* (q.v.). The GCSS closely cooperated with the General Council of Burmese Associations (GCBA) (q.v.) and was instrumental in developing Bamar (q.v.) nationalism as a popular movement in the 1920s. Although at least some "political" *pongyis*, namely U Ottama (q.v.), were modern-minded, on the whole, the *pongyis'* movement of the 1920s was a resurgence of traditional nationalism interpreting the contemporary demand for "home rule" as the restoration of an independent Myanmar kingdom. The *pongyi* agitators attempted to achieve their objectives by intimidation and defiance of the authority of the colonial state, as represented by civil servants, the police, tax collectors and village headmen. The GCSS was a dominant factor in Myanmar nationalist politics of the 1920s. The 1930s saw the decline of their former authority as independent and often supreme nationalist leaders, namely in the rural areas.

GERMANY *see* FEDERAL REPUBLIC OF GERMANY (RELATIONS WITH).

GLASS PALACE CHRONICLE *see* HMANNAN YAZAWIN.

GOLDEN TRIANGLE. The mountainous region, a large part of which is located in the Hsenwi and Kengtung (q.v.) areas of Shan State (q.v.), and which also encompasses parts of Laos, Thailand and Yunnan. The Golden Triangle is notorious for growing opium poppy (*papaver somniferium*) from which heroin is derived. The tribes living in the region have been involved in the opium trade, as producers or middlemen, and many insurgent organizations operating there use the revenue from the opium trade to support their struggle against the Myanmar government. Several opium warlords are also active here. The Myanmar sector of the Golden Triangle, where about 80 percent of Southeast Asia's opium is harvested, produced almost 2,400 tons of raw opium in 1991. Much of it is processed in local heroin laboratories and exported, mainly to the United States. (*See also* Drug Abuse.)

GOSHAL, H. N. (aka BA TIN, THAKIN.) A Myanmar-born Bengali, one of the founding members of the Communist Party of Burma (CPB) (q.v.) in 1939 and a leading CPB ideologue after 1948. Although one of the veteran leaders, he was summarily tried by a radical faction of the party, inspired by the Chinese "Cultural Revolution," branded "Myanmar's Liu Shaoqi" and executed in the Bago Yoma (q.v.) on 18 June 1967.

GOVERNMENT OF BURMA ACT OF 1935. Also referred to as the 1935 Constitution, it came into effect on 1 April 1937, upon separation of Myanmar from India, and it functioned until the Japanese occupation of Myanmar (1942–1945) (q.v.). The Myanmar government, with the British Governor as its head, came directly under the British government in London. The Governor was solely responsible for defense, finance, foreign affairs, the "Excluded Areas" (q.v.) and certain specific cases, while in all other matters he was bound to act on advice of his ministers. The cabinet, headed by the Prime Minister, was vested with supreme executive power and was responsible to the legislature (Parliament). The Parliament consisted of a Senate with 36 seats, of which half were nominated by the Governor and the other half were elected by a House of Representatives. This popular chamber had 132 members, of whom 92 were filled on a non-communal territorial constituency basis, while the rest were reserved for communal and special interest. (*See also* Administration of Myanmar, British Colonial Era.)

GREAT BRITAIN (RELATIONS WITH). As the former metropolitan country, Great Britain continued to exercise a good deal of influence in Myanmar during the early postindependence years, providing much of the economic, military and technical aid. However, during the 1950s, the former close ties between the two countries became looser. By 1953, the backing of Myanmar's finance by a Currency Board in London and the Ottawa Tariff Agreement were both terminated. In 1954, Myanmar formally abrogated British military assistance under the Bo Let Ya-Freeman Defence Agreement of 1947. Former leading British firms in the country, such as the Bombay Burmah Trading Corporation and the Irrawaddy Flotilla Company (qq.v.), were nationalized as early as 1948, while others, such as the Burma Corporation (q.v.), were first transformed into joint ventures with the Myanmar government, then nationalized following the military coup of 1962 (q.v.). Although Great Britain was no longer Myanmar's major aid donor and trading partner, it continued to give support to various Myanmar development projects in the fields of education, culture and public health, partly also through Colombo Plan (q.v.) projects. Following the military coup of 1988 (q.v.), Great Britain was among the countries which suspended aid to Myanmar pending an improvement in Myanmar's human rights record.

GUARDIAN MAGAZINE. An English-language monthly which prints articles on culture and religion as well as translations of Myanmar poetry and short stories. Founded in 1953, and nationalized in 1964, it is published in Yangon (q.v.).

-H-

HAKA. The capital of Chin State (q.v.), a hill resort town, situated about 54 kilometers (34 miles) south of Falam, the former capital of the state.

HALIN. Also known as Halingyi and Hanlin. The former, now ruined Pyu (q.v.) capital, located about 16 kilometers (10 miles) southeast of Shwebo (q.v.). Halin was probably built between the 2nd and the 6th century A.D. It served as the last Pyu capital from the 8th century until 832 A.D., when it was overrun by the Nan-Chao.

HALL, DANIEL GEORGE EDWARD (1891–1979). One of the leading British historians of Southeast Asia who devoted many of his writings to Myanmar. From 1921 to 1934, he was professor of history at the University of Yangon (q.v.); during this period he also served as member of the Legislative Council (1923–1924). He returned to Myanmar after independence as visiting professor at the University of Yangon (1952–1953).

HARVEY, GODFREY ERIC (1889–1965). An official of the Indian Civil Service in Myanmar, from 1912 to 1932, Harvey later became lecturer of Myanmar history and law at Oxford University. His writings include *History of Burma* and its sequel, *British Rule in Burma, 1824–1942*.

HINTHA. Also *hamsa*. A mythological bird which was the national and sacred bird of the Mons (q.v.) and their kingdom with its capital at Bago (q.v.).

HLAING RIVER. Also known as the Yangon River. A river about 297 kilometers (185 miles) long which flows from the Bago Yoma down to Yangon (qq.v.). It then continues another 30 kilometers (20 miles) and empties into the Gulf of Martaban.

HLUTTAW. Also (incorrectly) *hlutdaw*. A Myanmar term meaning literally "place of release," which refers to the Council of Ministers at the court of precolonial Myanmar. The *hluttaw* was primarily responsible for the public affairs of the state. It registered royal edicts, issued royal letters and tried most important cases. It was composed of the chief ministers, *wungyi* (q.v.), normally four in number. Each was a sort of secretary of state; together they controlled every department of the government. The sessions of the *hluttaw* were presided over by the king, the heir apparent or a senior *wungyi*. (*See also* Administration of Myanmar, Precolonial Era; Byedaik.)

HMANNAN YAZAWIN. *The Glass Palace Chronicle*, the standard version of the Myanmar chronicles. Its compilation, ordered by King Bagyidaw (q.v.) in 1829, was undertaken by a group of learned scholars and it covered Myanmar history up to 1752. (*See also* Kula, U; Literature.)

HOME RULE PARTY. Nationalist party formed in 1925 as a breakaway group from the General Council of Burmese Associations (q.v.) by Tharrawaddy U Pu. The party rejected the dyarchy (q.v.) reform of 1923 and demanded "home rule" for Myanmar along the lines of the program of the Indian National Congress (q.v.). Later, it opposed the separation of Myanmar from India (q.v.). It merged with the Nationalist Party (q.v.) to form the People's Party (q.v.) in the late 1920s.

HSINBYUSHIN (r. 1763–1776). King of the Konbaung Dynasty (q.v.). His reign began with a massive Myanmar invasion of Thailand, which culminated in 1767 with the seizing and ransacking of Ayutthaya. At about the same time, in the years 1765 to 1769, the Myanmars successfully defended their country against a series of attacks by Chinese imperial armies. In 1770, the Myanmar army invaded Manipur. The Myanmars under Hsinbyushin also conquered the Thai province of Chiang Mai and the Laotian kingdom of Vientiane to the north. These campaigns brought numerous captives and rich booty, while the military successes boosted Bamar national pride. Hsinbyushin's reign was, however, not stable and was marked by Mon and Shan (qq.v.) revolts. The Thais also put up a strong resistance and established their new capital at Bangkok in 1768. Hsinbyushin's successor to the throne, his son Singu (1776–1782), had to terminate the campaign in Thailand and recall the Myanmar troops. (*See also* Third Myanmar Empire.)

HTAY, YEBAW. Along with H. N. Goshal (q.v.), one of the main theoreticians of the Communist Party of Burma (CPB) (q.v.) in the 1950s and in the early 1960s. In 1963, Yebaw Htay led the CPB delegation in the peace talks with the Revolutionary Council in Yangon (qq.v.). He was branded "Myanmar's Deng Xia Ping" by party radicals, inspired by the Chinese "Cultural Revolution," and executed in the Bago Yoma (q.v.) on 18 June 1967.

HTI. A Myanmar word meaning "umbrella." Another and related meaning is the upper part or crowning "umbrella" of a pagoda or temple, usually ornamented with small metal bells and sometimes gilded or bejeweled. (*See also* Architecture.)

HTILOMINLO. The Myanmar expression literally meaning "he whom the umbrella wished to be the king." The nickname of Nantaungmya (r. 1210–1234), the son of Narapatisithu (q.v.) and a king of the Bagan Dynasty (q.v.). He is said to have been chosen king by the white umbrella, a symbol of royalty in Myanmar, which pointed to him in preference to his brothers. Devoting himself to religion, he left the state affairs to his four brothers. They ruled jointly, sitting together in the Council of State, which is supposed to be the origin of the *hluttaw* (q.v.).

HTIN AUNG, DR. (1909–1978). Myanmar educationist, lawyer and scholar. He was Professor, Rector (1946–1958) and Vice-Chancellor of the University of Yangon (q.v.). He also served as Myanmar's ambassador to Ceylon (Sri Lanka) (1959–1962). Since then he has held several visiting professorships, namely in the United States and Great Britain. He wrote many books about Myanmar. His major publications include *Burmese Drama* (1937), *Burmese Folk-Tales* (1947), *Folk Elements in Burmese Buddhism* (1962) and *A History of Burma* (1967). As a historian, he represents a nationalist tradition and is noted for his defense of the Myanmar chronicles as a source of information about old Myanmar.

HUNTER THA HMWE, SAW. Also known as Saw Hunter Kawkasa. Former prominent Kayin (q.v.) rebel leader. In 1947, he joined the Karen National Union (KNU) and became one of the regional commanders of the Karen National Defence Organization (KNDO) (qq.v.). In 1949, he went underground. A year later he was appointed successor to Saw Ba U Gyi as head of the Kawthoolei government (qq.v.). In 1959, he founded the Karen Revolutionary Council (KRC); in 1963, he withdrew from the KNU. As KRC delegate to the 1963 peace talks with the Revolutionary Council in Yangon (qq.v.), he signed an agreement with the Revolutionary Council whereby the KRC agreed to lay down its arms and return to the legal fold, the only underground organization which did so at that time.

-I-

IMMIGRATION *see* MIGRATION.

INDEPENDENCE DAY. The major public holiday. It is observed on 4 January to commemorate the date in 1948 that Myanmar became a sovereign, independent state, the Union of Burma (q.v.), which chose to leave the British Commonwealth of Nations. (*See also* Independence Movement.)

INDEPENDENCE MOVEMENT. The origin of the independence movement in Myanmar dates back to the armed patriotic resistance by Bamars, Chins, Kachins, Shans (qq.v.) and some other ethnic groups against the British annexation of northern Myanmar in 1885, which was only crushed around 1895. These struggles, as well as the more recent Saya San Rebellion in 1930 (q.v.), demonstrated that the people of Myanmar were never reconciled to alien domination.

Modern Myanmar nationalism initially took the form of a movement for the defense of Buddhism (q.v.) as the national religion, and it was mainly headed by the Young Men's Buddhist Association (YMBA) founded in Yangon in 1906 (qq.v.). World War I (q.v.) was an important watershed in the evolution of Myanmar nationalism. In 1920, the YMBA was reorganized into the General Council of Burmese Associations (GCBA) which openly entered politics. The GCBA, which coordinated its efforts with the "political" monks, *pongyis,* rallied in the General Council of Sangha Sammeggi (qq.v.), dominated nationalist politics until the 1930s.

In the 1930s, the *Thakins* of the *Do Bama Asi Ayon* (qq.v.) came to the fore of the independence movement. Essentially nationalists, some *Thakins* turned to "radical" ideologies, including Marxism, in their struggle against British rule. In 1939, the Communist Party of Burma (q.v.) was formed. The first nationwide trade unions—the All Burma Peasants' Organization (1939) and the All Burma Trade Union Congress (1940) (qq.v.)—were also established.

The outbreak of World War II (q.v.) in 1939 gave a strong impetus to the nationalist quest for independence, but most nationalist leaders, rallied in the Freedom Bloc (q.v.), were arrested by the British or forced into hiding between 1940 and 1942. The leaders of the underground sections of the movement, namely of the People's Revolutionary Party (q.v.), seeking arms and military assistance, established contacts with Japanese military agents operating in the country prior to the outbreak of the Pacific War. One of the results of their cooperation was the smuggling out of the country, for military training by the Japanese, of a group of 30 young volunteers, including Aung San, who subsequently became known as the "Thirty Comrades" and who founded the Burma Independence Army in December 1941 (qq.v.).

The independence movement during the period of the Japanese occupation of Myanmar (1942–1945) (q.v.) was essentially an anti-fascist and anti-colonial struggle, with the genuine independence of Myanmar as its ultimate objective. Thousands of people, Bamars and other ethnic groups, were drawn into the anti-fascist resistance (q.v.). It culminated in March 1945 with an armed uprising by the Burma National

Army (q.v.) which greatly facilitated the Allied reconquest of the country and also influenced postwar political developments.

In August 1945, the Anti-Fascist People's Freedom League (q.v.), founded in August 1944, was reconstituted as a broad national front. It became the main political force which ultimately led Myanmar to independence on 4 January 1948. (*See also* Aung San-Attlee Agreement; Constitution of the Union of Burma; Interim Government; Nu-Attlee Agreement; Pacification of Burma; Panglong Agreement.)

INDIA (RELATIONS WITH). Historically, Myanmar's relations with India have been complex, namely as a result of the recent legacy of British colonial rule under which there was a large Indian migration into Myanmar, a province of British India between 1886 and 1937, and Indians assumed control over a large part of Myanmar's colonial economy.

After Myanmar's independence in 1948, the successive Myanmar governments tried to cultivate friendly relations with India while resolving outstanding problems between the two countries. In 1951, the treaty of friendship between India and the Union of Burma (q.v.) was signed and, until the early 1960s, both countries also cooperated closely in international diplomacy and in the non-aligned movement. After the military coup of 1962 (q.v.), the Revolutionary Council (q.v.) began a campaign to nationalize Myanmar's economy and about 200,000 people of Indian origin were forced to leave the country. Myanmar's relations with India in the next two decades were correct, but not close. The sensitive issues of bilateral relations included the status of Indians in Myanmar (q.v.), the demarcation of the maritime boundary between the two countries and the problem of Naga (q.v.) rebels in border areas. After the military coup of 1988 (q.v.), India, virtually alone among Myanmar's neighbors, was vocal in criticism of Myanmar's military government. (*See also* Indians.)

INDIAN NATIONAL CONGRESS. Due to the administrative association of Myanmar with British India, from 1886 to 1937, and the large Indian (q.v.) resident community there, the Indian National Congress exercised an influence on Myanmar's Indians as well as successive generations of Myanmar nationalist politicians. In 1908, the Myanmar branch of the Indian National Congress, the Burma Provincial Congress Committee, was founded by P. J. Mehta in Yangon (q.v.). It drew some support from resident Indian urban middle classes and, in the 1920s, it gained backing from several leaders of the General Council of Burmese Associations (GCBA), such as U Chit Hlaing, as well as U Ottama (qq.v.). While, in the 1920s, Gandhism—as an ideology and method of anti-colonial struggle—was copied to some extent by GCBA politicians, the leaders of the *Do Bama Asi Ayon* (q.v.) found their inspiration rather in the Congress Left, represented by Jawaharlal Nehru and Subhas Chandra Bose. From 1938, the *Do Bama Asi Ayon* sent its delegates to the sessions of the Indian National Congress. During the Japanese occupation of Myanmar (q.v.), the Provisional Government of Azad Hind led by Subhas Chandra Bose was located in Myanmar (1943–1945), while relations with the Indian National Congress in India were continued by some exiled Myanmar nationalist politicians, such as Thakin Thein Pe Myint (q.v.). After the war, the cooperation of the Myanmar independence movement (q.v.) with the Indian National Congress was best exemplified by contacts between Jawaharlal Nehru and Aung San, and also his successor, U Nu (qq.v.).

INDIANS (IN MYANMAR). The Indians, along with the Chinese (q.v.), are the largest non-indigenous ethnic group in Myanmar, though now the Chinese are probably more numerous than Indian residents whose numbers have been reduced to some 100,000 in recent decades. The Indian population of Myanmar consists largely of descendants of the migrants who came to the country especially from southern India and Bengal, during the British colonial era in the early 20th century. While not all of the Indian immigrants chose to live in the country for good, by the 1930s about one million Indians resided in Myanmar, forming about half of the population of Yangon (q.v.). Educated and rich Indians occupied the middle levels of administration and business, with the

Chettiars (q.v.) playing a prominent role as money-lenders and absentee-landlords. Poor Indians came and worked as seasonal agricultural workers and contract laborers. The Indian community was distinct from the Bamar majority and was not easily integrated into Myanmar society. There was resentment against the *Chettiars* and also against the largely unrestricted influx of Indian labor which, combined with a different culture and religion, aroused feelings which were manifested in two anti-Indian riots in 1930 and 1938. On the other hand, Myanmar nationalists drew inspiration from the Indian National Congress (q.v.). In 1942, at the beginning of the Japanese occupation of Myanmar (1942–1945) (q.v.), about half of the Indian population left the country for India, and several hundred thousands died on the trek.

After 1945, many Indians came back to Myanmar, but, since Myanmar's independence in 1948, there have been rigid restrictions on the number permitted to enter Myanmar. The Indians were gradually excluded from public services, dispossessed of their lands and discriminated against in commerce and trade. Indian interests were particularly affected by the nationalization of the Myanmar economy during the Burma Socialist Programme Party era (q.v.) in the 1960s. The present Indian community is made up mostly of poorer classes who earn their living in menial jobs. A majority of the Indians born in Myanmar are Muslims (q.v.), the minority are Hindus. (*See also* Nationality; Riots, British Colonial Era.)

INDUSTRY. All major industries introduced by the British were disrupted during World War II and the Japanese occupation of Myanmar (1942–1945) (qq.v.), and post-war progress towards industrial recovery was slow. Industrial development in Myanmar is still not far advanced and is mainly concentrated around certain cities and larger urban centers, such as Mandalay and Yangon (qq.v.). Currently, the proclaimed priority aim is the establishment of industries producing consumer goods for the domestic market, export-oriented industries and other industries based on domestic raw materials.

There were 35,279 factories and industrial establishments in Myanmar in 1991. Of these, 14,669 were processing food and beverages and 5,756 were producing clothing and wearing apparel. Other important industries included personal goods (3,644), processing of mineral and petroleum products (2,641) and of industrial raw materials (2,079). Although major industries were nationalized after 1962, the private (or cooperative sector) is most important in terms of both the number of establishments (predominantly small-sized) and of employment. The main constraints of Myanmar's industrial development, aside from the unstable political situation, are the lack of foreign exchange and investments, shortage of energy supplies and poor infrastructure. Myanmar's heavy industry is almost entirely defense-oriented while the manufacturing sector is declining due to recurring power (q.v.) shortages.

INLE LAKE. Also Inlay Lake. The best known of Myanmar's lakes and a popular tourist resort, Inle Lake is situated in Shan State (q.v.) at an elevation of about 853 meters (2,800 feet) on the Shan Plateau (q.v.). The lake is shallow, about 19 kilometers (12 miles) long and 6 kilometers (4 miles) wide. Its inhabitants, known as Inthas, gather the patches of floating weed and anchor them to their houses, to make vegetable or fruit floating gardens. The Inthas are also famous as leg-rowers. At the annual festival, held in the Myanmnar month of *Tawthalin* (September-October), the boat races and leg-rowing competitions take place. Silk-weaving is done in some villages around the lake and Inle silk is well-known in Myanmar.

INTERIM GOVERNMENT. The body formed by the Executive Council of the British Governor in Myanmar under the terms of the Aung San-Attlee Agreement (q.v.) of January 1947. It was agreed that the Interim Government would be regarded as that of a dominion country and would exercise full ministerial authority. Aung San (q.v.) was *de facto* head of the Interim Government until his assassination on 19 July 1947. Shortly thereafter, on 23 July 1947, the Interim Government became the Provisional Government with Thakin Nu (q.v.) as Prime Minister.

INTERNAL TRADE. After the military coup of 1962 (q.v.), much of the country's internal trade was nationalized. By the mid-1960s, the state officially controlled almost 60 percent of internal trade, but a considerable proportion of internal trade activities remained in the hands of the private and partly also cooperative sectors. The moves to decontrol and liberalize both foreign trade (q.v.) and domestic trade activities, which started in the late 1970s, are being continued by the present government, the State Law and Order Preservation Council (q.v.). Owing to the continuing shortage of consumer goods, including many basic necessities, as a result of the declining output of industry (q.v.), the "black market," supplied with illegally imported goods, continues to play an important role in trading, though some of its activities were recently legalized by the government and thus brought under its control. (*See also* Finance.)

INWA. An ancient, now ruined capital located a few kilometers from Mandalay (q.v.). Founded in 1364 A.D. by King Thadominbya, Inwa was the capital until the early period of the Toungoo Dynasty (qq.v.), and then again, from 1634 to 1752, when the Konbaung Dynasty (q.v.) came to power. King Bodawpaya moved to Amarapura in 1782 (q.v.), but Inwa enjoyed the status of capital city during the reign of King Bagyidaw (1819–1837) (q.v.). However, after an earthquake in 1837, King Tharrawaddy brought the capital back to Amarapura. For centuries prior to the British annexation of Myanmar in the 19th century, Myanmar was widely known abroad as Inwa ("Ava").

IRRAWADDY DELTA *see* AYEYARWADY DELTA.

IRRAWADDY DIVISION *see* AYEYARWADY DIVISION.

IRRAWADDY FLOTILLA COMPANY. A Scottish firm, founded in 1865, originally as the Irrawaddy Flotilla and Burmese Steam Navigation Company Limited, it became the leading public carrier of larger-scale river freight and passenger service in Myanmar prior to World War II and the Japanese occupation of Myanmar (1942–1945) (qq.v.).

Together with the Araccan Flotilla Company, the Irrawaddy Flotilla Company operated some 4,100 kilometers (2,550 miles) of waterways and carried 1,500,000 tons of freight and around 8 million passengers a year. Most of the company's boats (about 650 units in the 1930s) were sunk and destroyed and thus denied to the Japanese in 1942. The postwar years witnessed some reconstruction, but traffic did not return to normal. On 1 June 1948, the Irrawaddy Flotilla Company was nationalized by the government of the Union of Burma (q.v.) (*See also* Water Transport.)

IRRAWADDY RIVER *see* AYEYARWADY RIVER.

IRRIGATION. Irrigated agriculture has a long tradition in Myanmar, dating back to King Anawrahta (q.v.) in the 11th century. Irrigation works built at that time are still in use through constant maintenance and repair. In addition to existing works, new irrigation works and systems are constructed. Recent schemes have been designed to provide supplementary water in the wet season, rather than to allow for double cropping, or to provide flood control. As reservoirs are built in central Myanmar for storage of agricultural water, embankment works are also built in the Ayeyarwady Delta (q.v.) to prevent cultivated fields from being inundated. The total irrigated area in 1991 was 1,184,734 hectares (2,927,512 acres) or about 12 percent of the total arable land. (*See also* Agriculture; Rice.)

ISLAM. One of the religions of the Union of Myanmar. It was professed by 3.9 percent of the population according to the 1983 census. (*See also* Muslims.)

-J-

JAPAN (RELATIONS WITH). Memories of the Japanese occupation of Myanmar (1942–1945) (qq.v.) significantly marked the early postwar relations between the two countries. The Myanmar government refused to attend the peace conference at San Francisco in 1951 because the proposed peace treaty with Japan did not provide for reparations to Myanmar. Only in November 1954, after protracted negotiations, was the peace treaty between Myanmar and Japan signed. Japan agreed to pay US $200 million in reparations and another US $50 million in investments.

Initially cautious development of Japanese investments and joint-venture projects was followed by a rapid expansion of bilateral economic and trade cooperation since the late 1970s. Japan saw Myanmar as a country with vast economic and resources potential while Myanmar found in Japan a developed nation willing to assist with the modernization of the economy and development of natural resources, namely petroleum (q.v.) exploration. Over recent years, Japan has become Myanmar's major foreign trade (q.v.) partner.

Japan has also emerged as the leading donor among the countries providing aid to Myanmar. Prior to 1988, Japanese aid totalled some US $224 million a year. It is estimated that Myanmar owes almost half of its total external debt to Japan. After the military coup of 1988 (q.v.), Japan joined other major donors who froze their aid to Myanmar pending an improvement in Myanmar's human rights record. However, in February 1989, Japan partially resumed its aid, although indicating that aid payments would continue only for existing projects. In 1990, Japan provided Myanmar with US $33 million in terms of Overseas Development Assistance.

JAPANESE OCCUPATION OF MYANMAR (1942–1945). Myanmar figured in the Japanese plans to build an Asian Pacific Empire, such as in the "New Order Plan in East Asia" and the "Greater East Asia Co-Prosperity Sphere," which had been formulated prior to the outbreak of the Pacific War in December 1941. Myanmar was important to Japan because of its strategic geographic location and the "Burma Road" (q.v.) leading to China. After the outbreak of World War II (q.v.), between 1940 and 1941, Japanese military agents operating secretly in Myanmar and Japanese agencies, such as the *Minami Kikan* (q.v.), were instrumental in training the "Thirty Comrades" and in formation in Bangkok on 28 December 1941 of the Burma Independence Army (BIA) (qq.v.).

The Japanese military campaign in Myanmar, waged by the 15th Japanese Army under the Command of Lieutenant General Shojiro Iida, started in December 1941 in Tanintharyi (q.v.). By May 1942, the Japanese controlled most of Myanmar and the British troops were forced to retreat into India. During their campaign, the Japanese were assisted by the BIA and *Thakins* of the *Do Bama Asi Ayon* (q.v.) whose expectations that Myanmar would be given independence after the British retreat did not, however, materialize. On 5 June 1942, the Japanese military administration assumed responsibility over all Myanmar. On 1 August 1942, the Burmese Provisional Administrative Committee, with Dr. Ba Maw as its Head, was set up in Yangon (qq.v.). It was under strict Japanese control, which was exercised jointly by the 15th Japanese Army Command and the Military Administration (*Gunseikanbu*). Another Japanese agency, the *Kempeitai*, the Japanese military police, was entrusted with maintaining internal security. Much of Myanmar's economy was in the hands of Japanese monopolies. Agricultural and industrial production declined substantially, transport was disrupted and many people left the war-devastated or threatened urban centers to live in rural areas. Some 800,000 people were recruited into forced labor corps, many of them sent to build the Thai-Burma Railway (q.v.).

The political structure of Japanese-occupied Myanmar was greatly simplified by allowing only one party, the *Do Bama-Sinyetha* coalition (q.v.). The Japanese, still attempting to retain the support of Myanmar nationalists, granted Myanmar independence on 1 August 1943. Though largely nominal in character, this independence, nonetheless, produced a considerable political effect. The government of Myanmar with Dr. Ba Maw as Head of State and several leaders of the independence movement, such as Aung San, Nu and Than Tun (qq.v.), holding posts of cabinet ministers, gained invaluable administrative experience and an opportunity to build up the national military organization. Most of the nationalist leaders were secretly involved in anti-fascist resistance and the armed uprising of the Burma National Army (BNA) (qq.v.) in March 1945. This took place at a time when the Allied military reconquest of the country was already in progress. The BNA and resistance forces helped the British Army to fight the Japanese troops in the country until their formal surrender on 12 August 1945.

JATAKA. The collection of tales of the Buddha's former births. The *Jatakas*, 547 in number, also include secular tales and fables of any kind, provided that one of the characters in the tale is the future Buddha. In Myanmar, knowledge of the

Jataka tales is a necessary part of the religious upbringing of every Buddhist believer. (*See also* Buddhism.)

JUDSON, ADONIRAM (1788–1850). One of the early American Baptist missionaries to come to Myanmar in 1815. During the First Anglo-Myanmar War he was imprisoned in Inwa (q.v.). In 1827, he moved to Mawlamyine (q.v.) and began his missionary work among the Kayins (q.v.) in southern Myanmar. Judson mastered the Myanmar language (q.v.) and translated the Holy Bible into Myanmar. He also wrote a Myanmar grammar and compiled the first large Myanmar-English and English-Myanmar dictionaries which have since been revised and republished several times. (*See also* Anglo-Myanmar War, First; Christianity.)

JUDSON COLLEGE. Originally known as the American Baptist Intermediate College, it was started in 1875 in Yangon (q.v.) by American missionaries to provide higher education mainly to the Kayins (q.v.). It was renamed Judson College in 1918 and, in 1920, it became one of the two constituent colleges of the newly established University of Yangon (q.v.). After independence in 1948, the facilities of Judson College were absorbed by the University of Yangon. (*See also* Colonial Education; Education; Universities and Colleges.)

JUTE. Strong, glossy fiber used for making burlap sacks, mats, ropes, etc. The production of jute, one of the "industrial crops," has been encouraged by the government with the ultimate aim of making it a major export product (q.v.). Cultivation of jute is undertaken mainly in Ayeyarwady Division (q.v.). In 1991, the area under jute was 37,232 hectares (92,000 acres) and production reached some 29,000 tons. (*See also* Agriculture.)

-K-

KACHIN. A Tibeto-Burman ethnolinguistic group. The majority of Kachins living in Myanmar are settled in Kachin State and in the adjacent northern part of Shan State (qq.v.). Kachin refers to the people who call themselves *Jinghpaw* (also spelt *Chinghpaw* and *Singhpo*) as well as to their ethnic subgroups—such as the Atsi, Lashi and Maru—who live mainly along the Myanmar-China border. According to the 1983 census, the Kachins numbered 465,484, making up about 1.4 percent of the total population of the country.

Traditionally, the Kachins lived in villages situated on ridge tops or the upper portions of slopes. More recently, they began to settle in valley bottoms as well. Their main occupation is swidden agriculture.

The basic crop is rice, alternating with buckwheat, millet and barley. Agriculture is supplemented by hunting, gathering and fishing. Cattle, buffalo, pigs, dogs and fowl are bred for sacrifices.

Descent is traced in the male line. The superior kin group is a sib, a unilinear (patrilinear) group descended from a remote ancestor. Parents play an important role in the choice of a mate (marriage partner) for their children. As to the form of marriage among Kachins, polygyny is permitted, but monogamous marriages seem to be more common. As for inheritance rights, the younger son customarily inherits the father's property and position.

The Kachin were the latest ethnic group to arrive and settle in Myanmar in the late 19th century. Their previous history is not quite clear. The Kachins appear to have had closer contacts with the Shans (q.v.) and in certain localities were assimilated to their culture. There was no centralized state or political authority encompassing all the Kachins prior to the creation of Kachin State as part of the Union of Burma (q.v.) in 1948. In precolonial days, the Kachins were only loosely connected with Myanmar state and under British rule their territory was administered separately from Burma proper (q.v.). After 1962, Kachin State harbored several rebel armies and organizations which were fighting the Myanmar government.

The Kachins still maintain some patterns of their traditional form of organization, based on social stratification. Under the *gumsa* pattern, predominant in the north and in the highlands of Kachin State, the communities are ruled by hereditary chiefs, *Duwa* (q.v.), while under the *gumlao* system there is no hereditary status or aristocracy. During the period of British rule, the Kachins had intensive contacts with American Protestant and European Catholic missions and a number of them were converted to Christianity (q.v.).

Later, some became Buddhists, while the majority of the Kachins are still adherents of traditional religious beliefs and practices, not quite accurately labeled animism (q.v.).

KACHIN INDEPENDENCE ORGANIZATION/ARMY (KIO/KIA). Until quite recently, one of the largest and best organized armed ethnic opposition groups in Myanmar. Begun in 1961, as a Kachin (q.v.) response to then Prime Minister U Nu's promotion of Buddhism (qq.v.) as the state religion of the Union of Burma (q.v.), it succeeded in forging a united movement encompassing the Kachins (Jinghpaws) as well as several other ethnic sub-groups, such as the Lashi, Lisu and Maru. The KIO/KIA operated in a large part of Kachin State and in the northeastern regions of Shan State (qq.v.) inhabited by Kachins. It was affiliated with the National Democratic Front (q.v.).

KACHIN STATE. It covers an area of 89,041 square kilometers (34,379 square miles) and occupies the northernmost mountain zone of the country. Except for a few valleys and plains, it is mostly hilly.

Kachin State has international boundaries with the People's Republic of China in the east and the northeast and India in the west; it adjoins Sagaing Division on the west and Shan State (qq.v.) on the south. It consists of 18 townships and 614 village tracts. Its (1983) population was 904,794. The capital is Myitkyina (q.v.); other important towns include Bhamo (q.v.), Mogaung and Putao. While most of the people are Kachins (q.v.) and other hill groups, there are also Bamars and Shans (qq.v.) who mostly live in the valleys. The principal occupation is agriculture (q.v.) and the chief crop is rice (q.v.). The forests produce teak (q.v.) and other valuable woods. The mineral (q.v.) resources of the state are rich; most noteworthy is jade mining.

KALA. Also *Kula*. A Myanmar term for foreigners which was largely applied to Indians (q.v.) and Europeans. The latter were also called *Kalabyu*, meaning "white *Kala*." The term is assumed to be derived from a Pali (q.v.) word for "clan."

KALAW. A town in Shan State (q.v.). It is situated at an altitude of 1,319 meters (4,333 feet) on the western edge of the Shan

Plateau and about 70 kilometers (44 miles) north of Taunggyi (qq.v.). One of the former hill stations and summer resorts for British colonial officials, Kalaw is still a favorite tourist and recreation place.

KAN. A Myanmar expression derived from the Pali (q.v.) *kamma* and known as *karma* in Sanskrit. The belief of Buddhists according to which a person's fate is the outcome of all his acts during his present existence and the cumulative record of his present behavior. The idea of *kan* implies one's own responsibility for one's fate. (*See also* Buddhism; Kutho; Nirvana; Samsara.)

KAREN *see* **KAYIN**.

KAREN NATIONAL ASSOCIATION (KNA). Also known as the National Karen Association. Founded in 1881 by prominent Sgaw Christian Kayins (q.v.), the KNA was the first modern political organization in Myanmar. Led by San Crombie Po and Sydney Loo Nee (qq.v.), the KNA's declared objectives were to defend Kayin national interests and to bring about economic, cultural, social and political advancement of the Kayin people. Since the late 1920s, the KNA envisaged the future Kayin state as a separately administered region in British-ruled Myanmar. Despite its proclaimed goal of promoting a broader sense of unity of all Kayins, it remained basically a platform of the Kayin Christianized elite which provided most of its leadership and policy. The KNA was a forerunner of the Karen National Union (q.v.) established in 1947.

KAREN NATIONAL DEFENCE ORGANIZATION *see* **KAREN NATIONAL UNION**.

KAREN NATIONAL LIBERATION ARMY *see* **KAREN NATIONAL UNION**.

KAREN NATIONAL LIBERATION COUNCIL *see* **KAREN NATIONAL UNION**.

KAREN NATIONAL UNION (KNU). The major Kayin (q.v.)

rebel organization led by General (Bo) Mya (q.v.) which mainly operates in the territory of Karen Free State, Kawthoolei (q.v.). Founded in April 1947, the KNU rallied a majority of Kayin leaders, including its first President, Saw Ba U Gyi (q.v.), who asked for a separate Kayin state, under British protection, and Kayin armed forces. In July 1947, the KNU formally inaugurated the Karen National Defence Organization (KNDO) which consisted of Karen ex-servicemen and subsequently became the KNU's military arm. The KNU did not recognize the Union of Burma (q.v.) in January 1948, insisting on its former demand of an independent Kayin state which would include the entire Ayeyarwady and Tanintharyi Divisions (qq.v.) and a large part of southern Myanmar.

In January 1949, the majority of the KNU went underground to join the KNDO rebellion which broke out in that month. During 1949, the KNU and KNDO, supported by mutineers from the Kayin military police and the Burma Army (q.v.), controlled large areas in southern and central Myanmar. In June 1949, Karen Revolutionary Government was set up by the KNU with its headquarters at Toungoo (q.v.), which was designed as the center of a future Kawthoolei state. The KNDO allied temporarily with the Communist Party of Burma (CPB) (q.v.) and also with the remnants of the Kuomintang troops which withdrew into Myanmar after 1949. From 1950, the Kayin rebels were forced to retreat to the rural areas of southeastern Myanmar.

In the 1950s, the KNU underwent a complex evolution marked by several fractional splits, reorganizations and leadership changes. In 1953, the "second program" was adopted, based largely on Marxism, and a vanguard party, known as the Karen National United Party (KNUP), structured along CPB lines, was formed. The Kawthoolei People's Liberation Army (KPLA) and a guerilla force were also set up. However, the new policy was not endorsed by all Kayin rebels. Conflicts arose namely between the leftist-oriented Mahn Ba Zan, on one side, and the anti-Communist group led by Saw Hunter Tha Hmwe (qq.v.), on the other. In the early 1960s, aside from the KNU and KNUP, another body also existed, known as the Karen Revolutionary Council (KRC), and there was some division of the zones of influence between the various Kayin rebel forces.

In 1963, the main Kayin rebel organizations, the KNU, KNUP and KRC, participated in the peace talks with the Revolutionary Council in Yangon (qq.v.), but only the KRC agreed to return to the legal fold. In 1966, Bo Mya withdrew from the KNUP to form a separate organization known as the Karen National Liberation Council (KNLC), which was joined in 1966 by Mahn Ba Zan and some other former leaders of the KNUP. In 1968, the KNLC was dissolved and replaced by the Karen National United Front (KNUF), formed and led by Bo Mya and Mahn Ba Zan. In the late 1960s, the KNUF and KNUP became the main competitors for control of the Kayin underground movement. The KNUF, allied with the CPB, became an extremist organization, practicing the Maoist policy of "Red Power" and committing many excesses in the territories under its control, as result of which it lost much of its former support.

The KNUF changed its name back to KNU in 1976 when its Chairman Mahn Ba Zan was replaced by Bo Mya, KNU's current President. This change also brought about a shift in the KNU's policy toward a more conservative, nationalist and anti-Communist course. Under Bo Mya's command, the Karen National Liberation Army (KNLA) was regrouped and reorganized in the Kawthoolei state's border regions with Thailand. The KNU maintains its own administration and operates several military bases to protect Kawthoolei territory from the Myanmar army. After 1949, the KNU became a constituent member of several ethnic fronts, most recently of the National Democratic Front (q.v.). (*See also* Civil War.)

KAREN NATIONAL UNITED PARTY *see* **KAREN NATIONAL UNION.**

KAREN REVOLUTIONARY COUNCIL *see* **KAREN NATIONAL UNION.**

KAREN STATE *see* **KAYIN STATE.**

KARENNI NATIONAL PROGRESSIVE PARTY (KNPP). The ethnic rebel organization of Kayahs (q.v.), Kayans, Pakus and some other groups of Kayah State (q.v.). Founded in

1957 by Saw Mah Reh, the KNPP promoted the cause of a separate Karenni (Kayah) State and it gained control over much of Kayah State throughout the late 1960s. However, later its strength waned due to factional splits and desertions, such as that of the Karenni State Nationalities Liberation Front (KSNLF) set up in 1978. At present, the KNPP operates mainly in the area lying between the Thanlwin (q.v.) and the Myanmar-Thai border. The KNPP is affiliated with the National Democratic Front (q.v.). (*See also* Civil War.)

KARMA *see* KAN.

KAWTHAUNG. Also known as Victoria Point. Myanmar's southernmost town in Taninthayri Division (q.v.), located at the mouth of the Pachan River opposite the Thai town of Ranong.

KAWTHOOLEI. Also Kawthulay or Kawthulei. The Kayin (q.v.) word which is usually translated into English as "flowery land," but sometimes as "black land," i.e. the "country which went black" and must be fought for.
    This designation has two usages. Firstly, it is the name of Karen Free State, the territory of Myanmar adjacent to the Thai border and presently under control of the Karen National Union (q.v.). Secondly, the term is used to denote the region in southern Myanmar which was designed, in the Constitution of the Union of Burma (1947) (q.v.) to become the core of the proposed Karen (now Kayin) State. In 1954, Karen State was formed under an amendment of the constitution, with its capital at Hpa-an. In 1964, the Revolutionary Council (q.v.) changed its name to Kawthoolei. In 1974, the name reverted to Karen State, presently Kayin State (q.v.).

KAYAH *see* KAYIN.

KAYAH STATE. Originally known as Karenni State. It covers an area of 11,733 square kilometers (4,530 square miles), being the smallest of the seven states of the Union of Myanmar (q.v.). Kayah State is bounded by Thailand on the east, Shan State (q.v.) on the north and Kayin State (q.v.) on the south and west. Kayah State is mostly hilly, with several large lakes and waterfalls. It consists of 6 townships and 79 village tracts. Its 1983 population was 168,429. The capital is Loikaw. The state is inhabited by Kayahs (formerly Karenni), Padaungs (q.v.), Pa-os, Shans and Bamars (qq.v.). The main crop is rice (q.v.). There is an important hydroelectric power station at Lawpita. Teak (q.v.) is the main forest product and tin and tungsten are exploited in Mawchi mines (q.v.).

KAYIN. A Sino-Tibetan ethnolinguistic group which lives in Myanmar and Thailand. About one third of the Kayins who reside in the Union of Myanmar live in Kayin State; the rest are found in Kayah State and Mon State (qq.v.) and in some areas of Ayeyarwady and Tanintharyi Divisions (qq.v.). The Bamar (q.v.) term "Kayin," which has now replaced the term Karen in official usage, refers to the speakers of Kayin languages and, more broadly, also includes some minor ethnic groups which are akin to the Kayins linguistically or culturally. The major Kayin ethnolinguistic subgroups are: Kayah, Paku, Pao, Pwo and Sgaw. The Bamar term for Pao is Taungthu, which means literally "hillman." The former name for the Kayahs, Kayinni (or Karenni) meaning "Red Karens," originated because red was the favorite color of their wardrobe. Presently, the Kayah are classified as a separate ethnic group from the Kayins in Myanmar official materials. According to the 1983 census, there were 2,122,285 Kayins (6.2 percent of the total population) and 141,028 Kayahs (0.4 percent).

Kayin settlements exist in three distinct regions: the plains, the Bago Yoma (q.v.) and the Shan (q.v.) upland. The Pwo Kayins live mainly in the Ayeyarwady Delta (q.v.) and Sgaw Kayins inhabit Ayeyarwady, Bago and Tanintharyi Divisions (qq.v.) and Kayin State (q.v.). The Pao (Taungthu) are mostly found near Taunggyi and in Tanintharyi (q.v.) while the Kayahs predominate in Kayah State (q.v.). Another minor group related to the Kayins are Padaungs, most of whom live around Loikaw in Kayah State. Plains-dwelling Pwo Kayins are in many ways assimilated to Bamars and their main occupation is wet rice cultivation. Sgaw Kayins, who practice swidden agriculture in the hills, are less integrated into Myanmar society.

Kayin descent is bilateral. Kinship is matrilineal. Marriages are not preferential and are monogamous as a rule. Inherited property is equally shared by the children. Age and wealth are determinants of status.

The Kayins are supposed to have migrated to Myanmar in stages. Prior to the British annexation of the country in the 19th century, the Kayins were subjected to Mon, Myanmar or Shan control. During the British colonial era, the Kayins were one of the ethnic groups most affected by the Western impact. Most Kayins living within Burma proper (q.v.) were given a communal representation in the legislature, while the Kayahs were never officially incorporated into Myanmar, maintaining nominal independence in several feudatory principalities, known as the Karenni States.

Although the importance of Kayin acculturation as result of Western missionary activities is still accentuated, many Kayins seem to have been subjected to strong Bamar cultural influence. The Pwo Kayins and Pao are largely Buddhists and so are many Sgaw Kayins, although about one third were converted to Christianity (q.v.). Many hill Kayin groups and the Kayahs are mainly animistic. (*See also* Karen National Union; Kawthoolei.)

KAYIN STATE. Formerly Karen State, it covers an area of 30,383 square kilometers (11,731 square miles). It borders Mandalay Division (q.v.) on the north, Bago Division and Mon State (qq.v.) on the west, Thailand and Kayah State (q.v.) on the east, and Shan State (q.v.) on the northeast. Nearly half of the state's territory is covered with evergreen forests. The Thanlwin River (q.v.) which flows through the territory of Kayin State is the main communication line there. The state runs parallel to the Tanintharyi (q.v.) coast, extending about 523 kilometers (325 miles) from north to south, but is only 30 to 110 kilometers (20 to 70 miles) wide. Kayin State consists of 7 townships and 377 village tracts. Its 1983 population was about 1,055,359. The capital is Hpa-an; other towns include Hlaingbwe, Kawkareik and Myawaddy. Most of the people are Kayins (q.v.) and related ethnic groups. The chief occupation is agriculture (q.v.), mainly rice (q.v.) cultivation. Teak (q.v.) is the most important timber and source of income.

KENGTUNG. Also Keng Tung. The name of a former state and a municipality. Before 1948, Kengtung was the largest of the Southern Shan States. In 1943, under Japanese pressure, it was ceded to Thailand, but at the war's end it was returned to Myanmar. In 1948, it became the part of Shan State (q.v.). The municipality of Kengtung is a town, located in the eastern part of Shan State, which was previously the capital of Kengtung State.

KHIN KYI, DAW (1912–1988). The widow of Aung San and mother of Aung San Suu Kyi (qq.v.), Daw Khin Kyi was a prominent public figure of postindependence Myanmar. After 1948, she devoted herself to social welfare services and was a leading member of the All Burma Women's Freedom League (q.v.). In 1960, as the first Myanmar woman, she was appointed an ambassador and served in India and Nepal (1960–1967).

KHIN NYUNT, BRIGADIER-GENERAL (1939-). Head of the Directorate of the Defense Services Intelligence since 1984, and Secretary of the ruling State Law and Order Restoration Council (q.v.), Khin Nyunt is considered to be the strongman of the present military regime in Myanmar.

KHUN SA (aka CHANG CHI- FU). One of the veteran opium warlords who lives and is active in Shan State (q.v.). Of Chinese descent, Khun Sa served formerly as commander of the government-sponsored local defense militia, *kakweye*, and came into prominence as the leader of the Shan United Army. He was jailed in 1960, but released in 1967. In 1986, Khun Sa's Shan United Army joined with Moh Meng's Shan Revolutionary Army to form the Tai Revolutionary Council (q.v.) which is involved in cross-border drug trade, allegedly in cooperation with both Myanmar and Thai military officers. (*See also* Drug Abuse.)

KINGSHIP, CONCEPT OF. The concept of kingship in precolonial Myanmar was largely shaped by Buddhism (q.v.). The power and authority of the king were mainly justified by his *kan* (q.v.), which destined him to be born in a noble family and become king. The most positive basis on which popular allegiance to the king was acknowledged by the Myanmars was not secular, but rather religious, and derived from royalty's function of promoter and defender of the Buddhist faith, responsible also for the preservation and "purification" of the Buddhist order, the *sangha* (q.v.). The king's function of *dhammaraja*, lord of the law, included his responsibility of providing for the material well-being of his subjects as well as proper moral order. In Myanmar Buddhism, the supreme temporal ideal in Buddhist kingship was embodied in the *cakkavati*, or the universal emperor concept, which was, however, subordinated to and incorporated in the *boddhisatta* ideal of an emergent Buddha. The concept of kingship also drew heavily on Hinduism whose ethics provided a more effective rationalization for the pragmatic policy decisions of a monarch, and more broadly of royal power as such, then could the Buddhist ethos of universal suffering. (*See also* Adminstration of Myanmar, Precolonial Era.)

KINWUN MINGYI (aka KAUNG, U; KYIN, U) (1821–1908). A Myanmar court official who, from 1864, served as minister under King Mindon and his successor, King Thibaw (qq.v.). In 1872, Kinwun Mingyi led the Myanmar diplomatic mission to Europe. The mission was received by Queen Elizabeth in London and it also visited France and Italy where it concluded commercial treaties. In 1874, Kinwun Mingyi led another Myanmar mission to Europe which visited France and Italy. Kinwun Mingyi remained minister until 1885, but with the accession to the throne of King Thibaw his influence at the court waned. When the British annexed Mandalay (q.v.) in 1885, he accompanied King Thibaw en route to exile, but he returned to Mandalay, In 1886, he retired, but, in 1897, he was appointed advisor to the British Lieutenant Governor of Myanmar. Kinwun Mingyi is known as the author of two diaries in which he described his experience as head of the Myanmar diplomatic missions to Europe in 1872 and 1874. (*See also* Anglo-Myanmar War, Third; European Colonial Expansion; Third Myanmar Empire.)

KODAW HMAING, THAKIN (aka LUN, U) (1875–1964). A prominent Myanmar poet, journalist and politician, Thakin Kodaw Hmaing was born at Wale near Shwedaung in Pyay (q.v.) district. He received traditional education at a Buddhist monastery, *pongyi kyaung* (q.v.), in Mandalay (q.v.). In 1894, he became editor of *Myanma Nezin* (*Myanma Daily*) in Mawlamyine (q.v.) and, from 1911 to 1921, he worked as editor of *Thuriya* (*The Sun*) in Yangon (q.v.). In 1920, he became Professor at the National College which was established during the national school movement (q.v.), but retired and returned to journalism. He took an active part in the independence movement (q.v.) and in the late 1930s became one of the main leaders of the *Do Bama Asi Ayon* (q.v.). After independence in 1948, he was active in the World Peace Congress (Burma) and in the Internal Peace Committee. In 1954, he was awarded the International Stalin Peace Prize.

As a writer, Thakin Kodaw Hmaing is noted particularly for his commentaries, *tikas*, in which he expressed his attitudes on current public affairs of Myanmar. In *tikas*, which were written mainly in the 1920s and 1930s, he criticized British rulers and ridiculed Myanmar Anglophiles as well as corrupt nationalist politicians. (*See also* Literature.)

KO MIN KO CHIN APHWE. Also *Komin Kochin Aphwe*, literally "One's Own King, One's Own Kind Association." The name of the organization founded by the leaders of the *Do Bama Asi Ayon* (q.v.) to participate in the 1936 parliamentary elections. The *Ko Min Ko Chin Aphwe*, later headed by Thakin Mya (q.v.), won three seats in the House of Representatives. (*See also* Government of Burma Act of 1935.)

KONBAUNG DYNASTY. Also known as Alaungpaya Dynasty. The third and last all-Myanmar dynasty which ruled from 1752 to 1885. The name Konbaung is an ancient name for Shwebo (q.v.), which was the first capital of the Konbaung Dynasty, from 1752 to 1763.

Aside from Alaungpaya (1752–1762) (q.v.), the successive kings of the Konbaung Dynasty were Naungdawgyi (1760–1763), Hsinbyushin (1763–1776) (q.v.), Singu (1776–

1782), Bodawpaya (1782–1819) (q.v.), Bagyidaw (1819–1837) (q.v.), Tharrawaddy (1837–1846) (q.v.), Bagan (1846–1853), Mindon (1853–1878) (q.v.) and Thibaw (1878–1885) (q.v.). There was also a seven-day usurper king Maung Maung in 1782. (*See also* Third Myanmar Empire.)

KOYIN. A novice at a Buddhist monastery, *pongyi kyaung* (q.v.), who has not yet been ordained; one of the grades in the Buddhist monastic order, the *sangha* (q.v.).

KULA, U (1714–1733). The author of the major historical work, *Maha Yazawingyi* (Great Chronicle) which was the first Myanmar chronicle written in prose. It is an account of the lives of Myanmar kings from the earliest times up to the reign of King Taninganwe (1714–1733) of the Toungoo Dynasty (q.v.). U Kula also compiled the *Yazawinlat* (Middle Chronicle) and *Yazawingyok* (Concise Chronicle). (*See also* Hmannan Yazawin; Literature.)

KUTHO. The merit which may be acquired by following Buddhist moral precepts, by meditation and by performance of good religious deeds, such as making offerings to monks, *pongyis* (q.v.), and building pagodas. These deeds are seen as the main means to improve one's karma, *kan* (q.v.), by Myanmar Buddhists. (*See also* Buddhism.)

KYA DOE, SAW, BRIGADIER (1907–   ). A Kayin (q.v.) professional soldier and political leader. The first Myanmar graduate from the Royal Military College at Sandhurst (1932), he served in the Burma Army and in the Burma National Army (qq.v.). After the war, he became Brigadier and Vice-Chief of Staff of the Burma Army, but in 1954 was forced to resign. In the early 1970s, Kya Doe joined U Nu's exile-based resistance against Ne Win's Revolutionary Council (qq.v.). In 1980, he returned to Myanmar with an amnesty. (*See also* Civil War.)

KYANZITTHA. Also Kyansittha. A king of the Bagan Dynasty (q.v.). He successfully defended Bagan (q.v.) against Mon (q.v.) attacks. As a ruler, he followed a policy of reconciliation with the Mons and of unifying the diverse people who lived within his realm. He was the first Bagan king to send missions to Yunnan, in 1103 and again in later years. He is also remembered as the builder of the famous Ananda temple (q.v.). (*See also* First Myanmar Empire.)

KYAT. A unit of Myanmar currency which replaced the Indian rupee in 1952. There are 100 *pya* in one *kyat*.

KYAUKSE. A town in Mandalay Division (q.v.) located on the Yangon-Mandalay railroad about 48 kilometers (30 miles) from Mandalay. It is the center of the Kyaukse Plain.

KYAW NYEIN, U (1915–1986). One of the major figures of postindependence Myanmar politics. After completing his studies at the University of Yangon (q.v.), where he was active as one of the student leaders, he joined the People's Revolutionary Party (q.v.). During the Japanese occupation of Myanmar (1942–1945) (q.v.), Kyaw Nyein served in Dr. Ba Maw's (q.v.) administration and was also active in the anti-fascist resistance (q.v.). He was one of the founding members of the Socialist Party of Burma (q.v.) in 1945. In October 1946, he succeeded Thakin Than Tun (q.v.) as Secretary General of the Anti-Fascist People's Freedom League (AFPFL) (q.v.). He served as cabinet member (1948–1949), but resigned in 1949 and returned in 1951. He then served as Minister of Industry (1953), Acting Foreign Minister (1954) and Deputy Prime Minister (June 1956). He was concurrently Secretary General of the AFPFL. After the AFPFL split in 1958, he and U Ba Swe (q.v.) were the main leaders of the faction known as the Stable AFPFL. Following the military coup of 1962 (q.v.), he was arrested and interned. He was released in 1966. (*See also* Independence Movement; Socialism.)

KYAW ZAW, BO (aka SHWE, THAKIN) (1919-). One of the "Thirty Comrades" (q.v.), Bo Kyaw Zaw served in the Burma Independence Army (q.v.) and successive wartime military organizations. In 1942, he joined the anti-fascist resistance (q.v.) and organized a group of younger army officers. He joined the Communist Party of Burma (CPB) (q.v.) and became a member of the party's Central Committee in July 1945. In 1946, Kyaw Zaw was commissioned in the

Burma Army (q.v.). He then served in the armed forces (q.v.) of the Union of Burma, rising to the rank of Brigadier. In 1956, however, he had to resign on charges of leaking secret information to the CPB. He lived in retirement until 1976 when he went underground. He was a member of the Central Committee of the CPB and Vice Chief of General Staff of its armed force. After the 1989 mutiny, he was forced to leave for China, along with other veteran CPB leaders.

-L-

LAHU. A Tibeto-Burman ethnolinguistic group. The Lahus in Myanmar live mainly in the Thanlwin and Kengtung areas of Shan State (qq.v.) and near Putao in Kachin State (q.v.). The 1960 estimate put the number of Lahus in Myanmar at 60,000. Lahu villages are often located above 1,220 meters (4,000 feet) on flat ridge tops below summits of high ranges. The Lahus are swidden agriculturalists. Their staple crops are dry rice, maize (qq.v.) and buckwheat; their cash crops are opium and pepper. Their diet is supplemented by hunting and gathering. Domestic animals, pigs and chickens are raised for food and sacrifice.

They have patrilineal descent, formalized courtship and monogamous marriages. The village chief functions as the final authority. In Lahu religion, labeled animism (q.v.), there is an absence of ancestral cult observances. Larger Lahu communities usually contain a religious leader or village priest, *pawku*, a shaman or seer, *mawpa*, and a medicine man, *shepa*.

LAHU NATIONAL UNITED PARTY (LNUP). A rebel organization which grew out of a Lahu (q.v.) uprising in 1972 led by Paya Kyaw Long, who subsequently became head of the LNUP. The LNUP represented a loosely organized militia, which was composed mainly of animist Lahus and was active in the Mong Hset region of Shan State (q.v.). Paya Kyaw Long's death in 1976 was followed by the LNUP split, with one faction going to the Communist Party of Burma (q.v.) and another, led by Paya Kya Oo (the son of Paya Kyaw Long), forming a new group, the Lahu National Organization (LNO). The LNO operates in southern Shan State.

LANZIN PARTY. Another name for the Burma Socialist Programme Party (BSPP) (q.v.). It is derived from an abridged designation for the BSPP in Myanmar language which is *Myanma Hsoshelit Lanzin Pati.*

LANZIN YOUTH ORGANIZATION. A subsidiary organization of the Burma Socialist Programme Party (BSPP) (q.v.). It was organized in 297 townships and some educational institutions. In 1985, it claimed over 1,000,000 members, of whom around 200,000 were BSPP members. The Lanzin Youth Organization, designed for young people between 15 and 25 years of age, had two subordinate bodies: *Shesaung* (Forward) Youth, for youths between ten and 15 years of age; and *Teza* Youth (named after the *nom de guerre* of Aung San [q.v.]), for children. The main aim of the organization was to mobilize Myanmar's youths (q.v.) as a reserve force of the BSPP.

LASHIO. A town in northern Shan State (q.v.) at an altitude of some 850 meters (2,800 feet). It is an important trade and communications center, the terminus on the railroad line from Mandalay (q.v.).

LAW YONE, U (1911-). A well-known Myanmar journalist of the postindependence era. In July 1948, he established *The Nation*, the leading English-language daily in Myanmar throughout the 1950s, and was its long-time editor. He served as President of the Burma Journalists Association (1954–1955). He was interned in 1963. After his release in 1968, he went abroad, assumed U.S. citizenship and organized Myanmar exile groups. In the 1970s, he became associated with former Prime Minister U Nu's Parliamentary Democracy Party (q.v.). (*See also* Press.)

LEAD. One of the non-ferrous metals which is mined mainly in the Bawdwin-Namtu mines (q.v.). A new, expanded lead processing plant came into operation at Bawdwin in 1987, boosting the production of refined lead to some 6,000 tons. More recently, in 1991, the production of refined lead declined to 2,750 tons. (*See also* Minerals.)

LEDI SAYADAW. A venerable Buddhist monk, *pongyi* (q.v.), who is remembered mainly as the author of the booklet (in Myanmar) entitled "On the Impropriety of Wearing Shoes on Pagoda Platforms." This booklet provided religious authority in the controversy which arose in early colonial Myanmar as a result of the practice of Europeans of wearing shoes while walking on Buddhist pagoda premises, contrary to the custom which required the removal of footwear. The controversy grew into a nationalist campaign in the 1920s, referred to variously as the "no footwear campaign" or "pagoda footwear" controversy. (*See also* General Council of Burmese Associations.)

LEDO ROAD. Also known as Stilwell Road. The road, about 800 kilometers (500 miles) long, which was built by the Allies during World War II (q.v.) and was a vital link between India and China. It started at Ledo in Assam and reached Myitkyina in Kachin State (qq.v.), where it joined the Burma Road (q.v.). (*See also* Roads.)

LET YA, BO (aka HLA PE, THAKIN) (1911–1978). One of the "Thirty Comrades" (q.v.) who served in the Burma Independence Army (q.v.) and successive national military organizations. He negotiated with the British the defense agreement of 1947 which is known as the "Let Ya-Freeman Defence Agreement" and which was included in the Nu-Attlee Agreement (q.v.) of October 1947. He then served as Deputy Prime Minister and Minister of Home and Defense (1947–1948). In 1948, he resigned from his posts and went into business. After being interned in 1963, Bo Let Ya joined U Nu's exile Parliamentary Democracy Party (q.v.) in the late 1960s. In 1969, he was made commander of the Patriotic Liberation Army and in 1973, he became Chairman of the People's Patriotic Party. In November 1978, Bo Let Ya was killed by Kayin (q.v.) rebels.

LISU. A minor Tibeto-Burman ethnolinguistic group whose original home is in Yunnan (People's Republic of China). In Myanmar, the Lisu settlements are found between the Thanlwin (q.v.) and Mekong Rivers in Shan State (q.v.) and also in Bhamo, Myitkyina and some other places of Kachin State (qq.v.). Lisu villages are located high up on ridge and mountain tops, at an elevation ranging from 1,524 to 2,740 meters

(5,000–9,000 feet). The main subgroups are the White Lisu (Pai or Pe), the Long Lisu or Hua (Hwe) and the Black Lisu (He). These color designations refer to the dominant color or pattern of each group's clothing. Swidden agriculture and hunting are the main sources of food; gathering is a supplementary one. Major food crops are maize, mountain rice (qq.v.), barley and millet. The Lisu are known as opium producers. Social life is characterized by institutionalized courtship and a free choice of marriage partners. Among the Black Lisu of the Thanlwin area, control over the villages is exercised by hereditary chiefs. In the Myanmar Shan State portion of Thanlwin, Lisu villages were subject to local *Sawbwa* (q.v.). The Lisu religion is animism, with an emphasis on ancestor worship and exorcism.

LITERACY. The monastic school, *pongyi kyaung* (q.v.), system which still prevails in the rural areas of Myanmar assured a relatively high rate of literacy of the population, estimated to be 58 percent in 1965. Nonetheless, complete literacy has been the goal of all successive Myanmar governments since independence in 1948. From 1965, the drive to wipe out illiteracy assumed the form of a mass literacy movement. According to official figures, the percentage of illiteracy was reduced to 23 percent in 1981. Myanmar won the UNESCO Mohamed Reza Pahlevi Prize for its work in the literacy campaign. In 1983, the official estimate of the country's literacy was 78.6 percent. However, when applying for the status of "Least Developed Nation" for Myanmar in the United Nations, the Myanmar government argued that the figure was "mainly a reflection of monastic education level literacy" only. It claimed "a functional literacy rate" of merely 18 percent, the figure which was finally accepted by the UN, though not without reservations. (*See also* Education.).

LITERATURE. The history of Myanmar literature is customarily divided into two main periods: classical literature (prior to the British annexation of Myanmar in the 19th century) and modern literature produced during the colonial and postindependence era.

The earliest evidence of literature in Myanmar language (q.v.) are stone inscriptions dating back to the period of the

First Myanmar Empire at Bagan (qq.v.), between the 11th and 13th centuries A.D. These inscriptions, the oldest of which, the Myazedi inscription, dates to 1112 A.D., came mainly from the kings, royal officials and their families. Dedicatory in nature and religious in motif, they contain valuable historiographical evidence as the only literary production of that time which has been preserved.

After the fall of Bagan in 1287, learned and religious themes predominated in literature. From the 13th century onward, commentaries and texts based on the Buddhist scriptures, *Tipitaka* (q.v.), were made by Buddhist scholars. From about the same period, the courtiers also produced secular literature, though still influenced by the ideals of Buddhism (q.v.). Poetry dominated Myanmar's literary production from the 15th century until the end of the monarchy in 1885, while prose literature during the same period was limited mainly to chronicles and law treatises, *dhammathats* (q.v.). Book literature, in the form of palm leaves, *peiza*, or folded paper, known as *parabaik*, probably came into existence after the 15th century. The main poetic themes were religious, royalty, love and nature; only as of the 18th century were poems describing the lives of common people also produced. The main prosodic genres were *eigyin*, poems resembling ballads, *mawgun*, odes composed as records of notable events at the royal court, *pyo*, poems taking up a religious theme or rendering an episode of the *Jataka* (q.v.) tales, and *yadu*, lyrical or love poems.

The most prominent poets of the later 15th century, active at Inwa (q.v.), were Shin Maha Thilawuntha and Shin Maha Rattathara who developed the *pyo* genre. During the period of the Second Myanmar Empire (q.v.), Nawade became noted for his *yadus* on heroic themes, while Prince Natshinnaung gained prominence for his fine love poems, and Padetha Yaza as a poet describing the life of commoners. The most important prose works were chronicles compiled by U Kula (q.v.). The Myanmar literature produced during the Konbaung dynasty (q.v.) period consisted mainly of poems, dramas and chronicles. Princess Hlaing excelled as a court poetess who invented the *bawle* form, or plaintive songs combining verse with music, while Myawaddy Mingyi U Sa is remembered for his adaptations of Thai court plays. U Kyin U and U Ponnya were founders of Myanmar national drama, while the most remarkable prose work was the *Hmannan Yazawin* (q.v.).

The British annexation of northern Myanmar in 1886, which brought about the spread of printing and Western education, had a great impact on Myanmar literature. Printed plays aimed at a wider audience appeared, followed by novels, as a new literary genre, at the beginning of the 20th century. In 1904, Jamese Hla Gyaw produced the first Myanmar novel which was, in fact, an adaptation in Myanmar language of part of Dumas' *Count of Monte Cristo*. There followed similar novels by other authors, mostly imitations or adaptations of sometimes rather mediocre Western writers. Of greater literary merit were the works of early Myanmar novelists, U Kyi, U Lat and Pi Mo Nin.

With the development of the independence movement (q.v.) after World War I (q.v.), writings attempting to revive old Myanmar literary traditions and utilizing traditional forms for contemporary themes and settings appeared. This trend was best exemplified by the works of Thakin Kodaw Hmaing (q.v.). Maha Swe also became popular in the 1930s with his novels and short stories based on patriotic appeals. At the same time, a new trend arose in the mainstream of Myanmar literature—the *Khitsan* (The Test of the Age) movement. It was represented mainly by Min Thuwun, Zawgyi and Theippan Maung Wa, who propagated a simple, direct style, yet one able to convey modern emotions and feelings and leaving a deep impression on all subsequent Myanmar writing. In the late 1930s, Myanmar literature was influenced to some extent by leftist, Marxist ideas, as evident in the production of the *Nagani* (Red Dragon) Book Club (q.v.). The important writers of the period included Thein Pe Myint (q.v.) and Zawana.

At the end of World War II (q.v.), several writers attempted to depict life in Myanmar under the Japanese. Of special interest is Maung Htin's novel *Nga Ba*. After independence in 1948, along with mediocre, commercial literature, including various adventure, detective and love stories, there also appeared works of higher literary merit. Even more prominently than before, the political struggles of the newly independent state became reflected in literary production, with some poets and writers, such as Dagon Taya, Banmo Tin Aung and Ludu U Hla connected with critical, radical and reforming trends, and others, including Prime Minister U Nu (q.v.), writing with an anti-Communist bias. Between 1948 and 1961, the best literary works of the year received Sarpay Beikman (q.v.) awards. Among the rewarded writers, Gyanegyaw Ma Ma Lay's novel *Mon ywe mahu* (Not Out of Hate) is probably best known abroad, in English and Russian translations. Popular novelists of the postindependence era also include Min Aung, Min Shin, Tet Toe and Thadu, aside from those who had established their reputation in earlier years. Well-known poets of post-independence Myanmar are Ngwe Tayi, Tin Moe and Min Yu We. A younger generation of Myanmar writers and poets has been attempting to develop new themes and genres while also promoting the use of modern literary language.

LIVESTOCK AND FISHERIES. The livestock sector has been of lesser importance than agriculture (q.v.), both in terms of providing employment and in contributing to the GDP. There is relatively little commercial production of cattle for beef and most of the mutton, chicken, duck, pork and milk are produced in private, small-scale production units. In 1991, the total production of meat for consumption amounted to 104,922 tons. Cattle are raised mainly for draught as agricultural mechanization is modest. In recent years, there has been an increase in production, namely of chicken, duck and milk, while the consumption level remains very low.

Fish is the main source of animal protein in the Myanmar diet and *ngap*i (fermented paste of fish or shrimp) is almost a national dish. The fisheries sector has great potential, given Myanmar's extensive marine and fresh-water resources. Fish production, predominantly in private hands, has been hampered by obsolete equipment. Recently, there have been more attempts by the government to boost inland and coastal fisheries. Several companies from Thailand, Malaysia, Singapore, Korea and other countries have been granted fishing licences or entered into joint-ventures with the Myanmar Fishing Enterprise.

LO HSING HAN. One of the opium warlords who, like Khun Sa (q.v.), served originally as a commander of the government-sponsored local defense militia, *kakweye*. After 1973, he went underground, allied with other rebel groups, became involved in the narcotics trade and took refuge in Thailand. He was extradited from Thailand, and sentenced to death, but released from jail in Yangon (q.v.) in the 1980 amnesty. He still remains a powerful political figure and is widely believed to have established close links with some top-ranking Myanmar military officers. (*See also* Drug Abuse.)

LOKTHA PYITHU NEZIN. Myanmar-language daily established in 1963 by the Revolutionary Council (q.v.), after September 1988 the organ of the State Law and Order Restoration Council (q.v.), with a circulation of 135,000 copies. In April 1993, it was renamed *Myanmar Alin*. It has an English-language counterpart, *The New Light of Myanmar* (formerly *The Working People's Daily*), with a circulation of about 14,000. Both newspapers carry national and international news and are published in Yangon (q.v.). (*See also* Press.)

LOO NEE, SYDNEY. Barrister and one of the main leaders of the Kayin (q.v.) Christians in the preindependence period. In 1946, he was a member of the Karen goodwill mission to Great Britain and figured among the leaders of the Karen National Association (q.v.).

LOWER BURMA. Before the annexation of entire Myanmar, in 1886, Lower Burma was the term applied to the British territory, while Upper Burma (q.v.) denoted the independent Myanmar kingdom in the north. After the British annexation, these terms were used in both a geographical and a political sense. Thus, Lower Burma meant the region of the Ayeyarwady Delta, Bago, Tanintharyi and Rakhine (qq.v.), comprising four of the total seven administrative divisions of Burma proper (q.v.). (*See also* Administration of Myanmar, British Colonial Era.)

LUCE, GORDON (1889–1979). British scholar who spent most of his life in Myanmar. His major work *Old Burma-Early Pagan* (1969–1970) indicates his main academic interest and is the result of Luce's more than 50 years of pioneering research and writing about old Myanmar. (*See also* Burma Research Society.)

-M-

MA MA LAY, GYANEGYAW (1917–1985). Myanmar journalist and one of the most prominent women writers. With her husband U Chit Maung, she published the *Gyanegyaw* Magazine prior to World War II (q.v.). After independence in 1948, she was Vice-President of the World Peace Congress (Burma) and President of the Burma Writers' Association (1955). Ma Ma Lay produced short stories and novels. Her best novel, *Mon ywe mahu* (Not Out of Hate) (1955), depicting the tragic conflict of a young woman brought up in the traditional way with her "modern," Anglicized husband, won her the *Sarpay Beikman* (q.v.) Prize and was translated into English and Russian. (*See also* Literature.)

MAGWAY. The name of a territorial division and of its capital. Magway Division has an area of 44,820 square kilometers (17,305 square miles) and is located in the Dry Zone (q.v.) in central Myanmar. It borders Mandalay Division on the east, Sagaing Division on the north, Chin State and Rakhine State on the west and Bago Division on the south (qq.v.). The Division is generally flat and is drained by the Ayeyarwady (q.v.) and its tributaries. It consists of 25 townships and 1,696 wards and village tracts. Its (1983) census population was 3,243,166, mostly Bamars, Chins and Rakhines (qq.v.). The main products are cooking oil, groundnuts and sesame; other crops include maize, rice and tobacco (qq.v). Myanmar's main petroleum production area around Chauk and Yenangyaung (qq.v.) also falls within the Division. It has rice and saw mills, cement and fertilizer plants as well as important handicrafts. The town of Magway, located on the bank of the Ayeyarwady River, is an important communications and industrial center.

MAGWE *see* **MAGWAY.**

MAHA. The Pali (q.v.) word meaning "great."

MAHA BAMA ASI AYON. Known as the Greater Burma Association or Organization, it was formed on 1 August, 1944 by Dr. Ba Maw to replace the *Do Bama Sinyetha Asi Ayon* (qq.v.). In 1946, it was reorganized by Dr. Ba Maw, but did not develop into a mass party and suffered defeat in the 1951 elections.

MAHA MUNI PAGODA. The "Great Sage" Pagoda. Also known as the Arakan Pagoda or Payagyi, "Great Pagoda." One of the most famous religious buildings in Mandalay (q.v.), the pagoda enshrines the Maha Muni Buddha image which was brought in 1784 from Myohaung in Rakhine (qq.v.) by King Bodawpaya's (q.v.) troops as religious war booty. The pagoda was built in 1784 and reconstructed after a fire in 1884.

MAIZE. Also known as "Indian corn," maize has undergone an increase in production since the late 1970s, being grown both as a mixed and monoculture crop. In 1991, about 186,000 tons of maize were produced on 137,594 hectares (340,000 acres). (*See also* Agriculture.)

MANDALAY. The capital of Mandalay Division (q.v.) located on the bank of the Ayeyarwady River about 560 kilometers (350 miles) north of Yangon (qq.v.). With its (1983) population of about 533,000, it is the second largest city of Myanmar. Founded in 1857 by King Mindon (q.v.), Mandalay served as the last capital of the Third Myanmar Empire (q.v.) from 1860 until the British annexation of northern Myanmar in 1885. The central, fortified city, known as the "Golden City," which also contained a royal palace, was destroyed during World War II (q.v.). Mandalay still boasts a large number of famous pagodas, monasteries and other monuments and is still regarded by many as the true center of Myanmar culture. It houses the Arts and Science University and the State School of Fine Arts, Music and Dancing. Mandalay represents a repository of several traditional arts and crafts, while modern industry includes a brewery and distillery. It is also an important communications and commercial center. (*See also* Architecture; Artisanal Industries; Maha Muni Pagoda; University of Mandalay.)

MANDALAY DIVISION. It has an area of 37,024 square kilometers (14,295 square miles) which falls within the Dry Zone (q.v.) of central Myanmar. The Division is situated between the Ayeyarwady River and the Shan Plateau and borders Bago Division on the south, Magway Division on the west, Sagaing Division on the north and Shan State on the east (qq.v.). Mandalay Divison is low-lying, except for some higher places, such as the Shan Plateau and part of the Bago Yoma (q.v.). The Division is drained by the Ayeyarwady and Sittoung (q.v.). It consists of 29 townships and 1,796 wards and village tracts. Its (1983) population was 4,577,762, mainly Bamars, Chins, Kayins, Kayahs, Mons and Shans (qq.v.). Mandalay Division is the core region of Myanmar encompassing the ancient capitals of Amarapura, Inwa, Bagan, Pinya and Mandalay (qq.v.). Agriculture, based on an ancient, well-preserved system of irrigation (q.v.) works, is the chief occupation. The main crops are rice (q.v.), wheat, maize (q.v.), groundnuts, sesame, cotton (q.v.), pulses, chili, onions and tobacco (q.v.). Most of the industries are based on agriculture and forestry (q.v.) products. The Division is rich in minerals (q.v.), namely gems, mined in Mogok (qq.v.). The main communication lines, aside from the Ayeyarwady River, are the Yangon-Mandalay railroad and highway.

MANUHA. Also Makuta. The Mon king who was brought as a captive to Bagan after King Anawrahta's conquest of Thaton in 1057 A.D. (qq.v.). Manuha, who was given residence at Myinkaba, south of Bagan, built the Manuha Temple there in 1059. (*See also* First Myanmar Empire.)

MARTABAN. A town in Mon State located at the mouth of the Thanlwin River (qq.v.). A road and railroad terminus, it is linked by a ferry service across the river to Mawlamyine (q.v.). Known as an old sea port, Martaban was the capital of a Mon kingdom founded by Wareru in 1287 A.D. (q.v.). Later, in the 16th century, it was the site of a Portuguese trading settlement. (*See also* European Colonial Expansion; Portuguese and Myanmar.)

MARTYRS' DAY. A public holiday in the Union of Myanmar, known in Myanmar as *Azani Ne* (qq.v.). It is observed on 19

July to commemorate that day in 1947 when Bogyoke Aung San (q.v.) and several other members of the Interim Government of Burma (q.v.) were assassinated by their political adversaries. (*See also* Independence Movement.)

MARXISM *see* SOCIALISM.

MASS MEDIA *see* PRESS; RADIO; TELEVISION.

MAUNG MAUNG, DR. (1924–). Former President of the Union of Myanmar and Chairman of the Burma Socialist Programme Party (BSPP) (qq.v.) in 1988. Born in 1924 in Mandalay (q.v.), he served in the Burma Defence Army during the Japanese occupation of Myanmar (1942–1945) (qq.v.). After the war, he left the army and became a scholar. He was educated at Mandalay College and the University of Yangon (q.v.). In 1950, he was called to the Bar at Lincoln's Inn. He studied further at the University of Utrecht and at Yale University. He was editor of the *New Times of Burma*. He started the monthly *Guardian Magazine* (q.v.) in 1954 and the *Guardian* daily in 1956.

Dr. Maung Maung served as Government Advocate (1953–1955) and as Assistant Attorney under the Caretaker Government of General Ne Win (1958–1960) (q.v.). After the military coup of 1962, he was made Chief Justice and was one of the main authors of the Constitution of the Socialist Republic of the Union of Burma (1974) (qq.v.). In July 1988, he became a member of the Central Committee of the BSPP and, from 19 August to 18 September 1988, he held the posts of BSPP Chairman and President of the Union of Myanmar. Dr. Maung Maung's writings on Myanmar law, modern history and politics include *Burma's Constitution* (1960) and *Burma and General Ne Win* (1966). (*See also* Pro-Democracy Movement.)

MAW SHANS. Non-Buddhist Shans (q.v.) who were known in Myanmar's history as rivals of both the Mongols and Shans settled in northern Myanmar. In the 13th century, the Maw Shans attempted to restore Tai rule in Nan-Chao (a Chinese province in Yunnan), and later they launched attacks on northern Myanmar. (*See also* Three Shan Brothers.)

MAWCHI MINES. The mines at Mawchi in Kayah State (q.v.). Prior to World War II (q.v.), the Mawchi Mines produced half of Myanmar's tin and tungsten, ranking first in the world among tungsten mines and third among tin mines. The wartime damages and the civil war (q.v.) in the postindependence era were the main factors causing the rapid decline of ore production at Mawchi. In 1991, 350 metric tons of tin concentrates (75 percent), 146 tons of tin and tungsten mixed concentrates (65 percent) and 1,300 tons of tin, tungsten and shellite mixed concentrates were produced. (*See also* Minerals.)

MAWLAMYINE. The capital of Mon State (q.v.) situated at the mouth of the Attaran, Gyaing and Thanlwin (q.v.) Rivers on the Gulf of Martaban about 160 kilometers (100 miles) southeast of Yangon (q.v.). Its (1983) population was 219,961.

In the mid-19th century, Mawlamyine was the chief town of British-held southern Myanmar, an important center for the export of rice, rubber and teak (qq.v.). It remained so until the 1890s, when it was superseded by Yangon (q.v.). Mawlamyine is a railroad terminal and a gateway to southern Mon State and to Thailand.

MAY OUNG, U (1880–1926). A Myanmar lawyer and one of the early nationalist leaders in the preindependence period. He was one of the founders of the Young Men's Buddhist Association and a founding member and President (1923) of the Burma Research Society (q.v.). (*See also* Independence Movement.)

MAYMYO *see* **PYIN-Oo-LWIN.**

MEIKTILA. A town in Mandalay Division (q.v.) located on the railroad about 112 kilometers (70 miles) south of Mandalay (q.v.). The nearby Meiktila Lake was supposedly built by the Pyu (q.v.) people in the 7th century A.D.

MERGUI *see* **BEIK.**

MIGRATION. Between the years 1852 to 1900, there was a substantial migration of people from the Dry Zone (q.v.) into the sparsely populated Ayeyarwady Delta (q.v.) in connection with the development by the British of rice (q.v.) cultivation there. Southern Myanmar then became the center of administration, commerce and trade, with Yangon (q.v.) as a major urban center. Under British rule, prior to the Japanese occupation of Myanmar (1942–1945) (q.v.), there was a considerable immigration of Indians, and partly also of Chinese (qq.v.), into Myanmar. After independence, and mainly after the military coup of 1962 (q.v.), many Indians were forced to leave the country as a result of restrictive measures introduced by Myanmar's governments and the nationalization of the economy. More recently, in 1978 and in 1991, there was a mass exodus of Rohingya Muslims (q.v.) to neighboring Bangladesh. Throughout the postindependence period, illegal migration from and to China has continued across the frontier. There has also been a large-scale migration of many Myanmar nationals abroad after the suppression of the pro-democracy movement of 1988 (q.v.). Presently, refugees from Myanmar found in Bangladesh, India, Malaysia, Thailand and some other Asian countries, are estimated at 360,000. (*See also* Nationality; Population.)

MILITARY COUP (1962). The coup staged on the night of 2 March 1962 by the armed forces (q.v.) which were concerned with the danger of secession by some Union states from the Union of Burma (q.v.). The Constitution of the Union of Burma (1947) (q.v.) was abrogated, the Union Parliament dissolved, and many members of the government as well as leaders of the ethnic minority groups arrested. All power was seized by a 17-member Revolutionary Council headed by General Ne Win (qq.v.). The 1962 coup ushered in a long period of military rule (q.v.). (*See also* Burma Socialist Programme Party Era; Parliamentary Era.)

MILITARY COUP (1988). The military coup of 18 September 1988, which took place at the time the pro-democracy movement (q.v.) was gathering momentum, is widely believed to have been precipitated by several incidents, at least some of which are suspected to have been engineered by the armed forces (q.v.), and which were used as a pretext for intervention by the military. Another factor was the rapid deterioration of law and order in the country. On the day of the coup, General Saw Maung (q.v.) announced that the military had assumed power and set up the State Law and Order Restoration Council (SLORC) (q.v.) which has since been the ruling authority in the Union of Myanmar.

MILITARY RULE (1962–1974). During the greater part of more than a decade of military rule, the ruling Revolutionary Council (RC) (q.v.) strove to replace the political system of the previous parliamentary era (q.v.) with a new arrangement based on the military leadership of the nation, the existence of one governing political party—the Burma Socialist Programme Party (BSPP) (q.v.) and the ideology of the Burmese Way to Socialism.

The RC's policy attempted to treat the Union of Burma (q.v.) as a unitary state. With effect from 9 May 1962, the system of Security and Administrative Councils (SAC), which originated during the tenure of the Caretaker Government of General Ne Win (1958–1960) (q.v.), was reorganized from the center downward to all levels of administration including the village tract and ward, and staffed with army and police officers and some civil servants. Very few civilians were ever appointed members of the RC or cabinet ministers.

Although the military held a monopoly of political power, it was faced from the beginning with the problem of winning popular support. Generally, the people were mobilized under the BSPP's programs. As another means of popular mobilization, the RC convened annual peasants' and workers' seminars, starting in 1963. In 1977, two "class organizations," the Peasants' *Asi Ayons* and the Workers' *Asi Ayons* (qq.v.) were formed. Other mass organizations, such as the Lanzin Youth Organization (q.v.), were also initiated.

In 1963, the RC conducted peace talks with major underground organizations, seeking an end to the civil war (q.v.) and insurgency in Myanmar. However, the talks failed, except with the Karen Revolutionary Council (q.v.). The RC thus resumed military operations, particularly against the Communist Party of Burma (CPB) (q.v.), which brought success to the government troops between 1967 to 1969. At the same time, in a bid to win the support of former political leaders of the parliamentary era, many of them were gradually released from detention. In December 1968, 33 former political and ethnic leaders were invited by General Ne Win to submit their ideas on the means of establishing internal unity and formally organized as the Internal Unity Advisory Board. The majority report (supported by 18 members of the Board), which recommended a return to the system based on the first constitutional law of 1947, however proved to be unacceptable to General Ne Win.

In 1971, preparations began to draw up a new constitution of the Union of Burma. In April 1972, General Ne Win and 20 senior army commanders retired and became civilian members of the government which replaced the RC and was headed by U Ne Win as Prime Minister. Altogether three drafts of a new constitution were prepared between 1972 and 1973. The final draft was approved by a national referendum held in December 1973. The Constitution of the Socialist Republic of the Union of Burma (q.v.) became effective on 3 January 1974.

After the 1962 coup, the RC carried out an extensive nationalization. By 1965, foreign trade, banking, and a major portion of internal trade and industry came under state control. Agricultural and peasant land remained largely in private hands, but the farmers were required to deliver crops to the state at fixed prices. The cumulative effect of the radical nationalization was very disruptive in the lives of the majority of the people. Industrial and agricultural production declined, commodity distribution faltered and "black market" activities increased. From 1966, the government began to relax its strict control over certain sectors of the economy, but state direction and planning on the national level were retained. The popular image and reputation of the military leaders were further damaged as a result of their encouraging power and wealth.

Military rule was formally terminated on 2 March 1974 when elections for all levels of government were held under the new constitution. (*See also* Military Coup (1962); Socialist Constitutional System.)

MINAMI *see* SUZUKI, KEIJI.

MINAMI KIKAN. Japanese term meaning South Intelligence Organization. Formally set up in February 1941 in Tokyo by the Imperial Army General Headquarters, and headed by Colonel Keiji Suzuki (q.v.) (known also as Minami), the Minami Kikan started as a collective venture of the Japanese army, some navy officers and civilians. It was entrusted with the task of closing the Burma Road (q.v.) and assisting the independence movement (q.v.) in Myanmar. The Minami Kikan was responsible for smuggling out of Myanmar most of the "Thirty Comrades" (q.v.) and their subsequent military training by Japanese instructors in Hainan and Formosa (Taiwan) in 1941. In early December 1941, the Minami Kikan and the "Thirty Comrades" were transferred to Bangkok and assisted there in establishing the Burma Independence Army (BIA) (q.v.) on 28 December. The Minami Kikan was dissolved with the disbanding of the BIA in July 1942. (*See also* Japanese Occupation of Myanmar.)

MINDON. A king of the Konbaung Dynasty (1853–1878) (q.v.) regarded as one of the most capable rulers of traditional Myanmar. In 1857, Mindon founded Mandalay (q.v.), which he built up as the last royal capital (1860–1885). In 1871, he convened the Fifth Great Buddhist Council (q.v.). Mindon also introduced coined money, confirmed the uniform system of measures and weights, introduced the *thathameda* tax, improved communications and established factories. He tried to maintain good relations with the British in the vain hope that they would restore to Myanmar the territories lost in two wars. He also attempted to establish contacts with other foreign states, sending an embassy to Europe in 1872 which was headed by Kinwun Mingyi (q.v.). Mindon's attempts at modernizing the country were only partly successful. (*See also* Anglo-Myanmar War, First; Anglo-Myanmar War, Second).

MINERALS. Myanmar has formidable, albeit still little explored mineral wealth. Petroleum and natural gas (qq.v.) deposits, originally found and exploited in the central Ayeyarwady (q.v.) area and, more recently, in other parts of the country, are the most important. A variety of metals, including lead, silver and zinc (qq.v.) are found in the Shan Plateau (q.v.), while Tanintharyi Division (q.v.) is a tin zone. Antimony, cobalt, copper (q.v.), iron ore and tungsten are also found. Myanmar is also rich in gems (q.v.). The export of gems and minerals accounted for 11 percent of Myanmar's exports in 1988. (*See also* Bawdwin-Namtu Mines; Mawchi Mines.)

MINKHAUNG. The king of Inwa (1401–1422) (q.v.). His reign was marked by prolonged wars for supremacy which the Bamars waged with the Mons, led by Razadarit, and with the Shans (qq.v.)

MIN KO NAING. Meaning literally "conqueror of kings" or "I shall defeat you." *Nom de guerre* of Baw Oo Tun, who gained prominence as a student leader in Yangon during the pro-democracy movement of 1988 (qq.v.). After the military coup of 1988 (q.v.), Min Ko Naing went underground, but was captured and interned in March 1989.

MISSIONARIES *see* CHRISTIANITY.

MOGOK. A town in Mandalay Division (q.v.) about 112 kilometers (70 miles) northeast of Mandalay (q.v.), Mogok is Myanmar's leading producer of rubies, sapphires and some other gems (q.v.). The local mines, exploited since the 16th century, have been state-controlled since 1962.

MON. A Mon-Khmer ethnolinguistic group now found in the Union of Myanmar and in Thailand. In Myanmar, the majority of Mons inhabit the territory of Mon State (q.v.). Smaller Mon groups are settled in the Ayeyarwady, Sittoung and Thanlwin River (qq.v.) valleys and deltas. According to the 1983 census, the Mons totalled 826,801 (2.4 percent of the total population).

For centuries, the Mons were known to the Bamars (q.v.) as Talaings, probably meaning people from Telingana, a place on the eastern coast of India. They are supposed to have reached Myanmar around the 3rd century B.C. By the 9th century A.D., when the Bamars arrived in the center of Myanmar, the Mons had been settled in the Ayeyarwady Delta (q.v.) and in the Sittoung valley. The Mons transmitted Hindu-Buddhist culture to the Bamars and also gave them a script. It is largely on the foundations they laid that Myanmar civilization, as witnessed by the early Bagan (q.v.) period, was built. After the fall of Bagan in 1287, there was a prolonged struggle for supremacy between the Bamars and the Mons which lasted until 1757 when the Mons were defeated by King Alaungpaya (q.v.). During the last two centuries, the Mons have undergone an intensive acculturation to the Bamars.

The Mons are primarily peasant agriculturalists who pioneered irrigation (q.v.) and wet rice (q.v.) cultivation in Myanmar. Hunting and fishing are important supplementary activities, as well as trade and crafts.

There are bilateral descent groups. Early marriage is general. The Mons are mostly Theravada Buddhists with similar monastic organizations and religious ceremonies to Bamar and Thai Buddhists.

MON NATIONAL DEFENCE ORGANIZATION (MNDO). The military wing of the Mon Freedom League (subsequently known as the Mon United Front) formed in 1947 and led by Nai Shwe Kyin and Nai Hla Maung. The MNDO, set up in the same year under the command of Nai Hla Maung, represented the main force of Mon insurgency after 1949, when the MNDO went underground. Closely allied with the Karen National Defence Organization (q.v.), the MNDO was active mainly in the Mon-inhabited areas of Tanintharyi (q.v.), originally claiming to fight for an independent Mon-Karen state there.

MON STATE. It covers an area of 12,297 square kilometers (94,748 square miles). Mon State is bounded by Bago Division (q.v.) on the north, Kayin State (q.v.) on the east, Tanintharyi Division (q.v.) on the south and the Gulf of Martaban on the west. It is a coastal region, elongated in shape, like Rakhine State (q.v.), and it is fringed with many islands. Generally, the region is hilly, the only large plain being the Mawlamyine (q.v.) Plain. The Thanlwin (q.v.) with its tributaries is the most important river of the state. Mon State consists of ten townships and 443 wards and village tracts. Its (1983) population was 1,680,157. The capital is Mawlamyine (q.v.); other important towns include Bilin, Martaban (q.v.), Mudon and Thaton (q.v.). The state is inhabited mainly by Bamars and Mons (qq.v.). The chief crops are rice, rubber, sugarcane (q.v.), groundnuts, coconuts, durian, rambootan and mangosteen. Fishing and salt-making are also important occupations. There are rich deposits of minerals (q.v.).

Mon State was constituted on 3 January 1974 of that part of Tanintharyi Division comprising the former Mawlamyine and Thaton districts.

MONASTERY, BUDDHIST *see* PONGYI KYAUNG.

MONASTIC SCHOOLS *see* PONGYKI KYAUNG.

MONK, BUDDHIST *see* PONGYI.

MOUNTBATTEN, LORD LOUIS (1900–1979). As Supreme Allied Commander for Southeast Asia (1943–1946), Mountbatten significantly affected military operations leading to the Japanese defeat in Myanmar in August 1945. He also played an important role in shaping the wartime British policy of military cooperation with the anti-fascist resistance in Myanmar, represented by the Anti-Fascist People's Freedom League, with Aung San as its main leader (qq.v.).

MUJAHID. Arabic term for one who fights a holy war for Islam (q.v.). Also the name for the Muslim (q.v.) insurgents in north Rakhine (q.v.) who started an armed rebellion in 1948, ostensibly to create in Rakhine a separate Muslim state. (*See also* Civil War.)

MUSIC. Music forms part of the daily life of the Myanmar people and it accompanies various forms of entertainment. Myanmar music lacks the chromatic scale and it sounds a bit strange to Western ears. Another difference is that Myanmar music developed melodic patterns, rather than harmony.

Originally the major musical instrument was the *bongyi*, a big drum made of a piece of *padaung* wood. Since the 19th century, central to Myanmar music is the orchestra, dominated by percussion instruments, and known as the *saing* or *saing waing*. The centerpiece of the orchestra is the *saing waing*, or *patwaing*, a series of 21 cylindrical drums mounted on a circular gilded frame of wood and rattan. Around this are a series of 18 (or less) bell-metal gongs, *kyi waing*, a single large drum, *patma*, the oboe, *hne*, the bamboo flute, *palwe*, cymbals, *lagwin*, bamboo clappers, *wa let khok*, and a bamboo xylophone, *pattala*. Probably the oldest Myanmar musical instrument is the harp, *saung kauk*. Another ancient musical instrument is the crocodile-shaped zither, *migyaung*.

Modern Myanmar music reflects contacts with Western musical styles. Several Western instruments, such as the guitar, piano, saxophone and violin, found their way into Myanmar musical compositions. Among the youths, pop music is very popular. (*See also* Pwe; Theater.)

MUSLIMS. About 3.9 percent of Myanmar's population is Muslim, 3.8 percent being Sunnis and 0.1 percent Shiites. The original nucleus of the local Muslim community was formed by the descendants of Arab, Persian and Indian Muslim traders who had settled in the country prior to the British annexation in the 19th century. Under British rule, along with a huge immigration of Indians (q.v.) into Myanmar, there was also a considerable expansion of the local Muslim community. There were two main groups of Myanmar's Muslims: Indian Muslims and Myanmar Muslims, the former still constituting the bulk. Many Muslims live in the north of Rakhine where they form a special group known as the Rohingya. There are also Chinese Muslims, referred to in Myanmar as Panthay, and a group of Zerbadee, the offspring of mixed marriages.

Historically, there have been some clashes between the Muslims and Buddhists; there has been a resentment particularly against Indian Muslims who tended to emphasize their separate identity by religious orthodoxy. More recently, in 1978, and, again, in 1991, the trouble developed in north of Rakhine as a result of specific policies of Myanmar government towards a Rohingya community there, causing the Muslim exodus into neighboring Bangladesh. (*See also* Bangladesh; Rohingya.)

MYA, BO (aka MYA, SAW BO) (1927–). President of the Karen National Union (KNU) (q.v.). He went underground in 1949 and was active in various underground Kayin (q.v.) organizations. He reorganized the Karen rebel forces as the

Karen National Liberation Army. In 1976, he assumed the chairmanship of the Karen National United Front (q.v.), which returned to the original name of Karen National Union. Bo Mya is also Chairman of an insurgent front known as the Democratic Alliance of Burma (q.v.). (*See also* Civil War.)

MYA, THAKIN (1897–1947). A Myanmar nationalist leader and politician in the preindependence period. He was one of the leaders of the *Do Bama Asi Ayon*, a member of the House of Representatives for the *Ko Min Ko Chin Aphwe* (1936), the first president of the All Burma Peasants' Organization (ABPO) (1939), and the leader of the All Burma Trade Union Congress (1940) (qq.v.). After being interned by the British (1940–1942), from 1943 to 1945 he served as Deputy Prime Minster in Dr. Ba Maw's (q.v.) government. After the war he became President of the Socialist Party of Burma (q.v.). He was also President of the ABPO and, from 1946 to 1947, he served in the Governor's Executive Council and Interim Government (q.v.). He was assassinated along with Aung San (q.v.) on 19 July 1947. (*See also* Anti-Fascist People's Freedom League; Socialism.)

MYANMAR. The English transcription of the Bamar (q.v.) literary term for the country which has been used by the State Law and Order Restoration Council since 18 June 1989 instead of the previous name, Burma (qq.v.). The term Myanmar, sometimes also spelled Myanma, has also replaced the previous terms Burman and Burmese (qq.v.). It is a Bamar literary term of self-reference, probably derived from the Chinese term *mien*. (*See also* Union of Myanmar.)

MYANMAR ALIN *see* LOKTHA PYITHU NEZIN.

MYANMAR BROADCASTING SERVICE *see* RADIO; TELEVISION.

MYANMAR ERA. The Myanmar era begins in March 638 A.D. It is assumed that it was originally inaugurated by the Vikrama Dynasty which reigned in the Pyu capital of Sri Ksetra (qq.v.). The Myanmar Era is still widely used, along with the Christian Era. There is also a Buddhist Era which begins with the birth of Gautama Buddha in 543 B.C.

MYANMAR LANGUAGE. The Myanmar language is a member of the Tibeto-Burman subgroup of the Sino-Tibetan language family. It is the official language of the Union of Myanmar, spoken as a native tongue by Bamars (q.v.), but also used by other ethnic groups as a *lingua franca*.

There are several dialects of which some, such as Intha, Tavoyan and Rakhine (q.v.), are sometimes considered to be separate languages. The Central Dialect, based on Yangon (q.v.) speech, is the basis of the standard national language. Myanmar is a tonal language. Many Myanmar words are monosyllabic. There is a number of loanwords from Pali (q.v.) and, more recently, from English. A special feature of the language is the use by speakers of different modes of address, including the choice of specific pronouns and other words, depending upon their age, prestige or social status.

The Myanmar alphabet consists of 33 basic single letters. It is written and read from left to right, from top to bottom. The Myanmar script is derived from the Pallava script of southern India and it came to the Bamars from the Mons in the early Bagan (qq.v.) period. Except for a rounding of the originally square characters, the script has remained largely unchanged to the present day. (*See also* Literacy; Literature.)

MYITKYINA. The capital of Kachin State (q.v.). Located in the upper navigable section of the Ayeyarwady (q.v.), Myitkyina is a traditional trading center. it is also the northernmost railroad terminus and a point on the Burma Road (q.v.).

MYO. A Myanmar term for a town, city or administrative area. Originally, it meant a fortified place, a country town and the center of a domain. (*See also* Administration of Myanmar, Precolonial Era.)

MYOHAUNG. Also Mrohaung. "Old City." A jungle-infested site in Rakhine State (q.v.), close to the Myanmar-Bangladesh border, which is one of the former capitals of the kingdom of Rakhine. Originally known as Mrauk-U, it was built by King Minsawmun and it served as capital from the 15th century to the late 18th century.

MYOTHUGYI. The hereditary chieftain of a tract based on a provincial town, or on a *myo* (q.v.), under the precolonial state. (*See also* Administration of Myanmar, Precolonial Era.)

MYOZA. Also MYOSA *see* APPANAGE.

-N-

NAGA. A mythological serpent, half-snake, half-dragon, with a hooded head. The *naga* cult was widespread in pre-Buddhist Myanmar, and later it was incorporated into a popular form of Buddhism (q.v.).

NAGA. A Tibeto-Burman ethnolinguistic group. Most Nagas now live in the Indian state of Nagaland. Relatively few Naga tribes are settled in Myanmar, where they inhabit the upper Chindwinn River (q.v.) area of Sagaing Division and of Chin and Kachin States (qq.v.). Many Naga tribes were notorious for warfare and head hunting. Now they lead a more peaceful existence. Their villages are situated at higher mountain elevations some 900 to 1,200 meters (3,000–4,000 feet) above sea level. They practice swidden agriculture, but their villages are permanent. Rice (q.v.) is their staple crop, fishing and hunting are supplementary to agriculture. Naga home-woven textiles are famous. Their social structure is archaic. The Nagas in Myanmar live in exogamous patrilineal clans. Monogamy is the usual pattern, but polygyny is also practiced. There is no group hierarchy and no legal institution above the village level. Most Nagas are animists. (*See also* Animism.)

NAGA HILLS. A hill range in India and in Myanmar forming part of the Rakhine Yoma (q.v.) mountain system. The Naga Hills divide the Brahmaputra River valley in India from the Chindwinn (q.v.) River valley in Myanmar. Their highest peak, Saramati, reaches an altitude of 3,810 meters (12,500 feet).

NAGANI BOOK CLUB. "Red Dragon" Book Club. Founded in December 1937 by Thakin Nu, Thakin Than Tun (qq.v.), U Ohn Kin and several other persons, it organized public lectures on current topics. It also published the *Nagani* Journal and a variety of original as well as translated books, including Marxist literature. (*See also* Do Bama Asi Ayon; Socialism.)

NANDABAYIN. The last king of the First Toungoo Dynasty (1581–1599). He put down major rebellions against his rule, but his military campaigns against the Thai capital of Ayutthaya were largely a failure. In 1599, his capital Bago (q.v.) was besieged by the Thais who joined forces with the Rakhines (q.v.). The local ruler of Toungoo (q.v.), who was allied with the Rakhines, sacked Bago, seized Nandabayin and his son and later put them to death. On Nandabayin's death, Myanmar broke into a number of petty states, with Thanlyin (q.v.) taken by a Portuguese mercenary Felipe de Brito, and the country south of Martaban (q.v.) subjected to Thai rule. (*See also* Portuguese and Myanmar; Second Myanmar Empire; Toungoo Dynasty.)

NARAPATISITHU. A king of the Bagan Dynasty (1173–1210) (q.v.). He built many pagodas and several large temples at Bagan (q.v.), such as Gawdawpalin and Sulamani, as well as irrigation (q.v.) works in the Kyaukse and Shwebo (qq.v.) regions. He is mainly remembered for his efforts to introduce a Sinhalese form of Buddhism in Myanmar. (*See also* First Myanmar Empire.)

NARATHIHAPATI. The last king of the Bagan Dynasty (1254–1278) (q.v.). In 1271, Narathihapati refused to receive the envoys sent to him by the Governor of Yunnan, who acted on orders of Kublai Khan, the Emperor of China, and to pay the Chinese the usual annual tribute. In 1273, when the second Mongol mission came to Bagan (q.v.), he put the ambassador to death. In 1277, in an engagement with the troops of the Governor of Yunnan at the frontier fort at Ngazaunggyan, the Myanmar army was defeated. In 1283, when the Mongols sent another expedition, this time to Bagan, King Narathihapati fled in panic to Pathein (q.v.), earning his nickname *Tayokpyay min*, "the King Who Ran Away from the Chinese." Although Narathihapati offered his submission to Kublai Khan, he lost his prestige and was killed by his own son Narathu in Pyay (q.v.). The central government broke up and the Mons and Rakhines (qq.v.) started to revolt. (*See also* First Myanmar Empire.)

NAT. The Myanmar term for a spirit or spirit being. *Nat* worship is the native Myanmar animistic religion which had existed long before the introduction of Buddhism (q.v.) into the country in the 11th century A.D. The original form of animism (q.v.) still prevails among some of the hill tribes in Myanmar, while many animistic beliefs and practices have been integrated into popular, folk Buddhism. Originally, the *nats* were local and impersonal, such as those of the rain, the wind or *nats* who inhabited villages and lakes. Later, they became identified as distinct personages with their own life stories around whom a nationwide animistic worship revolved. King Anawrahta (q.v.), unable to completely eliminate the *nat* propitiation when introducing Buddhism, simplified animistic practices, adding a new 37th *nat*, Thagya, to the existing pantheon of 36 nats. These 37 *nats* (or lords) are still worshipped in Myanmar, though some of the original group have been replaced by historical figures over the centuries.

Nat worship continues to be an important part of folk Buddhism in Myanmar. Many houses contain a coconut as the representation of the most famous of the 37 nats, Min Mahagiri, and offerings are regularly made to the *nat*. The official government efforts to reeducate the people to abandon animistic practices seem to have achieved only partial success. (*See also* Animism.)

NATIONAL ANTHEM *see* DO BAMA SONG.

NATIONAL COALITION GOVERNMENT OF THE UNION OF BURMA *see* NATIONAL LEAGUE FOR DEMOCRACY.

NATIONAL COLLEGE *see* NATIONAL SCHOOL MOVEMENT.

NATIONAL DEMOCRATIC FRONT (NDF). An umbrella organization of originally 11 major ethnic rebel organizations and forces in Myanmar. The NDF is led by Saw Maw Reh (President), Nor Mong Onn (Vice-President) and Tu Ja (Secretary General). Set up in 1976, the NDF has become the ethnic front with a real impact on the course of the civil war (q.v.) in the country. The objectives of the NDF include the formation of the Union of Myanmar as a truly federal union based on the principles of democracy, self-determination and equality of all nationalities of the country. After the suppression of the pro-democracy movement—of 1988 (q.v.), the "liberated" zones established by the NDF were the main refuge for thousands of students and other leaders of the movement who fled there from the towns.

NATIONAL DEMOCRATIC UNITED FRONT (NDUF). The first successful united front representing various ethnic insurgent groups, including Bamars (q.v.). It was founded in 1959 by the Communist Party of Burma (CPB) (q.v.), the New Mon State Party (NMSP) and the Karen National United Party (KNUP) (q.v.) and joined later by organizations of several other nationalities. The core of the NDUF were the CPB and KNUP which cooperated, both militarily and politically, until the virtual demise of the NDUF in 1975.

NATIONAL LEAGUE FOR DEMOCRACY (NLD). The main legal opposition party in the Union of Myanmar. Founded on 24 September 1988 and initially led by Aung Gyi (President), Tin U and Aung San Suu Kyi (Secretary General) (qq.v.), the NLD registered with the State Law and Order Restoration Council (SORC) (q.v.) authorities as a political party on 27 September. The NLD drew much popular support, mainly as a result of public campaigns conducted in late 1988 and in early 1989 by Aung San Suu Kyi. In December 1988, Aung Gyi split from the NLD and was replaced in his post by Tin U. On 20 July 1989, Aung San Suu Kyi and Tin U were placed under house arrest, originally for a period up to one year. Despite these and other SLORC-inspired measures, the NLD won a landslide victory in the May 1990 elections, gaining 392 out of the 485 seats in the *Pyithu Hluttaw* (q.v.).

However, the military refused to honor the outcome of the elections and to sanction a transfer of power to a civilian government. In late 1990 and throughout 1991, the SLORC cracked down on the NLD, arresting many of its members and activists, including 45 elected candidates. In July 1990, Aung San Suu Kyi's house arrest was extended, while Tin U had been earlier tried and sentenced to three years' imprisonment. Hundreds of other NLD activists fled from the towns to the Myanmar-Thai border. On 18 December 1990, a "parallel government," known as the National Coalition Government of the Union of Burma, headed by Dr. Sein Win (q.v.) and containing a dozen other elected NLD candidates, was formed at a Karen National Union (q.v.) base at Manerplaw. In April 1991, under intensive persuasion by the military authorities, the NLD leaders still remaining in Yangon (q.v.) were forced to drop Aung San Suu Kyi and Tin U from the party's membership.

NATIONAL SCHOOL MOVEMENT. The movement started in the wake of a strike at the University of Yangon (q.v.) in 1920, with the objective of establishing national (Myanmar) schools in order to emancipate education in Myanmar from the influence of the British administration.

Between December 1920 and January 1921, national schools were set up in many districts of Myanmar. The National College was also started in Shwegyin Kyaundaik monastery in Yangon (q.v.) on 14 August 1921, with several prominent Myanmar intellectuals, such as Thakin Kodaw Hmaing (q.v.), serving the college as teachers. However, the National School Movement eventually lost its initial strength as it became evident that the whole scheme was premature at the time. Many national schools were not well run and withered away, as did the National College. Some national schools, however, accepted aid from the government and were integrated into the colonial education system (q.v.).

NATIONAL UNITY. One of the basic concepts advocated by the successive postindependence Myanmar governments. The official pronouncements tend to emphasize that the ethnic and cultural differences among the indigenous people are only minor and that the existing divisions are mainly the legacy of the "divisive" policy of British colonialism in the past. More recently, during the Burma Socialist Programme Party era (q.v.), the official statements indicated the common "racial" origin of all indigenous people of Myanmar as an important factor which could facilitate their integration in one broader national community. The opponents of the government policies, who are found mainly among the country's numerous ethnic minority groups, rather emphasize their own separate identities, based on different language and, often, also culture or religion. (*See also* Federalism.)

NATIONAL UNITY FRONT (NUF). Also known as National United Front. The legal opposition front formed in 1955 by the Burma Workers' and Peasants' Party (q.v.), several minor leftist parties and organizations and the Justice Party. The NUF contested the 1956 elections as the main rival of the ruling Anti-Fascist People's Freedom League (AFPFL) (q.v.) and it won over 30 percent of the votes and 47 seats in the parliament. At the AFPFL split, the NUF supported U Nu (q.v.) and the Justice Party broke away from the NUF and joined the Clean AFPFL (q.v.) in October 1958. During the tenure of the Caretaker Government of General Ne Win (1958–1960) (qq.v.), most NUF leaders were jailed and in the 1960 elections the NUF failed to win a single parliamentary seat. After the military coup of 1962, some NUF leaders assisted the Revolutionary Council (RC) in drawing up the program of the Burmese Way to Socialism (qq.v.), but the NUF was not exempted from the RC's ban on political parties and organizations in March 1964.

NATIONAL UNITY FRONT OF ARAKAN (NUFA). Also known as National United Front of Arakan. The Rakhine (q.v.) nationalist alliance formed in 1989 which brought together the Arakan Independence Organisation (AIO), the Arakan Liberation Party (ALP), the Arakan National Liberation Party (ANLP) (q.v.) and the Communist Party of Arakan (CPA) (q.v.).

NATIONAL UNITY PARTY (NUP). A successor to the Burma Socialist Programme (BSPP) (q.v.), the NUP was formed shortly after the military coup of 1988 (q.v.). Led by U Tha Kyaw, a former army officer, it rallied behind a number of smaller parties and organizations made up mostly of former BSPP members. In the 1990 elections, the NUP won ten seats in the 185-seat Constituent Assembly.

NATIONALIST PARTY. Originally known as the "21 Party," to denote a splinter group of 21 nationalist politicians led by U Ba Pe (q.v.) who decided to cooperate with the government in carrying out the dyarchy (q.v.) reform. In 1925, the Nationalist Party merged with the Home Rule Party to form the People's Party (q.v.).

NATIONALITY. Under the Burma Citizenship Law of October 1982, which superseded the Union Citizenship Act of 1948 (amended in 1954), Myanmar citizens are classified into full, associate and naturalized citizens. Full citizens are those born of parents at least one of whom is a Myanmar national, i.e. a Bamar (q.v.) or a member of indigenous ethnic groups, such as the Chins, Kachins, Kayins, Kayahs, Shans (qq.v.) etc., and who are 18 years old. They are given full political and economic rights. Associate and naturalized citizenship is granted to foreign nationals who had lived in Myanmar continually for five years, or to those born in any part of the British Empire and who had lived in Myanmar for eight out of ten years before 1942 or before Myanmar's independence in 1948. Associate and naturalized citizens have the right to "pursue their legitimate means of livelihood" but are barred from holding public office concerned with the "affairs of the country and the duty of the state." The 1982 law has been widely interpreted as a law designed to restrain the activities of Chinese, Indians (qq.v.) and other resident foreigners in the armed forces (q.v.) and politics.

NATURAL GAS. Natural gas is found in huge quantities along with petroleum (q.v.) deposits in the central Ayeyarwady (q.v.) basin area. There had been a rapid increase in natural gas production in the late 1980s, with a peak production of some 1,146,700,000 cubic meters reached in 1988. Most of the natural gas output comes from the wells on the west bank of the Ayeyarwady. New deposits of natural gas were found off the Martaban coast.

NAW SENG (1922–1972). A Kachin (q.v.) rebel leader who went underground in 1949 and who founded the first Kachin rebel army, known as the Pawngyawng National Defence Force. In 1950, Naw Seng retreated to the People's Republic of China. He returned to Myanmar in 1968 and became the military commander of the Communist Party of Burma's (q.v.) Northeast Command. He died, under mysterious circumstances, in 1972.

NE WIN, U (aka SHU MAUNG, THAKIN) (1911–   ). One of the "Thirty Comrades" (q.v.) and a key figure in Myanmar's politics after 1962. Born on 14 May 1911, in Paungdale, Pyay (q.v.) district, he was educated at the University of Yangon (q.v.), but left without a degree. He joined the *Do Bama Asi Ayon* (q.v.) and allied himself with a conservative faction led by Thakin Ba Sein and Thakin Tun Ok (qq.v.), which was also known as the Ba Sein-Tun Ok *Do Bama*. During the Japanese occupation of Myanmar (1942–1945) (q.v.), Ne Win was the commanding officer of the Burma Independence Army and of the Burma Defence Army (qq.v.), Commander in Chief of the Burma National Army (1943–1945) and of the Patriotic Burmese Forces (1945) (qq.v.). He participated in the anti-fascist resistance (q.v.).

After the war, Ne Win was the commanding officer and (from 1947) Brigadier of the Burma Army (q.v.). He later entered the cabinet as Deputy Prime Minister and Minister of Defense and Home (1949–1950). He served as Commander in Chief of the armed forces (q.v.) from 1949 to 1972. From October 1958 to March 1960, U Ne Win was Prime Minister of the Caretaker Government (q.v.). Following the military coup of 1962 (q.v.) and until March 1974, he held the post of Chairman of the Revolutionary Council (q.v.). He was President of the Union of Burma (1974–1980) and Chairman of the Burma Socialist Programme Party (qq.v.), from July 1962 to 23 July 1988. Although, in July 1988, he officially retired from government and active politics, his influence in Myanmar's public life is still strong. (*See also* Military Rule.)

NEGRAIS, TREATY OF *see* **EUROPEAN COLONIAL EXPANSION.**

NEW LIGHT OF MYANMAR *see* **LOKTHA PYITHU NEZIN.**

NIRVANA. *Nibban* or *neikban* in Myanmar usage. In the teaching of Buddhism (q.v.), the state of non-existence. However, only some Myanmar Buddhists consider *nirvana* to be a state of total extinction; many regard it rather as a state of supreme pleasure, a sort of superheaven.

NU, THAKIN, U (1907–   ). One of the leading nationalist politicians of the preindependence period, former Prime Minister of the Union of Burma (q.v.). Born on 25 May 1907 in Wakema, Myangmya District, he was educated at the University of Yangon (q.v.), became President of the Rangoon University Students Union (1935–1936) and, in 1937, joined the *Do Bama Asi Ayon*. He was also a co-founder of the *Nagani* Book Club (qq.v.). After being interned by the British (1940–1942), during the Japanese occupation of Myanmar (1942–1945) (q.v.) Nu served as Minister of Foreign Affairs in Dr. Ba Maw's (q.v.) government (1943–1945). He was Vice-President and (from July 1947) President of the Anti-Fascist People's Freedom League (AFPFL) (q.v.) and President of the Constituent Assembly (1947). As *de facto* Prime Minister of Myanmar, he negotiated the final independence treaty with Britain in October 1947.

U Nu's role was crucial during the postindependence era, in particular as Prime Minister of the Union of Burma (1948–1956, 1957–1958, 1960–1962). He was instrumental in promoting Buddhism (q.v.) and in making it the state religion in 1960. At the AFPFL split in 1958, he became one of the main leaders of the Clean AFPFL which he reorganized in 1960 as the *Pyidaungsu* Party (q.v.). Interned from 1962 to 1966, he left Myanmar in 1969 and until 1973 he organized armed resistance against Ne Win's Revolutionary Council (qq.v.) from Thailand. Thereafter, he lived in exile, first in the United States (1973–1974) and then in India (1974–1980). U Nu returned to Myanmar after the 1980 amnesty. He initially retired, but reemerged as one of the leading opposition politicians in the pro-democracy movement of 1988 (q.v.). He proclaimed his own interim government on 9 September 1988. In December 1989, he was put under house arrest, but was released in April 1992. U Nu is also known as a writer. (*See also* Nu-Attlee Agreement.)

NU-ATTLEE AGREEMENT. Officially, the "Treaty between the Government of the United Kingdom and the Provisional Government of Burma Regarding the Recognition of Burmese Independence and Related Matters." The treaty, recognizing "The Republic of the Union of Burma as a fully independent, sovereign state," was signed on 17 October 1947 in London, by Clement Attlee and Thakin Nu (q.v.). A separate Defence Agreement (Let Ya-Freeman Agreement) and Financial Agreement were also signed in Yangon (q.v.). The Burma Independence Bill was passed by the British Parliament on 10 December 1947. The Myanmar government chose 4 January 1948 as the day for the formal declaration of independence.

NYAUNGYAN DYNASTY *see* TOUNGOO DYNASTY.

-O-

OIL-FIELD WORKERS' STRIKE (1938). One of the largest workers' strikes in Myanmar during the British colonial era, it was started in January 1938 by Burmah Oil Company (BOC) (q.v.) workers at Chauk and Yenangyaung (qq.v.) in central Myanmar. As the BOC did not respond to workers' demands for better living and working conditions, in November 1938, some 2,000 oil-field workers, led by Thakin Po Hla Gyi, set out on a 600 kilometers (400 miles) long protest march to Yangon, to demonstrate their grievances to government authorities. The oil-field workers' strike won the enthusiastic support of the nationalist press and the people who provided the strikers with meals, clothing and other necessities. This sparked a sympathy students' strike, a protest march of peasants from southern Myanmar and other public campaigns, marking the year 1938 as a "year of revolution." One of the results of the strike was the formation (in 1940) of the first nationwide labor union, the All Burma Trade Union Congress (q.v.). (*See also* Independence Movement; Student Strikes, British Colonial Era.)

ORWELL, GEORGE (1900–1953). The British novelist whose real name was Eric Hugh Blair. His first novel, *Burmese Days* (1934), is a largely autobiographical account of his experiences in Myanmar where he served from 1922 to 1927 with the Indian Imperial Police.

OTTAMA, U (1880–1939). The most prominent of the "political" monks, *pongyis* (q.v.), in the preindependence period. Before World War I (q.v.), U Ottama visited Japan and also lived for some time in India where he was closely associated with the Indian National Congress (q.v.) and was also President of Hindu Mahasabha. After his return to Myanmar, he was one of the founders and leaders of the General Council of Sangha Sammeggi (q.v.). U Ottama led public campaigns blaming the British for the decline of Buddhism (q.v.) as well as the culture and morals of the Myanmar people. He exhorted the *pongyis* to take up the nationalist struggle and, while not inciting Myanmars to armed rebellion, he did not reject the use of violence in principle. But he was tolerant of other religions and did not allow Buddhist appeals to become a divisive factor in the independence movement (q.v.). From 1921 until his death in 1939, U Ottama served a series of jail sentences on charges of sedition.

-P-

PACIFICATION OF BURMA. The title of a book by Sir Charles Crosthwaite, Chief Commissioner of Myanmar (1887–1890), published in 1890. Also a reference to the British campaigns to suppress the patriotic resistance of Bamars, Chins, Kachins, Shans (qq.v.) and other ethnic groups of the country to the establishment of colonial rule in northern Myanmar after 1885. To "pacify" Myanmar, the British employed a variety of means, ranging from ruthless and brutal to more subtle and persuasive. Thousands of resistance fighters were killed in battle or executed on capture. Decapitation of dead bodies of guerillas and the exposure of their heads in public also occurred. Villages suspected of being in sympathy with the guerillas were burned and their rebuilding prohibited. By 1890, the British had succeeded in crushing the resistance against their rule in the greater part of Myanmar, but in the Chin Hills and Kachin Hills the armed struggle continued for several more years. (*See also* Adminstration of Myanmar, British Colonial Era; Independence Movement.)

PADALIN CAVES. An important site of proto-Neolithic culture located in the west of the Shan Plateau (q.v.). Systematic exploration of the caves, carried out in 1969, yielded over 1,600 stone artifacts. Most of those found are crude and without signs of secondary flaking resembling paleolithic tools. But flake scrappers with ground surfaces were also excavated. The caves were presumably not merely a habitation site but also a tool-making workshop. The most interesting other find is the mural painting on the wall of one cave on which the figures of a human hand, a bison, a deer, elephant hinds, a huge fish and the sun, as seen from the cave, can be traced.

PADAUNG. A minor ethnic group in the Union of Myanmar related to the Kayins (q.v.). The Padaungs, about 7,000 in number, live in Kayah State (q.v.) near Loikaw, and are known mainly for their "giraffe women." Padaung women's necks give the appearance of being elongated by 9 kilograms (20 pounds) of copper or brass rings. This unusual custom probably comes from the time the Padaungs were subject to slave raids and deformed their wives to prevent their being stolen.

PADDY. Unhusked rice (q.v.).

PAGAN *see* BAGAN.

PAGAN DYNASTY *see* BAGAN DYNASTY.

PAGODA *see* ARCHITECTURE.

PAGODA FOOTWEAR CONTROVERSY *see* LEDI SAYADAW.

PALAUNG. A Mon-Khmer ethnolinguistic group, mostly found in the northern part of Shan State, in Kengtung and also in the southern part of Kachin State (qq.v.). Despite their ethnolinguistic affiliation, many Palaungs speak Shan and also use it as their written language. Palaungs live in compact villages, located on hill-tops, spurs or ridges between hills, ranging in size from two to 50 houses. They are swidden agriculturalists, raising mainly dry rice (q.v.). Tea is their principal cash crop produced for export.

Descent is uncertain. The marriage is by conventional elopement. Polygyny is permitted, but rarely practiced. Villages are controlled by chiefs who until recently owed their allegiance to a Shan *Sawbwa* (q.v.). Animism (q.v.) is widespread, although some Palaungs have accepted Buddhism (q.v.) as their faith.

PALI. A classical language of India in which the sacred Buddhist scriptures, the *Tipitaka* (q.v.), the Pali Buddhist Canon, are written. Over the centuries after the introduction of Buddhism into Bagan (qq.v.) in the 11th century A.D., the influence of Pali on the literature (q.v.) of the Myanmar people was considerable. The Myanmar language (q.v.) has adopted many philosophical and religious terms of Pali origin.

PANGLONG AGREEMENT. An agreement concluded on 12 February 1947, at a conference held at Panglong in Shan State (q.v.), by Chin, Kachin and Shan (qq.v.) traditional leaders and Bogyoke Aung San (q.v.), on behalf of the Executive Council of the Governor of Myanmar. The Panglong Agreement ruled that the people of Burma proper (Ministerial Burma) and of the Frontier Areas (qq.v.) would act in concert with each other, based on the principle of equality. Shortly after the agreement was signed, a Frontier Areas Committee of Enquiry was formed by the British Parliament which, after hearing testimonies of ethnic groups, recommended the unification of Ministerial Burma and the Frontier Areas in one state. The Kayins (q.v.) did not become a party to the Panglong Agreement, expressing their wish to live in a separate state under British protection. (*See also* Constitution of the Union of Burma; National Unity.)

PARLIAMENTARY DEMOCRACY PARTY (PDP). An exiled, Bangkok-based party founded in 1969 by former Prime Minister U Nu and some other Myanmar politicians, such as Bo Yan Naing, Bo Let Ya, Bohmu Aung, U Law Yone (qq.v.) and Zali Maw. The PDP's main objective was to overthrow Ne Win's Revolutionary Council (qq.v.). It therefore attempted to bring non-Communist Bamar (q.v.) nationalist groups at the Myanmar-Thai border into an alliance with some Chin, Karen and Mon (qq.v.) rebel organizations, which was formally established in 1970 as the National United Liberation Front (NULF). The NULF pledged to form a "Federal Union Republic" of Myanmar and it organized an armed wing, known as the Patriotic Liberation Army, which operated along the frontier. The PDP also conducted radio propaganda and sent several guerilla units on sabotage or terrorist missions into Myanmar. However, all these efforts were largely a failure. In 1973, U Nu resigned from his post as PDP President. The PDP was renamed the People's Patriotic Party, but it disintegrated into several rival factions. Most PDP leaders returned to Myanmar in the 1980 amnesty while the NULF ceased to exist in 1974. (*See also* Military Rule.)

PARLIAMENTARY ERA (1948–1962). The postindependence period when Myanmar existed as a political democracy which operated within the framework of the Constitution of the Union of Burma (1947) (q.v.). The constitution provided for an elected bicameral legislature (Union Parliament). There was an independent judiciary which served, along with the parliament, as the main pillars of political democracy. The Union of Burma consisted of Burma proper, four union states and one special division. In theory, a federal system was created under which the union states and a special division enjoyed certain common powers. In practice, however, the federal structure was only nominal as effective power was in the hands of central (Union) government which also administered Burma proper.

At independence in 1948, the ruling party was the Anti-Fascist People's Freedom League (AFPFL), headed by U Nu (qq.v.), who was also the first Prime Minister. From its inception, the AFPFL government was faced with serious rivals, in particular the Communist Party of Burma (q.v.) which started the civil war (q.v.) shortly after independence, later joined by other political organizations and some ethnic groups such as the Kayins and Mons (qq.v.). By the late 1950s, the government had regained control of most of the urban areas, but, as a result of the civil war and foreign threats, namely the intervention of Kuomingtang troops in the early 1950s, the Myanmar armed forces (q.v.) were projected onto Myanmar political scene as of 1949.

The chief problem at independence was the rehabilitation of the country torn by World War II (q.v.). The main economic tasks were to restore economic output to the prewar level and to diversify an economy based on the production of primary products. During the earlier part of the 1950s, the government attempted to guide the economy through planning and by pursuing various socialist and welfare state goals, such as the *pyidawtha* (q.v.), as well as by nationalizating several sectors. From 1957, a new road to economic recovery, stressing the role of private capital and joint-ventures, was sought.

Another major task during the parliamentary era was to solve the ethnic question and to bring unity to the diverse peoples of the Union. While initially some progress was achieved with the Chins, Kachins and Shans (qq.v.), the Kayins and Mons (qq.v.) remained in opposition.

In the Union Parliament, the AFPFL was the dominant force, gaining an overwhelming victory in the first (1951) general elections. In the second elections in 1956 the AFPFL again scored a victory, but the margin was smaller, as many votes went to the National Unity Front (q.v.). Meanwhile, the AFPFL faced a serious crisis as the result of internal friction and, in 1958, it split into two rival factions. Under these circumstances, the Caretaker Government of General Ne Win

(1958–1960) (q.v.) was entrusted with the task of preparing the country for new elections.

The elections held in March 1960 returned to power U Nu's *Pyidaungsu* Party (q.v.). Although U Nu dedicated his administration to the firm establishment of democracy in Myanmar, as well as to improving the economy, internal dissensions within the ruling party, increased demands of Kachin and Shan leaders for autonomy, or even secession from the Union, which were partly a reaction to making Buddhism (q.v.) the state religion in 1960, prevented the government from attaining its goals. The military coup of 1962 led by Ne Win (qq.v.) brought the parliamentary era in Myanmar to an end. (*See also* Federalism; National Unity.)

PATHEIN. The capital of Ayeyarwady Division (q.v.). With its (1983) population of 144,096, Pathein is one of the major cities of Myanmar and the second largest inland seaport. It is situated on the left bank of the Pathein River (q.v.) some 160 kilometers (100 miles) west of Yangon (q.v.). Pathein is an important center of rice (q.v.) processing and export and of the timber trade. It is also noted for the production of pottery and painted umbrellas.

PATHEIN RIVER. A river about 320 kilometers (200 miles) long in Ayeyarwady Division (q.v.). Known for its upper course as the Ngamun River, the Pathein River is the westernmost tributary of the Ayeyarwady River (q.v.). It empties into the Andaman Sea some 32 kilometers (20 miles) south of Pathein (q.v.).

PATRIOTIC BURMESE FORCES (PBF). A wartime Myanmar nationalist military organization and a successor to the Burma National Army (BNA) (q.v.). The BNA, renamed the Patriotic Army of Burma on 30 May 1945, acquired the status of a temporary British ally on 25 July 1945, under the name of the PBF, through British payment, provisioning and a promise of incorporation into the Burma Army (q.v.). Under the terms of the agreement reached at Kandy between the Supreme Allied Commander Lord Louis Mountbatten (q.v.) and Myanmar anti-fascist resistance (q.v.) leaders in September 1945, some 5,200 PBF servicemen were brought into the Burma Army. The remainder later rallied to the People's Volunteer Organization under Aung San's (qq.v.) command. (*See also* Independence Movement.)

PAW TUN, SIR (1883–1955). The last Prime Minister (January-June 1942) before the Japanese occupation of Myanmar (1942–1945) (q.v.). During the wartime years he was an advisor to the Government of Burma in exile at Simla. In 1946, Paw Tun served in the Governor's Executive Council.

PEASANTS' ASI AYON. "Peasants' Association." One of the two "class" organizations of the Burma Socialist Programme Party era (q.v.). It was formed in 1977 by reorganizing the People's Councils at different levels. In 1983, the Peasants' *Asi Ayon* claimed a total membership of 7,830,959 peasants. (*See also* Workers' Asi Ayon.)

PEGU *see* BAGO.

PEGU DIVISION *see* BAGO DIVISION.

PEGU RIVER *see* BAGO RIVER.

PEGU YOMA *see* BAGO YOMA.

PE MAUNG TIN, U (1888–1974). Myanmar literary historian, scholar and professor. Pe Maung Tin received his education at Yangon College, Calcutta University and Oxford University. He had a long career at the University of Yangon (1912–1945) (q.v.). Upon retirement, he was appointed Emeritus Professor of Pali (1948–1950) and Emeritus Professor of Myanmar language (1961). After 1948, U Pe Maung Tin also served in other capacities, including that of Chairman of the Burma Historical Commission (q.v.). He wrote and published on various aspects of Myanmar and Pali philology and also compiled *Myanma Sablei Thamaing* (History of Myanmar Literature) (1958). (*See also* Literature.)

PEOPLE'S DEMOCRATIC FRONT (PDF). The alliance set up

by the Communist Party of Burma, the People's Volunteer Organization and the Revolutionary Burma Army at Pyay (qq.v.) in March 1949. The alliance, in fact, broke down with the seizure of Pyay by government troops in 1950. The term PDF was then used to denote several other leftist insurgent fronts of the 1950s, none of which was successful. (*See also* Civil War; Parliamentary Era.)

PEOPLE'S PARTY. The collective term for referring to three Myanmar nationalist parties, the Home Rule Party, the Nationalist Party (qq.v.) and the Swaraj Party, which worked together in the Legislative Council in the late 1920s. The People's Party, led by U Ba Pe (q.v.), propagated the "Burma for the Burmans" program and, in the 1930s, it favored separation of Myanmar from India. In 1936, it formed a coalition with four minor factions known as *Ngabwinsaing*.

PEOPLE'S REPUBLIC OF CHINA (RELATIONS WITH).
The Union of Burma (q.v.) was the first non-communist country to recognize the People's Republic of China (PRC), on 16 December 1949. A long, indefensible and, until 1960, also undemarcated land border between the two countries, a large Chinese (q.v.) community in Myanmar, as well as the civil war (q.v.) with the Chinese-backed Communist Party of Burma (CPB) (q.v.) were the main reasons for Myanmar's paying special attention to its relations with the PRC. From the Chinese point of view, there was an interest in keeping Myanmar a neutral country. The signing of the border agreement, together with the treaty of friendship and mutual non-aggression on 28 January 1960, were hallmarks of what used to be termed "*paukpaw*" or (cousin) friendship between the two countries. The period of the "Cultural Revolution," accompanied by anti-Chinese riots in Yangon (q.v.) and Beijing's open backing of the CPB's campaigns against Ne Win's Revolutionary Council (qq.v.) in 1967, soured the official relations. Ne Win's visit to the PRC in 1971 signaled a return to normalcy and the former active cooperation between the two countries in various fields.

Since the 1980s, a shift towards greater cooperation was strengthened after the collapse of the communist insurgency in northeastern Myanmar in 1989. An agreement on cross-border trade between the two countries was signed on 6 August 1988 to legitimize previous illegal cross-border trading. By 1991, the PRC had emerged as Myanmar's most important foreign trade (q.v.) partner. In the early 1990s, the PRC is one of the few foreign states still providing fresh economic assistance to Myanmar; it is also regarded as the major supporter of Myanmar's ruling State Law and Order Restoration Council (q.v.). Myanmar has also become the PRC's closest ally in the region, developing active military cooperation as a major purchaser of Chinese arms and ammunition. (*See also* Foreign Policy.)

PEOPLE'S REVOLUTIONARY PARTY (PRP). Also known as the Burma Revolutionary Party or National Revolutionary Party. Founded in late 1939, or in early 1940, by Aung San, Ba Hein, Ba Swe, Kyaw Nyein, Let Ya, Nu (qq.v.) and some other national leaders, it represented the underground section of the independence movement (q.v.) which aimed at overthrowing British colonial rule in Myanmar. The PRP was active among students, peasants and trade unionists, distributing propaganda pamphlets and providing rudimentary paramilitary training for its members. The PRP was instrumental in making arrangements to send out of the country, for military training by the Japanese, a group of volunteers, subsequently known as the "Thirty Comrades" (q.v.). During the Japanese occupation of Myanmar (1942–1945) (q.v.), some PRP organizations joined the anti-fascist resistance (q.v.). In September 1945, the PRP was reorganized as the Socialist Party of Burma (q.v.). (*See also* Minami Kikan.)

PEOPLE'S VOLUNTEER ORGANIZATION (PVO). A paramilitary organization set up in 1945 to bring together ex-servicemen of the Patriotic Burmese Forces (q.v.) to work for the reconstruction of Myanmar. Under Aung San's (q.v.) command, the PVO developed into the military force of the Anti-Fascist People's Freedom League (AFPFL) (q.v.). After Aung San's assassination in July 1947, some AFPFL leaders called for the disbandment of the PVO, while the PVO insisted on remaining a paramilitary force or developing as an independent political party. In February 1948, the PVO split over the issue of disbanding itself as a military force. The majority group, subsequently known as the White Band PVO, led by Bo Po Kun and Bo La Yaung, opposed disbanding. The minority group, subsequently known as the Yellow Band PVO, headed by Bohmu Aung (q.v.), was willing to cooperate with the AFPFL. While the White Band PVO took up arms against the government, the Yellow Band PVO joined U Nu's (q.v.) government. The White Band PVO became one of the main insurgent organizations in Myanmar during the early 1950s. However, in the 1958 amnesty, many members of the (underground) PVO surrendered their arms and formed a legal People's Comrade Party (PCP). This was subsequently banned in 1964. Some former PCP and PVO leaders reemerged in Myanmar politics after the military coup of 1988 (q.v.). In February 1989, the PVO joined the League of Democratic Allies.

PETROLEUM. Petroleum and natural gas (q.v.) are viewed by the ruling State Law and Order Restoration Council (q.v.) as major components of overall energy (q.v.) development which is regarded as a prerequisite for the economic development of the Union of Myanmar. Petroleum production reached a peak of some 11 million US barrels in 1985, but since has declined steadily to 5,800,000 barrels in 1991. The fall of production, which led the government to impose restriction on the use of petroleum and its rationing, was probably caused by over-pumping the original wells in the Central Basin (q.v.) area. The main state agency, Myanmar Oil and Gas Enterprise, has entered into production sharing contracts with ten international petroleum companies for participation in onshore exploration and future participation in offshore exploitation of petroleum deposits.

PINYA. A capital of the Shan (q.v.) kingdom in northern Myanmar founded in 1312 by Thihathu. Thihathu established a dynastic line of Pinya kings which linked its genealogy to the kings of the Bagan Dynasty (q.v.) and which ruled until 1364. (*See also* Three Shan Brothers.)

PLURAL SOCIETY. The term originally used by J. S. Furnivall (q.v.) to refer to Myanmar's colonial society. In the plural society of Myanmar, as Furnivall saw it, Europeans, Chinese (q.v.) and Indians (q.v.) lived side by side with Bamars (q.v.) and other indigenous peoples, but each group possessed its own separate identity, language, religion and way of life. As a result, the colonial society lacked the cultural and social bonding of an integrated political unit or nation. (*See also* Colonial Education; Economy, British Colonial Era.)

POLITICAL ORGANIZATIONS. Following the military coup of 1988, the State Law and Order Restoration Council (qq.v.) permitted the political organizations to function on condition that they obtain official registration. By February 1989, a total of 233 political parties had been registered with the military authorities. Of these, a total of 93 parties contested the general elections held in May 1990. The National League for Democracy (NLD) (q.v.) which had established itself as the main legal opposition group, won almost 60 percent of the votes cast and 392 seats in the *Pyithu Hluttaw* (q.v.). On the opposite side of the political spectrum, the National Unity Party (q.v.) gained 21 percent of the votes and 10 seats. Other parties which won more than three seats in the *Pyithu Hluttaw* were the Shan Nationalities League for Democracy, the Rakhine Democracy League and the Mon National Democratic Front, all regional parties allied with the NLD. Among the many other parties and organizations which failed to gain any significant public support were some led by major political figures of the 1950s or groups which were without clearly formulated objectives and programs.

Many more political organizations, parties and groups, Bamar (q.v.) as well as ethnic, were operating illegally, in armed confrontation with the government. (*See also* Civil War.)

"POLITICAL" PONGYI. An expression used for Buddhist monks who were active in Myanmar nationalist politics after World War I (q.v.) and instrumental in developing Myanmar nationalism as a popular movement in the 1920s. (*See also* General Council of Sangha Sammeggi; Independence Movement; Ottama, U.)

PONGYI. Also *hpongyi* and *phongyi*. The title of a Buddhist monk meaning literally "great glory." Almost any man can become a *pongyi*, either temporarily or for life. A *pongyi* must renounce worldly life and must submit himself to the 227 rules of the Buddhist order, *sangha* (q.v.). *Pongyi* is also the general term of address to a member of the *sangha*, which includes *upazin, pongyi* and *sayadaw* (qq.v.) grades. In this hierarchy, *pongyi* denotes a monk with about 20 years of continuous service in the order. In relation to the laity, the *pongyi* performs two main tasks, attendance at Buddhist rituals and teaching youths at monastery schools, *pongyi kyaungs* (q.v.). (*See also* Buddhism.)

PONGYI KYAUNG. Also *hpongyi kyaung*. Monastic schools which were of major importance in forming the traditional Myanmar society. The *pongyi kyaung* was generally available in almost every village throughout the country and open to all Buddhists youths (boys). The pupils went there for a period of one or two years to learn the rudiments of the *dhamma* (q.v.) as well as to receive training in reading, writing and arithmetic. The official British policy after the annexation of Myanmar in 1885 was to link the *pongyi kyaungs* to the government's educational system, but these efforts largely failed as most of the *pongyi kyaungs* resisted the appeals for a change of curricula and also because many Bamars (q.v.) lost interest in traditional education. Despite this, many *pongyi kyaungs* survived and after independence in 1948 some were gradually absorbed by the state system. The functioning of the *pongyi kyaungs* has been linked to a relatively high rate of literacy (q.v.) in Myanmar. (*See also* Colonial Education; Education.)

POPULATION. The population of the Union of Myanmar was estimated to be 44,500,000 in 1993 as compared to the (1983 census) figure of 33,307,913. Males make up 49.56 percent and females 50.44 percent of the total population. With a population growth rate of 2.1 percent (1993), the population projection for 2000 is estimated at more than 54 million. Presently, with a density of only about 58 persons per square kilometer, Myanmar is far below the level not only of neighboring India, Bangladesh and People's Republic of China, but also the Southeast Asian average.

The population is irregularly distributed. The greatest concentration occurs in the deltas and in the lowlands of some great rivers, especially the Ayeyarwady, as well as in Rakhine and Tanintharyi, where the Bamars (qq.v.) form the majority. Uplands are more sparsely populated by minority ethnic groups. Most people live in rural areas while only about 25 percent are urban dwellers. The major cities are Yangon, Mandalay, Mawlamyine, Bago and Pathein (qq.v.). All other towns have less than 100,000 inhabitants. (*See also* Migration; Nationality.)

PORTUGUESE AND MYANMAR. The Portuguese were the first Europeans to arrive and reside in Myanmar as early as the 16th century. In 1519, they established a trading center at Martaban (q.v.), which functioned for almost a century. They also founded a trading center at Tanintharyi (q.v.). The Portuguese had a major impact on the course of Myanmar history by bringing firearms to the country and serving as mercenary gunners in the royal army of several Myanmar kings, including Tabinshwehti and Bayinnaung (qq.v.). The best known of the Portuguese mercenaries was Felipe de Brito, who was placed in charge of Thanlyin (q.v.) by King Minyazagyi of Rakhine (q.v.), but actually established his rule over part of southern Myanmar between the years 1610 and 1612. In 1613, Anaukpetlun (q.v.) laid siege to Thanlyin, defeated and slew De Brito. Also executed was Natshinnaung, the ruler of Toungoo and a brilliant poet, who had allied with the Portuguese.

After De Brito's death some four hundred Portuguese were taken captive and settled in villages in northern Myanmar between the Chindwinn (q.v.) and Mu Rivers. Their descendants, known as *bayingyi* or *feringhi* (qq.v.), are still found in that area. (*See also* European Colonial Expansion.)

POWER, ELECTRIC. Electric power generation in Myanmar comes from hydroelectric plants, steam, gas and thermal (diesel) stations. The hydroelectric program has been the most vital item in successive governments' industrial policies. Major hydroelectric plants have been constructed on the Baluchun River in Kayah State, or the Bago River (qq.v.) and elsewhere. The total generated energy in 1991 was 2,478,000,000 KWH, of which about 48 percent was by hydroelectric plants, 50 percent by natural gas plants and remainder by steam power and diesel plants. Supply still falls short of demand.

PRESS, THE. Myanmar's first newspaper was the English-language *The Maulmain Chronicle* started by the British in 1836 in Mawlamyine (q.v.). After 1852, the press center in the British-held territory of the country shifted to Yangon (q.v.). In northern Myanmar, then still under the rule of Myanmar kings, *Yadana Neipyidaw* was launched in Mandalay in 1874.

The British colonial era and the years following Myanmar's independence in 1948 saw a great increase in the number of newspapers and periodicals, in English, Myanmar and some other languages. Of the Myanmar-language newspapers, the most popular were *Hanthawaddy, Kyeimon, Thuriya*, and *Myanma Alin* and, of the English-language newspapers, *The Nation* and *The New Times of Burma*. After the military coup of 1962 (q.v.), many independent newspapers were either closed or nationalized. In 1966 a decree was issued that newspapers could only print in English or Myanmar, thereby eliminating several Chinese, Indian and Pakistani newspapers.

Presently there are two dailies, both published in Yangon and state-owned, *Myanmar Alin* and *The New Light of Myanmar* (qq.v). In addition, there are about ten periodicals in English or Myanmar on a number of subjects, including *Guardian Magazine* (q.v.).

The government news agency, the News Agency of Myanmar (NAM), formerly the News Agency of Burma, was established in 1963 in Yangon.

PRO-DEMOCRACY MOVEMENT (1988). The political protests which ushered in a popular, pro-democracy movement during 1988 were set in motion by growing discontent with the authoritarian rule of the Burma Socialist Programme Party (BSPP) (q.v.), worsening economic conditions and deteriorating living standards of the people. An immediate cause for the unrest was the demonetization of some higher banknotes in September 1987. This provoked concern in the University of Yangon (q.v.) as early as December 1987. In March 1988, student demonstrations broke out again and the students' protest march into the center of Yangon, joined also by ordinary citizens, was put down by the riot police. Again, in June 1988, university students clashed with riot police and regular army units. Up to 120 people were killed in Yangon alone and the protest movement spread to some other cities and places. The universities were closed indefinitely, but the movement continued to grow.

The election of General Sein Lwin as Chairman of the State Council and State President on 26 July, following resignations offered by U Ne Win and San Yu (qq.v.) at the BSPP's extraordinary congress, caused even more unrest. Martial law was imposed on Yangon and more than 2,000 unarmed demonstrators were killed by the armed forces throughout the country. The pro-democracy movement was becoming more organized by August. A general strike, including massive demonstrations, was started on 8 August, to bring down the BSPP government. The armed forces responded with unprecedented brutality, killing an estimated 1,000 to 3,000 people in Yangon alone, before General Sein Lwin stepped down on 12 August.

General Sein Lwin was replaced by a more moderate, civilian President Dr. Maung Maung (q.v.), who proposed a peaceful and legal transition to the reforms wanted by the people. But the demonstrations continued and the demands put by the largest opposition group, later known as the National League for Democracy (q.v.), was that the BSPP regime should step down and be replaced by an interim government before holding general elections. The extraordinary congress of the BSPP called on 10 September agreed to hold multi-party general elections within three months. But, on 18 September, the military, headed by General Saw Maung, assumed power through a coup, using the deterioration of law and order as a pretext. A new, military-dominated junta, known as the State Law and Order Restoration Council with General Saw Maung as Chairman (qq.v.), was formed.

PROME *see* PYAY.

PULSES AND BEANS. Pulses and beans have ranked second after rice (q.v.) among Myanmar's agricultural products. Production grew by more than 100 percent in the years up to 1983 and exports have also been increasing. In 1991, the production of pulses and beans totalled 1,260,000 tons, of which 500,000 tons were exported. (*See also* Agriculture; Export Products.)

PWE. A Myanmar word to refer to an entertainment or festival. The generic term for various theatrical performances and dance shows.

PYAY. A town in Bago Division located on the bank of the Ayeyarwady River (qq.v.). An important river port and trade center, Pyay is close to the site of the ancient Pyu capital of Sri Ksetra (qq.v.).

PYIDAUNGSU PARTY. The Union Party. The new name (in March 1960) for the Clean Anti-Fascist People's Freedom League (AFPFL) led by U Nu (qq.v.). Although the party won a landslide victory in the 1960 parliamentary elections, shortly thereafter the integrity of the party was disrupted by factional disputes over the composition of the party's Executive Council. The division of the *Pyidaungsu* Party into two main factions, resembling the AFPFL split in 1958, was one of the factors causing the crisis in U Nu's second premiership which ultimately led to the military coup of 1962 (q.v.). (*See also* Parliamentary Era.)

PYIDAWTHA. A Myanmar term meaning literally "sacred, happy country." The term refers to a welfare state program initiated in 1952 during the parliamentary era (q.v.).

PYIN-Oo-LWIN. A town located on the Shan Plateau (q.v.) at a height of 1,050 meters (3,448 feet), about 70 kilometers (43 miles) east of Mandalay (q.v.). Its original name, Maymyo (Maytown) was after British Colonel May. During the British colonial era, the town was used as a summer resort of the government.

PYITHU HLUTTAW. The 489-member People's Assembly, a unicameral legislature, and the highest organ of state power in the Burma Socialist Programme Party era (q.v.). After the military coup of 1988 (q.v.), the *Pyithu Hluttaw*, together with all other state organs, was abolished. General elections were held in May 1990, but it was subsequently announced that the new body was to serve as a constituent assembly with no legislative power.

PYU. An early Tibeto-Burman group which is assumed to have reached the upper Ayeyarwady River (q.v.) valley around 500 B.C. The Pyu gradually gained control of the entire Ayeyarwady valley, south to present day Pyay (q.v.). They established several city-states there which reached a high level of economic and cultural development. (*See also* Beikthano; Halin; Sri Ksetra.)

-R-

RADIO. There is one broadcasting station in the Union of Myanmar, the state-owned Myanmar TV and Radio Department, located in Yangon (q.v.). It broadcasts in Myanmar language (q.v.) and also in English and in the languages of Myanmar's major ethnic groups, Chin, Kachin, Kayah, Kayin, Mon, Shan and Rakhine (qq.v.). (*See also* Television.)

RAILROADS. Myanmar's railroad network, built by the British in the late 19th century, was largely disrupted during the Japanese occupation of Myanmar (1942–1945) (q.v.). Due to the civil war (q.v.), its postindependence rehabilitation only proceeded slowly.

In 1989, the railroad network comprised 3,137 kilometers (1,949 miles) of track operated by the state-owned Myanmar Railways Corporation. The major rail tracks are Yangon-Mandalay-Myitkyina (qq.v.); Mandalay-Lashio (q.v.); Yangon-Pyay (q.v.); and Bago-Mawlamyine-Ye (qq.v.). Myanmar has no rail communication across the border with the neighboring countries, although a link with Thailand is under consideration. (*See also* Air Transport; Roads; Thai-Burma Railway; Water Transport.)

RAKHINE. An ethnic group, akin to the Bamars (q.v.), which lives mostly in the western part of Myanmar, namely Rakhine State (q.v.). In the 1983 census, the Rakhines accounted for some 4.5 percent of the total population of the Union of Myanmar (qq.v.).

RAKHINE STATE. It covers an area of 36,778 square kilometers (14,200 square miles). Situated in the western part of Myanmar, Rakhine State is a long, narrow and hilly region, separated from the rest of Myanmar by the Rakhine Yoma (q.v.). The only important plain, and also the major rice (q.v.) producing area, is the Sittwe Plain. Rakhine State consists of 17 townships and 11,041 village tracts. Its (1983) population was 2,045,559. Its capital is Sittwe (q.v.); other towns include Kyaukphu and Thandwe. Most of the people are Rakhines (q.v.) who are Buddhists, but there is also a Rohingya (q.v.) Muslim minority. Rakhine, formerly a region, became a state on 3 January 1974. In the past, Rakhine was an independent kingdom which was annexed to Myanmar in 1785. (*See also* Third Myanmar Empire.)

RAKHINE YOMA. A mountain range in Rakhine State (q.v.). It is the southernmost part of the mountain chain stemming from the eastern extension of the Himalayas, stretching through the Naga Hills and Chin Hills (qq.v.), very close to the coast, before descending into the Andaman Sea at Cape Negrais. The Rakhin Yoma rises to a maximum altitude of some 11,200 meters (7,000 feet), constituting a natural barrier between Rakhine State and the rest of Myanmar. It is traversed by several passes of which An Pass, Gwa Pass and Taungup Pass are the most important.

RANCE, SIR HUBERT. British Army General. He was chief of the Civil Affairs Service (Burma) (q.v.) from 10 June 1945 to October 1945. In August 1946, he succeeded Sir Dorman-Smith (q.v.) as the last British Governor of Myanmar.

RANGOON see YANGON.

RANGOON DIVISION see YANGON DIVISION.

RANGOON UNIVERSITY see UNIVERSITY OF YANGON.

RANGOON UNIVERSITY STUDENTS' UNION (RUSU). Formed in 1930, originally to carry on usual students' social activities, it became involved in politics following the 1936 strike at the University of Yangon (q.v.) when the leadership of the RUSU was captured by radical students, of whom Aung San, Kyaw Nyein, Nu and Raschid (qq.v.) later became prominent as *Thakin* (q.v.) politicians. The RUSU, along with the All Burma Students' Union, was instrumental in assisting the cause of the oil field workers' strike (1938) (qq.v.). The RUSU supported the Anti-Fascist People's Freedom League (q.v.) in the years 1945 to 1947, though at independence it came under strong influence of the Communist Party of Burma (q.v.). During the parliamentary era (1948–1962) (q.v.), the RUSU remained an influential, politically active students' body. After the military coup of 1962 (q.v.), RUSU-led students clashed with the military. On July 7, 1962, the original RUSU building at the university campus was destroyed by the army, many student leaders were arrested, while others went underground, to join the Communist Party of Burma (CPB). The RUSU was reconstituted during the March 1988 students' riots in Yangon (q.v.) which sparked the pro-democracy movement of 1988 (q.v.).

RASCHID, M. A. (1912–). Born in 1912 in Allahabad (India) of an Indian Muslim family, he grew up and was educated in Myanmar where he also became one of the nationalist politicians of the preindependence and postindependence era. He was the first Secretary General of the Rangoon University Students' Union and the first President of the All Burma Students' Union (1936–1937) (qq.v.). During the parliamentary era (1948–1962) (q.v.), Raschid served in several ministries and was also a leader of the *Pyidaungsu* Party (q.v.). Following the military coup of 1962, he was interned for some time by the Revolutionary Council (qq.v.).

RAZADARIT. A Mon (q.v.) king (1385–1423). A brave warrior and able ruler, he is remembered mainly for the wars with Inwa (q.v.) where his main rivals were King Minkhaung (q.v.) and Thihathu.

RAZAK, ABDUL (1897–1947). A Myanmar Muslim (q.v.) who was Minister of Education and National Planning in the Executive Council, later Interim Government (q.v.), from 1946 to 1947. He also held the post of President of the All Burma Muslim Congress (q.v.). Razak was assassinated, along with Aung San (q.v.), on 19 July 1947.

RESISTANCE DAY. Also known as Armed Forces Day. It is observed on 27 March, marking that day in 1945 when the Burma National Army (q.v.) launched an armed anti-Japanese uprising. (*See also* Anti-Fascist Resistance.)

RESTORED TOUNGOO DYNASTY *see* **TOUNGOO DYNASTY.**

REVOLUTIONARY BURMA ARMY (RBA). The name used to denote the mutineers of the Burma Army, under the command of Bo Zeya, who joined other rebel forces in the civil war in 1948 (qq.v.). The RBA became a founding member of the People's Democratic Front (q.v.). In 1950, the RBA merged with the armed forces of the Communist Party of Burma (q.v.) into a single force known as the People's Army of Burma.

REVOLUTIONARY COUNCIL (RC). A body originally composed of 17 senior military officers, headed by Bogyoke Ne Win (q.v.), which took power in the military coup of 2 March 1962 (q.v.). Following the first congress of the Burma Socialist Programme Party (q.v.) in 1971, the RC was reconstituted, its members reduced to 15, including, for the first time, 4 civilians.

The line between the RC and the military government was not clearly defined throughout the period of military rule (1962–1974) (q.v.). Initially, the government was known as the Council of Ministers and it consisted of eight members, of whom six were drawn from the RC. In 1972, Ne Win and other senior commanders retired from the armed forces (q.v.) and became civilian members of the government which had been renamed the Government of the Union of Burma (q.v.), with U Ne Win as Prime Minister. The Revolutionary Council was formally dissolved on 2 March 1974.

RICE. Myanmar's principal crop and also the staple food. Prior to World War II and the Japanese occupation of Myanmar (1942–1945) (qq.v.), approximately two-thirds of the country's total acreage was planted with rice and Myanmar was the largest exporter in the world. During the wartime years, rice production fell dramatically and not until 1964 did the area under rice reach the prewar level. Rice production recovered considerably between 1973 and 1983, mainly reflecting a rapid increase in yield per hectare as a result of successful promotion by the government of a high-yield variety paddy (q.v.) project in several parts of Myanmar.

In 1991, the total area under rice was 4,936,003 hectares (12,197,000 acres), while the production figure was 13,691,000 tons. About 168,000 tons of rice were exported in the same year. Rice production is concentrated in the lower Ayeyarwady and Sittoung (qq.v.) valleys and in the Ayeyarwady Delta (q.v.) which account for about two-thirds of the rice crop. Rice is also grown in extensive regions under irrigation in the Dry Zone (qq.v.) and in some other parts of the country. In 1987, the government decontrolled domestic trade in rice and several other products, ending restrictions which came into force in 1966. (*See also* Agriculture; Foreign Trade; Internal Trade.)

RIOTS, BRITISH COLONIAL ERA. Myanmar nationalism, prior to World War II (q.v.), manifested itself not only in hostility towards British rulers but also towards other foreigners, mainly the Indians, and partly also the Chinese (qq.v.), who, as British intermediaries in business and commerce or as agricultural and industrial laborers, were the prime source of Myanmar resentment. Under normal conditions, peace and harmony among the diverse ethnic and religious communities were preserved, but at times of economic and social hardship, racial antipathies turned into violence.

Serious Indo-Bamar riots broke out in Yangon (qq.v.) in May 1930 as a result of clashes between immigrant Indian laborers and Bamar workers at the Yangon docks. Again, in January 1931, there were Sino-Bamar riots, which developed out of a small matter, but at an rather early stage came under police control. The origin of the anti-Indian riots of 1938, the most extensive ones in pre-war Myanmar, was religious. The riots developed as a reaction of Bamar Buddhists to a religious pamphlet by a Muslim, Saya Shwe Pyi, which was taken as a deliberate insult to Buddhism (q.v.). The riots, which erupted in July 1938 in Yangon, lasted for several weeks, claiming several hundred Indian Muslims killed or injured.

ROADS. Myanmar has about 23,220 kilometers (14,416 miles) of roads, of which more than 8,000 kilometers are unpaved. The natural lines of road communications are from north to south; east-west roads are less numerous. The main road runs up the valley of the Sittoung River from Yangon to Mandalay (qq.v.). There is an alternative road running from Yangon to Mandalay up the Ayeyarwady (q.v.) valley. The road east from Mandalay runs through the Shan Plateau to Myitkyina (qq.v.). There is a road from Meiktila in central Myanmar to the Myanmar-Thai border, and a southern highway branch from Bago to Beik (qq.v.). Roads provide an important means of transport both for passengers and freight traffic.

The state-owned Road Transport Corporation operates buses and trucks on the main highways and handles passenger transport in Yangon and major cities. Most road traffic is handled by the private sector. Recently, there has been a reduction in motor transport and traffic due to the shortage of fuel. Bullocks and buffalo carts remain the major form of transport in the rural areas where water transport (q.v.) is not available. (*See also* Air Transport; Burma Road; Ledo Road; Railroads.)

ROHINGYA. A term for the Muslims who live in the northern part of Rakhine State of the Union of Myanmar (qq.v.). (*See also* Bangladesh; Islam; Muslims.)

RUBBER. Though never on a large scale, rubber production had been developed prior to Myanmar's independence in 1948, mainly in Tanintharyi, with most local estates owned by Steel Brothers and Company (qq.v.). Recently, rubber was included among the "industrial crops" which were given priority in the government's agricultural policy. Still, rubber production, estimated at 15,000 tons in 1991, has been modest. (*See also* Agriculture.)

-S-

SAGAING. A town in Mandalay Division located on the bank of the Ayeyarwady River (qq.v.). Sagaing was the capital of a Shan kingdom in northern Myanmar after the fall of Bagan (qq.v.), around 1322 A.D. It served again as the capital of the Konbaung Dynasty (q.v.) from 1760 to 1764. The Sagaing Hills, dotted with pagodas and monasteries, are a well-known place of Buddhist studies and meditation.

SALON. The Myanmar name for a minor Malayo-Polynesian group, belonging to the Sea Gypsies, which calls itself Moken (Mawken). The Salons are semi-nomadic boat people who mostly inhabit the islands of the Beik (Mergui) Archipelago.

SALWEEN *see* THANLWIN.

SAMSARA. A term for the wheel of rebirth, known in Myanmar as *thantaya*. One of the basic tenets of Buddhism (q.v.), according to which all creatures are involved in an endless cycle of existences. The escape from this circle is the core of Buddhist teaching and the ideal goal of Buddhist believers.

SAN CROMBIE, PO. A Kayin (q.v.) doctor and nationalist leader in the preindependence period. He is the author of *Burma and the Karens* (1928), a tract in which he publicly advocated the idea of a separate Kayin state and self-government for the Kayins under British protection. (*See also* Karen National Union.)

SAN, SAYA *see* SAYA SAN REBELLION.

SAN YU, U (1918-). Former President of the Union of Burma and a top-ranking military leader of the Burma Socialist Programme Party (BSPP) era (qq.v.). San Yu was a member of the Revolutionary Council (1962) (q.v.), Vice Chief of Staff (Army) and Deputy Minister of Defense and Planning (1963–1972). He served as Minister of Defense (1962–1974) and President of the Union of Burma (1981–1988). He was also Secretary General of the BSP (1964) and the party's Vice-Chairman (1985–1988). In 1988, San Yu retired from all his posts.

SANGERMANO, VINCENTIUS. A Barnabite missionary of Italian origin who lived in Yangon (q.v.) from 1783 to 1808. He is the author of *A Description of the Burmese Empire*, written originally in Italian and translated into English. The value of Sangermano's account of precolonial Myanmar is mainly that it is based on his personal experience and on Myanmar sources. (*See also* Christianity.)

SANGHA. A Buddhist monastic order. In precolonial Myanmar, there was a close link between the secular power and religion which was made explicit through the king's appointment of a leading senior monk to the office of *thathanabaing* ("lord of the religion"), the primate and head of the *sangha*. The British withdrew this state patronage from the *sangha* after their annexation of Myanmar in 1885, failing to perpetuate the Buddhist ecclesiastical hierarchy and to enforce its decisions. During the British colonial era, the structure of the *sangha* became loose and many monks got involved in politics, namely the so-called "political" *pongyi* (q.v.).

After independence in 1948, during the paraliamentary era (q.v.), efforts were made to reinforce the structure of the *sangha*. In 1965, the Revolutionary Council (q.v.) attempted to register *sangha* members in a move which was strongly opposed by the majority of the *sangha*. More recently, in May 1980, the government convened a nationwide congregation "for the purification, perpetuation and propagation of Buddhism," which created a centralized authority to control the *sangha* and to issue identification cards for monks and nuns. In 1981, the religious courts were revived. While part of the *sangha* was brought under state control, many individual monks resisted such attempts, as witnessed by the active role they played in the pro-democracy movement of 1988 (q.v.) as well as in opposition to the ruling State Law and Order Restoration Council (q.v.). (*See also* Koyin; Pongyi; Sayadaw; Upazin.)

SARPAY BEIKMAN. Literally "Palace of Literature." Also known as the Burma Translation Society, it was established in 1947 by the government to translate and publish books in Myanmar and other indigenous languages for general readers and to encourage research in Myanmar culture. Since 1955, Sarpay Beikman has also published the *Myanmar Encyclopedia*. Between 1948 and 1961, it distributed annual awards for the best literary works. (*See also* Literacy; Literature.)

SAW, U, GALON (1900–1948). A Myanmar pleader and politician in the preindependence period. He took the title *Galon* after his defense of Saya San (qq.v.) at the court trial in 1931. In 1938, he formed the *Myochit* ("Patriotic") Party and from 1940 to 1941, he served as Prime Minister. In this capacity, Saw went to Great Britain and the United States in 1941, but was arrested by the British on his way back home, because of secret contacts with the Japanese Embassy in Lisbon, and detained in Africa for the duration of the war. In 1946, on his return to Myanmar, he reorganized the *Myochit* Party. From 1946 to 1947, Saw was a member of the Governor's Executive Council. While a member of a Myanmar delegation to London in January 1947, he refused to sign the Aung San-Attlee Agreement (q.v.). Attempting to seize power, Saw organized a conspiracy which led to the assassination of his political rival, Aung San (q.v.), and some other Interim Government (q.v.) members in July 1947. He was arrested, tried, sentenced to death in December 1947 and executed in May 1948. (*See also* Anti-Fascist People's Freedom League.)

SAW MAUNG, SENIOR GENERAL. (1928–). A postindependence military and political leader. Saw Maung served as Vice Chief of Staff (Army) (1983–1985) and Chief of Staff (from

1985), also holding the posts of Deputy Minister of Defense (1985–1988) and Minister of Defense (1988). Following the military coup of 1988 (q.v.), Saw Maung became Chairman of the State Law and Order Restoration Council (q.v.) as well as Head of State. He also held the posts of Minister of Defense and Minister of Foreign Affairs in the military government which was formed on 20 September 1988. On 23 April 1992, he retired and was replaced by General Than Shwe (q.v.).

SAWBWA. English term for a hereditary Shan (q.v.) ruler known as *Saopha*. In precolonial Myanmar, there were 34 *Sawbwas* who were nominal vassals of Myanmar kings, but who ruled in separate feudal principalities in the present Shan State (q.v.). *Sawbwas'* privileges were recognized by the British as well as in the Constitution of the Union of Burma (1947) (q.v.). During the tenure of General Ne Win's Caretaker Government (1958–1960) (q.v.), in April 1959, the *Sawbwas* signed agreements with the government renouncing their hereditary rights for a fixed compensation and retention of their titles and property. Most of the *Sawbwas*, however, remained active in politics, getting involved in campaigns for federalism (q.v.) in the early 1960s. After the military coup of 1962 (q.v.), some *Sawbwas* were arrested and interned while others went underground or abroad, organizing armed resistance against the Revolutionary Council (q.v.). (*See also* Parliamentary Era.)

SAYA SAN REBELLION. The greatest peasants' rebellion in Myanmar during the British colonial era which broke out in Tharrawaddy District in southern Myanmar on 22 December 1930. Sometimes referred to as the Tharrawaddy Rebellion, it is better known after its main leader, Saya San, a former Buddhist *pongyi* (q.v.) and alchemist and a nationalist politician associated with a radical fraction of the General Council of Burmese Associations (q.v.) led by U Soe Thein.

The main reasons for the rebellion were economic, reflecting the desperate situation of Myanmar peasants adversely affected by the fall in rice (q.v.) purchase prices. The major aim of the rebellion was the revival of the traditional political and social order. Saya San had himself crowned king of Myanmar, assuming the title of *Thupannaka Galon Raja*, the *Galon* (q.v.) King. He organized his followers, the *galons*, who were to defeat their enemies, the British, symbolized as *naga* (q.v.), into troops equipped with traditional weapons, oaths, amulets and tattooing believed to guarantee invulnerability to modern arms.

The core of the rebellion was in southern Myanmar, but some northern Myanmar districts were also affected. The rebels attacked and killed forest officials, village headmen and Indian *Chettiars* (q.v.), also destroying railroads and telegraphs and occasionally attacking smaller towns. The rebellion reached its peak in June-August 1931, when about 11,000 soldiers of the Burma Army (q.v.) and additional troops from India were deployed in operations against the rebels. "Peace missions" headed by senior Buddhist monks, such as Aletawya Sayadaw, were also formed to persuade the rebels to accept the government's offer of amnesty. Ultimately, Saya San escaped to the Shan States (q.v.) where he was captured in August 1931, while his closest associate, Bo Myat Aung, was arrested in November 1931. Following the arrests of the main leaders and their trials by special tribunals, the rebellion began to disintegrate. Saya San was sentenced to death and hanged on 28 November 1931. Also executed were another 78 rebel leaders, while more than 200 rebels were subject to deportation.

Although most of Myanmar's nationalist parties did not support the rebellion, many Myanmars felt sympathy for Saya San and the rebellion aroused national pride. (*See also* Independence Movement.)

SAYADAW. Also *hsayadaw*. A Myanmar royal title for a senior, respected Buddhist monk, or the abbot of a monastery or group of monasteries in precolonial Myanmar. Presently, the *sayadaw*, in charge of a monastery, is mainly a teacher of other monks who also preaches to laymen. (*See also* Buddhism; Pongyi; Pongyi Kyaung; Sangha.)

SECOND MYANMAR EMPIRE. An empire which existed from about 1531 to 1752 and was ruled by successive kings of the Toungoo Dynasty (q.v.). Under the first Toungoo Dynasty kings, namely Tabinshwehti and Bayinnaung (qq.v.), the capital was moved from Toungoo to Bago (qq.v.). Making use of Portuguese (q.v.) gunners, the kings waged successful military campaigns between 1540 and 1580 which brought all of present-day Myanmar, except Rakhine (q.v.), and large areas in Manipur, Yunnan, Laos and Thailand, under Toungoo control, thereby creating one of the greatest empires in traditional mainland Southeast Asia. But the empire's stability was weak, mainly due to the lack of a firm, impersonal administration. Rebellions of subject peoples, the Rakhines, Mons (qq.v.) and Thais, caused the disintegration of the empire under King Nandabayin (q.v.) in 1599.

At about the time that Nandabayin's empire collapsed, his younger brother, who was known as Nyaungyan, proclaimed himself king and established a new royal line, referred to as the Nyaungyan Dynasty and, more recently, as the Restored Toungoo Dynasty. His son, Anaukpetlun (q.v.), restored the empire, including Thanlyin, temporarily ruled by Felipe de Brito (qq.v.). The rule of Anaukpetlun and his successors until 1648 was characterized by a discontinuation of military conquests of neighboring countries, moving the capital from Bago to Inwa (1634) (q.v.), and reforms of the provincial administration. Still, the empire began to fall apart as of the late 17th century, largely due to increasing rivalries among the ruling elite. There were also devastating Chinese, Manipuri and Thai raids as well as a series of Mon attacks on Inwa, the latter bringing the Second Myanmar Empire to an end in 1752. (*See also* Third Myanmar Empire.)

SEIN LWIN, GENERAL. A senior Myanmar military officer who was a member of the Council of State (1981–1988) and Joint Secretary of the ruling Burma Socialist Programme Party (BSPP) (1983–1988) (q.v.). Sein Lwin served for 18 days (26 July-12 August 1988) as President of the Union of Burma (q.v.) and as Chairman of the BSPP. He ordered the brutal repression of peaceful demonstrations in Yangon during the pro-democracy movement of 1988 (qq.v.).

SEIN WIN, DR. A cousin of Daw Aung San Suu Kyi and an elected member of the Constituent Assembly in the 1990 elections as a candidate of the National League for Democracy (qq.v.). On 18 December 1990, Dr. Sein Win became head of a "parallel" government, known as the National Coalition Government of the Union of Burma, which established its headquarters at the Karen National Union (q.v.)–controlled base of Manerplaw at the Myanmar-Thai border.

SHAN. A Western Tai ethnolinguistic group who call themselves *Tai*, meaning literally "free people." They are called Shans by the Bamars (q.v.), a term which was also used by the British. Their largest concentration is in Shan State, where they inhabit the Shan Plateau (qq.v.). Elsewhere, they are scattered and assimilated with Bamars. A small group of Hkamti Shans, which resides mainly in the Hukawng valley and upper Chindwinn (q.v.) valley, retains its Shan identity. There are also Shans, referred to in Myanmar as *Shan Tayok* (Shan Chinese), or Chinese Shans in British sources, representing the Thai immigrants from Yunnan, presently settled in Kachin State (q.v.). According to the 1983 census, there were 2,890,437 Shans, constituting some 8.5 percent of the total population and forming the second largest ethnic group after the Bamars.

The Shans are primarily wet-rice agriculturalists living in permanent village settlements. Villages are located in river valleys or on level land in the hills at an average altitude of 1,000 metres (3,280 feet). Their main crops are rice, tobacco, cotton, sugarcane, maize (qq.v.), coffee and tea.

There is patrilineal descent among the nobility and bilateral descent among commoners. The choice of a partner is subject to parental approval as a rule. A cash bride price is negotiated by a go-between. Polygamy occurs among the nobility, monogamy among commoners. Inheritance rules are guided by *dhammathat* (q.v.).

The Shans formed their principality of Mogaung, north of Bhamo (q.v.), in 1215 A.D. The fall of the First Myanmar Empire of Bagan (qq.v.) in 1287 enabled the Shans to establish their rule over northern Myanmar until 1531 when they were pushed onto the Shan Plateau. Shan hereditary rulers, *Sawbwas* (q.v.), have officially enjoyed their traditional privileges until 1959. Since the 1960s, Shan State has become one of the centers of insurgent ethnic movements seeking to gain greater autonomy or a federal status, with some groups aiming at separation from the Union of Myanmar. The large Shan population of Myanmar seems to have been a result of the assimilation of various non-Tai people, while, on the other hand, many Shans came under the influence of Myanmar culture. Many Shans are Buddhists.

SHAN PLATEAU. The huge tableland, with an average altitude of 914 meters (3,000 feet), which covers the eastern part of Shan State (q.v.). The plateau, rising abruptly from the Central Basin (q.v.), is a succession of mountain chains and plateaux, marking Myanmar's border with China, Laos and Thailand. The Shan Plateau is traversed by the Thanlwin (q.v.) and many other minor rivers.

SHAN STATE. The largest of the states in Myanmar, it covers an area of 155,801 square kilometers (60,155 square miles). It is bounded on the north by Kachin State (q.v.) and the People's Republic of China (PRC), on the south by Kayin State (q.v.) and Thailand, on the east by the PRC and Laos, and on the west by Mandalay and Sagaing Divisions (qq.v.). Shan State lies in the region of the Shan Plateau (q.v.). It consists of 52 townships and 1,932 wards and village tracts. Its (1983) population was 3,716,841. The capital is Taunggyi (q.v.); other towns include Kalaw, Kengtung, Lashio (qq.v.) and Hsipaw. About half of the inhabitants are Shans (q.v.), the remainder being Palaungs and Was as well as some Kachins and Bamars (qq.v.). Agriculture is the main occupation, and rice (q.v.), tea, coffee and tobacco (q.v.) are the main crops, in addition to poppy cultivation in the area east of the Thanlwin (q.v.). There are teak (q.v.) forests and rich, though little explored, mineral (q.v.) resources, with mining done mainly in two places: Bawdwin-Namtu (q.v.) and Bawsaing.

Previously, the region was known as the Shan States and was divided into the Northern and Southern Shan States. Most of these became incorporated into the Federated Shan States in 1922. On Myanmar's independence in 1948, the Federated Shan States were integrated with Wa States (bordering on China) to form a state of the Union of Burma (q.v.).

SHAN STATES *see* SHAN STATE.

SHAN STATE ARMY (SSA). Established in 1964 by merging the Shan National United Front, one of the largest Shan (q.v.) rebel organizations, with the Shan State Independence Army (SSIA), led by some dissident Shan *Sawbwas* (q.v.), and the Kokang Resistance Force. It has since been the main and best organized Shan rebel force. In 1972, its political wing, known as the Shan State Progress Party (SSPP), was formed and subsequently became an affiliate member of several insurgent fronts, more recently (in 1976) of the National Democratic Front (q.v.). During the 1980s, the SSA and SSPP suffered from internal rivalries and splits, namely over cooperation with the Communist Party of Burma (q.v.) which part of the SSPP favored. Following the collapse of the CPB in 1989, the bulk of the fighting force of the SSA made a truce with the ruling State Law and Order Restoration Council (q.v.), while the remainder was allied with the Kachin Independence Organization (q.v.).

SHAN STATE PROGRESS PARTY *see* SHAN STATE ARMY.

SHETHO. A Myanmar-language monthly published in Yangon (q.v.) by the Ministry of Information. It has a circulation of 36,000 copies. It is also published in English as *Forward*. (*See also* Press.)

SHINSAWBU. A Queen of the Mon kingdom of Bago (1453–1472) and successor of her father, King Razadarit (qq.v.). She was the only woman ruler of a major state known in Myanmar's history. During her reign, the country prospered and Bago, Thanlyin (q.v.) and other towns in southern Myanmar developed as trade centers. Shinsawbu spent her retirement building the Shwedagon Pagoda in Yangon (qq.v.) almost to its present height.

SHOE QUESTION. One of the incidents illustrating the deterioration of Anglo-Myanmar official relations under the last kings of the Konbaung Dynasty (q.v.). According to habits, observed even in present-day Myanmar, shoes are taken off when entering a house or a religious building as a sign of respect. In precolonial Myanmar, all visitors to the king, including Europeans, had to remove their shoes and sit upon the floor at royal audiences. The British objected to this practice and ultimately, in King Mindon's (q.v.) reign, the British Resident at Mandalay (q.v.) was instructed by the British government in India not to comply with the practice. As King Mindon did not give way, no British resident could thereafter be received in royal audience. On Thibaw's (q.v.) succession to the throne in 1878, the British were not given access to the new king, losing an opportunity to improve their status and diplomatic relations. (*See also* European Colonial Expansion; Third Myanmar Empire.)

SHWE THAIK, SAO. Also Shwe Thaik, Saw. The Shan *Sawbwa* (q.v.) of Yawnghe, who played a crucial role in the Panglong conference in February 1947. He was the first President of the Union of Burma ((1948–1952)) (q.v.), Speaker of the Chamber of Nationalities of the Union Parliament (from 1952) and one of the leading Shan politicians of the parliamentary era (1948–1962) (q.v.).

SHWEBO. Originally Moksobo, a town located about 100 kilometers (60 miles) northwest of Mandalay (q.v.). It is noted as the birthplace of Alaungpaya, the founder of the Konbaung Dynasty in 1752 (qq.v.). Shwebo, along with Sagaing (q.v.), was the capital from 1760 to 1764.

SHWEDAGON PAGODA. Also Shwe Dagon. One of the most venerated Buddhist shrines, believed to have been originally built in 585 B.C. to enshrine relics of the Gautama Buddha and of three preceding Buddhas. The pagoda stands on Singuttara Hill in Yangon (q.v.) and rises 99 meters (326 feet) above the base which has a perimeter of 432 meters (1,420 feet). It is entirely covered with gold leaf, up to the top; above the umbrella, *hti* (q.v.), are a jewelled vane and diamond orb studded with some 6,000 diamonds and over 2,000 other precious stones.

The Shwedagon pagoda also figured prominently in modern Myanmar history as a place where many public gatherings, demonstrations and political events occurred during the British colonial era as well as in postindependence years.

SHWELI. A river about 643 kilometers (400 miles) long, it is the largest of the left-bank tributaries of the Ayeyarwady (q.v.) in northern Myanmar. It originates in Yunnan (China) and it empties into the Ayeyarwady below Katha in Sagaing Division (q.v.).

SINYETHA PARTY. Known variously as the "Poor Man's" or "Proletarian" Party. Founded in 1936 by Dr. Ba Maw (q.v.), the party designed its name, its symbol, a hewing knife, *dahma*, and its program to draw support from the rural electorate. Winning only 16 seats in the 1936 elections to the legislature, Dr. Ba Maw nonetheless managed to form a minority coalition government which lasted until February 1939. Thereafter, the *Sinyetha* Party joined the nationalist opposition and, in October 1939 it was one of the founding members of the Freedom Bloc (q.v.). During the Japanese occupation of Myanmar (1942–1945) (q.v.), the *Sinyetha* Party fused with the *Do Bama Asi Ayon* into the *Do Bama Sinyetha* Party (qq.v.).

SITTANG *see* SITTOUNG.

SITTOUNG. A river about 500 kilometers (350 miles) long which runs parallel to the Ayeyarwady River (q.v.). The Sittoung flows through the Bago Yoma (q.v.) and empties into the Gulf of Martaban. The Sittoung valley is one of the most populated areas of Myanmar.

SITTWE. The capital and major sea port of Rakhine State (q.v.), situated at the mouth of the Kaladan River on the Bay of Bengal, with a (1983) population of 107,607. Sittwe, formerly Akyab, grew from a small village into a rice milling and exporting port after the British annexation of Rakhine in 1826.

SIXTH GREAT BUDDHIST COUNCIL. The Council which was convened in Yangon (q.v.) in May 1954 by Prime Minister

U Nu (q.v.). Its chief aim was to codify and edit the Pali Buddhist Canon, *Tipitaka* (q.v.). The session of the Council, attended by Myanmar and foreign Buddhist scholars, lasted a full two years. It was held in Maha Pasana Guha, a huge artificial cave, built on the grounds of Kaba Aye (World Peace) Pagoda, in preparation of the Council. Also located on the premises of the Kaba Aye Pagoda is the International Institute for Advanced Buddhist Studies founded in 1955. (*See also* Fifth Great Buddhist Council.)

SMITH-DUN, GENERAL (1906–1979). A Kayin (q.v.) professional soldier. He served with the Burma Army during World War II (qq.v.). In 1948, he became Commander in Chief of the armed forces of the Union of Burma (qq.v.), but in January 1949 was forced to resign due to the Kayin insurrection. (*See also* Civil War.)

SOCIALISM. Socialism, in the broadest sense of the term, was introduced to Myanmar during the British colonial era and became a source of inspiration for the leaders of the independence movement, mainly the *Thakins* of the *Do Bama Asi Ayon* (qq.v.). The *Thakins'* version of socialism included a rather wide spectrum of concepts, including some basic tenets of Marxist socialism and British reformist socialism as well as some elements of Buddhism (q.v.). In general, the *Thakins'* vision of the future social and economic system of independent Myanmar, however vague, preferred socialism to capitalism which was equated with colonialism.

From independence in 1948 until quite recently, socialism was proclaimed as the program, policy and ultimate goal by successive Myanmar governments as well as by some of its formidable political opponents, whether legal or underground. The doctrine of the post-independence Anti-Fascist People's Freedom League, a ruling body during the parliamentary era, was mainly worked out by the Socialist Party of Burma (qq.v.). Known as "democratic socialism," it was a syncretic doctrine drawing mainly from Western sources, such as the British Labour Party or Social Democratic parties' programs. Attempts were also made, mainly by U Nu (q.v.), to reconcile socialist principles with traditional religious values. The final form of "Buddhist socialism," as espoused by U Nu in the early 1960s, however, rejected Marxism as a component part of the doctrine which became more firmly embedded in traditional Buddhist roots.

After the military coup of 1962 (q.v.), the "Burmese Way to Socialism" (q.v.) became the main platform and officially declared objective of the new ruling regime. As evident from this policy declaration, as well as from other documents of the ruling Burma Socialist Programme Party (q.v.), the ideology of the military elite was on the whole, a result of adapting Marxist socialism to the philosophy and worldview of Buddhism. The building of a "socialist society" in Myanmar was an avowed aim of the Constitution of the Socialist Republic of the Union of Burma (q.v.), which remained in force until the coming to power of the State Law and Order Restoration Council (q.v.) in September 1988. Only then, the former socialist orientation was scrapped in favor of a more pragmatic economic policy based on the principles of a market economy and multi-party democracy. (*See also* Burma Workers' and Peasants' Party; Communist Party of Burma.)

SOCIALIST CONSTITUTIONAL SYSTEM (1974–1988). The system established after the formal termination of military rule (1962–1974), during the Burma Socialist Programme Party (BSPP) era (qq.v.). All state organs, under the new Constitution of the Socialist Republic of the Union of Burma (SRUB) (q.v.), were elected on 2 March 1974. The Constitution confirmed the structure of the State as a Union, but the State became, in fact, unitary. Real power remained in the hands of the BSPP, with virtually the same leaders who had seized power in the military coup of 1962 (q.v.). The leading figure was U Ne Win (q.v.), who was elected Chairman of the Council of State and became the first President of the SRUB, the post he held until 1981.

Despite the institutional changes, serious economic problems persisted. Serious riots and demonstrations of students and workers took place in 1974, and again in 1975, while ethnic and political rebellions continued. These negative developments could not have been stopped by greater state expenditure on education and health and increased imports of consumer goods.

The continuing political unrest and economic shortcomings forced the ruling elite to make several attempts at improving the situation. The general amnesty order in 1980 brought back to the legal fold many Bamar (q.v.) politicians. More recently, the government also freed the purchase, sale, transport and storage of basic foodstuffs from state control. The positive effects of these measures were, however, largely offset by the demonetization of the 23, 25 and 72 *kyat* (q.v.) banknotes in September 1987, which virtually wiped out nearly 80 percent of the currency in circulation, without any effective offer of repayment. The demonetization, ostensibly directed against growing "black market" operations, provoked immediate protests by students and gave an impetus to the pro-democracy movement of 1988 (q.v.). This, in turn, brought an end to the one-party socialist constitutional system in September 1988. (*See also* State Law and Order Restoration Council.)

SOCIALIST PARTY OF BURMA. Established in September 1945 out of the People's Revolutionary Party, with Thakin Mya as President, and U Ba Swe and U Kyaw Nyein (qq.v.) as prominent leaders, the Socialist Party was the main rival of the Communist Party of Burma in attempts to draw support for the independence movement and to gain control of the Anti-Fascist People's Freedom League (AFPFL) (qq.v.). After independence in 1948, the Socialist Party leaders established themselves as an influential group in the AFPFL leadership and in official trade unions, such as the All Burma Peasants' Organization and the Trade Union Congress of Burma (qq.v.). During the parliamentary era (1948–1962) (q.v.) they also held important cabinet posts.

In 1946, the Socialist Party of Burma adopted its program of establishing a "Burmese socialist society" and the ideology of "socialism based on Marxism." In fact, the party leaders' platform was more influenced by reformist socialism, one of the reasons for the party's split and subsequent formation, by left-wing Socialists, of their own Burma Workers' and Peasants' Party (q.v.) in 1950. The Socialist Party remained the main source of political ideology of the AFPFL, though the personal relations of Socialist Party leaders with U Nu were not without problems. When the AFPFL split in 1958, most Socialist Party leaders joined the Stable AFPFL, a rival faction to U Nu's Clean AFPFL. (*See also* Military Rule; Socialism.)

SOCIALIST REPUBLIC OF THE UNION OF BURMA (SRUB). The official English name for Burma introduced in January 1974 and used up to September 1988. By a decree of the State Law and Order Restoration Council, the state again assumed its former name, the Union of Burma (qq.v.), with effect from 18 September 1988. It was in use until 18 June 1989, when it was replaced by the term Union of Myanmar (q.v.).

SOE, THAKIN (1905–1989). A leading Marxist and top-ranking Communist leader during the war and in the post-independence period. A member of the *Do Bama Asi Ayon*, he was active in the *Nagani* Book Club and was one of the founders of the Communist Party of Burma (CPB) in 1939 (qq.v.). From 1940 to 1942, Soe was imprisoned by the British. During the Japanese occupation of Myanmar (1942–1945) (q.v.), he was one of the main organizers of the anti-fascist resistance (q.v.) and Secretary General of the CPB (1943–1945). However, in February 1946, he split with the CPB, set up a separate Communist Party (Red Flag) (q.v.) and went underground. He headed the party until 1970, when he was captured by government troops in the area of the Rakhine Yoma (q.v.). Soe was imprisoned, but released in the 1980 amnesty. He reemerged shortly during the pro-democracy movement of 1988 (q.v.) and he sponsored the Unity and Development Party established in September 1988. Soe translated Marxist literature into the Myanmar language and compiled some original political tracts.

SRI KSETRA. Also known as *Thayekhittaya*. The Pyu city-state, the remains of which are located about eight kilometers (five miles) east of Pyay (qq.v.). Sri Ksetra, which covers an area of about 12 square kilometers (5 square miles), has been intensively explored by archaeologists since 1907. It has been established that Sri Ksetra was built in the form of a circle, surrounded by a massive wall with 12 gates and moats. Some pagodas and temples have been partly preserved. The terra cotta tablets and stone reliefs recovered in Sri Ksetra bear the influence of east Indian art and iconography and date back to the period from 6th to 10th century A.D. (*See also* Beikthano; Halin.)

STABLE ANTI-FASCIST PEOPLE'S FREEDOM LEAGUE *see* ANTI-FASCIST PEOPLE'S FREEDOM LEAGUE.

STATE LAW AND ORDER RESTORATION COUNCIL (SLORC). The military junta which came to power through a coup on 18 September 1988. The SLORC has abolished the existing state organs, imposed military control on the country and governed directly since that time. It is composed of military commanders from the divisional commands of the armed forces (q.v.) as well as from central military structures. Until 23 April 1992, the SLORC was headed by Senior General Saw Maung, who was then replaced in that post by Brigadier General Than Shwe (qq.v.). Another prominent leader of the junta is Brigadier General Khin Nyunt (q.v.). Some SLORC members also constitute the governing cabinet. In January 1992, the SLORC was expanded with the addition of three new members. The cabinet was also reorganized with the creation of a number of new ministers and the appointment of some new, civilian ministers. (*See also* Military Coup (1988); Political Organizations; Pro-Democracy Movement.)

STEEL BROTHERS AND COMPANY. One of the major British enterprises in colonial Myanmar. The company, incorporated in 1890 as a joint Steel Company, was extensively represented in cotton, petroleum, rice, rubber and teak (qq.v.). It engaged in import and export, shipping agency, insurance and general trade. On 1 January 1963, it was nationalized by the Revolutionary Council (q.v.). (*See also* Bombay Burmah Trading Corporation; Burma Corporation; Burmah Oil Company; Economy, British Colonial Era.)

STUDENT STRIKES, BRITISH COLONIAL ERA.

After World War I (q.v.), student strikes were increasingly used as a tool of the nationalist struggle against British rule, becoming part of the independence movement (q.v.).

The first, and greatest, strike, often referred to as the University Boycott, was declared on 5 November 1920 by the students of the newly established University of Yangon (q.v.) in protest against what they considered to be an anti-national University Act. The strike, gaining popular support, ushered in the national school movement (q.v.). The main importance of the second university strike, which began on 25 February 1936, in protest against the decision of the authorities to expel from the university Aung San and Nu (qq.v.) for their political activities, was that it brought together these and other radical-minded students who came to the forefront of the independence movement in the early 1940s. The third major prewar student strike broke out in December 1938. It occurred in protest against the arrest of some student leaders sent to assist the oil-field workers' strike (q.v.). The student demonstration in Yangon on 20 December 1938 was charged by the mounted police injuring many students and killing one, Aung Gyaw, who became a national martyr.

The tradition of politically-motivated student strikes has continued after independence in 1948.

SUGARCANE.

The production of sugarcane, as one of the "industrial crops," has been encouraged by the government. There was a three-fold increase in sugarcane production between 1975 and 1985, reaching a peak of 3,368,000 tons in 1988. In 1991, production totalled about 2,000,000 tons. (*See also* Agriculture; Economy.)

SUVANNABHUMI.

Also Suvarnabhumi. "The Land of Gold." The name of a Mon-Khmer kingdom which is supposed to have existed around the 3rd century B.C. The exact location of Suvannabhumi is not known and probably it meant the entire region occupied by the Mons (q.v.) in western mainland Southeast Asia. The capital of Suvannabhumi was evidently Thaton (q.v.) in present-day Myanmar, though some Thai scholars insist it was rather Nakorn Pathom in Thailand.

SUZUKI, KEIJI (aka MINAMI; MOGYO, BO). The Japanese army officer who came to Myanmar in 1940, supposedly as a newspaper reporter, but actually to collect military intelligence and develop contacts with sympathetic Myanmar nationalist leaders. Suzuki was instrumental in founding the *Minami Kikan*, in training the "Thirty Comrades" and in establishing, in December 1941, the Burma Independence Army (BIA) (qq.v.). He participated in the military campaign in Myanmar in 1942 as the Commander in Chief of the BIA. He had the leave Myanmar when the BIA was disbanded in June 1942. (*See also* Independence Movement; Japanese Occupation of Myanmar.)

SWA SAWKE. The king of Inwa (1367–1400) (q.v.). He descended from the Bagan Dynasty line and from the family of the Three Shan Brothers (qq.v.). He was brought up as a Shan (q.v.), but spent many years in Myanmar. In 1371, Swa Sawke met King Binnya U and made peace with the Mons (q.v.), which was maintained until his death. The king repaired irrigation (q.v.) systems, reclaimed considerable arable land in northern Myanmar and brought much needed stability to Ava.

SYMES, MICHAEL. British envoy sent on two missions, in 1795 and 1803, to the court of Inwa (q.v.). His main aim was to prevent the French from using Myanmar's ports and to impress the Myanmar king with the greatness of British power. He described the experience of his missions, providing interesting insights into life in 18th century Myanmar. (*See also* Cox, Hiram; European Colonial Expansion.)

SYRIAM *see* THANLYIN.

-T-

TABINSHWEHTI. The founder of the Toungoo Dynasty and of the Second Myanmar Empire (1531–1550) (qq.v.) He achieved the unity of the Bamars and their supremacy over the Shans and conquered the Mons (qq.v.). Himself a Bamar,

Tabinshwehti, however, followed a policy of reconciliation with the population of the conquered Mon territories and had himself crowned for the second time in Bago (q.v.), which he also made his capital. His forces were composed of men of diverse ethnic origin, including many Portuguese (q.v.) mercenaries. His main concerns were military campaigns, while he paid little attention to the proper administration of his empire. After reverses in his campaigns in Rakhine (1546–1547) and Thailand (1547–1548), he took to drinking. The empire began to fall apart and Tabinshwehti was murdered by Mon rebels in 1550.

TAGAUNG. A town on the bank of the Ayeyarwady some 200 kilometers (125 miles) south of Bhamo (qq.v.). Tagaung is reputed to have been the site of a kingdom established by King Abhiraja (q.v.) which flourished in the 6th century B.C. Although these data are not corroborated by historical evidence, many Bamars tend to believe that their history began with Tagaung.

TAI REVOLUTIONARY COUNCIL (TRC). The Tai Revolutionary Council, with its Möng Tai Army, is the main private warlord force which operates in northern and southern areas of Shan State (q.v.). It was formed in 1986, when Moh Meng's Shan United Revolutionary Army, a breakaway group from the Shan State Army (q.v.), joined its forces with the Shan United Army led by opium warlord Khun Sa (q.v.). Despite its name, the TRC's main occupation is to protect its heroin refineries along the Myanmar-Thai border and to carry on cross-border narcotics trade. (*See also* Drug Abuse.)

TANINTHARYI DIVISION. It covers an area of 43,343 square kilometers (16,735 square miles). Tanintharyi is Myanmar's southernmost division, bordering Thailand on the east and southeast, Mon State (q.v.) on the north and the Andaman Sea on the west. It is a narrow, coastal region, backed by the Tanintharyi Yoma which is the continuation of the Shan Plateau (q.v.), with numerous islands along its coast. Tanintharyi Division consists of 10 townships and 317 wards and village tracts. Its (1983) population was 917,247, mostly

Bamars, Kayins and Mons (qq.v.). The capital is Dawei; other important towns, all situated on the seacoast, include Beik and Kawthaung (qq.v.). The chief crops are coconut, maize, pulses, rice, sugarcane and rubber (qq.v.). Equatorial fruits, such as durian, mangosteen and rambutans, are also grown there on a large scale. Almost about 70 percent of the tin and tungsten produced in the country comes from Tanintharyi Division. It is also known for cultured pearls.

TATMADAW. The Myanmar term currently used to refer to the armed forces (q.v.), the military.

TAUNGGYI. The capital of Shan State (q.v.). Located on a plateau at an altitude of 1,430 meters (4,690 feet), Taunggyi is noted for its market as well as being an important center of Shan (q.v.) culture.

TAVOY *see* DAWEI.

TEAK. Teak (*tectona grandis*) is Myanmar's most important forest product. It grows in areas below an altitude of about 914 meters (3,000 feet) in the basins of streams and rivers. Presently, Myanmar produces about 90 percent of the world's teak. In 1991, its production totalled 415,000 tons, of which 229,000 were exported. However, the official statistics do not record any teak production in the private sector, although the illegal felling of teak and its smuggling into neighboring Thailand has become a major problem. Since September 1988, the ruling State Law and Order Restoration Council (SLORC) (q.v.) has also made efforts to increase foreign exchange reserves by signing a series of logging deals with some Thai companies. This has resulted in a rapid increase in the rate of felling, in disregard of the country's earlier good record in forest conservation. In January 1990, the SLORC announced an 80 percent reduction in the level of timber exports allowed for the Thai companies and a halt in new timber contracts. In June of the same year, the export fees for teak and other hardwoods were increased by more than 100 percent.

Myanmar is also a major producer and exporter of other

hardwoods, such as *in-kanyin* (*diptero-carpus*), *padauk* (*pterocarpus mecrocarpus*) and *pyinkado* (*xylia dolabriformis*). In 1991, the production of these hardwoods totalled 871,000 tons.

TELEVISION. Television service is provided by the Myanmar TV and Radio Department. Regular color television transmissions began in November 1980. About six hours of daily programming are provided, including news, sporting events, entertainment and education. In 1988, there were about 68,000 television receivers in use. (*See also* Radio.)

TENASSERIM *see* TANINTHARYI.

THADOMINBYA. The founder of Inwa in 1364 A.D. (q.v.). He was of mixed, Shan-Bamar (qq.v.) descent and he united, for a time, the whole of central and northern Myanmar under his rule. (*See also* Three Shan Brothers.)

THAI-BURMA RAILWAY. Also known as the Burma-Thai Railway and the Burma-Siam Railway. Built by the Japanese during World War II (q.v.), this rail link, about 416 kilometers (267 miles) long, connected the Mawlamyine-Ye line at Thanbyuzayat, south of Mawlamyine (q.v.) in Myanmar, with Banpong on the Bangkok-Singapore line. The rail link was put into operation in December 1943. About 330,000 Asian laborers, including many Myanmars, and some 16,000 Allied war prisoners worked and died there through starvation, disease and ill-treatment, giving the railway an infamous reputation as the "Death Railway." Since the war's end, the link has been out of operation. In 1992, the ruling State Law and Order Restoration Council (q.v.) proposed the construction of a rail link with Thailand along the route of the Thai-Burma Railway. (*See also* Railroads.)

THAILAND (RELATIONS WITH). Historically, Myanmar and Thailand were often war enemies and mistrust and suspicion between Myanmars and Thais persisted, to some extent, up to the recent past. In 1956, a treaty of friendship was signed between Myanmar and Thailand. But closer cooperation did not develop, partly due to different foreign policy orientations of the two countries. More recently, bilateral relations were strained because of the large-scale illegal trade across the common border, the provision of sanctuary for rebels from Myanmar in Thai territory and disputes over maritime boundaries.

A radical change in bilateral relations only came after the visit of Thai Supreme Commander General Chaovalit to Yangon (q.v.) in December 1988. Agreements were signed by the Myanmar-ruling State Law and Order Restoration Council (SLORC) (q.v.) giving the Thais teak logging and fishing concessions in Myanmar in return for foreign exchange. Thereafter, official ties and economic cooperation were vastly expanded. The Thai-Myanmar border trade has in effect been regulated. By 1991, Thailand, and especially its overseas Chinese community, has become one of the major foreign investors in Myanmar.

Aside from commerce and trade benefits, for Myanmar this close relationship with Thailand also establishes a kind of diplomatic legitimacy for the SLORC. The Thai motivation in developing contacts with Myanmar is more complex. Close military-to-military relations are said to bring financial rewards to both partners. More important are evidently Thai foreign policy and strategic considerations, namely to counterbalance the growing influence of the People's Republic of China (q.v.) in Myanmar. More recently, there have been official protests in Thailand over incursions by Myanmar troops fighting the ethnic minority rebel groups along the border. Another nagging problem of bilateral relations is caused by refugees from Myanmar to Thailand, whose number (excluding those seeking job opportunities) is estimated to be about 70,000 and who are regarded as illegal immigrants by the Thai authorities. (*See also* Association of Southeast Asian Nations; Foreign Policy; Foreign Trade; Teak.)

THAKIN. A Myanmar word meaning literally "master," used like "sahib" by the British in Myanmar during their rule. The expression was also used by the members of the nationalist party, the *Do Bama Asi Ayon* (q.v.), in the late 1930s to demonstrate that Myanmars were the real masters of their country.

THALUN. A king of the Toungoo Dynasty (1629–1648) (q.v.). In 1634, he moved his capital from Bago back to Inwa (qq.v.). Thalun discontinued the warlike activities of his predecessors, trying rather to maintain peace and stability, to restore order and social organization. Under his rule, the first law book in Myanmar, *Maharaja Dhammathat*, was compiled by his minister Kaingsa Manu. Thalun reorganized the local administration and also reconstructed the irrigation (q.v.) works in Kyaukse (q.v.) region. His major accomplishment was the revenue inquest which he took in 1638, for the first time in Myanmar's history. Thalun promoted relations with both the British and Dutch East India Companies, but he was reluctant to relax the royal monopoly on foreign trade. (*See also* Dhammathat; European Colonial Expansion; Second Myanmar Empire.)

THAN SHWE, BRIGADIER GENERAL. The present Chairman of the State Law and Order Restoration Council, succeeding Senior General Saw Maung (qq.v.) whom he replaced on 23 April 1992. Than Shwe also assumed the function of Prime Minister of the Union of Myanmar, in addition to the post of Minister of Defense.

THAN TUN, DR. (1923–). A leading, internationally-known Myanmar historian. Than Tun started his academic career at the University of Yangon (q.v.) in 1948. Between 1952 and 1956, he studied at the London School of Oriental and African Studies and, in 1956, he obtained his Ph.D. at London University. In 1960, he became Lecturer in Myanmar history at the Department of Oriental History of the University of Yangon. More recently, he was transferred to Mandalay (q.v.), where he is presently Professor of Myanmar History at the University of Mandalay (qq.v.). During the 1980s, he received a visiting scholarship at Tokyo University of Foreign Studies. Than Tun has done research and published, in both the English and Myanmar languages, on various aspects of Myanmar's precolonial history. He also edited and published ten volumes of *Royal Orders of Burma (1598–1885)*.

THAN TUN, THAKIN (1911–1968). One of Myanmar's most prominent Communist leaders in the wartime and postindependence periods. In the 1930s, Than Tun was active in the *Do Bama Asi Ayon* and became one of the founders of the *Nagani* Book Club (1937) and of the Communist Party of Burma (CPB) (1939) (qq.v.). He was interned by the British from 1940 to 1942. During the Japanese occupation of Myanmar (1942–1945) (q.v.), he served as Minister of Agriculture and as Minister of Transport in Dr. Ba Maw's (q.v.) government. He figured among the main leaders of the antifascist resistance and the founders of the Anti-Fascist People's Freedom League (AFPFL) (qq.v.) in August 1944. From May to August 1946, he was Secretary General of the AFPFL. He became the actual leader of the CPB at the Second Congress in July 1945 and led the party underground in March 1948. In 1950, he was elected the CPB's Chairman and retained this post until 24 September 1968, when he was killed in the Bago Yoma (q.v.) by his bodyguard. (*See also* Civil War; Socialism).

THANLWIN RIVER. A river about 2,735 kilometers (1,700 miles) long, of which about 1,600 kilometers (1,000 miles) are in the territory of Myanmar. Thanlwin enters Myanmar in the northern part of the Shan Plateau (q.v.). Interrupted, particularly in its upper part, by ravines and waterfalls, it is navigable only in certain sections and is of lesser importance for water transport than the Ayeyarwady or Chindwinn (qq.v.). The Thanlwin, joined by two other rivers, the Attaran and Gyaing, empties into the Gulf of Martaban.

THANLYIN. A town located on the bank of the Hlaing River just opposite Yangon (qq.v.). It has a petroleum (q.v.) refinery and a candle factory. Once the center of foreign trade for southern Myanmar, Thanlyin attained its greatest significance as a seat of Portuguese (q.v.) mercenary De Brito in the early 17th century. (*See also* Second Myanmar Empire.)

THANT, U (1909–1974). Former Secretary General of the United Nations, one of the internationally best known Myanmars. After independence, from 1948 to 1953, U Thant served at the Ministry of Information. In 1954, he became Secretary to Prime Minister U Nu (q.v.). In 1957, U Thant was appointed Myanmar's permanent representative to the UN. In November 1961, he became Secretary General of the UN and retained this post until 1971. He died in November 1974 in New York. His burial in Yangon (q.v.) in December of the same year, as arranged by the government, was found unfitting to U Thant's significance by the opponents of the ruling regime. The issue of U Thant's burial sparked large-scale anti-government demonstrations initiated by students of the University of Yangon (q.v.).

THARRAWADDY. A town in Bago Division (q.v.) located on the Bago-Pyay railroad some 96 kilometers (60 miles) north of Yangon (q.v.). It is a trading center for collecting and transporting teak (q.v.) products from the Bago Yoma (q.v.) to Yangon.

THARRAWADDY. A king of the Konbaung Dynasty (1837–1846) (q.v.). He came to power after deposing his brother Bagyidaw (q.v.). During his reign, the capital was moved from Inwa to Amarapura (qq.v.). He repudiated the Treaty of Yandabo (q.v.) and his relations with the British were strained. In 1845, he went insane and was put under restraint by his sons. (*See also* Third Myanmar Empire.)

THATON. A town in the Mon State about 48 kilometers (30 miles) north of Mawlamyine (qq.v.). Thaton was presumably the capital of Suvannabhumi (q.v.) and of the Mon (q.v.) kingdom which existed in southern Myanmar before Bagan (q.v.) rose to power. Little of the ancient town has been preserved and the modern town was built on the top of the old site.

THEATER. The stage, or the theater, as understood in the West does not exist in Myanmar. Myanmar theatrical performances or dramatic shows go under the generic term of *pwe* (q.v.).

Myanmar *pwe* are usually classified into three main categories: 1. *zat pwe*, plays taking themes from Buddhist lore or from the Indian epic *Ramayana*; 2. *anyein pwe*, plays without much plot and a lot of clowning and dancing; 3. *yein pwe*, comprising group dancing and singing. A more recent theater form is that of a musical comedy known as *pyazat*.

Myanmar drama has its roots in religious pageants depicting the life of the Buddha. Innovations were made over the centuries, also under the impact of Thai court drama. U Kyin U and U Ponnya, well-known playwrights of the 19th century, active at the court of Konbaung Dynasty (q.v.) kings, are remembered as founders of Myanmar national drama. Their plays were produced on stage. Later, more plays based on the *Jataka* (q.v.) tales, the *Ramayana* or other popular themes were compiled. In the late 19th century, some of the most popular stage plays were printed. But the British annexation of Myanmar in 1885 brought a new departure for dramatic plays.

The marionette or puppet show, *yokthe pwe*, was an original and popular art in precolonial Myanmar. However, at present there are only a few traditional puppet troupes which occasionally perform at festivals.

THEIN MAUNG, DR. (1891–1946). A Myanmar politician active in the 1920s and 1930s. From 1937 to 1939, he served as Minister of Commerce and Industry. He was close to Dr. Ba Maw (q.v.) and, during the Japanese occupation of Myanmar (1942–1945) (q.v.), he worked in his government as Minister of Finance (1943). From 1944 to 1945, he served as Myanmar's ambassador to Japan.

THEIN PE MYINT, THAKIN (1914–1978). A Myanmar politician, journalist and writer. One of the leaders of the 1936 strike at the University of Yangon (q.v.), he became a member of the Executive Committee of the *Do Bama Asi Ayon* (q.v.) in the same year. From 1937 to 1938, he studied at Calcutta University and he joined Bengal Students' Federation. He was one of the founders and leaders of the People's Revolutionary Party (q.v.) and was close to the Communist Party of Burma (CPB) (q.v.). During the Japanese occupation of Myanmar (1942–1945) (q.v.), he stayed in India where he worked as a liaison of the anti-fascist resistance in Myanmar (q.v.) with the Allies. He was elected Secretary General of the CPB in July 1945, but did not join the party when it went underground in March 1948. In the 1950s, Thein Pe Myint was active in various legal leftist organizations. In 1956, he was elected a Member of Parliament for the National Unity Front (q.v.). Following the military coup of 1962 (q.v.), he became an adviser to Ne Win's Revolutionary Council and also a member of the Burma Socialist Programme Party (qq.v.).

As a writer, he is remembered for his short stories, novels and political memoirs, the latter based largely on his experience as a student and political leader in Myanmar and wartime activities in India. (*See also* Independence Movement; Literature.)

THERAVADA BUDDHISM *see* BUDDHISM.

THIBAW. The last king of the Konbaung Dynasty (1878–1885) (q.v.). Thibaw, the junior son of King Mindon (q.v.), came to the throne in a court plot of Kinwun Mingyi (q.v.). Thibaw, however, fell under the influence of his wife, Supayalat, who persuaded the king to order a huge massacre of his kinsmen and to install in key positions her favorites, other than Kinwun Mingyi. Faced with growing discontent of the Kachins and Shans (qq.v.) and mounting British pressure, Thibaw decided to strengthen his position by resuming relations with France and to play off the French against the British. Thibaw's efforts to develop relations with France and other European countries, and his action against the Bombay Burmah Trading Corporation (q.v.), served the British as a welcome pretext for starting the Third Anglo-Myanmar War which led to the annexation of the Myanmar kingdom. Thibaw surrendered on 28 November 1885, when the British took Mandalay (q.v.). He was sent, with his wife and family, into exile at Ratnagiri in India, where he died on 15 December 1916. (*See also* Anglo-Myanmar War, Third; Pacification of Burma.)

THIRD MYANMAR EMPIRE. The last Myanmar empire which existed, under the rule of the kings of the Konbaung Dynasty (q.v.), from 1752 to 1885.

The empire was founded by Alaungpaya (q.v.) who defeated the Bamars' traditional rivals, the Mons (qq.v.), by 1757 and reunified the country. The traditional policy of conquest and of suppressing the rebellions of the diverse peoples who inhabited the empire was continued by Alaungpaya's immediate successors, in particular Hsinbyushin (q.v.). The empire reached its zenith under Bodawpaya (q.v.) who annexed Rakhine (q.v.) to Myanmar in 1785. Bodawpaya's attempts to expand eastward were, however, ultimately checked by the Thais who forced the Myanmars to withdraw from Chiangmai and Laos. The annexation of Rakhine, on the other hand, brought Myanmar closer to British power in India. It also incited a series of border clashes and incidents leading up to the First Anglo-Myanmar War (1824–1826), in which Bodawpaya's successor, King Bagiydaw (q.v.), lost about two-fifths of the empire.

During the first half of the 19th century, the empire had no capable rulers. Only with Mindon (q.v.), did Myanmar once again have a good king. But his efforts to modernize and reform the country were only partly successful and came too late to prevent the British annexation of Myanmar, under the last king Thibaw (q.v.), bringing the Third Myanmar Empire to an end in 1885. (*See also* Anglo-Myanmar War, First; Anglo-Myanmar War, Second; Anglo-Myanmar War, Third.)

THIRTY COMRADES. *Yebaw Thongyeit*. Also known as Thirty Heroes. The group of thirty young Myanmars, most of whom were smuggled out of Myanmar with the assistance of the *Minami Kikan* (q.v.) between March and July 1941. They were given military training by the Japanese at Hainan and shortly after the outbreak of the Pacific War were moved to Bangkok. The group, headed by Aung San (q.v.), then founded the first national military organization, the Burma Independence Army (q.v.) on 28 December 1941. The Thirty Comrades held a traditional military ceremony, pledging to fight for Myanmar's independence. All of them, except Thakin Tun Ok (q.v.), also chose their auspicious *noms de guerre*. The Thirty Comrades were: Aung San (Bo Te Za) (q.v.); San Hlaing (Bo Aung); Hla Pe (Bo Let Ya) (q.v.); Hla Myaing (Bo Yan Aung) (q.v.); Ko Shwe (Bo Kyaw Zaw); Tun Shwe (Bo Lin Yone); Ba Gyan (Bo La Yaung); Aung

Thein (Bo Ye Htut); Soe (Bo Myin Aung); San Mya (Bo Tauk Htain); Ko Hla (Bo Min Yaung); Tun Lwin (Bo Ba La); Than Nyunt (Bo Zin Yaw); Maung Maung (Bo Nyana); Khin Maung U (Bo Taya); Saw Lwin (Bo Min Gaung); Than Tin (Bo Than Tin); Hsu Maung (Bo Ne Win) (q.v.); Aung Than (Bo Set Kya) (q.v.); Tun Khin (Bo Myint Swe); Kyaw Sein (Bo Mo Nyo); Aye Maung (Bo Mo); Thit (Bo Saw Naung); Ngwe (Bo Saw Aung); Than Tin (2) (Bo Than Tin); Tun Ok; Tun Shein (Bo Yan Naing) (q.v.); Hla Maung (Bo Zeya) (q.v.); Saung (Bo Htain Win); Ko Tin Aye (Hpone Myint). (*See also* Bo; Independence Movement.)

THREE SHAN BROTHERS. The sons of a Shan chieftain and Bamar lady (q.v.). They served under King Narathihapati of the Bagan Dynasty (qq.v.) and, along with their sister, who was married to the king, founded a Shan ruling family in northern Myanmar in the 13th century. Narathihapati's son Kyawzwa, who succeeded his father to the throne, recognized the eldest brother Athinkhaya as the chief of Myinsaing, the second brother Yazathinkyan as the chief of Mekkaya and the third and youngest brother Thihathu as the chief of Pinle. The three brothers were involved in a plot leading to the dethronement and murder of the last king of the Bagan Dynasty, Sawhnit, and thereafter became the real rulers of northern Myanmar. Later, Thihathu murdered his two brothers and ruled alone, with Pinya as his capital, from 1312 to 1324. His son Sawyun (1315–1323) founded a rival kingdom at Sagaing (q.v.). Thihathu's rule was recognized by the Bamars, but he had to resist attacks by the Maw Shans (q.v.) who sacked both Pinya and Sagaing in 1368. However, they withdrew and a new Shan ruler, Thadominbya (q.v.), who was related to the Three Shan Brothers, founded Inwa (q.v.) in 1364 and became the first king of a new Shan-Bamar dynasty.

THUGYI. A Myanmar term designating hereditary local chieftains in the precolonial state. The *thugyi* was in charge of a tract called in some places a *myo* (q.v.), a town, or a *taik*, usually translated as a circle, elsewhere. The *thugyi* (*myothugyi* or *taikthugyi*) represented the lowest level of the administrative system. In addition to levying taxes, of which a certain percentage constituted their own income, the *thugyi* were responsible for the supervision of *corvée* labor demands, military service requirements, the maintenance of law and order and some other duties. (*See also* Administration of Myanmar, Precolonial Era.)

TIN PE, BRIGADIER GENERAL. The Minister of Mines in the Caretaker Government of General Ne Win (1958–1960) (q.v.). An assistant to Ne Win, and co-conspirator in the military coup of 1962, Tin Pe became the leading ideologue of the Revolutionary Council and one of the authors of the "Burmese Way to Socialism" program (qq.v.). He was also a member of the military government and of the Central Committee of the Burma Socialist Programme Party (q.v.). He resigned from all of his posts in 1968. (*See also* Military Rule.)

TIN TUT, U (1895–1948). One of the first Myanmars to be admitted to the Indian Civil Service. During the Japanese occupation of Myanmar (1942–1945) (q.v.), he served as Adviser to the Government of Burma in exile at Simla. From 1945 to 1947, he was a member of the Governor's Executive Council and of the Interim Government (q.v.). After independence, he served briefly as Minister of Foreign Affairs and as Inspector General of the Auxiliary Forces. He was assassinated in December 1948, probably by hirelings of his political opponents.

TIN U, U (1927–   ). Former Chief of Staff and Minister of Defense (1974–1976). He was accused of involvement in an abortive army officers' coup attempt in July 1976 and imprisoned. He was released in the 1980 amnesty. In August 1988, he reemerged as one of the principal leaders of the pro-democracy movement (q.v.). He became Vice-Chairman (later Chairman) of the National League for Democracy (q.v.). In July 1989, he was placed under house arrest and, in December, sentenced to three years' imprisonment.

TIPITAKA. A Pali (q.v.) term for the Sanskrit *tripitaka*, meaning literally "three baskets." The scriptures of the Pali Buddhist canon, containing the basic teachings of Theravada Buddhism (q.v.). The three baskets, or three grand divisions, of the canon are: 1. the *Vinaya Pitaka* (The Collection of Discipline), a code of conduct and rules for the Buddhist monastic order, the *sangha* (q.v.); 2. the *Sutta Pitaka* (The Collection of Discourses), Buddhist discourses or religious readings; 3. the *Abhidhamma Pitaka* (The Collection of Philosophy) which interprets the philosophy and psychology of Buddhism. (*See also* Dhamma.)

TIYATANA. Also *Tiratana*. A Pali (q.v.) term meaning literally "three jewels." These are the Buddha, the *dhamma* (q.v.), the law, and the *sangha* (q.v.), the Buddhist monastic order. (*See also* Buddhism.)

TOUNGOO. A town in Bago Division on the bank of the Thanlwin River (qq.v.). Toungoo is an important juncture of the Yangon-Mandalay railroad and a trade center. It was the center of one of the major states of Myanmar from the late 13th century and the capital of the Second Myanmar Empire, from 1486 to 1539 (q.v.).

TOUNGOO DYNASTY. The Toungoo Dynasty ruled from 1531 to 1752. Traditionally, this is divided into two sub-periods, the Toungoo Dynasty (1531–1597) and the Nyaungyan Dynasty (1597–1752). The more recent terminology is the First Toungoo Dynasty and the Restored Toungoo Dynasty. The rulers of the Toungoo Dynasty include: Tabinshwehti (1531–1550) (q.v.), Bayinnaung (1551–1581) (q.v.), Nandabayin (1581–1599) (q.v.), Nyaungyan (1599–1606), Anaukpetlun (1606–1628) (q.v.), Minyedeikpa (1628–1629), Thalun (1629–1648) (q.v.), Pindale (1648–1661), Pye (1661–1672), Nayawaya (1672–1673), Minyekyawdin (1673–1698), Sane (1698–1714), Taninganwe (1714–1733) and Maha Damma Yaza Dipati (1733–1752). (*See also* Second Myanmar Empire; Toungoo.)

TRADE UNION CONGRESS (BURMA) (TUC)(B). The trade union formed in 1945 by the Socialist Party of Burma (q.v.). In 1950, the then President of the TUC(B), Thakin Lwin, along with several other leftist Socialist leaders who broke away from the Socialist Party, organized a separate Burma Trade Union Congress (BTUC). While the BTUC became affiliated with the Burma Workers' and Peasants' Party (q.v.), the TUC(B) remained under the control of the Socialist Party. Led by Ba Swe and M. A. Raschid (qq.v.), the TUC(B) became the largest trade union in the country in the 1950s.

TRANSPORT *see* AIR TRANSPORT; RAILROADS; ROADS; WATER TRANSPORT.

TREATY OF YANDABO. This was signed on 24 February 1826, formally ending the First Anglo-Myanmar War. By the terms of the treaty, Myanmar, which lost the war, undertook to pay a war indemnity of one million pounds; to cede Rakhine and Tanintharyi (qq.v.) to the British, while recognizing Assam, Manipur and other regions in India as British territory; to sign a commercial treaty with the British East India Company; and to maintain a resident envoy in Calcutta and receive a British resident representative in Inwa (q.v.). Yangon (q.v.), occupied during the war by British troops, was to revert to Myanmar upon the payment of the second installment of the indemnity, within one hundred days of the signing of the treaty. (*See also* Anglo-Myanmar War, First.)

TUN AUNG GYAW, U. One of the main leaders of the students' protest campaigns against the military regime in Myanmar in 1974 and 1976, he spent several years in jail. He reemerged during the pro-democracy movement of 1988 (q.v.). In November 1988 he became the first Chairman of the Central Committee of the All Burma Students' Democratic Front (q.v.).

TUN OK, THAKIN (1907–1970). One of the "Thirty Comrades" (q.v.). Tun Ok was one of the leaders of the *Do Bama Asi Ayon* (q.v.) and President of the splinter organization, the Ba Sein-Tun Ok *Do Bama*, from 1939 to 1941. During the Japanese occupation of Myanmar (1942–1945) (q.v.), he was the Chief Administrator (Head) of the Burma Administrative Headquarters. In 1943, he became Minister of Forests and Mines in Dr. Ba Maw's (q.v.) government and, between

1943 and 1946, he was in Singapore. After his return to Myanmar, he was nominated as a member of the Governor's Executive Council, but he opposed the Aung San-Attlee Agreement (q.v.) signed in 1947. In 1946, he reorganized the *Do Bama Asi Ayon* as an opposition party to the Anti-Fascist People's Freedom League (q.v.). After independence he retired from politics. (*See also* Burma Independence Army; Independence Movement.)

-U-

UNION DAY. A public holiday celebrated on 12 February to commemorate the day in 1947 that the Panglong Agreement, paving the way for the formation of the Union of Burma (qq.v.), was signed.

UNION KAREN LEAGUE (UKL). One of the legal organizations among the Kayins (q.v.) in the 1950s. It was formed in 1951, by reorganizing the Karen Youth Organization. Led by Mahn Win Maung (q.v.), the UKL drew its primary support from the Kayins living in the plains of southern Myanmar. In 1956, the UKL was absorbed into the Anti-Fascist People's Freedom League (q.v.). (*See also* Parliamentary Era.)

UNION LABOUR ORGANIZATION (ULO). A trade union formed in 1958 after the split of the ruling Anti-Fascist People's Freedom League (AFPFL) (q.v.). It was set up by U Nu's Clean AFPFL (*Pyidaungsu* Party) (qq.v.) and affiliated with it.

UNION OF BURMA, THE. The official English name of the country which was in use from Burma's Independence Day (q.v.), 4 January 1948, until 4 January 1974, when the new constitution came into force, changing the official name to the Socialist Republic of the Union of Burma (q.v.). The former name, the Union of Burma, was reintroduced by the State Law and Order Restoration Council (q.v.) with effect from 18 September 1988 and used up to June 1989. (*See also* Myanmar; Union of Myanmar.)

UNION OF MYANMAR. The official English name for the country which was introduced by the State Law and Order Restoration Council (q.v.) on 18 June 1989. The alternative Myanmar terms, which are also used in English-language material published in the country, are *Myanma(r) Naing Ngan* and *Myanma(r) Naingngandaw*, with the word *naing ngan* meaning "the state." (*See also* Burma; Socialist Republic of the Union of Burma; Union of Burma.)

UNITED HILL PEOPLE'S CONGRESS. An organization of the leaders of various ethnic groups of Myanmar which was politically active in the 1950s as an affiliate organization of the Anti-Fascist People's Freedom League (q.v.). (*See also* National Unity; Parliamentary Era.)

UNITED STATES OF AMERICA (RELATIONS WITH). Myanmar gained recognition from the United States in 1947, on the eve of its Independence Day (q.v.). The US aid program to Myanmar began in 1950, but was suspended in 1952 and terminated in March 1953, due to Myanmar's charges of American involvement in the Kuomintang intervention in Shan State (q.v.). It was renewed in 1956 and cooperation between the two countries expanded in the late 1950s. After the military coup of 1962 (q.v.), US aid and technical assistance that had been concluded prior to the coup continued, but private aid, such as that from the Ford Foundation and the Asia Foundation, was terminated. The educational exchange program under the Fulbright Act was also temporarily suspended between 1962 and 1970. Since 1976, Myanmar has cooperated with the United States in restricting the illegal drug traffic from the Golden Triangle (q.v.). Other areas where US assistance was provided to Myanmar from the 1970s included agriculture and health. US military assistance, though never publicly discussed by either side, was provided to Myanmar from 1958 to 1970, totalling some US $80 million.

Following the military coup of 1988, US aid to Myanmar was suspended and the US government continued to apply moral pressure on the State Law and Order Restoration Council (q.v.) to bring about democratic change in Myanmar. (*See also* Foreign Policy.)

UNITED WA STATE ARMY (UWSA). A rebel Wa (q.v.) organization set up in November 1989, following the mutiny in the Communist Party of Burma (CPB) (q.v.). The UWSA rallied non-Communist Wa forces with the Burma National United Army, another rebel group which emerged after the collapse of the CPB and the fall of its leadership at Panghsang.

UNIVERSITIES AND COLLEGES. There are three universities and 28 colleges and institutes of higher education in the Union of Myanmar, with a total of 5,974 teachers and 218,848 students enrolled in 1991.

The University of Yangon (Yangon University) traces its origin to Rangoon College, founded in 1885, and the American Baptist Intermediate College, started in 1875 in Yangon (q.v.). In 1918, Baptist College was renamed Judson College (q.v.) and, in 1920, it merged with Rangoon College and became the University of Rangoon (Rangoon University). After independence in 1948, it was reorganized as a unitary university. Under the University Education Law of 1964, the university system was reorganized and the name of the university changed to Rangoon Arts and Sciences University. Detached faculties became independent institutes and the affiliated colleges ceased to be constituents of the university. Presently, the University of Yangon has about 560 teachers and 12,500 students. Other bodies of higher education in Yangon are the Institute of Education, the Institute of Dental Medicine, two Institutes of Medicine, the Institute of Economics and Yangon Institute of Technology, all founded in 1964.

The University of Mandalay was founded in 1925, originally as the Intermediate College. It gained its full-fledged status in 1958. In 1964, it was renamed the Mandalay Arts and Sciences University. Presently, the University of Mandalay consists of 14 departments and 9 affiliated colleges. There is also an Institute of Medicine founded in 1964.

Mawlamyine University, founded as a college in 1953, gained its full university status in 1986. It comprises 13 departments and two affiliated colleges in Bago (q.v.) and Hpa-an.

A regional college system provides two-year pre-university arts and sciences courses at regional colleges. (*See also* Education.)

UNIVERSITY OF MANDALAY *see* UNIVERSITIES AND COLLEGES.

UNIVERSITY OF YANGON *see* UNIVERSITIES AND COLLEGES.

UPANZIN. A junior monk in the Buddhist order, the *sangha* (q.v.), who has undergone the ordination ceremony. (*See also* Koyin; Pongyi; Sayadaw.)

UPPER BURMA. Before the annexation of all Myanmar in 1886, the term used by the British to refer to the independent Myanmar kingdom in the north of the country. After 1886, the term Upper Burma referred to the central and northern regions of Burma proper (q.v.), while the remainder of the latter was known as Lower Burma (q.v.). Upper Burma consisted of three administrative divisions, Magway, Mandalay and Sagaing (qq.v.). (*See also* Administration of Myanmar, British Colonial Era.)

-V-

VAISALI. Also Vesali. A town in Rakhine (q.v.) which is assumed to have been the capital of the Candra Dynasty and whose origin dates back to the 4th century A.D.

VICTORIA POINT *see* KAWTHAUNG.

VISHNU CITY *see* BEIKTHANO.

VOICE OF THE PEOPLE OF BURMA (VOPB). A former clandestine radio station operated by the Communist Party of Burma (CPB) (q.v.), broadcasting news and propaganda. Set up in April 1971, it was originally located in the People's Republic of China; later it was transferred to the Myanmar-China border area under CPB control. The VOPB broadcasting facilities were seized by the Wa (q.v.) rebels on 12 April

1989. Thereafter, the VOPB began broadcasting under the new name of the Burma Nationalities Broadcasting Service.

VUM KO HAU (1917–). A Chin (q.v.) national leader and diplomat. During World War II and the Japanese occupation of Myanmar (1942–1945) (qq.v.), he served in the Chin Levies. He led a Chin delegation to the Panglong Conference in February 1947 and was appointed a Counselor for Chin Affairs in the Interim Government (q.v.). He participated in drafting the Constitution of the Union of Burma (1947) and co-signed the U Nu-Attlee Agreement (qq.v.). After independence in 1948, he joined the Foreign Service and later served as Myanmar's ambassador to various countries. (*See also* Panglong Agreement.)

-W-

WA. A Mon-Khmer ethnolinguistic group found mainly in a mountain range along the Thanlwin River (q.v.) and eastward to the watershed between the Thanlwin and the Mekong. Their true country is the former Wa States, a region situated along the Myanmar-China border. Some Was also live in the Kengtung area of Shan State (q.v.) and in the Kachin (q.v.) portion of North Hsenwi. The (1960) population estimate, including population on both sides of the border, was 300,000. The Wa language belongs to the Wa-Palaung group of Mon-Khmer languages and has numerous dialects. Ethnically, the Was are subdivided into two main groups: the Pagan or "Wild" Was and the "Tame" Was. Under British rule, the Wa States was an area disputed between Myanmar and China and was not properly administered because of the hostility of the Was against all strangers who penetrated into their territory. After independence in 1948, the Was were recruited into various military or political rebel forces operating in Shan State. More recently, they formed the core of the armed forces of the Communist Party of Burma (qq.v.).

"Wild" Wa villages are usually located on the higher mountain slopes. Originally, the "Wild" Was were swidden agriculturalists, with rice (q.v.) as their main crop; more recently, opium poppy has become the principal cash crop.

Since the 1960s, the Was have been the main suppliers of raw opium in the Golden Triangle (q.v.). The Was are organized into clans. The wives are purchased with bullocks and other goods. Polygyny is permissible but rare. The villages of "Wild" Was are autonomous. A confederation of villages, under a common chief, known as the *ramang*, may be formed for mutual defense, while each village in a confederation retains its own chief, known as a *kraw*. Among the "Tame" Was, villages are smaller and are united in relatively large numbers under separate chiefs. The Was have won a reputation for being warlike and hostile to strangers. Most "Tame" Was are Buddhists while the "Wild" Was are animists, who were known as headhunters offering human skulls to their spirits.

WA NATIONAL ARMY (WNA). Wa (q.v.) rebel army, formed in 1973 and led by a former Wa chieftain Mahasang, who in 1989 encouraged the Wa soldiers to rise against the veteran Bamar leadership of the Communist Party of Burma (qq.v.). The WNA operated mainly in areas of Shan State (q.v.) close to the Myanmar-Thai border. In November 1989, the WNA became the nucleus of the newly formed United Wa State Army (q.v.).

WARERU. A Shan (q.v.) adventurer from Sukhotai in Thailand who ruled as king of a Mon (q.v.) state in southern Myanmar (1287–1296). This state, with its capital in Martaban and (from 1369) in Bago (qq.v.), lasted until 1539. Wareru is remembered for the earliest law book in Myanmar which was compiled at his command by one of his ministers and is known as the Wareru *dhammathat* (q.v.).

WATER TRANSPORT. Myanmar's rivers provide more than 8,000 kilometers (5,000 miles) of navigable routes. Shipping is the most important means of transport in the southern and central regions of the country as well as along the coast of Rakhine (q.v.). The main arteries are the Ayeyarwady (q.v.), navigable for about 1,450 kilometers (900 miles) of its length, and the Chindwinn, navigable for about 627 kilometers (390 miles). The rivers and central network of the Ayeyarwady Delta (q.v.) provide a further 3,200 kilometers (2,000 miles) of navigable inland waterways, of which part are ship canals. Only about 400 kilometers (250 miles) of navigable inland waterways are available in the south, around Mawlamyine (q.v.). There are boat services between Yangon and deltaic towns, and also services along the coast of Rakhine and Tanintharyi (qq.v.). The state-owned Inland Water Transport Corporation operates several passenger and freight services on internal waterways, but most inland water transport is privately owned. The main seaport of Myanmar is Yangon; other ports include Dawei, Mawlamyine, Pathein and Sittwe (qq.v.). International passenger and freight services are provided by the Myanmar Five Star Line, a state-owned company founded in 1959. (*See also* Air Transport; Railroads; Roads.)

WELFARE STATE *see* PYIDAWTHA.

WHITE PAPER ON BURMA (1945). The Statement of Policy on Burma by the British Government issued on 7 May 1945. The White Paper envisaged three years of British Governor's rule in Myanmar until December 1948. At that time, elections were planned to reconstitute parliament and a government, more or less along the lines of the Government of Burma Act (1935) (q.v.). As a final stage, Burma proper (q.v.) should have attained the status of a dominion, while the remainder of the country, the Frontier Areas (q.v.), should stay under British Governor's control until their people signified their desire for amalgamation with Burma proper.

From the outset, the White Paper was criticized and opposed by the main Myanmar political force, the Anti-Fascist People's Freedom League led by Aung San (qq.v.). Ultimately, the White Paper, as official British policy on Myanmar, was replaced by the Aung San-Attlee Agreement (q.v.) concluded in London in January 1947.

WIN MAUNG, MAHN (1916–1989). A Kayin (q.v.) nationalist and former President of the Union of Burma (q.v.). In 1940, he joined the Burma Army and, in 1944, he made his way into India where he was trained by the British and, in early 1945, parachuted into Toungoo area where he joined the anti-fascist resistance (qq.v.). A member of the Anti-Fascist People's Freedom League (q.v.) he was elected Vice-President of the Karen Youth Organization and President of the Union

Karen League (1951) (q.v.). Win Maung was Minister of Transport and Communications (1948–1956) and then President of the Union of Burma (1952–1962). After the military coup of 1962 (q.v.), he was interned. He re-entered active politics during the pro-democracy movement (1988) (q.v.) and became one of the main leaders of the League for Democracy and Peace, a post he held until his death in July 1989. (*See also* Political Organizations.)

WISARA, U. One of the leading "political" *pongyis* (q.v.) active in Myanmar during the 1920s. He died in jail in September 1929 as the result of a hunger strike which he undertook to secure the right to wear the yellow robe of a Buddhist monk while in prison. Wisara is remembered as one of the heroes of the independence movement (q.v.).

WORKERS' ASI AYON. "Workers' Association." One of the two "class" organizations of the Burma Socialist Programme Party era (q.v.). It was formed in 1977 by reorganizing the People's Workers' Councils at different levels. In 1983, the Workers' *Asi Ayon* claimed a total membership of 1,603,814 workers. (*See also* Peasants' Asi Ayon.)

WORKING PEOPLE'S DAILY *see* LOKTHA PYITHU NEZIN.

WORLD WAR I. The direct impact of World War I on Myanmar was only slight. Although Myanmar, as part of British India, was a belligerent country on the side of Great Britain, Myanmar's participation in war campaigns was limited. Only about 12,000 men, of whom about 8,000 were Myanmars, saw service in France, Mesopotamia and Palestine. The indirect effect of the war, mainly on the people's political consciousness was, however, very considerable. The people of Myanmar learned about the Allied war aims, particularly the "fourteen points" proposed by US President Woodrow Wilson, as well as about the revolution in Russia. Even more significantly, they became aware of the political developments in neighboring India and of the campaigns waged there by the Indian National Congress (q.v.). On the whole, World War I was instrumental in the rebirth of Myanmar nationalism and in its entrance on the political scene in the early 1920s. (*See also* General Council of Burmese Associations; Independence Movement; Wunthanu; Young Men's Buddhist Association.)

WORLD WAR II. Myanmar was severely hit by World War II. It became a major battlefield during the Japanese campaign (1941–1942) and again during the Allied reconquest of the country from late 1944 to May 1945. As a result of wartime operations, including the demolition of strategic communications, industries, etc., during Britain's retreat from the country, of wartime Allied bombings, and of the destructive effects of Japanese policies, Myanmar's economy was more or less ruined by war's end in 1945. Most affected were agricultural production and public transport and some sectors of industry. There were also immense losses of human lives and property. The wartime destruction of Myanmar's economic and human resources impeded, to a large extent, the process of economic rehabilitation and development in the postwar and postindependence period.

Viewed from a political perspective, the wartime years, particularly the Japanese occupation of Myanmar (1942–1945), gave a strong impulse to the progress of the independence movement (q.v.), accelerating the process of decolonization and gaining Myanmar's independence in January 1948.

WUNGYI. Literally "great-burden" or "great-burden bearer." The king's minister or a member of the *hluttaw* (q.v.) under the precolonial state. Later used as a term to refer to a cabinet minister.

WUNTHANU. "Protector of national interest" or "patriot." A term used for a Myanmar nationalist and the nationalist movement in the early 1920s. (*See also* General Council of Burmese Associations.)

-Y-

YAN AUNG, BO (aka HLA MYAING, THAKIN) (1908–1967). One of the "Thirty Comrades" (q.v.). In 1940, he accompanied Aung San (q.v.) on a secret trip abroad to Amoy and to Japan. During the Japanese occupation of Myanmar (1942–1945) (q.v.), he served with the national army and took part in the anti-fascist resistance (q.v.). After the war, Yan Aung joined the Communist Party of Burma (CPB) (q.v.), but declined to go underground with the party in March 1948. First arrested, he was later released to negotiate with the party. He rejoined the CPB and became an elected member of its central committee. Accused of "revisionism" by party radicals inspired by the Chinese "Cultural Revolution," Yan Aung was executed in the Bago Yoma (q.v.) on 26 December 1967. (*See also* Civil War; Independence Movement.)

YAN NAING, BO (aka TUN SHEIN, KO) (1918–1989). One of the "Thirty Comrades" and son-in-law of Dr. Ba Maw (qq.v.). Active in the prewar student movement, he was Secretary General of the Rangoon University Students' Union (1938–1941) and of the All Burma Students' Union (1939–1941) (qq.v.). Yan Naing won fame as a commander of the Burma Independence Army (q.v.) fighting the British at Shwedaung in 1942. From 1943 to 1944, he was Chief of the Operations Department and, from 1944 to 1945, Commanding Officer of the Military Academy at Mingaladon. In 1946, Yan Naing joined and led the *Maha Bama* (q.v.) party. After many years in active politics, he retired in 1960. Following the military coup of 1962 (q.v.), he joined the armed opposition against General Ne Win's Revolutionary Council (qq.v.). He was the founder of the National Liberation Council. In 1969, he joined U Nu's exile-based Parliamentary Democracy Party and became one of the commanders of the Patriotic Liberation Army (qq.v.). Yan Naing returned to Myanmar in the 1980 amnesty. After the military coup of 1988, he helped U Nu (qq.v.) to build the League for Democracy and Peace. (*See also* Political Organizations.)

YANGON. The capital of Yangon Division and also the capital of the Union of Myanmar (qq.v.). With 2,513,123 inhabitants (1983), Yangon is also the biggest city of the country and its political, economic and cultural center. It is located on the

Hlaing River (q.v.), some 30 kilometers (20 miles) from the Andaman Sea.

An ancient Mon (q.v.) settlement, known as Dagon, it was rebuilt and renamed Yangon, meaning "the end of strife," by King Alaungpaya (q.v.) in 1753. From then on, Yangon developed as a sea port, particularly under the British who made it the capital of the country following their annexation of northern Myanmar in 1885. Yangon was severely damaged as result of World War II and of the Japanese occupation of Myanmar (1942–1945) (qq.v.). It became the national capital in January 1948.

Yangon has a commercial center which is surrounded by residential areas that were mainly built in British colonial days. The city center includes banks, bazaars, cinemas, stores, the Independence Monument and the National Museum. The most famous religious building is the Shwedagon Pagoda (q.v.). There are many other Buddhist pagodas and temples as well as Christian churches and other places of worship. To the northwest of the city is the campus of Yangon University (q.v.). The more centrally-located districts of Yangon are surrounded by satellite towns and sites, such as Okkalapa, Thakita and Thuwanna, all built in postindependence years. Yangon port handles more than 80 percent of Myanmar's trade. Yangon is also the transportation hub of the country. The city's industries include rice and timber processing and the manufacture of aluminum goods, cigarettes, matches, soap, pharmaceuticals, etc.

YANGON DIVISION. It has an area of 10,171 square kilometers (3,927 square miles). The Division came into being relatively recently and was formed out of Bago Division (q.v.). It occupies the eastern part of the Ayeyarwady Delta (q.v.). It is bounded on the north and east by Bago Division, on the south by the Gulf of Martaban and on the west by Ayeyarwady Division (q.v.). The Division is generally low-lying, except the southern extension of the Bago Yoma (q.v.) which reaches as far as Yangon (q.v.). The Division is watered by three main rivers which all flow into one, Hlaing River (q.v.), which enters the sea south of Yangon. The Division consists of 39 townships and 1,144 wards and village tracts. Its (1983) population was 3,965,916, mostly Bamars, but also other ethnic groups, including Chinese, Eurasians and Indians, who are concentrated in Yangon. Yangon Division is commercially and industrially the most developed of all the divisions and states of the Union of Myanmar. Aside from Yangon, there are some smaller towns, including Hmawbi, Thanlyin (q.v.) and Twante. Yangon Division is one of the major rice (q.v.) producing areas. Main crops also include groundnuts, jute (q.v.), pulses, rubber and sugarcane (qq.v.). The important industries are aluminum, glass, steel, pharmaceuticals and various artisanal (q.v.) branches. Yangon Division is the center of the country's air, railroad, road and water transport (qq.v.).

YANGON RIVER see HLAING RIVER.

YENANGYAUNG. A town in Magway Division located on the bank of the Ayeyarwady River (qq.v.). Along with nearby Chauk (q.v.), it is one of the petroleum (q.v.) industry centers in central Myanmar.

YOMA. A Myanmar term for a range of hills or mountains. (*See also* Bago Yoma; Rakhine Yoma.)

YOUNG MEN'S BUDDHIST ASSOCIATION (YMBA). An organization formed in 1906 in Yangon (q.v.) along the lines of the Young Men's Christian Association. The YMBA's founders included Ba Pe, May Oung (qq.v.), Maung Gyee and several other young people, mostly graduates of Rangoon University College (q.v.) who later gained prominence as national leaders. Initially, the YMBA was a non-political organization, composed mainly of senior government servants, barristers, teachers and traders. Their aim was to preserve traditional cultural and religious values while adopting some Western instrumentalities in order to advance Myanmar's progress as a modern nation. This was combined with an exhortation to their own countrymen for moral self-reform. Within a decade, the YMBA had become a nationwide organization. Meanwhile, more radical members emerged within its ranks and began to expand its activities.

In 1916, the YMBA's criticism of the practice of Europeans in Myanmar of wearing shoes on pagoda precincts created a nationalist issue. Under the impact of World War I (q.v.), there was an increase in Myanmar nationalistic aspirations. By 1917, politics had surfaced and subsequently changed the YMBA into a political body known as the General Council of Burmese Associations (q.v.). (*See also* Ledi Sayadaw.)

YOUTHS. Historically, youths in Myanmar played an important role in awakening the political consciousness of the people during the early British colonial period as well as in more recent stages of the independence movement (q.v.).

Today, Myanmar's youth is quite varied, including children and adolescents, students and dropouts, the unemployed and working people. Overall, youths figure prominently among Myanmar's age groupings. The age group under 15 years constituted around 37 percent of the population in 1991.

During the Burma Socialist Programme Party era (qq.v.), the BSPP attempted to channel young people's energies towards the goals of national development and socialist construction, through the Lanzin Youth Organization (q.v.) as well as through the *Luyechun* (Outstanding Student) scheme, so as to nurture suitable young people for their future role as the nation's vanguard. Despite these and other similar efforts, youths in Myanmar continue to be heavily affected by serious problems, including widespread unemployment and drug abuse (q.v.). After the military coup of 1962 (q.v.), university students in particular joined in the agitation against the ruling BSPP. They also sparked the events leading to the pro-democracy movement of 1988 (q.v.).

YULE, HENRY (1820–1889). A British engineer and Under-Secretary in the Public Works Department in India. In 1855, Yule was appointed secretary to Arthur Phayre's mission to the court of Inwa (q.v.) with the primary goal of improving official Anglo-Myanmar relations after the Second Anglo-Myanmar war. The narrative of this mission, produced by Yule in 1859, is a valuable report on contemporary Myanmar, its life, people and history. (*See also* Anglo-Myanmar War, Second.)

-Z-

ZAT. A term for a caste, kind or race. Also applied to the accounts of different existences of the Buddha. (*See also* Jataka.)

ZAU SENG. The Kachin (q.v.) rebel leader who founded the Kachin Independence Organization/Army (q.v.) in 1961. Previously, he had served with British Force 136, with the Burma Army (q.v.), and the Kayin (q.v.) resistance. He died in 1975.

ZEDI. A Myanmar term for "pagoda" or "stupa."

ZERBADEE *see* MUSLIMS.

ZEYA, BO (aka HLA MAUNG, THAKIN) (1920–1968). One of the "Thirty Comrades" (q.v.). From 1940 to 1941, he was President of the Rangoon University Students' Union (q.v.). During the Japanese occupation of Myanmar (1942–1945), he served in the Burma Independence Army and, from 1942 to 1943, he was Chief of Staff of the Burma Defence Army (qq.v.). After the war, Zeya served in the Burma Army (q.v.). He joined the army mutineers and set up the Revolutionary Burma Army (q.v.). In 1950, he became Vice-Chairman of the People's Army. He went to China in 1953. In 1963, he returned to Myanmar to attend peace talks with the Revolutionary Council (q.v.). Zeya then served as a military commander of the forces of the Communist Party of Burma (q.v.). He was killed in action near the Bago Yoma (q.v.) in April 1968.

ZIN, THAKIN (1912–1975). Chairman of the Communist Party of Burma after the death of Thakin Than Tun (qq.v.), in October 1968. He held this post until March 1975, when he was killed in action by government troops in the Bago Yoma (q.v.).

ZINC. Zinc is mined and produced mainly at the Bawdwin-Namtu mines in Shan State (qq.v.). In 1989, the ruling State Law and Order Restoration Council (q.v.) signed an agreement with a Thai tin smelter company for the exploration and production of zinc. In 1991, about 4,500 tons of zinc concentrate were produced. (*See also* Minerals.)

ZOMI NATIONAL FRONT (ZNF). A Chin (q.v.) rebel organization. It was set up in 1965 and was affiliated with the United Nationalities Front, a broader ethnic rebel alliance which existed between 1965 and 1966.

THE BIBLIOGRAPHY

INTRODUCTION

I. GENERAL

1. Bibliographies and Research Guides

2. Directories, Handbooks, Statistical Abstracts and Yearbooks

3. Guides

4. Interdisciplinary and General Studies

5. Travel and Description

II. CULTURE

1. General Works

2. Archaeology and Prehistory

3. Architecture

4. Arts

5. Languages and Linguistics

6. Literature

7. Publishing and Mass Media

III. ECONOMY

1. General Works and Economic History

2. Agriculture, Fisheries and Forestry

3. Development and Planning

4. Finance, Credit and Banking

5. Foreign Aid, Trade and Investment

6. Industry and Mining

7. Labor

8. Transport and Communications

IV. HISTORY

1. General

2. Pre-1824

3. Colonial (1824–1948)

4. World War II and the Japanese Occupation (1941–1945)

5. Post-Independence (1948–)

V. LAW AND CONSTITUTION

VI. POLITICS

1. Domestic

2. Foreign Relations

VII. SCIENCE

1. Botany

2. Climate

3. Geography and Geology

4. Zoology

VIII. SOCIETY

1. Anthropology and Ethnology

2. Demography

3. Education

4. Health

5. Urbanization

6. Religion

7. Sociology

INTRODUCTION

Myanmar is a relatively under-researched country, particularly after 1962, when it became virtually closed to foreign scholarship. Despite this negative research environment, which is reflected in the paucity of modern studies of Myanmar anthropology, economy and science, studies in other fields, such as historiography, political science, and linguistics, have continued in various countries of the world. M. P. Herbert, *Burma*, is the most recent and annotated guide to English-language publications about Myanmar. Another useful book is *Burma: A Study Guide* by the Asia Program of the Woodrow Wilson International Center for Scholars which also contains a survey of Myanmar studies worldwide.

Good coverage of events in Myanmar is found in the *Far Eastern Economic Review*. Articles, book reviews and other materials relating to Myanmar also appear in *Contemporary Southeast Asia, Journal of Asian Studies* (which publishes an annual bibliography of Asian Studies) and *Journal of Southeast Asian Studies*. Annual surveys of political and economic events are available in *Asian Survey, Asia Yearbook, The Far East and Australasia* and *Southeast Asian Affairs*.

Standard general works on Myanmar history by Western scholars are J. F. Cady, *A History of Modern Burma*, D. G. E. Hall, *Burma*, G. E. Harvey, *Outline of Burmese History*, F. N. Trager, *Burma from Kingdom to Republic*, and D. Woodman, *The Making of Burma*. Of works in English by Myanmar scholars, Htin Aung, *A History of Burma* and *The Stricken Peacock* are most relevant.

The classic works of the Bagan period are G. H. Luce, *Old Burma-Early Pagan*, and Michael Aung-Thwin, *Pagan: The Origins of Modern Burma*. Michael Aung-Thwin has also contributed on various aspects of kingship and society in traditional Myanmar. More recent periods of Myanmar's precolonial history are covered in V. B. Lieberman, *Burmese Administrative Cycles* and his essays relating mostly to the Toungoo Dynasty era, and W. J. Koenig, *The Burmese Polity, 1752–1819*. Refer also to Mya Sein, *The Administration of Burma*. Relevant also are editions of Myanmar-language source materials relating to precolonial Myanmar, translated into English, such as *The Royal Orders of Burma*, compiled by Than Tun, and *Burmese Sit-Tans* by F. N. Trager et al.

The British colonial era (1824–1948) is well covered in a number of works including memoirs and various accounts of participants. Among Western scholarly studies of the colonial era, mention should be made of J. S. Furnivall, *The Fashioning of Leviathan*, E. G. Harvey, *British Rule in Burma 1824–1924*, and more recently O. B. Pollak, *Empires in Collision*. Of importance are studies of the independence movement in Myanmar during the British colonial era by Western and Myanmar scholars which include Khin Yi, *The Dobama Movement in Burma (1930–1938)*, (Brigadier) Maung Maung, *Burmese Nationalist Movements* and *From Sangha to Laity*, (Dr.) Maung Maung, *Aung San of Burma* and *A Trial in Burma*, A. D. Moscotti, *British Policy and the Nationalist Movement in Burma*, and Ni Ni Myint, *Burma's Struggle Against British Imperialism*.

The period of World War II and the Japanese occupation of Myanmar (1941–1945) is recorded in a vast number of accounts of participants in war events, mainly British and American as well as some Japanese and Myanmar. Among scholarly works dealing with various aspects of the military campaigns, administration, etc., refer namely to L. Allen, *Sittang: The Last Battle* and *Burma: The Longest War 1941–1945*, F. S. V. Donnison, *British Military Administration in the Far East*, and J. L. Christian, *Burma and the Japanese Invader*. The problems of the political impact of the wartime period, including the anti-fascist resistance, are treated in J. Bečka, *The National Liberation Movement in Burma during the Japanese Occupation Period*, D. H. Guyot, *The Political Impact of the Japanese Occupation of Burma*, R. H. Taylor, *Marxism and Resistance in Burma 1942–1945*, and Won Zoon Yoon, *Japan's Scheme for the Liberation of Burma*. Ba Maw's *Breakthrough in Burma* and Nu's *Burma Under the Japanese* are both important in providing a Myanmar perspective of wartime events. For a relevant account of British policies in the wartime (and postwar) years refer to *Burma: The Struggle for Independence, 1944–1948*, edited by H. Tinker.

R. H. Taylor, *The State in Burma*, is a recent major work by a Western political scientist which presents Myanmar's political development in a historical perspective. Examining both legal and political aspects of post-war Myanmar are two works by Dr. Maung Maung, *Burma's Constitution* and *Burma in the Family of Nations*. Equally important for learning about modern Myanmar's political development is Dr. Maung Maung's book *Burma and General Ne Win*. R. Butwell, *U Nu of Burma*, also gives an account of a parliamentary era in Myanmar. The interaction of religion and politics in postindependence Myanmar is treated in D. E. Smith, *Religion and Politics in Burma*, and E. Sarkisyanz, *Buddhist Backgrounds of the Burmese Revolution*. The political evolution of Myanmar after 1962 is well covered in J. Silverstein, *Burma: Military Rule and the Politics of Stagnation*, and essays and studies by R. H. Taylor. Refer also to D. I. Steinberg, *The Future of Burma*. The civil war, insurgencies and events of the prodemocracy movement of 1988 are studied in a number of books and articles. See especially B. Lintner, *Land of Jade*, *Outrage: Burma's Struggle for Democracy*, and *The Rise and Fall of the Communist Party of Burma*, and M. Smith, *Burma: Insurgency and the Politics of Ethnicity.* Foreign relations are analyzed in W. C. Johnstone, *Burma's Foreign Policy: A Study in Neutralism,* although this is somewhat dated. A more recent account is Chi Shad Liang, *Burma's Foreign Relations.* See also Daw Than Han, *Common Vision: Burma's Regional Outlook.*

There is a number of recent studies on Myanmar economic history. Aside from books depicting the history of British economic enterprises and firms in colonial Myanmar, the following works are especially helpful: M. Adas, *The Burma Delta,* Aung Tun Thet, *Burmese Entrepreneurship,* and Hwa Siok Cheng, *The Rice Industry of Burma.* There is no comprehensive up-to-date survey of the Myanmar economy. Agriculture has received more attention. Refer especially to essays and articles by Mya Than. He is also the author of *Myanmar's External Trade* published recently. Also relevant is Mya Than and J. L. H. Tan, eds., *Myanmar Dilemmas and Options.*

Comprehensive studies on Myanmar art are virtually non-existent, but there are several important works on some aspects of the arts. There are two publications devoted to Bagan architecture, P. Pichard, *The Pentagonal Monuments of Pagan,* and an older book, P. Strachan, *Pagan: Art and Architecture of Old Burma.* H. L. Tilly compiled several monographs on various artisanal industries in Myanmar which were mostly published at the beginning of the 20th century. Recently, this topic was treated in articles and studies by S. Fraser-Lu, who is also the author of *Burmese Lacquerware.* Htin Aung, *Burmese Drama,* and J. R. Brandon, *Theater in Southeast Asia,* are important for an understanding of Myanmar dramatic art. On Myanmar music, see Khin Zaw, *Burmese Music: A Preliminary Enquiry.*

There exists no comprehensive account of the history of Myanmar literature in the English language. References to various aspects of Myanmar literature can be found in articles by A. Allott and also in Hla Pe, *Burma: Literature, Historiography, Scholarship, Language, Life and Buddhism.* The works of two Myanmar writers were recently published in English translation, Ludu U Hla, *The Caged Ones,* and Ma Ma Lay, *Not Out of Hate.* There are several published volumes of Myanmar folk tales. Refer namely to Htin Aung.

Myanmar is a country inhabited by numerous and varied ethnic groups. General information on them can be obtained in

P. Kunstadter, ed., *Southeast Asian Tribes, Minorities and Nations*, and F. M. Le Bar et al., *Ethnic Groups of Mainland Southeast Asia*. There are several books reporting on various aspects of life and customs of specific ethnic communities, but most of them were compiled by Christian missionaries during the British colonial era and are dated now. Among recent scholarly works, two specific studies are important, E. R. Leach, *Political Systems of Highland Burma: A Study of Kachin Social Structure*, and F. K. Lehman, *The Structure of Chin Society*. Also relevant is the recent publication by M. Spiro, *Anthropological Other or Burmese Brother?*

Studies of religion in Myanmar relate mainly to Buddhism. Standard works on Buddhism in Myanmar are E. M. Mendelsohn, *Sangha and State in Burma*, M. E. Spiro, *Buddhism and Society*. M. E. Spiro, *Burmese Supernaturalism*, and Htin Aung, *Folk Elements in Burmese Buddhism*, are also significant. There are many works relating to Christianity in Myanmar, often focusing on the life and activities of Christian missionaries in the country. For an account of missionaries in Myanmar see H. F. Trager, *Burma Through Alien Eyes*. Refer also to Moshe Yegar, *The Muslims of Burma: A Study of a Minority Group*, which analyzes the history of Islam and the Muslim community in Myanmar.

I. General

1. Bibliographies and Research Guides

Aung-Thwin, Michael. *Southeast Asian Research Tools: Burma.* Honolulu: Southeast Asian Studies, Southeast Asian Studies Program, University of Hawaii, 1979. (Southeast Asia Paper, No. 16, Part 3).

Bernot, Denise. *Bibliographie birmane: années 1950–1960.* Paris: Editions du Centre National de la Recherche Scientifique, 1960. (Atlas Ethno-Linguistique: Recherche Coopérative sur Programme 61, Troisième Série Bibliographies).

Bernot, Denise et al. *Bibliographie birmane: années 1960–1970.*

Paris: Editions du Centre National de la Recherche Scientifique, 1982–83. 2 vols.

Berton, P. and A. Z. Rubinstein. *Soviet Works on Southeast Asia. A Bibliography of Non-Periodical Literature, 1946–1965.* Los Angeles, California: University of Southern California, Far Eastern and Russian Research Series No. 3, 1967.

Burma. A Selective Guide to Scholarly Resources. Edited by Anita Hibler and William P. Tuchrello. Washington, D.C.: Woodrow Wilson International Center for Scholars, Asia Program, 1986.

Burma: A Study Guide. Washington, D.C.: Woodrow Wilson International Center for Scholars, Asia Program, 1987.

Burma Research Group, ed. *Burmese Studies in Japan, 1868–1985. Literary Guide and Bibliography.* Tokyo: Burma Research Group, Tokyo University of Foreign Studies, 1985.

Herbert, Patricia M., comp. *Burma.* Santa Barbara, California: Clio, 1991. (The World Bibliographical Series, Volume 132).

———. "Burma" in *South Asian Bibliography: A Handbook and Guide.* Compiled by the South East Asia Library Group, General Editor J. D. Pearson. Hassocks, England: Harvester; Atlantic Highlands, New Jersey: Humanities, 1979, pp. 328–51.

Herbert, Patricia M. and Anthony C. Milner, eds. *South-East Asia Languages and Literatures*: *A Select Guide.* Whiting Bay, Scotland: Kiscadale, 1988; Honolulu: University of Hawaii Press, 1989.

Quigly, E. Pauline. *Some Observations on Libraries, Manuscripts and Books of Burma from the 3rd Century AD to 1886.* London: Arthur Probsthain, 1956.

Shulman, Frank Joseph. *Burma: An Annotated Bibliographical*

Guide to International Doctoral Dissertation Research on Burma 1898–1985. Lanham, Maryland; New York; London: University Press of America, in Association with the Wilson Center, 1986.

Trager, Frank N. *Burma. A Selected and Annotated Bibliography*. With the Assistance of Janelle Wang, Dorothea Schoenfeldt, Ann Riotto, Mary Parker, Aung San Suu Kyi; and Robert Bordonaro and Frank Simonie. New Haven, Connecticut: Human Relations Area Files, 1973. (Behavior Science Bibliographies).

Trager, Frank N. et al. *Burma: Japanese Military Administration, Selected Documents, 1941–1945*. Edited with Introduction by Frank N. Trager. Translated by Won Zoo Yoon. Assisted by Thomas T. Winant. Philadelphia: University of Pennsylvania Press, 1971.

Trager, Frank N., comp., ed. *Furnivall of Burma: An Annotated Bibliography of the Works of John S. Furnivall*. New Haven, Connecticut: Yale University Southeast Asia Studies in Cooperation with University of British Columbia, Department of Asian Studies, 1963. (Bibliography Series, No. 8).

Trager, Frank N., ed. *Japanese and Chinese Language Source on Burma: An Annotated Bibliography*. New Haven, Connecticut: Human Relations Area Files, 1957.

Whitbread, Kenneth J. *Catalogue of Burmese Printed Books in the India Office Library*. London: H. M. Stationery Office, 1969.

2. Directories, Handbooks, Statistical Abstracts and Yearbooks

Asia Yearbook. Hong Kong: Review Publishing, 1960– , annual.

Facts About Burma, A Handbook. Yangon: 1982.

The Far East and Australasia. London: Europa Publications, 1969– , annual.

Henderson, John W. et al. *Area Handbook for Burma.* Washington, D.C.: U.S. Government Printing Office, 1971.

Socialist Republic of the Union of Burma. *Burma: 1983 Population Census.* Yangon: Ministry of Home Affairs, 1986.

Southeast Asian Affairs. Singapore: Institute of Southeast Asian Affairs, 1974– , annual.

Statistical Yearbook for Asia and the Pacific/Annuaire Statistique pour l'Asie et le Pacifique. Bangkok: United Nations Economic and Social Commission for Asia and the Pacific (ESCAP), 1966– , annual.

The Union of Myanmar. *Review of the Financial, Economic and Social Conditions for 1991/92.* (Yangon): Ministry of Planning and Finance, 1991.

Who's Who in Burma. Yangon: People's Literature Committee and House, 1961.

3. Guides

Courtauld, Caroline. *Collins Illustrated Guide to Burma.* London: Collins, 1988. (Asian Guide Series).

Department of History, University of Yangon, Myanmar. *Glimpses of Glorious Pagan.* Yangon: The Universities Press, 1986.

Esche, Annemarie. *Die goldene Pagoda: Shwedagon-ein Sinnbild des Buddhismus.* Hanau, Germany: Muller and Kiepenheuer, 1985.

Hla Myint, U. *Tourguide Map of Famous Pagodas and Important Places of Pagan/Nyaung-U Area.* Yangon: Syriam Literature House, 1984.

Hoskin, John. *Burma.* Singapore: Times Editions, 1987.

Klein, Wilhelm. *Burma.* Directed and Designed by Hans Johannes

Hoefer. Edited by John Anderson. 7th ed, London: Apa Productions (HK), 1988. (Insight Guide Series).

Morse, Stephen A. *Burma. A Briefing Book*. Bloomington, Indiana: The Author, 1990.

Myat Yin, Saw. *Burma*. Singapore: Times Books International, 1990.

Tin Yee, Ma. *The Golden Shwedagon*. Yangon: Daw Khin Htwe Yee, 1984.

Wheeler, Tony. *Burma: A Travel Survival Kit*. 5th ed. South Yarra, Australia: Lonely Planet, 1985.

4. Interdisciplinary and General Studies

Ba Shin, Jean Boisselier and Alexander B. Griswold, eds. *Essays Offered to G. H. Luce by His Colleagues and Friends in Honour of His Seventy-Fifth Birthday*. Ascona, Switzerland: Artibus Asiae, 1966. 2 vols.

Bunge, M., ed. *Burma: A Country Study*. Prepared by Foreign Area Studies, The American University. 3rd ed. Washington, D.C.: U.S. Government Printing Office, 1983.

Donnison, Frank S. V. *Burma*. London: Ernest Benn, 1970; New York: Praeger, 1970.

Fergusson, John P., ed. *Essays on Burma*. Leiden, The Netherlands: E. J. Brill, 1981.

Hall, Fielding H. *The Soul of a People*. London: Macmillan, 1898.

Khin Myo Chit. *Colourful Burma*. Yangon: Yangon University Press, 1988.

Landry, Lionel. *The Land and the People of Burma*. Philadelphia: J. B. Lippincott, 1968.

Maring, Joel M. and Ester G. Maring. *Historical and Cultural Dictionary of Burma*. Metuchen, New Jersey: Scarecrow Press, 1973. (Historical and Cultural Dictionaries of Asia, No. 4).

Mi Mi Khaing. *Burmese Family*. Bombay, India; Calcutta, India: Longmans Green, 1946.

———. *The World of Burmese Women*. London: Zed, 1984; Singapore: Times Books International, 1986.

Sangermano, Father Vincentius. *A Description of the Burmese Empire, Compiled Chiefly from Burmese Documents*. Translated from the Italian and Latin by William Tandy, with a Preface and Note by John Jardine. London: Susil Gupta, 1966.

Scott, James G. (Shway Yoe). *The Burman, His Life and Notions*. London: Macmillan, 1883; Norton, 1963.

Steinberg, David I. *Burma: A Socialist Nation of Southeast Asia*. Boulder, Colorado: Westview, 1982.

Trager, Helen G., ed. *We the Burmese: Voices from Burma*. New York: Frederick A. Praeger, 1969.

White, Arthur John Stanley. *The Burma of "AJ": Memoirs of AJS White*. London: British Association for Cemeteries in South Asia, 1991.

5. Travel and Description

Abbott, Gerry. *Back to Mandalay: An Inside View of Burma*. Bromley, Kent: Impact Books, 1990. (Travellers' Tales).

Aung San Suu Kyi. *Let's Visit Burma*. London: Burke, 1985.

Barber, Cecil Thomas. *A Geologist in the Service of the Raj*. Henfield, England: The Author, 1978.

Bixler, Norma. *Burma. A Profile.* New York: Praeger Publishers, 1971; London: Pall Mall Press, 1971.

Boucaud, Andre. *Birmanie: sur la piste des seigneurs de la guerre.* Paris: L'Harmattan, 1985.

Boudignon, Francoise. *A Letter from Burma.* Yangon: UNICEF, 1984.

Collis, Maurice. *The Land of the Great Image: Being Experiences of Friar Manrique in Arakan.* London: Faber and Faber, 1953.

———. *Lords of the Sunset: A Tour in the Shan States.* London: Faber and Faber, 1938.

Damrong, Rajanubhab. *Journey Through Burma in 1936. A View of Culture, History and Institutions.* By H. R. H. Prince Damrong Rajanubhab. Bangkok: River Books, 1991.

Enriquez, Colin Metcalf Dallas. *A Burmese Wonderland: A Tale of Travel in Burma, the Southern Shan States and Keng Tung.* Calcutta, India: Thacker, Spink, 1922.

———. *A Burmese Wonderland: A Tale of Travel in Lower and Upper Burma.* Calcutta, India: Thacker, Spink, 1922.

Ferrars, Max and Bertha Ferrars. *Burma.* London: Sampson, Low, Marston, 1901.

Hunt, Gordon. *The Forgotten Land.* London: Geoffrey Bles, 1967.

Jones, Charles Braimer. *Not Forgetting the Elephants.* Lewes, England: The Book Guild, 1983.

Kelly, Robert Talbot. *Burma Painted and Described.* London: Charles Black, 1905.

Khin Myo Chit, Daw. *Flowers and Festivals Round the Burmese Year.* With Nature Poems by Po Thudaw U Min. Translated by Maung Tha Noe. Yangon: Theikdi Sarzin, 1980.

———. *A Wonderland of Burmese Legends*. Bangkok: Tamarind, 1989.

Lawson, A. A. *Life in the Burmese Jungle*. Lewes, England: The Book Guild, 1983.

O'Brien, Harriet. *Burma Through the Wastelands*. London: M. Joseph, 1991.

———. *Forgotten Land: A Rediscovery of Burma*. London: M. Joseph, 1991.

O'Connor, Vincent Clarence Scott. *The Silken East: A Record of Life and Travel in Burma*. London: Hutchinson, 1904. 2 vols. Bangkok: White Lotus, 1993. 1 vol.

Trager, Frank N. and Helen G. Trager. *Burma: Land of Golden Pagodas*. New York: Foreign Policy Association, 1954.

Wheeler, J. Talboys. *Journal of a Voyage up the Irrawaddy to Mandalay and Bhamo*. Yangon: J. W. Baynes; London: Trubner, 1871.

II. Culture

1. General

The Burma Research Group, ed. *Burma and Japan: Basic Studies on Their Cultural and Social Structure*. Tokyo: The Burma Research Group, Tokyo University of Foreign Studies, 1987.

Khin Zaw. *Burmese Culture: General and Particular*. Yangon: Sarpay Beikman, 1981.

Murari, Krishna. *Cultural Heritage of Burma*. New Delhi: Inter-India Publications, 1985.

Soni, R. L. *A Cultural Study of the Burmese Era*. Mandalay: World Institute of Buddhist Culture, 1955.

2. Archaeology and Prehistory

Aung Thaw, U. *Historical Sites in Burma*. Yangon: Ministry of Union Culture, Government of the Union of Burma, 1972.

——. *Report of the Excavations at Beikthano*. Yangon: Ministry of Union Culture, Government of the Union of Burma, 1968.

——. "The 'Neolithic' Culture of Padahlin Caves," *Journal of the Burma Research Society*, vol. 52, pt. 1 (June 1969), pp. 9–23.

Aung-Thwin, Michael. "Burma Before Pagan: The Status of Archaeology Today," *Asian Perspectives,* vol. 35, no. 2 (1982–83), pp. 1–21.

Ba Shin, U. *The Lokahteikpan*. Yangon: Burma Historical Commission, Ministry of Union Culture, Revolutionary Government of the Union of Burma, 1962.

Luce, Gordon H. *Phases of Pre-Pagan Burma: Language and History*. Oxford: Oxford University Press, 1985. 2 vols.

——. "The Ancient Pyu," *Journal of the Burma Research Society*, vol. 27, pt. 3 (December 1937), pp. 239–53. Reprinted, Yangon: Burma Research Society, *Fiftieth Anniversary Publications*, no. 2 (1961), pp. 307–21.

——. "A Century of Progress in Burmese History and Archeology," *Journal of the Burma Research Society*, vol. 32, pt. 1 (June 1949), pp. 79–94.

——. "Dvaravati and Old Burma," *Journal of the Siam Society*, vol. 53 (1965), pp. 10–26.

——. "The Early Syám in Burma's History," *Journal of the Siam Society*, vol. 46, pt. 1 (August 1958), pp. 123–214; vol. 47, pt. 1 (June 1959), pp. 59–101.

———. "Old Kyaukse and the Coming of the Burman," *Journal of the Burma Research Society*, vol. 42, pt. 1 (June 1959), pp. 59–101.

Myint Aung. "The Capital of Suvannabhumi Unearthed?," *Shiroku*, vol. 10 (1977), pp. 41–53.

———. "The Excavations at Halin," *Journal of the Burma Research Society*, vol. 53, pt. 2 (1970), pp. 53–63.

Saimong Mangrai. "Did Son and Uttara Come to Lower Burma?," *Journal of the Burma Research Society*, vol. 59, pts. 1–2 (1976), pp. 155–66.

Stargardt, Janice. *The Ancient Pyu of Burma: Vol. 1. Early Pyu Cities in a Man-Made Landscape*. Cambridge, England: Publications on Ancient Civilizations in Southeast Asia (PSCSEA) in association with the Institute of Southeast Asian Studies, Singapore, 1990.

Terra, Helmut de and Hallam L. Movius. "Research on Early Man in Burma." With Supplementary Reports by Edwin H. Colbert and J. Bequaert, *Transactions of the American Philosophical Society*, New Series, vol. 32, pt. 3 (1943), pp. 267–464.

Tha Hla and Nyi Nyi. "Report on the Field Work at Hmawza (Sri-Ksetra) and Prome," *Journal of the Burma Research Society*, vol. 61, pts. 1–2 (1958), pp. 83–99.

Thin Kyi. "Arakanese Capitals: A Preliminary Survey of Their Geographical Setting," *Journal of the Burma Research Society*, vol. 53, pt. 2 (1970), pp. 1–13.

Tinker, Hugh. "The Place of Gordon Luce in Research and Education in Burma During the Last Decades of British Rule," *Journal of the Royal Asiatic Society*, no. 2 (1986), pp. 147–60.

3. Architecture

Franz, Heinrich Gerhard. *Von Gandhara bis Pagan: Kultbauten des Buddhismus u. Hinduismus in Sud und Zentralasien.* Graz, Austria: Akadem. Druck und Verlagsanst, 1979.

Pichard, Pierre. *Inventory of Monuments at Pagan.* Gartmore, Stirlingshire, Scotland: Kiscadale Publications, 1992–1993. 1–2 vols.

———. *The Pentagonal Monuments of Pagan.* Bangkok: White Lotus, 1991.

Soni, Sujata. *Evolution of Stupas in Burma, Pagan Period: 11th to 13th Centuries A.D.* New Delhi: 1991.

Stadtner, Donald M. "A Fifteenth Century Royal Monument in Burma and the Seven Stations in Buddhist Art," *Art Bulletin*, vol. 63, pt. 1 (March 1991), pp. 39–52.

Strachan, Paul. *Pagan: Art and Architecture of Old Burma.* Whiting Bay, Arran, Scotland: Kiscadale Publications, 1989. [Also Published by University of Hawaii Press under the title of *Imperial Pagan: Art and Architecture of Old Burma.*]

Traditional Burmese Architecture, Pagan Period. Yangon: Department of Higher Education, Ministry of Education, 1986.

4. Arts

Bailey, Jane Terry. "Some Burmese Paintings of the Seventeenth Century and Later," *Artibus Asiae*, vol. 38, pt. 4 (1976), pp. 267–86; vol. 40, pt. 1 (1978), pp. 41–61; vol. 41, pt. 1 (1979), pp. 41–63.

Bell, E. N. *A Monograph on Iron and Steel Work in Burma.* Yangon: Government Printing, 1907.

Brandon, James R. *Theater in Southeast Asia*. Cambridge, Massachusetts: Harvard University Press, 1967.

Bruns, Azel and Hla Thamein. *Birmanisches Marionettentheater*. Berlin: Firma Mandalay, 1990.

Burmese Art and Its Influence. London: Beurdeley Matthews, 1981.

Fraser-Lu, Sylvia. *Burmese Lacquerware*. Bangkok: Tamarind, 1986.

———. *Handwoven Textiles of South-East Asia*. Singapore: Oxford University Press, 1988.

———. "Buddha Images from Burma," *Arts of Asia*, vol. 11, nos. 1–3 (January-February; March-April; May-June 1981), pp. 72–82; pp. 62–72; pp. 129–136.

———. "Burmese Silverware," *Arts of Asia*, vol. 10, no. 2 (March-April 1980), pp. 77–83.

———. "Sadaik: Burmese Manuscript Chests," *Arts of Asia*, vol. 14, no. 3 (May-June 1984), pp. 215–254.

Frédéric, Louis. *The Temples and Sculptures of Southeast Asia*. Foreword by Jeannine Auboyer. Translated from the French by Arnold Rosin. London: Thames and Hudson, 1965.

Gear, Donald and Joan Gear. *Earth to Heaven: The Royal Animal-Shaped Weights of the Burmese Empires*. Harrow, England: Twinstar, 1992.

Herbert, Patricia. *The Art of the Painted Books in Burma*. Edinburgh: Kiscadale Publications, 1991.

Karrow, Otto. *Burmese Buddhist Sculpture*. The Johan *Möger Collection*. Bangkok: White Lotus, 1991.

Khin Zaw. *Burmese Music: A Preliminary Enquiry.* Yangon: Burma Research Society, 1941.

Laypway, Tetkatho. "Seven Decades of Burmese Film," *The Guardian* (Yangon) vol. 34, no. 12 (December 1987), pp. 10–15.

Lowry, John. *Burmese Art.* London: H. M. Stationery Office, 1974.

Luce, Gordon H. "The 550 Jatakas in Old Burma," *Artibus Asiae*, vol. 19, pts. 3–4 (1956), pp. 291–307.

Ono, Toru. *Pagan: Mural Paintings of the Buddhist Temples in Burma.* Tokyo: Kodansha, 1978.

Oshegowa, Nine and Sergej Oshegow. *Kunst in Burma: 2000 Jahre Architektur, Malerei und Plastik im Zeichen des Buddhismus und Animismus.* Translated from the Russian (*Iskusstvo Birmy*) by Christian Heidemann. Leipzig: VEB E. A. Seemann, 1988.

Pratt, H. S. *Monograph on Ivory Carving in Burma.* Yangon: Superintendent, Government Printing, 1901.

Prunner, Gernot. *Meisterwerke Burmanische Lackkunst.* Hamburg: Hamburgisches Museum für Völkerkunde und Vorgeschichte in Selbstverlag, 1966.

Sein, Kenneth and J. A. Withey. *The Great Po Sein: A Chronicle of the Burmese Theater.* Bloomington, Indiana; London: Indiana University Press, 1965.

Singer, Noel F. *Burmese Puppets.* Gartmore, Stirlingshire, Scotland: Kiscadale Publications, 1993.

———. "The Ramayana at the Burmese Court," *Arts of Asia*, vol. 19, no. 6 (November-December 1989), pp. 90–103.

Taw Sein Ko. *Monograph on the Pottery and Glassware of Burma, 1894–95.* Yangon: Government Printing, 1895.

Thein Han and Kin Zaw. "Ramayana in Burmese Literature and Arts," *Journal of the Burma Research Society*, vol. 59, pts. 1–2 (December 1976), pp. 137–154.

Tilly, Harry L. *Glass Mosaics of Burma*. Yangon: Superintendent, Government Printing, 1901.

———. *Modern Burmese Silverwork*. Yangon: Superintendent, Government Printing, 1904.

———. *Monograph on the Brass and Copper Wares of Burma*. Yangon: Superintendent, Government Printing, 1894.

———. *The Silverwork of Burma*. Yangon: Superintendent, Government Printing, 1902.

———. *Wood-Carving of Burma*. Yangon: Superintendent, Government Printing, 1903.

Wenk, Klaus. *Murals in Burma: Volume 1, Paintings from Pagan of the Late Period, 18th Century*. With a Contribution by Tin Lwin. Zurich: Verlag Inigo von Oppersdorff, 1977.

5. Languages and Linguistics

Allott, Anna J. "Language Policy and Planning in Burma," in *Papers in South-East Asian Linguistics No. 9: Language Policy, Language Planning and Sociolinguistics in South-East Asia*. Edited by David Bradley. Canberra: Department of Linguistics, Research School of Pacific Studies, Australian National University, 1985, pp. 131–54.

Armstrong, Lilias E. and Pe Maung Tin. *A Burmese Phonetic Reader*. London: University of London Press, 1925; Yangon: University of Yangon, 1960.

Ba Han. *The University English-Burmese Dictionary*. Yangon: Hanthawaddy, 1966. 2 vols.

Bernot, Denise. *Le prédicat en birman parlé*. Paris: Langues et civilisations de l'Asie du Sud-est et le Monde Insulindien, 1980.

Bernot, Denise et al. *Dictionnaire birman-français*. Paris: Centre de Documentation sur l'Asie du Sud-est et le Monde Insulindien, 1978– . 14 vols.

Bernot, Denise, Marie-Helene Cardinaud, and Marie Yin Yin Myint. *Manuel de birman: langue de Myanmar*. Paris: L'Asiathèque, 1990 (Langues de l'Asie-INALCO). Vol. 1.

Bradley, David. *Burmese Phrasebook*. South Yarra, Australia: Lonely Planet, 1988. (Language Survival Kits).

Bridges, James E. *Burmese Grammar*. Yangon: British Burma Press, 1915.

Brown, R. Grant. *Half the Battle in Burmese: A Manual of the Spoken Language*. London: Oxford University Press, 1910.

Burling, Robbins. *Proto Lolo-Burmese*. Bloomington, Indiana: Indiana University, 1967.

A Burmese-English Dictionary. Compiled under the Direction of the late J. A. Stewart and C. W. Dunn from Material Supplied by a Large Number of Contributors. London: School of Oriental and African Studies, 1981.

Cornyn, William S. *Outline of Burmese Grammar*. Baltimore: Linguistic Society of America, 1944.

———. *Spoken Burmese: Basic Course*. United States Armed Forces Institute, 1946; New York: Spoken Language Services, 1979.

Cornyn, William S. and John K. Musgrave, comp. *Burmese Glossary*. Washington, D.C.: American Council of Learned Societies, 1958.

Cornyn, William S. and D. Haigh Roop. *Beginning Burmese*. New Haven, Connecticut; London: Yale University Press, 1968. (Yale Linguistic Series).

Cushing, Josiah Nelson. *Elementary Handbook of the Shan Language*. Rev. 2d ed. Yangon: American Baptist Mission Press, 1906; Farnborough, England: Gregg International, 1971.

——. *Grammar of the Shan Language*. 2d ed. Yangon: American Baptist Mission Press, 1887.

——. *A Shan and English Dictionary*. 2d ed. (Reprint). Yangon: American Baptist Mission Press, 1914; Farnborough, England: Gregg International, 1971.

Esche, Annemarie. *Wörterbuch Burmesisch-Deutsch*. Leipzig: Verlag Enzyklopädie, 1976.

Esche, Annemarie and Eberhardt Richter. *Burmesisches Übungsbuch*. Leipzig: Verlag Enzyklopädie, 1988.

Gilmore, David. *A Grammar of the Sgaw Karen*. Yangon: American Baptist Mission Press, F. D. Phinney, 1898.

Grierson, George Abraham, ed. *Linguistic Survey of India*. Calcutta, India: Superintendent, Government Printing, 1903–28. 13 vols.

Hale, Austin. *Research on Tibeto-Burman Languages*. Berlin: Mouton, 1982. (Trends in Linguistics, State of the Art Reports, 14).

Halliday, Robert. *A Mon-English Dictionary*. Bangkok: Siam Society, 1922; Yangon: Mon Cultural Section, Ministry of Union Culture, Government of the Union of Burma, 1955.

Hanson, Ola. *A Dictionary of the Kachin Language*. Yangon: American Baptist Mission Press, 1906; Yangon: Baptist Board of Publications, 1966.

———. *A Grammar of the Kachin Language.* Yangon. American Baptist Mission Press, 1896.

———. *A Handbook of the Kachin or Jinghpaw Language: Including Grammar, Phrase-Book, English Kachin and Kachin-English Vocabularies.* Yangon: American Baptist Mission Press, 1917.

Henderson, Eugénie. *Tiddim Chin: A Descriptive Analysis of Two Texts.* London: Oxford University Press, 1965.

Hertz, Henry Felix. *A Practical Handbook of the Kachin or Chingpaw Language: Containing the Grammatical Principles and Pecularities of the Language, Colloquial Exercises and a Vocabulary, with an Appendix on Kachin Customs, Laws and Religion.* Yangon: Government Printing and Stationery, 1935.

Jones, Robert B., Jr. *Karen Linguistic Studies: Description, Comparison and Texts.* Berkeley: University of California Press, 1985.

Jones, Robert B. and Khin. *The Burmese Writing System.* Washington, D.C.: American Council of Learned Societies, 1953.

Judson, Adoniram. *A Grammar of the Burmese Language.* Rev. ed. Yangon: Baptist Board of Publications, 1951.

———. *Judson's Burmese-English Dictionary.* Revised and Enlarged by Robert C. Stevenson and F. H. Eveleth. Yangon: Baptist Board of Publications, 1986.

———. *Judson's English and Burmese Dictionary.* Revised and Enlarged by E. O. Stevens, Francis Mason, and F. H. Eveleth. 10th ed. Yangon: Baptist Board of Publications, 1966.

Khin, U. *Spoken Burmese.* Washington, D.C.: Department of State Foreign Service Institute, 1976.

Khin, U and Glen San Lwin. *Burmese-English Dictionary*. Washington, D.C.: Office of Training, National Security Agency, 1956.

Luce, Gordon H. *A Comparative Word-List of Old Burmese, Chinese and Tibetan*. (With an Introduction by Eugénie J. A. Henderson and References and Sources by Tin Htway). London: School of Oriental and African Studies, University of London, 1981.

Manam Hpang. *English-Kachin-Burmese Dictionary*. [Burma, n.p.], 1977.

Maran La Raw. *Burmese and Jinghpo. A Study of Tonal Linguistic Processes*. Urbana: Center for Asian Studies, University of Illinois, 1971.

Matisoff, James A. *The Dictionary of Lahu*. Berkeley, California; London: University of California Press, 1988. (University of California Publications in Linguistics, vol. 3).

―――. *The Grammar of Lahu*. Berkeley, California: University of California Press, 1973; rev. ed. Berkeley, California: University of California Press, 1982.

―――. *A Variational Semantics in Tibeto-Burman: The "Organic" Approach to Linguistic Comparison*. Philadelphia: Institute for the Study of Human Issues, 1978.

Milne, Mary Lewis (Mrs. Leslie). *A Dictionary of English-Palaung and Palaung-English*. Yangon: Superintendent, Government Printing, 1931.

―――. *An Elementary Palaung Grammar*. Oxford: Clarendon, 1921.

Mînn Latt Yêkháun. *Modernization of Burmese*. Prague: Oriental Institute in Academia, Publishing House of the Czechoslovak Academy of Sciences, 1966. (Dissertationes Orientales, Vol. 11).

Okell, John. *First Steps in Burmese*. London: School of Oriental and African Studies, University of London, 1989.

———. *A Guide to the Romanization of Burmese*. London: The Royal Asiatic Society of Great Britain and Ireland, 1971.

———. *A Reference Grammar of Colloquial Burmese*. London: Oxford University Press, 1969. 2 vols.

———. "Nissaya Burmese: A Case of Systematic Adaptation to a Foreign Grammar and Syntax," *Journal of the Burma Research Society*, vol. 50, pt. 1 (June 1967), pp. 95–123.

———. "The Yaw Dialects of Burmese" in *South-East Asian Linguistics: Essays in Honour of Eugénie J. A. Henderson*. Edited by Jeremy H.C.S. Davidson. London: School of Oriental and African Studies, University of London, 1989, pp. 199–218.

Richter, Eberhardt. *Deutsch-Burmesisches Gesprächsbuch*. Leipzig: Verlag Enzyklopädie, 1969.

———. *Lehrbuch des Modernen Burmesisch: Umgangssprache*. Leipzig: Verlag Enzyklopädie, 1983.

Roop, D. Haigh. *An Introduction to the Burmese Writing System*. New Haven, Connecticut; London: Yale University Press, 1972. (Yale Linguistic Series).

Shorto, Harry Leonard. *A Dictionary of Modern Spoken Mon*. London: Oxford University Press, 1962.

———. *A Dictionary of the Mon Inscriptions from the Sixth to the Sixteenth Centuries: Incorporating Materials Collected by the Late C.O. Blagden*. London: Oxford University Press, 1971.

Stewart, John Alexander. *Manual of Colloquial Burmese*. London: Luzac, 1955.

Tun Nyein. *The Students' English-Burmese Dictionary*. 3d ed. Yangon: Paw U Sa-pei, 1971.

Wheatley, Julian K. "Burmese" in *The Major Languages of East and South-East Asia*. Edited by Bernard Comrie. London: Routledge, 1990, pp. 106–26.

Young, Linda Wai Ling. *Shan Chrestomathy: An Introduction to Tai Mau Language and Literature*. Lanham, Maryland: University Press of America, 1985.

Yule, Henry and Arthur C. Burnell. *Hobson-Jobson: A Glossary of Colloquial Anglo-Indian Words and Phrases*. 2d ed. London: Routledge and Kegan Paul, 1985.

6. Literature

Allott, Anna J. *Inked Over, Ripped Out. Burmese Storytellers and the Censors*. A Pen American Center Freedom-to-Write Report. New York: Pen American Center, September 1993.

———. "Burmese Literature" in *Far Eastern Literatures in the Twentieth Century, a Guide: Based on the Encyclopaedia of World Literature in the Twentieth Century*. Edited by Leonard S. Klein. Harpenden, Hertfordshire: Oldcastle, 1988, pp. 1–9.

———. "The Short Story in Burma with Special Reference to Its Social and Political Significance" in *The Short Story in Southeast Asia: Aspects of a Genre*. Edited by Jeremy Davidson and Helen Cordell. London: School of Oriental and African Studies, 1982, pp. 101–38.

Badgley, John H. "Intellectuals and the National Vision: the Burmese Case" in *Essays on Literature and Society in Southeast Asia: Political and Sociological Perspectives*. Edited by Tham Seong Che. Singapore: Singapore University Press, 1981, pp. 36–55.

Bagshawe, Lionel Ewart, trans. *The Maniyadanabon of Shin Sandalinka*. Translated from the Burmese by Lionel Ewart Bagshawe. Ithaca, New York: Cornell University, South East Asia Program, 1981.

248 / Bibliography

Bates, Herbert Ernest. *The Jacaranda Tree*. London: Michael Joseph, 1949.

——. *The Purple Plain*. London: Michael Joseph, 1947.

Bechert, Heinz and Heinz Braun. *Pali Niti Texts of Burma: Dhammaniti, Lokaniti, Maharaniti, Rajaniti, A Critical Edition and Study*. London: Pali Text Society, 1981.

Bechert, Heinz, Daw Khin Su, and Daw Tin Tin Myint, comp. *Burmese Manuscripts*. Wiesbaden: Steiner, 1978.

Bode, Mabel Haynes. *The Pali Literature of Burma*. London: Royal Asiatic Society, 1909; 1966. (Prize Publications Fund, vol. 2).

Butterworth, Sidney. *Three Rivers to Glory*. London: Hutchinson, 1956.

Carr, Ray. *Love in Burma: A Tale of the Silken East*. London: Geoffrey Bles, 1928.

Chamales, Tom T. *Never So Few*. London: Allan Wingate, 1958.

Chan-Toon, M. *A Marriage in Burmah: A Novel*. London: Greening, 1905.

Chia, Hern Chek. *The White Elephant; a Burmese Folktale*. Artwork by Kwan Shan Mei. [Singapore]: Alpha Press, [1972].

Collis, Maurice. *The Dark Door*. London: Faber and Faber, 1960.

——. *Descent of the God*. London: Faber and Faber, 1948.

——. *Lord of the Three Worlds*. London: Faber and Faber, 1947.

——. *The Mystery of Dead Lovers*. London: Faber and Faber, 1951.

——. *Sanda Mala*. London: Faber and Faber, 1939. New York: Carrick and Evans, 1940.

———. *She Was a Queen*. London: Faber and Faber, 1937; 2d ed., 1952.

Esche, A., trans. *Der Markt von Pagan. Prose aus Burma*. Berlin: Volk und Welt, 1968.

George, Sidney Charles. *Burma Story*. London; New York: Frederic Warne, 1948.

Hla U Ludu. *The Caged Ones*. Translated by Sein Tu. Bangkok: Tamarind, 1986. (Asian Portraits).

———. *Prince of Rubies and Other Tales from Burma*. Translated by Than Tun and Kathleen Forbes. Mandalay: Kyipwayay, 1980.

———. *Tales of Indigenous Peoples of Burma*. English Version by Than Tun. Mandalay: Hla, 1974.

Hla Pe. *Burma: Literature, Historiography, Scholarship, Language, Life and Buddhism*. Singapore: Institute of Southeast Asian Studies, 1985.

———. *Burmese Proverbs*. London: John Murray, 1962.

———. "Burmese Poetry (1300–1971)," *Journal of the Burma Research Society*, vol. 54, pts. 1–2 (December 1971), pp. 59–114.

Htin Aung. *Burmese Drama: A Study, With Translations, of Burmese Plays*. Calcutta, India: Oxford University Press, 1937; Westport, Connecticut: Greenwood, 1978.

———. *Burmese Folk-Tales*. London; Calcutta, India: Oxford University Press, 1954.

———. *Burmese Monks' Tales*. Collected, Translated and Introduced. New York: Columbia University Press, 1966.

———. *Epistles Written on the Eve of the Anglo-Burmese War*.

Translated and Introduced by Htin Aung. The Hague: Martinus Nijhoff, 1968.

———. *Folk Tales of Burma*. New Delhi: Sterling Publishers, 1976.

———. *Thirty Burmese Tales*. London: Oxford University Press, 1952.

Htin Aung, Helen Trager. *A Kingdom Lost for a Drop of Honey and Other Burmese Folktales*. Illustrated by Paw Oo Thet. New York: Parent's Magazine Press, 1968.

Jesse, Fryniwyd Tennyson. *The Lacquer Lady*. London: Virago, 1979. (Virago Modern Classics).

Jung, Eugen, ed. *Märchen aus Burma*. Translated into German by Marie Louise Hitz and Walter Klinger. Bern: J. Morzsinary, 1980.

Keely, H. H. and Christine Price. *The City of the Dagger and Other Tales from Burma*. London: Frederic Warne, 1972.

Khin Myo Chit. *Anawrahta of Burma*. Foreword by Chief Justice Dr. Maung, Illustrations by U Ba Kyi. Yangon: Sarpay Beikman, 1970.

———. *The 13 Carat Diamond and Other Stories*. Illustrated by Ba Kyi. Yangon: Sarpay Beikman, 1970.

Lustig, Friedrich V. (Ashin Ananda). *Burmese Classical Poems*. Selected and Translated by Friedrich V. Lustig (Ashin Ananda). Yangon: Rangoon Gazette, 1966.

———. *Burmese Poems Through the Ages: A Selection*. Translated by Friedrich V. Lustig (Ashin Ananda). Yangon: Sabe-u, 1986.

———. *A Glimpse of Contemporary Burmese Poetry: A Selection*. Translated by Friedrich V. Lustig (Ashin Ananda). Yangon: Sabe-u, 1986.

Ma Ma Lay. *Not Out of Hate: A Novel of Burma*. Translated from the Burmese by Margaret Aung-Thwin. Edited by William Frederick, with Introduction by Anna Allott. Athens, Ohio: Ohio University Press, 1991. (Monographs in International Studies, Southeast Asia Series, No. 88).

McCrae, Alister et al., comp. *Tales of Burma*. Paisley: J. Paton, 1981.

Maung Maung Pye. *Burmese Sunshine: Sunbeams of Wit and Humor*. Yangon: Khittaya, 1956.

———. *Tales of Burma*. Illustrated by Thet Win. Calcutta, India; London: Macmillan, 1952.

Myint Thein. *Burmese Folk-Songs*. Collected and Translated from the Burmese by Myint Thein, Foreword by Htin Aung. 2d ed. Calcutta, India: P. Lal/Writers Workshop, 1987.

———. *Burmese Proverbs Explained in Verse*. Singapore: W. P. J. and N. Handmer, 1984.

Nováková, Dagmar. "Maurice Collis and His Novels on Burma," *Journal of the Burma Research Society*, vol. 42, pt. 2 (December 1959), pp. 15–23.

One Thousand Hearts and Other Modern Burmese Short Stories. Yangon: Sarpay Beikman, 1973.

Orwell, George. *Burmese Days*. London: Penguin, 1989.

Pok Ni. *Konmara Pya Zat: An Example of Popular Burmese Drama in the XIX Century*, Vol. 1. Introduction and Translation by Hla Pe. London: Luzac, 1952.

Sarkar, Himansu Bhusan. *Literary Heritage of South-East Asia*. Calcutta, India: Firma KLM, 1980.

Shute, Nevil. *The Chequer Board*. London: William Heinemann, 1947.

Siek, Margaret. *Favourite Stories from Burma*. Hong Kong; Singapore; Kuala Lumpur: Heinemann Asia, 1975.

———. *More Favourite Stories from Burma*. Hong Kong; Singapore; Kuala Lumpur: Heinemann Asia, 1978.

Silverstein, Josef. "Burma Through the Prism of Western Novels," *Journal of Southeast Asian Studies*, vol. 16, no. 1 (March 1985), pp. 129–40.

Singer, Noel F. "Palm Leaf Manuscripts of Myanmar (Burma)," *Arts of Asia*, vol. 21, no. 1 (January-February 1991), pp. 133–40.

Takeyama, Michio. *Harp of Burma*. Translated from the Japanese by Howard Hibbett. Rutland, Vermont; Tokyo: Tuttle, 1966. (UNESCO Collection of Contemporary Works, Library of Japanese Literature).

Thaung, U (aka Aung Bala). "Contemporary Burmese Literature" in *Essays on Burma*. Edited by John P. Fergusson. Leiden, The Netherlands: E. J. Brill, 1981, pp. 81–101.

Thein Han. "His Spouse." By Zawgyi (pseudonym). Translated (from the Burmese) by Win Pe in *A Treasury of Modern Asian Stories*. Edited by William Clifford and Daniel L. Milton. New York: New American Library, 1961, pp. 138–143.

Thein Pe (Myint). *Over the Ashes: A Play About Resurgent Burma*. Bombay: People's Publishing House, 1945.

———. *Selected Short Stories of Thein Pe Myint*. Translated from the Burmese, with Introduction and Commentary by Patricia M. Milne. Ithaca, New York: Cornell University Southeast Asia Program, 1973. (Cornell University Southeast Asia Program Data Papers, No. 91).

Tin Htway. "Notes on Rāmāyana in Burmese Literature," *South East Asian Review*, vol. 5, no. 2 (December 1980), pp. 85–94.

———. "The Role of Literature in Nation Building in Burma" in *Southeast Asia in the Modern World*. Edited by Bernhard Grossman. Wiesbaden: Otto Harrassowitz, 1972, pp. 35–60. (Schriften des Instituts für Asienkunde in Hamburg, vol. 33).

Webb, G. H. "Kipling's Burma: A Literary and Historical Review," *Asian Affairs*, vol. 15, no. 2 (1984), pp. 163–178.

Win Pe, trans. *Modern Burmese Poetry*. Translated by Win Pe. Yangon: Myawaddy Sazin, 1978.

7. Publishing and Mass Media

Allott, Anna. "The Media in Burma and the Pro-Democracy Movement of July-September 1988," *South-East Asia Library Group Newsletter*, no. 34–35 (December 1990), pp. 17–24.

———. "Prose Writing and Publishing in Burma Today: Government Policy and Popular Practice" in *Essays on Literature and Society in Southeast Asia: Political and Sociological Perspectives*. Edited by Tham Seong Chee. Singapore: Singapore University Press, 1981, pp. 1–35.

Bečková, Dagmar. "Nationalism and Tradition in Burma's Cultural Policy. A Case Study of the Burmese Press 1975–76," *Archív Orientální*, vol. 49, no. 1 (1981), pp. 32–44.

Blackburn, Paul P. "Burma" in *Newspapers in Asia: Contemporary Trends and Problems*. Edited by John A. Lent. Hong Kong; Singapore; Kuala Lumpur: Heinemann Asia, 1982, pp. 177–90.

Lent, John A., ed. *Broadcasting in Asia and the Pacific: A Continental Survey of Radio and Television*. Hong Kong; Singapore; Kuala Lumpur: Heinemann Asia, 1978.

Pearn, Bertie Reginald. "Burmese Printed Books Before Judson,"

Journal of the Burma Research Society, vol. 30, pt. 1 (1940), pp. 384–385.

III. Economy

1. General Works and Economic History

Adas, Michael. *The Burma Delta: Economic Development and Social Change on an Asian Rice Frontier, 1842–1941*. Madison, Wisconsin: University of Wisconsin Press, 1974.

———. "Moral Economy or Contest State? Elite Demands and the Origins of Peasant Protest in Southeast Asia," *Journal of Social History*, vol. 13, no. 4 (Summer 1980), pp. 521–46.

Ahmad, Nafis. *Economic Resources of the Union of Burma*. Natick, Massachusetts: Earth Sciences Laboratory, 1971.

Andrus, J. Russell. *Burmese Economic Life*. Foreword by J. S. Furnivall. Stanford, California: Stanford University Press, 1947.

Aung Tun Thet. *Burmese Entrepreneurship: Creative Response in the Colonial Economy*. Stuttgart: Steiner Verlag Wiesbaden GmbH, 1989. (Beitrage zur Südasienforschung, Südasien-Institut, Universität Heidelberg, vol. 126).

Aye Hlaing. *A Study of Economic Development of Burma, 1870–1940*. Yangon: Department of Economics, University of Yangon, 1964.

Bandyopadhyay, Sekhar. *Burma Today: Economic Development and Political Control Since 1962*. Calcutta, India: Papyrus, 1987.

Bečka, Jan. "Planning for New Burma: Major-General Aung San's Views of Economic Development," *Archív Orientální*, vol. 56, no. 1 (1988), pp. 1–15.

Braund, Harold E. W. *Calling to Mind: Being Some Account of the First Hundred Years (1870 to 1970) of Steel Brothers and Company Limited.* Oxford; New York: Pergamon, 1974.

Burmese Agriculture, 1924–1941. Yangon: Department of Economics, Statistics and Commerce, University of Yangon, 1959.

Cheng, Siok Hwa. *The Rice Industry of Burma.* Kuala Lumpur: University of Malaya Press, 1968.

Chubb, H. J. and C.L.D. Duckworth. *Irrawaddy Flotilla Company Limited 1865–1950.* London: National Maritime Museum, 1973.

Corley, Thomas Anthony Buchanan. *A History of the Burmah Oil Company: Vol. 1, 1886–1924; Vol. 2, 1924–1966.* London: Heinemann, 1983, 1988. 2 vols.

Diokno, Maria Serena Icasiano. *The British Firms and the Economy of Burma: With Special Reference to the Rice and Teak Industries, 1917–1937.* Ph.D. Dissertation, University of London, 1983.

The Economic Position of Burma. New York: New York University, Institute of International Finance, 1955.

Fenichel, Allen H. and W. G. Huff. *The Impact of Colonialism on Burmese Economic Development.* Montreal: Centre for Developing-Area Studies, McGill University, 1971. (Occasional Paper Series, no. 7).

Furnivall, John Sydenham. *Colonial Policy and Practice: A Comparative Study of Burma and Netherlands India.* Cambridge, England: Cambridge University Press, 1948; New York: New York University Press, 1956.

———. *An Introduction to the Political Economy of Burma.* 3d ed. Yangon: People's Literature Committee and House, 1957.

Hill, Hal and Jayasuriya Sisira. *An Inward-Looking Economy in Transition*. Singapore: Institute of Southeast Asian Studies, 1986. (Occasional Paper, no. 80).

Khin Maung Nyunt. "Burma's Rice Trade in the 17th Century," *The Guardian* (Yangon), vol. 17, no. 4 (April 1970), pp. 12–20.

Laird, Dorothy. *Paddy Henderson, 1834–1961*. Glasgow; London: George Outram, 1961.

Lieberman, Victor B. "Secular Trends in Burmese Economic History, c. 1350–1830, and Their Implications for State Formation," *Modern Asian Studies*, vol. 25, pt. 1 (February 1991), pp. 1–31.

Ling, Trevor. "Buddhist Values and the Burmese Economy" in *Buddhist Studies in Honour of I. B. Horner*. Edited by L. Cousins, A. Kunst and K. R. Normans. Dordrecht, The Netherlands; Boston, Massachussetts: D. Reidel, 1974, pp. 103–118.

M. B. K. *An Outline of Burma's Oil History*. Yangon: Myawaddy, 1982.

McCrae, Alister. *Scots in Burma. Golden Times in Golden Land*. Edinburgh: Kiscadale, 1990.

McCrae, Alister and Allen Prentice. *Irrawaddy Flotilla*. Paisley, Scotland: James Paton, 1978.

Mya Maung. *The Burma Road to Poverty*. New York: Praeger, 1991.

———. "The Burmese Way to Socialism Beyond the Welfare State," *Asian Survey*, vol. 10, no. 6 (June 1970), pp. 533–551.

———. "Cultural Value and Economic Change in Burma," *Asian Survey*, vol. 4, no. 3 (March 1964), pp. 757–84.

Mya Than and Joseph L. H. Tan, eds. *Myanmar Dilemmas and Options: The Challenge of Economic Transition in the 1990s.* Singapore: ASEAN Economic Research Unit, Institute of Southeast Asian Studies, 1990.

Pearn, Bertie Reginald. *A History of Rangoon.* Yangon: American Baptist Mission Press, 1939; Farnborough: Gregg International, 1971.

Pointon, A. C. *The Bombay Burmah Trading Corporation Limited 1863–1963.* Southampton, England: Millbrook, 1964.

———. *Wallace Brothers.* Oxford: Oxford University Press, 1974.

Schendel, Willem van. *Three Deltas: Accumulation and Poverty in Rural Burma, Bengal and South India.* New Delhi: Sage Publications India, 1991.

———. "Origins of the Burma Rice Boom, 1850–1880," *Journal of Contemporary Asia,* vol. 17, no. 4 (1987), pp. 456–472.

Scott, James C. *The Moral Economy of the Peasant: Rebellion and Subsistence in Southeast Asia.* New Haven, Connecticut: Yale University Press, 1976.

Sein Maung. *Socio-Cultural Values and Economic Backwardness: A Case Study of Burma.* Ph.D. Dissertation, New York University, 1964.

Shein, Maung. *Burma's Transport and Foreign Trade in Relation to the Economic Development of the Country 1885–1914.* Yangon: University of Yangon, Department of Economics, 1964.

Siegelman, Philip. *Colonial Development and the Chettyar: A Study in the Ecology of Modern Burma 1850–1941.* Ph.D. Dissertation, University of Minnesota, Minneapolis, 1962.

Steinberg, David I. "Democracy, Power and the Economy in Myanmar: Donor Dilemmas," *Asian Survey*, vol. 31 (August 1991), p. 729–42.

Thaung, Blackmore. "British Quest for China Trade by Routes Across Burma (1826–1876)" in *Symposium on Historical, Archaeological and Linguistic Studies on Southern China, South-East Asia and the Hong Kong Region*. Edited by F. S. Drake. Hong Kong: Hong Kong University Press, 1967, pp. 180–90.

Tin Maung Lat, ed. *City of Yangon Modernization Record*. Translated by Tin Nwe Maung. Yangon: Public Relations Information Division for Yangon City Development Committee, 1990.

Toe Hla. *Money Lending and Contractual "Thet Kayits": A Socio-Economic Pattern of the Later Kon-baung Period*, 1819–1885. Ph.D. Dissertation, Northern Illinois University, De Kalb, Illinois, 1987.

Tun Wai. *Economic Development of Burma from 1800 till 1940*. Yangon: University of Yangon, Department of Economics.

2. Agriculture, Fisheries and Forestry

Andrus, J. Russell. *Rural Reconstruction in Burma*. Bombay: Oxford University Press, 1936.

Asian Socialist Conference, Planning Information Bureau. *A Short Account of the Land Nationalization Programme in Burma*. Yangon: Asian Socialist Conference, February/March 1957.

Aye Hlaing. *Some Aspects of Seasonal Agricultural Loans in Burma and Agroeconomic Problems in Burma*. Yangon: Department of Economics, Statistics and Commerce, University of Yangon, 1958. (Economics Research Project, Papers Nos. 14 and 21).

Barker, Randolph, Robert W. Herdt, with Beth Rose. *The Rice Economy of Asia.* Washington, D.C.: Resources for the Future, 1985.

Binns, Bernard Ottwell. *Agricultural Economy in Burma.* Yangon: Superintendent, Government Printing, 1946.

Cost of Cultivation and Income of Sampled Farms in Lower Burma for the Year 1975–76. Yangon: Department of Research, Institute of Economics, 1977.

Demaine, Harvey. "Current Problems of Agricultural Development Planning in Burma," *Southeast Asian Affairs* (1978), pp. 95–103.

Khin. *Fisheries in Burma.* Yangon: Superintendent, Government Printing and Stationery, 1948.

Khin Maung Kyi. "Modernization of Burmese Agriculture: Problems and Prospects," *Southeast Asian Affairs* (1982), pp. 15–31.

Kyaw Zin. *Burma and the CGIAR Centers: A Study of Their Agricultural Research.* Washington, D.C.: World Bank, [1986].

Lubeigt, Guy. *Le palmier à sucre (Borassus flabellifer) en Birmanie centrale.* Paris: Publications du Département de Géographie de l'Université de Paris-Sorbonne, 1979. (Publications du Département de Géographie de l'Université de Paris-Sorbonne, no. 8).

———. "L'Introduction d'une nouvelle culture dans état socialiste: le cas de jute en Birmanie" in *Types de cultures commerciales paysannes en Asie du Sud-Est et dans le monde insulindien.* Paris: Centre d'Etudes de Géographie Tropicale, Centre Nationale de la Recherche Scientifique, 1975, pp. 235–74. (Travaux et Documents de Géographie Régionale, no. 20).

May Khin San. *The Australian Rice Industry in Relation to the In-*

ternational Rice Trade and Its Implications for Southeast Asian Rice Exporting Countries*. Canberra: Australian National University, Development Studies Centre, 1981.

Mya Maung. "Agricultural Co-Operation in Burma: A Study on the Value-Orientation and Effects of Socio-Economic Action," *Social and Economic Studies*, vol. 14 (1965), pp. 321–28.

Mya Than. *Growth Pattern of Burmese Agriculture: A Productivity Approach*. Singapore: Insitute of Southeast Asian Studies, 1988. (ISEAS Occasional Paper, no. 81).

———. "Agriculture in Myanmar. What Has Happened to Asia's Rice Bowl?," *Southeast Asian Affairs* (1990), pp. 240–254.

———. "Burma's Agricultural Development Since 1962: From Stagnancy to Breakthrough" in *Unreal Growth: Critical Studies on Asian Development*. Edited by Manh Lan. Delhi: Hindustan Publishing Corporation, 1984, pp. 84–177.

Nuttonson, M. Y. *The Physical Environment and Agriculture of Burma: A Study Based on Field Survey Data on Pertinent Records, Materials and Reports*. Washington, D.C.: American Institute of Crop Ecology, 1963.

Report on the Survey of Rural Household Expenditures, 1960–1961. Conducted by the Central Statistical and Economics Department, Revolutionary Government of the Union of Burma. Yangon: [1961–1962]. 3 vols.

Richter, H. V. *Burma's Rice Surpluses: Accounting for the Decline*. Canberra: Development Studies Centre, Australian National University, 1976.

———. "The Impact of Socialism on Economic Activity in Burma" in *Opportunity and Response: Case Studies in Economic Development*. Edited by T. Scarlett Epstein and David H. Penney. London: C. Hurst, 1972, pp. 216–39.

———. "The Union of Burma" in *Agricultural Development in Asia*. Edited by R. T. Shand. Canberra: Australian National University Press; London: George Allen and Unwin, 1969, pp. 140–80.

Rodger, Alex. *A Hand-Book of the Forest Products of Burma*. New Delhi: Ajay Book, 1984.

Saito, Teruko. "Farm Household Economy under Paddy Delivery System in Contemporary Burma," *Economic Development and Cultural Change*, vol. 19, no. 4 (December 1981), pp. 367–97.

Shao-Wen Ling. *Aquaculture in Southeast Asia: A Historical Overview*. Edited by Laura Mumaw. Seattle, Washington; London: University of Washington Press, 1977.

Supply, Marketing, Distribution, and Use of Fertilizer in Burma. Bangkok: Fertilizer Advisory, Development and Information Network for Asia and the Pacific, 1987.

Watabe, Todayo, ed. *Preliminary Report of the Kyoto University Scientific Survey to Burma, 1974*. [Kyoto]: Laboratory of Crop Science, Faculty of Agriculture, Kyoto University, 1976.

3. Development and Planning

Amin, Hassan M. *Technical Co-Operation and Comparative Models of Development: Lessons Drawn from the UNDP Experience in Egypt and Burma*. Brighton, England: Institute of Development Studies at the University of Sussex, 1977. (Discussion Papers).

Aye Hlaing. *Commercial Policy and Economic Development: Some Notes on the Burmese Experience*. Yangon: Department of Economics, Statistics and Commerce, University of Yangon, 1961. (Economics Research Project, Paper no. 15).

The Economic Development of Burma. Yangon: Yangon University, Economics Department, 1958.

Government of the Union of Burma. *Pyidawtha, the New Burma: a Report from the Government to the People of the Union of Burma on Our Long-Term Programme for Economic and Social Development.* Yangon: Economic and Social Board, Government of the Union of Burma, 1954.

Hagen, Everett E. *The Economic Development of Burma.* Washington, D.C.: National Planning Association, Center for Development, 1956.

Hla Myint. *Protection and Economic Development.* Yangon: University of Yangon, Department of Economics. Statistics and Commerce, 1961.

Kohama, Hirohisa. *Development Strategy and Growth Performance: A Comparison of Burma and Malaysia.* Tokyo: International Development Center of Japan, 1982.

Mya Maung. *Burma and Pakistan: A Comparative Study of Development.* New York: Praeger, 1971.

——. *The Genesis of Economic Development of Burma: The Plural Society.* Ph.D. Dissertation, Catholic University of America, Washington, D.C., 1961.

——. "Socialism and Economic Development of Burma," *Asian Survey*, vol. 4, no. 12 (December 1964), pp. 1182–90.

Sell, Axel. *Economic Structure and Development of Burma.* Berichte aus dem Weltwirtschaftlischen Colloquium der Universität Bremen, Nr. 5. Bremen: Fachbereich Wirtschaftwissenschaft der Universität Bremen, 1985.

Steinberg, David I. *Burma's Road toward Development: Growth and Ideology under Military Rule.* Boulder, Colorado: Westview, 1981.

———. "Burma's Third Four-Year Plan: Half-Way to Socialism and Industrialization," *Contemporary Southeast Asia*, vol. 5, no. 1 (June 1983), pp. 1–26.

———. "Burmese Economics: The Conflict of Ideology and Pragmatism" in *Military Rule in Burma Since 1962, A Kaleidoscope of Views*. Edited by F. K. Lehman. Singapore, Maruzen Asia: Issued under the Auspices of the Institute of Southeast Asian Studies, 1981, pp. 29–51.

———. "Economic Growth and Equity?: the Burmese Experience," *Contemporary Southeast Asia*, vol.4, no. 2 (September 1982), pp. 124–152.

Trager, Frank N. *Building a Welfare State, 1948–1956*. New York: Institute of Pacific Relations, 1958.

———. *Towards a Welfare State in Burma: Economic Reconstruction and Development, 1948–1954*. New York: International Secretariat, Institute of Pacific Relations, 1954.

United Nations. Development Project. *UNDP in Burma, 1985*. Yangon: UNIC, 1986.

Walinsky, Louis. *Economic Development in Burma, 1951–60*. New York: Twentieth Century Fund, 1962.

4. Finance, Credit and Banking

Burma, Committee on State Agricultural Bank. *Report 1948*. Yangon: Superintendent, Government Printing and Stationery, 1949.

Burma, Provincial Banking Enquiry Committee. *Banking and Credit in Burma*. Yangon: Superintendent, Government Printing and Stationery, 1930.

Mali, K. S. *Public Expenditures and Inflationary Impact in*

Burma, 1951 to 1959. By K. S. Mali. *Commercial Policy and Economic Development, Some Notes on the Burmese Experience.* By Aye Hlaing. [Yangon]: Department of Economics, Statistics and Commerce, University of Yangon, 1961.

Tun Wai. *Burma's Currency and Credit.* Rev. ed. Foreword by Hla Myint. Bombay, India: Orient Longmans, 1962.

5. Foreign Aid, Trade and Investment

Badgley, John H. *Burma's Foreign Economic Relations, 1948–1958. A Survey.* Yangon: Rangoon-Hopkins Center for Southeast Asian Studies, 1959.

Bell, Jonathan. *The Complete Guide to Countertrade and Offset in South East Asia, China and the Far East.* London: COI Publications (Countertrade and Offset Intelligence), 1988.

Export List of Myanmar. Yangon: Union of Myanmar Ministry of Trade, 1990.

Guide to Foreign Investment in Myanmar. Yangon: Union of Myanmar Foreign Investment Commission, 1989–90. 2 vols.

Hyndman, Vance. *U.S. Economic Assistance Programs in Asia: Report of a Study Mission to Thailand, Burma, Sri Lanka, and India, August 3–23, 1979 to the Committee on Foreign Affairs, U.S. House of Representatives.* Washington, D.C.: U.S. G.P.O., 1980.

Khin Maung Nyunt. *Foreign Loans and Aid in the Economic Development of Burma 1974/75 to 1985/86.* Bangkok: Institute of Asian Studies, Chulalongkorn University, 1990.

———. *Market Research of Principal Exports and Imports of Burma with Special Reference to Thailand (1970/71 to 1985/86).* Bangkok: Institute of Asian Studies, Chulalongkorn University, 1988.

Mya Than. *Myanmar's External Trade. An Overview in the Southeast Asian Context*. Singapore: Institute of Southeast Asian Studies, ASEAN Economic Research Unit, 1992. (ISEAS Current Economic Affairs Series).

Soe Saing. *United Nations Technical Aid in Burma: A Short Survey*. Singapore: Institute of Southeast Asian Studies, 1990.

Steinberg, David I. "International Rivalries in Burma: The Rise of Economic Competition," *Asian Affairs*, vol. 30, no. 6 (June 1990), pp. 587–601.

———. "Japanese Economic Assistance to Burma: Aid in the 'Tarenagashi' Manner?," *Crossroads*, vol. 5, No. 2 (1990), pp. 51–107.

Trade Directory of Myanmar. Yangon: Union of Myanmar Ministry of Trade, 1989.

Tun Wai. *Role of Foreign Capital in Southeast Asian Countries*. Singapore: Institute of Southeast Asian Studies, 1989.

6. Industry and Mining

Arumugab, Raja Segaran. *State and Oil in Burma: An Introductory Survey*. Singapore: Institute of Southeast Asian Studies, 1977. (Research Notes and Discussion Series, no. 3).

Burma Gems, Jade and Pearl Emporium. Yangon: Ministry of Mines, Myanma Gems Corporation, Government of Socialist Republic of the Union of Burma, 1984.

International Labour Office. *Report to the Government of the Union of Burma on Industrial Hygiene and Occupational Health*. Geneva: International Labour Office, 1971.

———. *Report to the Government of Burma on Occupational*

Safety and Health in Factories. Geneva: International Labour Office, 1968.

Khin Maung Gyi. *Memoirs of Oil Industry in Burma 1905–1980.* Yangon: n.p. 1989.

Myin Thein, U. *Industrial Management.* Yangon: Myanma Sapei Taik, 1982.

Phin Koeng Voon. "The Rubber Industry of Burma, 1876–1964," *Journal of Southeast Asian Studies*, vol. 5, pt. 2 (September 1973), pp. 216–28.

Thompson, J. *Silk-Weaving Cottage Industry in Burma.* New York: United Nations Technical Assistance Program, 1952.

Tin Htoo. "An Overall View of the Rubber Industry of Burma," *Journal of the Burma Research Society*, vol. 45, pt. 1 (June 1962), pp. 91–107.

Tin Maung Maung Than. "Burma's Energy Use: Perils and Promises," *Southeast Asian Affairs* (1985), pp. 68–95.

Turrell, Robert Vicat. "Conquest and Concessions: The Case of the Burma Ruby Mines," *Modern Asian Studies*, vol. 22 (February 1988), pp. 141–163.

United Nations. *Survey of Lead and Zinc Mining and Smelting in Burma. General Report Prepared for the Government of Burma.* New York: UN, 1966.

7. Labor

International Labour Office. *Report to the Government of the Union of Burma on Labour Statistics.* Geneva: International Labour Office, 1973.

———. *The Trade Union Situation in Burma: A Report of a Mission from the International Labour Office.* Geneva: International Labour Office, 1962.

Koop, John Clement. *Sample Survey of Labour Force in Rangoon: A Study in Methods*. Yangon: Government Printing, 1955.

Mya Than. "The Role of Women in Rural Burma: A Case Study," *Sojourn*, vol. 1, no. 1 (February 1986), pp. 97–108.

Myo Htun Lynn. *Labour and Labour Movement in Burma*. Yangon: Department of Economics, University of Yangon, 1961.

Thompson, Virginia. *Labor Problems in Southeast Asia*. New Haven, Connecticut: Yale University Press; London: Oxford University Press, 1947.

8. Transport and Communications

Ba Thann Winn. *Highways and Major Bridges of Burma*. Yangon: Security and Information Department, Construction Corporation, 1976.

Berger, Louis. *Rangoon-Mandalay Highway Project, Union of Burma. Report to Corps of Engineers, Gulf District, Burma Area*. Harrisburg, Pennsylvania: 1962.

Fenton, A. B. *Routes in Upper Burma, Including the Chin Hills and Shan States, to Which Are Added a Number of Routes Leading from Lower Burma and Siam into Those Districts*. Compiled for the Quartermaster-General of the Madras Army by A. B. Fenton. Delhi: Cultural Publication House, 1983.

Tan Pei-Ying. *The Building of the Burma Road*. New York; London: McGraw-Hill Book Company, 1945.

IV. HISTORY

1. General

Ba Hkain, U. *Myanma Pyi Naingnganyei Yazawin* [Political History of Myanmar]. Yangon: Bagan, 1964.

Ba Shin, Bohmu. *Pyidaungsu Myanma Naingngan Thamaing*. [History of the Union of Burma]. 7th ed. Yangon: Thuwanni, 1956.

Ba Swe. *Workers' Struggles in Burma. Being a Text of May Day Speech Delivered on May 1, 1951 at B.A.A. Stadium, Rangoon, by U U Ba Swe, President, Trade Union Congress, Burma*. Yangon: People's Literature House, 1951.

Ba U. *My Burma: The Autobiography of a President*. Foreword by J. S. Furnivall. New York: Taplinger, 1959.

Bečka, Jan. "The State in Burma," a Review Article, *Archív Orientální*, vol. 58, no. 1 (1990), pp. 79–85.

Bennet, Paul J. *Conference under the Tamarind Tree: Three Essays in Burmese History*. New Haven, Connecticut: Yale University Southeast Asian Studies, 1971. (Yale University Southeast Asia Studies Monograph Series, no. 15).

Cady, John Frank. *A History of Modern Burma*. Ithaca, New York: Cornell University Press, 1958.

———. *The United States and Burma*. Cambridge, Massachusetts; London: Harvard University Press, 1976.

Cowan, Charles D. and Oliver William Wolters, eds. *Southeast Asian History and Historiography: Essays Presented to D.G.E. Hall*. Ithaca, New York; London: Cornell University Press, 1976.

Desai, W. S. *A Pageant of Burmese History*. Bombay: Orient Longmans, 1961.

Grant, W. J. *The New Burma*, 2d ed. London: George Allen and Unwin, 1942.

Hall, Daniel George Edward. *Burma*. London: Hutchinson's University Library, 1950, 1960; 3d ed. New York: AMS Press, 1974.

———. *Europe and Burma: A Study of European Relations with*

Burma to the Annexation of Thibaw's Kingdom 1886. London; New York: Oxford University Press, 1945.

———. *History of South-East Asia.* 4th. rev. ed. London: Macmillan, 1981.

———. ed. *Historians of South-East Asia.* London: Oxford University Press, 1961. (Historical Writing on the Peoples of Asia).

Harvey, Godfrey Eric. *Outline of Burmese History.* Bombay, India: Longmans, Green, 1926, 1947.

Htin Aung. *A History of Burma.* New York; London: Columbia University Press, 1967.

———. *The Stricken Peacock: Anglo-Burmese Relations 1752–1948.* The Hague: Martinus Nijhoff, 1965.

Ishizawa, Yoshiaki, ed. *Historical and Cultural Studies in Burma.* Tokyo: Institute of Asian Cultures, Sophia University, 1988.

Lieberman, Victor B. "Reinterpreting Burmese History," *Comparative Studies in Society and History, An International Quarterly*, vol. 29, no. 1 (January 1987), pp. 162–94.

Maung Maung. *Burma and General Ne Win.* Yangon: Religious Affairs Department; London; New York: Asia Publishing House, 1969.

Sarkisyanz, Emmanuel. *Peacocks, Pagodas and Professor Hall: A Critique of the Persisting Use of Historiography as an Apology for British Empire Building in Burma.* Athens, Ohio: Ohio University Center for International Studies, Southeast Asia Program, 1972. (Papers in International Studies, Southest Asia Series, no. 24).

Sein Myin, U. *Hnit 200 Myanma Naingngan Thamaing Abidan.* [A Dictionary of 200 Years of Myanmar History]. Yangon: U Myat Kyaw, 1969.

Thaung, Blackmore. "Burmese Historical Literature and Native

Foreign Scholarship" in *Symposium on Historical, Archaeological and Linguistic Studies on Southern China, Southeast Asia and the Hong Kong Region*. Edited by F. S. Drake. Hong Kong: Hong Kong University Press, 1967, pp. 311–319.

Thein Hpei Myin (Thein Pe Myint). *Tawhlanyei Kala Naingnganyei Atwei Akyon mya* (The Political Experiences of the Revolutionary Period). Yangon: Shwei Pyi Tan, 1956.

Trager, Frank N. *Burma from Kingdom to Republic: A Historical and Political Analysis*. New York: Frederick A. Praeger, 1966; Westport, Connecticut: Greenwood Press, 1976.

Wilson, Constance M. and Lucien M. Hanks, eds., trans. *The Burma-Thailand Frontier Over Sixteen Decades: Three Descriptive Documents*. Edited and Translated by Constance M. Wilson and Lucien M. Hanks. Athens, Ohio: Ohio University Press, Center for International Studies, 1985.

Woodman, Dorothy. *The Making of Burma*. London: Cresset Press, 1962.

2. Pre-1824

Aung-Thwin, Michael. *Irrigation in the Heartland of Burma: Foundations of the Pre-Colonial Burmese State*. DeKalb, Illinois: Northern Illinois University, Center for Southeast Asian Studies, 1990. (Occasional Paper no. 15).

———. *Pagan: The Origins of Modern Burma*. Honolulu, Hawaii: University of Hawaii Press, 1985.

———. "Divinity, Spirit and Human: Conceptions of Classical Burmese Kingship" in *Centers, Symbols and Hierarchies: Essays on the Classical States of Southeast Asia*. Edited by Lorraine Gessick. New Haven, Connecticut: Yale University Southeast Asia Studies, 1983, pp. 45–86.

———. "Heaven, Earth and the Supernatural World: Dimensions of the Exemplary Center in Burmese History" in *The City as a Sacred Center: Essays on Six Asian Contexts*. Edited by Bardwell Smith and Holly Baker Reynolds. Leiden, The Netherlands: E. J. Brill, 1987, pp. 88–102.

———. "Jambudipa: Classical Burma's Camelot" in *Essays on Burma*. Edited by John P. Fergusson. Leiden, The Netherlands: E. J. Brill, 1981, pp. 38–61.

———. "Kingship, the Sangha and Society in Pagan" in *Exploration in Early Southeast Asian Statecraft*. Ann Arbor, Michigan: University of Michigan Center for South and Southeast Asian Studies, 1976, pp. 205–256.

———. "The Problem of Ceylonese-Burmese Relations in the 12th Century and the Question of an Interregnum in Pagan 1164–1174 AD," *Journal of the Siam Society*, vol. 64, pt. 1 (January 1976), pp. 53–74.

———. "Prophecies, Omens and Dialogue: Tools of the Trade in Burmese Historiography" in *Moral Order and the Question of Change: Essays on Southeast Asian Thought*. Edited by David K. Wyatt and Alexander Woodside. New Haven, Connecticut: Yale University, Southeast Asia Studies, 1982, pp. 78–103.

———. "The Role of Sasana Reform in Burmese History: Economic Dimensions of a Religious Purification," *Journal of Asian Studies*, vol. 38, no. 4 (August 1979), pp. 671–688.

Cox, Hiram. *Journal of a Residence in the Burmhan Empire and More Particularly at the Court of Amarapoorah*. London: John Warren and G. and W. B. Whittaker, 1821. Reprinted with Introduction by Daniel George Edward Hall. Farnborough, England: Gregg International, 1971.

Dalrymple, Alexander. *Reprint from Dalrymple's Oriental Repertory, 1791–7, of Portions Relating to Burma*. Selected by Godfrey Eric Harvey. Yangon: Superintendent, Government Printing, 1926.

Gutman, Pamela C. *Ancient Arakan: With Special Reference to Its Cultural History Between the 5th and 11th Centuries.* Ph.D. Thesis, Australian National University, Canberra 1977.

Hall, Daniel George Edward. *Early English Intercourse with Burma 1587–1743: With the Tragedy of Negrais as a New Appendix.* 2d ed. London: Frank Cass, 1968.

Hall, Kenneth R. and John K. Whitmore, eds. *Explorations in Early Southeast Asian History: the Origins of Southeast Asian Statecraft.* Ann Arbor: Center for South and Southeast Asian Studies, University of Michigan, 1976.

Harvey, Godfrey Eric. *History of Burma: From the Earliest Times to 10 March 1824, the Beginning of the English Conquest.* London: Longmans, Green, 1925; London: Frank Cass, 1967.

Htin Aung. *Burmese History Before 1287: A Defence of the Chronicles.* Oxford: Asoka Society, 1970.

Khin Maung Kyi, Tin Tin. *Administrative Patterns in Historical Burma.* Singapore: Institute of Southeast Asian Studies, 1973. (Southeast Asian Perspectives, no. 1).

Koenig, William J. *The Burmese Polity, 1752–1819: Politics, Administration, and Social Organization in the Early Konbaung Period.* Ann Arbor, Michigan: Center for South and Southeast Asian Studies, University of Michigan, 1990. (Michigan Papers on South and Southeast Asia, no. 34).

Langham-Carter, R. R. "Burmese Army," *Journal of the Burma Research Society*, vol. 27, no. 3 (1937), pp. 254–276.

Lieberman, Victor B. *Burmese Administrative Cycles: Anarchy and Conquest, c. 1580–1760.* Princeton, New Jersey: Princeton University Press, 1984.

———. "Ethnic Politics in Eighteenth-Century Burma," *Modern Asian Studies*, vol. 12, no. 3 (1978), pp. 455–482.

———. "Europeans, Trade and the Unification of Burma, c. 1540–1620," *Oriens Extremus*, 27 Jahrgang, Heft 2 (1980), Kommisionsverlag Otto Harrassowitz, Wiesbaden, pp. 203–26.

———. "How Reliable is U Kala's Burmese Chronicle? Some New Comparisons," *Journal of Southeast Asian Studies*, vol. 17, no. 2 (September 1986), pp. 236–255.

———. "The Political Significance of Religious Wealth in Burmese History: Some Further Thoughts," *Journal of Asian Studies*, vol. 39, no. 4 (August 1980), pp. 753–769.

———. "Provincial Reforms in Taung-Ngu," *Bulletin of the School of Oriental and African Studies*, University of London, vol. 43, pt. 3 (1980), pp. 548–569.

———. "The Transfer of the Burmese Capital from Pegu to Ava," *Journal of the Royal Asiatic Society*, no. 1 (1980), pp. 64–83.

Luce, Gordon H. *Old Burma-Early Pagán*. Locust Valley, New York: J. J. Austin for *Artibus Asiae* and Institute of Fine Arts, New York University, 1969–1970. 3 vols. (Artibus Asiae Supplementum 25).

———. "The Career of Htilaing Min (Kyanzittha)," *Journal of the Royal Asiatic Society*, New Series, vol. 1–2 (1966), pp. 53–68.

———. "Mons of the Pagan Dynasty," *Journal of the Burma Research Society*, vol. 36, pt. 1 (June 1953), pp. 1–19.

Mya Sein, Daw. *The Administration of Burma*. Introduction by Josef Silverstein. Kuala Lumpur; Singapore; London: Oxford University Press, 1973. (Oxford in Asia Historical Reprints).

Myo Min. *Old Burma as Described by Early Foreign Travellers*. Forward by Dr. Htin Aung. Yangon: Hanthawaddy Publication, 1947.

Pe Maung Tin and Gordon H. Luce, trans. *The Glass Palace*

Chronicle of the Kings of Burma. London: Oxford University Press, 1923; Yangon: Yangon University Press, 1960. New York: AMS Press, 1976.

Smith, Bardwell L. "The Pagan Period (1044–1287): A Bibliographic Note" in *Essays on Burma*. Edited by John P. Fergusson. Leiden, The Netherlands: E. J. Brill, 1981, pp. 112–30.

Symes, Michael. *Michael Symes: Journal of His Second Embassy to the Court of Ava in 1802*. Edited with an Introduction and Notes by Daniel George Edward Hall. London: George Allen and Unwin, 1955.

Than Tun, ed. *The Royal Orders of Burma, AD 1598–1885*. Edited with Introduction, Notes and English Summary by Than Tun. Kyoto, Japan: Center for Southeast Asian Studies, Kyoto University, 1983–1990. 10 vols.

———. "Ayut'ia Men in the Service of Burmese Kings, 16th and 17th Centuries," *Tonan Ajia Kenkyu* (Southeast Asian Studies), vol. 21, no. 4, March 1984, pp. 400–8.

———. "A Forgotten Town of Burma," *Shiroku*, Kagoshima University, no. 12, November 1979, pp 51–56.

———. "Social Life in Burma in the 16th Century," *Tonan Ajia Kenkyu* (Southeast Asian Studies), vol. 21, no. 3 (December 1983), pp. 267–74.

Trager, Frank N., William J. Koenig, and Yi Yi. *Burmese Sit-Tans 1764–1826: Records of Rural Life and Administration*. Translations from the Burmese by William J. Koenig. Tucson, Arizona: University of Arizona Press, for the Association for Asian Studies, 1979. (Association for Asian Studies Monographs, no. 36).

3. Colonial (1824–1948)

Anti-Fascist People's Freedom League. *The New Burma in the*

New World: From Fascist Bondage to New Democracy. Yangon: Nay Win Kyi, 1946.

Aung San. *Burma's Challenge 1946.* Yangon: New Light of Burma, 1946.

———. "Burma To-Day," *The Burma Digest* (Yangon), vol. I, no. 10 (1946), pp. 19–25.

———. "The Defence of Burma," *The Burma Digest* (Yangon), vol. I, no. 7 (1946), pp. 39–45.

———. "Economic Fascism in Burma," *The Burma Digest* (Yangon), vol. I, no. 5 (1946), pp. 13–17.

Aung San Suu Kyi. *Burma and India: Some Aspects of Intellectual Life Under Colonialism.* Simla, India: Indian Institute of Advanced Study, in Association with Allied Publishers, New Delhi, 1990.

Aung-Thwin, Michael. "The British 'Pacification of Burma': Order Without Meaning," *Journal of Southeast Asia Studies*, vol. 16, no. 2 (September 1985), pp. 245–61.

Banerjee, Anil Chandra. *Annexation of Burma.* Calcutta, India: A. Mukherjee, 1944.

Bečka, Jan. "The Ideology of the Dou Bămá Ăsîj Ăyôuṃ: A Study of the Evolution of Burmese Nationalism (1930–1940)," *Archív Orientalní*, vol. 54, no. 4 (1986), pp. 336–58.

———. "The Role of Buddhism as a Factor of Burmese National Identity in the Period of British Rule in Burma (1886–1948)," *Archív Orientální*, vol. 59, no. 4 (1991), pp. 389–405.

Brown, Riou Grant. *Burma As I Saw It*, 1889–1917, With a Chapter on Recent Events. London: Methuen, 1926.

Bruce, George L. *The Burma Wars 1824–1886.* London: Hart-Davis, MacGibbon, 1973.

Cady, John. *Contacts with Burma, 1935–1949: A Personal Account.* Athens, Ohio: Ohio University, 1983. (Center for International Studies, Papers in International Studies, Southeast Asia Series no. 61).

Chandran, J. *The Burma-Yunnan Railway. Anglo-French Rivalry in Mainland Southeast Asia and South China, 1859–1902.* Athens, Ohio: Ohio University Center for International Studies (Southeast Asia Program), 1971.

Collis, Maurice. *Trials in Burma.* London: Faber and Faber, 1938; New York: AMS Press, 1975.

Cooler, Richard M. *British Romantic Views of the First Anglo-Burmese War (1824–1826).* De Kalb, Illinois: Northern Illinois University, Department of Art, 1977.

Crosthwaite, Charles Haukes Todd. *The Pacification of Burma.* London: Edward Arnold, 1912; London: Frank Cass, 1968.

Dautremer, Joseph. *Burma under British Rule.* Translated and with Introduction by James George Scott. London: T. Fisher Unwin, 1913.

Dennis, Peter. *Troubled Days of Peace: Mountbatten and South East Asia Command, 1945–1946.* Manchester, England: Manchester University Press, 1987. (War, Armed Forces and Society).

Desai, Walter Sadgun. *Deposed King Thibaw of Burma in India, 1885–1916.* Bombay: Bharatiya Vidya Bhavan, 1967. (Bharatiya Vidya Series no. 25).

———. *History of the British Residency in Burma, 1820–1840.* Farnborough: Gregg International, 1972.

Devas, D. *Rebirth of Burma.* With Introduction by J. S. Furnivall. Madras, India: Associated Printers, 1947.

Drake, B. K. *Burma: Nationalist Movements and Independence.* Kuala Lumpur: Longman, 1979.

Foucar, Emil Charles Victor. *I Lived in Burma.* London: Dennis Dobson, 1946; 1956.

Furnivall, John Sydenham. *The Fashioning of Leviathan: The Beginnings of British Rule in Burma.* Canberra: Research School of Pacific Studies, Australian National University, in Association with the Economic History of Southeast Asia Project and the Thai-Yunnan Project, 1991. (Originally published in *Journal of the Burma Research Society*, vol. 29, pt. 2 [April 1939], pp. 1–137).

Ghosh, Parimal. *Peasant Resistance to British Imperialism in Burma, 1886 to 1891.* Calcutta: Centre for Southeast Asian Studies, University of Calcutta, 1983.

———. "Peasant Resistance to British Imperialism in Burma 1825–1870," *Bengal Past and Present*, vol. 102, pt. 2 (July-December 1983), pp. 30–62.

Glass, Leslie. *The Changing of Kings: Memories of Burma 1934–1939.* London: Peter Owen, 1985.

Hall, Daniel George Edward. *The Dalhousie-Phayre Correspondence 1852–1856.* Edited with Introduction and Notes by Daniel George Edward Hall. London: Oxford University Press, 1932.

———. *Henry Burney: A Political Biography.* London; New York; Kuala Lumpur: Oxford University Press, 1974.

Harvey, Godfrey Eric. *British Rule in Burma 1824–1942.* London: Faber and Faber, 1946; New York: AMS Press, 1974.

Herbert, Patricia M. *The Hsaya San Rebellion (1930–1932). Reappraised.* Melbourne, Australia: Monash University, Centre of Southeast Asian Studies, 1982.

Htin Aung. *Lord Randolph Churchill and the Dancing Peacock: British Conquest of Burma 1885.* New Delhi: Manohar, 1990.

———. "First Burmese Mission to the Court of St. James: Kinwun Mingyi's Diaries, 1872–74," *Journal of the Burma Research Society*, vol. 57, pts. 1–2 (December 1974), pp. 1–198.

Keeton, Charles Lee. *King Thebaw and the Ecological Rape of Burma: The Political and Commercial Struggle Between British India and French Indo-China in Burma 1878–1886.* Foreword by John F. Cady. Delhi: Manohar Book Service, 1974.

Khin Maung Nyunt. "A Profile of Alavaka," *The Guardian Monthly* (Yangon), vol. 17, no. 6 (1970), pp. 29–34.

———. "Supannaka Galuna Raja," *The Guardian Monthly* (Yangon), vol. 15, no. 4 (1968), pp. 9–13.

Khin Yi. *The Dobama Movement in Burma (1930–1938).* Foreword by Robert H. Taylor. Ithaca, New York: Southeast Asia Program, Cornell University, 1988. (Southeast Asia Program Monographs, no. 2).

———. *The Dobama Movement in Burma (1930–1938): Appendix (Documents in Burmese).* Ithaca, New York: Southeast Asia Program Publications (SEAP) Series no. 2 A, Cornell University, 1988.

Khin Zaw, Thakin. *Bama Lutlatyei hnin Alokthama Taikpwe.* [Burma's Independence and Workers' Struggle]. Yangon: Zwe Sapei, 1969.

Kin Oung. *Who Killed Aung San?* Bangkok: White Lotus, 1993.

Lu Pe Win. *History of the 1920 University Boycott.* Yangon: The Author, 1970.

Lwin, Thakin. *Myanma Naingngan Alokthama Hlokshahmu Thamaing.* [A History of the Labor Movement in Myanmar]. Yangon: Bagan, 1968.

Maung Maung, (Brigadier). *Burmese Nationalist Movements, 1940–1948.* Edinburgh: Kiscadale, 1989.

———. *From Sangha to Laity: Nationalist Movements of Burma 1920–1940.* New Delhi: Manohar, for the Australian National University, 1980. (Australian National University Monographs on South Asia, no. 4).

Maung Maung (Dr.), compil., ed. *Aung San of Burma.* Introduction by Harry J. Benda. The Hague: Martinus Nijhoff, for Yale University Southeast Asia Studies, 1962.

———. *A Trial in Burma: The Assassination of Aung San.* The Hague: Martinus Nijhoff, 1962.

Maung Maung Pye. *Burma in the Crucible.* Yangon: Khittaya Publishing House, 1952.

Moscotti, Albert D. *British Policy and the Nationalist Movement in Burma, 1917–1937.* Honolulu: University Press of Hawaii, 1974. (Asian Studies at Hawaii, no. 11).

Mukherjee, Aparna. *British Colonial Policy in Burma: An Aspect of Colonialism in South East Asia 1840–1885.* New Delhi: Malik Abhinav Publications, 1988.

Myo Mint. *The Politics of Survival in Burma: Diplomacy and Statecraft in the Reign of King Mindon, 1853–1878.* Ph.D. Dissertation. Cornell University, Ithaca, New York, 1987.

Ni Ni Myint. *Burma's Struggle Against British Imperialism, 1885–1895.* Yangon: The Universities Press, 1983.

Pollak, Oliver B. *Empires in Collision: Anglo-Burmese Relations in the Mid-Nineteenth Century.* Westport, Connecticut; London: Greenwood, 1979.

Preschez, Philippe. *Les Relations entre la France et la Birmanie au XVIIIe et au XIXe siècles.* Paris: Fondation Nationale des Sciences Politiques, 1967.

Saimong Mangrai. *The Shan States and the British Annexation.* Ithaca, New York: Cornell University Southeast Asia Program, 1965. (Cornell University Southeast Asia Program Data Paper, no. 57).

Silverstein, Josef, comp. *The Political Legacy of Aung San.* Compiled, with Introductory Essay by Josef Silverstein. Ithaca, New York: Cornell University, 1972. (Lovnell University Southeast Asia Program Data Paper, no. 86). Revised Edition, 1993 (Lovnell University Southeast Asia Program Series No. 11).

Singh, Surendra Prasad. *Growth of Nationalism in Burma 1900–1942.* Calcutta, India: Firma KLM, 1980.

Singh, Uma Shankara. "India and Burmese Nationalism (1885–1937), A Study in Indian Support to Burmese Nationalism," *The Modern Review* (October 1977), pp. 210–21.

Singhal, D. P. *British Diplomacy and the Annexation of Upper Burma.* 2d ed. New Delhi: South Asian Publishers, 1981.

Stewart, Anthony Terence Quincy. *The Pagoda War: Lord Dufferin and the Fall of the Kingdom of Ava, 1885–6.* London: Faber and Faber, 1972.

Tarling, Nicholas. *The Fourth Anglo-Burmese War: Britain and the Independence of Burma.* Gaya, India: South East Asian Review Office, for the Centre for South East Asian Studies, 1987.

———. "Lord Mountbatten and the Return of Civil Government to Burma," *Journal of Imperial Commonwealth History*, vol. 11, no. 2 (January 1983), pp. 197–226.

Thein Hpei Myin (Thein Pe Myint). *Ashei ka Neiwun Htwetthi Pama* [As the Sun Rises in the East]. Yangon: Myat Sapei, n.d. 3 vols.

———. *Bon Wada hnin Do Bama* [Communism and *Do Bama*]. Yangon: Pyidawso, 1954.

Tinker, Hugh, ed. *Burma: The Struggle for Independence, 1944–1948. Documents from Official and Private Sources.* London: Her Majesty's Stationery Office, 1983–84. 2 vols. (Constitutional Relations between Britain and Burma).

———. *The Foundations of Local Self-Government in India, Pakistan and Burma.* 2d ed. London: Pall Mall Press; New York: Frederick A. Praeger, 1968.

———. "Burma's Struggle for Independence: The Transfer of Power Thesis Re-Examined," *Modern Asian Studies*, vol. 20, no. 3 (July 1986), pp. 461–81.

Watson, James Kiers. *Military Operations in Burma, 1890–1892: Letters from Lieutenant J. K. Watson, K.R.R.C.* Ithaca, New York: Cornell University, Southeast Asia Program, 1967. (Cornell University Asia Program Data Paper, no. 65).

Yule, Henry. *A Narrative of the Mission to the Court of Ava in 1855; Together with The Journal of Arthur Phayre Envoy to the Court of Ava, and Additional Illustrations by Colesworthy Grant and Linnaeus Tripe.* Introduction by Hugh Tinker. Kuala Lumpur; London; New York: Oxford University Press, 1968. (Oxford in Asia Historical Reprints).

4. World War II and the Japanese Occupation (1941–1945)

Allen, Louis. *Burma: The Longest War 1941–1945.* London; Melbourne: J. M. Dent, 1984; London: J. M. Dent, 1986.

———. *Sittang: The Last Battle: The End of the Japanese in Burma, July-August 1945.* London: MacDonald and Company, 1973.

Anders, Leslie. *The Ledo Road: General Joseph W. Stilwell's Highway to China.* Norman, Oklahoma: University of Oklahoma Press, 1965.

Aung San. *Burma's Challenge 1946*. Yangon: New Light of Burma, 1946.

Aung San Suu Kyi. *Aung San of Burma: A Biographical Portrait by His Daughter*. 2d ed. Edinburgh: Kiscadale, 1991.

Ba Maw. *Breakthrough in Burma: Memoirs of a Revolution, 1939–1946*. Foreword by William C. Cornyn and Myint. New Haven, Connecticut; London: Yale University Press, 1968.

Ba Sein, Thakin. *Thakin mya Bama Lutlatyei Kyopamhmu* [The Struggle of the Thakins for Burma's Independence]. Yangon: Tainpyi, 1943.

Ba Than. *The Roots of the Revolution: A Brief History of the Defence Services of the Union of Burma and the Ideals for Which They Stand*. Yangon: Director of Information, 1962.

Baker, Alan D. *Merrill's Marauders*. New York: Ballantine Books, 1972.

Bečka, Jan. *The National Liberation Movement in Burma during the Japanese Occupation Period (1941–1945)*. Prague: Oriental Institute in Academia, Publishing House of the Czechoslovak Academy of Sciences, 1983. (Dissertationes Orientales, vol. 42).

———. "The Communists and the Anti-Fascist Resistance Movement in Burma (1942–1945)." Review Article, *Archív Orientální*, vol. 55, no. 3 (1987), pp. 284–87.

———. "The Dynamics of Burmese Liberation Movement During World War II," *The Oracle* (Calcutta), *A Quarterly Review of History, Current Affairs and International Relations*, vol. 2, no. 1 (January 1980), pp. 16–26.

———. "The Origin and Role of the National Armed Forces in Burma's Struggle for Freedom, 1941–1945," *Archív Orientální*, vol. 49, no. 4 (1981), pp. 344–363.

———. "Subhas Chandra Bose and the Burmese Freedom Movement" in *Netaji and India's Freedom*. Edited by Sisir K. Bose. Proceedings of the International Netaji Seminar. Calcutta, India: Netaji Bhawan, 1975, pp. 54–75.

Burma Intelligence Bureau. *Burma During the Japanese Occupation*. Simla, India: Government of India Press, 1943–44. 2 vols.

Callahan, Raymond. *Burma, 1942–1945*. London: Davis-Poynter, 1978. (The Politics and Strategy of the Second World War Series. Edited by Noble Frank and Christopher Dowling).

Calvert, Michael. *Chindits: Long Range Penetration*. London: Pan/Ballantine, 1974.

Chandra, Anil. *Indian Army Triumphant in Burma (The Burmese Campaign 1941–45)*. Delhi; Lucknow, India: Atma Ram, 1984.

Christian, John Leroy. *Burma and the Japanese Invader*. Foreword by Reginald Hugh Dorman-Smith. Bombay, India: Thacker, 1943.

Collis, Maurice. *Last and First in Burma (1941–1948)*. London: Faber and Faber, 1956.

Crew, F.A.E. *The Army Medical Services Campaigns: Vol. 5, Burma*. London: Her Majesty's Stationery Office, 1966. (History of the Second World War, United Kingdom Medical Series. Edited by Arthur S. MacNalty).

Cruickshank, Charles. *SOE in the Far East*. Oxford; New York: Oxford University Press, 1983.

Donnison, Frank Siegfried Vernon. *British Military Administration in the Far East, 1943–46*. London: Her Majesty's Stationery Office, 1956. (History of the Second World War, United Kingdom Military Series).

Dun, Smith. *Memoirs of the Four-Foot Colonel.* Introduction by David I. Steinberg. Ithaca, New York: Cornell University Southeast Asia Program, 1980. (Cornell University Southeast Asia Program Data Paper, no. 113).

Elsbree, Willard H. *Japan's Role in Southeast Asian Nationalist Movements, 1940–45.* Cambridge, Massachusetts: Harvard University Press, 1953.

Fellowes-Gordon, Ian. *Amiable Assassins: The Story of the Kachin Guerillas of North Burma.* London: Robert Hale, 1957.

———. *The Magic War; The Battle for North Burma.* New York: Scribner, 1972.

Fergusson, Bernard. *Return to Burma.* London: Collins, 1962.

Guyot, Dorothy Hess. *The Political Impact of the Japanese Occupation of Burma.* Ph.D. Dissertation, Yale University, 1966.

———. "The Burma Independence Army: A Political Movement in Military Garb" in *Southeast Asia in World War II; Four Essays.* Edited by J. Silverstein. New Haven, Connecticut: Yale University Southeast Asia Program, 1966, pp. 51–65.

Hla Pe. *U Hla Pe's Narrative of the Japanese Occupation of Burma.* Recorded by U Khin. Foreword by Hugh Tinker. Ithaca, New York: Cornell University Southeast Asia Program, 1961. (Cornell University Southeast Asia Program Data Paper, no. 41).

Izumiya, Tatsuro. *The Minami Organ.* Translated by Tun Aung Chain. Yangon: Universities' Press, for Translation and Publications Department, Higher Education Department, 1981.

Jones, F. C. *Japan's New Order in East Asia. Its Rise and Fall 1937–1945.* London: Oxford University Press, 1954.

Khin Myo Chit. *Three Years under the Japs*. Yangon: The Author, 1945.

Kirby, Stanley Woodburn. *The War Against Japan*. London: Her Majesty's Stationery Office, 1957–69. 5 vols. (History of the Second World War, United Kingdom Military Series. Edited by James Butler).

Lebra, Joyce C. *Japanese-Trained Armies in Southeast Asia: Independence and Volunteer Forces in World War II*. Hong Kong: Heinemann Educational Books (Asia); New York: Columbia University Press, 1977.

McKelvie, Roy. *The War in Burma*. London: Methuen, 1948.

Matthews, Geoffrey. *The Re-Conquest of Burma 1943–1945*. Aldershot, England: Gale and Polden, 1966.

Morrison, Ian. *Grandfather Longlegs: The Life and Gallant Death of Major H. P. Seagrim*. London: Faber and Faber, 1947.

Mountbatten of Burma, The Earl. *Report to the Combined Chiefs of Staff by the Supreme Commander, South-East Asia, 1943–1945*. London: Her Majesty's Stationery Office, 1951. New York: Philosophical Library, 1951.

Nu, U. *Burma Under the Japanese. Pictures and Portraits*. Edited and Translated with Introduction by J. S. Furnivall. London: Macmillan, 1954; New York: St. Martin's Press, 1954.

Ogburn, Charlton. *The Marauders*. New York: Quill, 1982. (Reprint).

On Kin. *Burma Under the Japanese*. With Additional Chapter by Brother Patrick. Lucknow, India: Lucknow Publishing House, 1947.

Owen, Frank. *The Campaign in Burma*. London: His Majesty's Stationery Office, 1946.

Pearn, Bertie Reginald. *The Burman: 1939–1944*. London: India-Burma Association, 1945.

Peers, William R. and Dean Brelis. *Behind the Burma Road*. Boston, Massachusetts: Little Brown, 1963; London: Robert Hale, 1964.

Prasad, Bishawar, gen. ed. *Official History of the Indian Armed Forces in the Second World War*. Calcutta, India: Combined Inter-Services Historical Section (India and Pakistan), 1944–59. 5 vols.

Sein, U, Bandoola. *Kyanyok to Atwinyei* [Our Internal Affairs]. Yangon: Yanponhlwin, 1946. 2 vols.

Selth, Andrew. "Race and Resistance in Burma, 1942–1945," *Modern Asian Studies*, vol. 20 (July 1986), pp. 483–507.

Slim, William Joseph. *Defeat into Victory*. London: Cassell, 1956; London: Papermac, 1986.

Smyth, John. *Before the Dawn: The Story of Two Historic Retreats*. London: Cassell, 1957.

Stilwell, Joseph Warren. *The Stilwell Papers*. Arranged and Edited by Theodore H. White. With Introduction by J. F. C. Fuller. London: Macdonald, 1949.

Tarling, Nicholas. " 'An Empire Gem': British Wartime Planning for Post-War Burma," *Journal of Southeast Asian Studies*, vol. 13, no. 2 (September 1982), pp. 310–48.

———. " 'A New and Better Cunning': British Wartime Planning for Post-War Burma," *Journal of Southeast Asian Studies*, vol. 13, no. 1 (March 1982), pp. 33–59.

Taylor, Robert H. *Marxism and Resistance in Burma 1942–1945: Thein Pe Myint's Wartime Traveller*. Athens, Ohio: Ohio University Press, 1984. (Southeast Asia Translation Series, vol. 4).

———. "Burma in the Anti-Fascist War" in *Southeast Asia Under Japanese Occupation*. Edited by Alfred W. McCoy. New Haven, Connecticut: Yale University Southeast Asia Studies, 1980, pp. 132–57. (Yale University Southeast Asia Studies Monograph Series no. 22.

Than Daing, Bo. *Lutlatyei Ayeidawbon Hmattan* [An Account of the Independence Struggle]. Yangon: Sarpay Beikman, 1967. 2 vols.

Thein Hpei Myin (Thein Pe Myint). *Mahameit hnin Bama Seitaman* [Burmese Envoy and the Allies]. Yangon: U Thain Tin, 1962.

———. *Sis Atwin Hkayithe* [Wartime Traveller]. 3rd ed. Yangon: Bagan, 1963.

Thein Pe (Myint). *What Happened in Burma*. Allahabad, Pakistan: Kitabistan, 1943.

Tin Mya, Thakin. *Bon Bawa hma hpyin* [In This Communist World]. Yangon: Bagan, 1971.

———. *Hpekhsit Tawhlanyei Htanakyok hnin Taing Hse Taing* [The Headquarters of the Anti-Fascist Revolution and Ten Zones of Resistance]. 2d ed. Yangon: Pyilonkyut, 1968.

Tun Ok, Thakin. *Kyanyok i Sunsahkan*. [My Adventures]. 2d ed. Yangon: Kyonpyaw, 1964.

Tun Pe. *Sun Over Burma*. Yangon: Rasika Ranjani, 1949.

Yoon, Won Zoon. *Japan's Scheme for the Liberation of Burma: The Role of the Minami Kikan and the "Thirty Comrades"*. Athens, Ohio: Ohio University Center for International Studies, Southeast Asia Program, 1973. (Papers in International Studies, Southeast Asia Series, no. 27).

Ziegler, Philip. *Mountbatten of Burma: The Official Biography*. London: William Collins, 1985.

5. Post-Independence (1948–)

Chit Maung, Thakin, Widura. *Lutlatyei Yapinauk Myanma Pyi* [Post-Independence Myanmar]. Yangon: Bagan, 1969.

Tinker, Hugh. *The Union of Burma: A Study of the First Years of Independence.* 4th rev. ed. London: Oxford University Press, Issued Under the Auspices of the Royal Institute of International Affairs, 1967.

V. LAW AND CONSTITUTION

Aye Kyaw. "Status of Women in Family Law in Burma and Indonesia," *Special Burma Studies Issue*, vol. 4, no. 1 (Fall 1988), *Crossroads: An Interdisciplinary Journal of Southeast Asian Studies*, Northern Illinois University, pp. 100–120.

Bečka, Jan and Alan Gledhill. "Burma" in *International Encyclopedia of Comparative Law. Volume I. National Reports.* Edited by V. Knapp, J. C. B. Mohr, and Paul Siebeck. Tubingen, The Hague, Paris: Mouton [1971], pp. 77–90.

The Constitution of the Socialist Republic of the Union of Burma. Yangon: Printing and Publishing Corporation, 1974.

The Constitution of the Union of Burma. Yangon: Superintendent, Government Printing and Stationery, 1954 (Reprint).

E Maung, U. *Burmese Buddhist Law.* Yangon: New Light of Burma Press, 1937; Yangon: Daw Than Tint Mya Sapay, 1970.

Fleischmann, Klaus. *Die Neue Verfassung der Union von Birma: Vorgeschichte, Inhalte, Wirklichkeit.* Hamburg: Institut für Asienkunde, 1976. (Mitteilungen des Instituts für Asienkunde, Nummer 82).

Forchhammer, Emil. *The Jardine Prize: An Essay on the Sources and Development of Burmese Law from the Era of the First Introduction of the Indian Law to the Time of the British Occupation of Pegu, With Text and Translation of King Wagaru's Manu Dhammathatham*. Yangon: Government Press, 1885.

Furnivall, John Sydenham. "Manu in Burma," *Journal of the Burma Research Society*, vol. 30, pt. 2 (1940), pp. 351–70.

Hooker, Michael Barry. *A Concise Legal History of Southeast Asia*. Oxford: Clarendon, 1978.

———. *Islamic Law in South-East Asia*. Singapore; Oxford: Oxford University Press, 1984.

———. "The 'Chinese Confucian' and the 'Chinese Buddhist' in British Burma 1881–1947," *Journal of Southeast Asian Studies*, vol. 21, no. 2 (September 1990), pp. 384–401.

Htin Aung. *Burmese Law Tales: The Legal Element in Burmese Folk-Lore*. London: Oxford University Press, 1962.

Jardine, John. *Notes on Buddhist Law*. By [John Jardine] the Judicial Commisioner, British Burma. Yangon: Office of the Superintendent, Government Printing and Stationery, 1883–1965. 8 vols.

Kyaw Win, Mya Han and Thein Hlaing. *Taingyintha Lumyo mya Ayei hnin 1947 Acheihkan Upadei*. [The Nationalities Issue and 1947 Constitution.] Yangon: Yangon University, 1990. 2 vols.

Kyin Swi. "The Origin and Development of the Dhammathats," *Journal of the Burma Research Society*, vol. 49, pt. 2 (1966), pp. 173–205.

Maung Maung (Dr.). *Burma in the Family of Nations*. 2d ed., rev. and enl. Amsterdam: Djambatan; New York: Institute of Pacific Relations, 1957.

———. *Burma's Constitution*. Foreword by John S. Furnivall. Rev. ed. The Hague: Martinus Nijhoff, 1961.

———. *Law and Custom in Burma and the Burmese Family*. The Hague: Martinus Nijhoff, 1963.

Moscotti, Albert D. *Burma's Constitution and Elections of 1974*. Singapore: Institute of Southeast Asian Studies, 1977.

Okudaira, Ryuji. "The Burmese Dhammathat" in *The Laws of South-East Asia: Vol. 1, The Premodern Texts*. Edited by Barry Michael Hooker. Singapore: Butterworth, 1986.

Pyihtaungsu Hsoshelit Thammata Myanma Naingngantaw Hpwetsipon Akhyeihkan Upadei hnin Patthet thaw Adeippe Shinlinhkyet mya. [Explanatory Points Regarding the Constitution of the Socialist Republic of the Union of Burma]. Yangon: Burma Socialist Programme Party, Printing and Publishing Corporation, 1973.

Taylor, Robert H. "Burma's National Unity Problem and the 1974 Constitution," *Contemporary Southeast Asia*, vol. 3, no. 3 (December 1979), pp. 232–48.

VI. POLITICS

1. Domestic

Amnesty International. *Burma: Extrajudicial Execution and Torture of Members of Ethnic Minorities*. London: Amnesty International, 1988.

———. *Myanmar (Burma): Continuing Killings and Ill-Treatment of Minority Peoples*. London: Amnesty International, 1991.

———. *Myanmar (Burma): Prisoners of Conscience, A Chronicle of Developments Since September 1988*. London: Amnesty International, 1989.

———. *Myanmar "In the National Interest": Prisoners of Conscience, Torture, Summary Trials Under Martial Law*. London: Amnesty International, 1990.

———. *Some Concerns about the Ill-Treatment, Torture and Killing of Members of Indigenous Populations: Oral Statement*. London: Amnesty International, 1988.

———. *Thailand: Concerns about Treatment of Burmese Refugees*. London: Amnesty International, 1991.

Aung San Suu Kyi. *Freedom from Fear and Other Writings*. New York: Viking, 1991; Calcutta, India: Penguin Books, 1991.

———. "The True Meaning of Boh," *Asian Survey*, vol. 31, no. 9 (September 1991), pp. 793–797.

Aye Saung. *Burman in the Back Row: Autobiography of a Burmese Rebel*. Hong Kong: Asia 2000; Bangkok, White Lotus, 1989. (Burma Reader Series.)

Ba Swe. *The Burmese Revolution*. Yangon: Union of Burma, Information Department, 1952.

———. *Guide to Socialism in Burma*. Yangon: Government Printing, 1956.

Badgley, John H. *Politics among Burmans: A Study of Intermediary Leaders*. Athens, Ohio: Ohio University Center for International Studies, 1970. (Southeast Asia Series no. 15).

———. "Burma's Political Crisis," *Pacific Affairs*, vol. 31 (1958), pp. 336–51.

———. "Burmese Communist Schisms" in *Peasant Rebellion and Communist Revolution in Asia*. Edited by John Wilson Lewis. Stanford, California: Stanford University Press, 1974, pp. 151–68.

———. "The Communist Parties of Burma" in *The Communist*

Revolution in Asia. Edited by Robert A. Scalapino. Englewood Cliffs, New Jersey: Prentice Hall, 1965, pp. 290–308.

Bečka, Jan. "Buddhist Revival in Post-Independence Burma: A Study of Interaction of Religion and Politics (1948–1962)" in *Religion and Society in India and Burma.* Edited by Stanislava Vavroušková. Prague: Oriental Institute of the Czechoslovak Academy of Sciences, 1991, pp. 7–32.

———. "The Ideological Aspects of Buddhist 'Revival' in Burma (1948–1962)," *Archív Orientální,* vol. 58, no. 4 (1990), pp. 337–53.

———. "The Military and the Struggle for Democracy in Burma: The Presentation of the Political Upheaval of 1988 in the Official Burmese Press," *Archív Orientální,* vol. 61, no. 1 (1993), pp. 63–80.

———. "Military Rule in Burma. A Political Analysis of General Ne Win's Revolutionary Council, 1962–1969," *Courrier de l'Extrême Orient* (Bruxelles), no. 37 (1970), Centre d'Etude du Sud Est Asiatique et de l'Extrême Orient.

Belanger, Francis W. *Drugs, the US and Khun Sa.* Bangkok: Editions Duong Kamal, 1987.

Bless, Roland. *Divide et Impera? Britische Minderheitenpolitik in Burma 1917–1948.* Stuttgart: Steiner, 1990.

Boucaud, André and Louis Boucaud. *Burma's Golden Triangle: On the Trail of the Opium Warlords.* Translated from the French by Diana-Lee Simon. Revised and Edited by Lesley D. Clark. Hong Kong: Asia 2000; Bangkok: Pacific Rim, 1988. (Burma Reader Series).

Burma Communist Party's Conspiracy to Take Over State Power. Yangon: Ministry of Information, 1989.

Burma Socialist Programme Party. *The Constitution of the Burma Socialist Programme Party for the Transitional Period of Its*

Construction. Adopted by the Revolutionary Council [on] July 4, 1962. Yangon: Burma Socialist Programme Party, 1962.

——. *The Specific Characteristics of the Burma Socialist Programme Party*. Yangon: Sarpay Beikman Press, 1964.

——. *The System of Correlation of Man and His Environment. The Philosophy of the Burma Socialist Programme Party*. Yangon: The Burma Socialist Programme Party, January 1963.

Butwell, Richard *U Nu of Burma*. 2d ed. Stanford, California: Stanford University Press, 1969.

——. "Civilians and Soldiers in Burma" in *Studies on Asia, 1961*. Edited by Robert K. Sakai. Lincoln, Nebraska: University of Nebraska Press, 1961, pp. 74–85.

Cady, J. F. *Political Institutions of Old Burma*. Ithaca, New York: Cornell University, Department of Far Eastern Studies, April 1954. (Cornell University Southeast Asia Program Data Paper, No. 12).

Chit Maung, Thakin. *Bama Pyi Nainnganyei Hmattan*. [An Account of Burma's Politics]. Yangon: Bama Pyi Alokthama Pati, 1959.

Clements, Alan. *Burma: The Next Killing Fields?* Berkeley, California: Odonian Press, 1992.

Donnison, Frank Siegfried Vernon. *Public Administration in Burma: A Study of Development During the British Connexion*. London and New York: Royal Institute of International Affairs. Published in Cooperation with the International Secretariat, Institute of Pacific Relations, 1953.

Falla, Jonathan. *True Love and Bartholomew: Rebels on the Burmese Border*. Cambridge, England: Cambridge University, 1991.

Fenichel, Allen and Afzar Khan. "The Burmese Way to Socialism" in *Socialist Models of Development.* Edited by C. K. Wiber and K. P. Jameson. Oxford: Pergamon, 1982, pp. 813–24.

Fistié, Pierre. *La Birmanie ou la quête de l'unité: le problème de la cohesion nationale dans la Birmanie contemporaine et sa perspective historique.* Paris: Ecole Française d'Extrême Orient, 1985. (Publications de l'Ecole Française d'Extrême Orient, vol. 139).

Fleischmann, Klaus. *Die Kommunistische Partei Birmas: von den Anfangen bis zur Gegenwart.* Hamburg: Institut für Asienkunde, 1989. (Mitteilungen des Instituts für Asienkunde Hamburg, no. 171).

———, ed. *Documents on Communism in Burma 1945–1977.* Hamburg: Institut für Asienkunde, 1989. (Mitteilungen des Instituts für Asienkunde Hamburg, no. 172).

Furnivall, John Sydenham. *The Governance of Modern Burma.* 2d ed. New York: Institute of Pacific Relations, International Secretariat, 1960.

Guyot, James F. "Bureaucratic Transformation in Burma" in *Asian Bureaucratic Systems Emergent from the British Imperial Tradition.* Edited by Ralph Braibanti. Durham, North Carolina: Duke University Press, 1966, pp. 354–443.

International Human Rights Law Group. *Post-Election Myanmar: A Popular Mandate Withheld.* Washington, D.C.: International Human Rights Law Group, 1990.

Khin Maung Gyi. *Patterns of Accommodation to Bureaucratic Authority in a Transitional Culture: A Sociological Analysis of Burmese Bureaucrats with Respect to Their Orientation Towards Authority.* Ph.D. Dissertation, Cornell University, Ithaca, New York, 1966.

Kin Aung. "Political Opposition in Burma, 1948–1981," *Journal of Asian Affairs,* vol. 9 (1984), pp. 86–116.

Kyaw Thet. "Burma: The Political Integration of Linguistic and Minority Groups" in *Nationalism and Progress in Free Asia*. Edited by Philip W. Thayer. Baltimore: Johns Hopkins, 1956, pp. 156–68.

Lawyers Committee for Human Rights. *Burma: The International Response to Continuing Human Rights Violations.* New York: Lawyers Committee for Human Rights, February 1992.

———. *Burma (Myanmar): Response to the Statement of the Union of Myanmar to the UN General Assembly.* New York: Lawyers Committee for Human Rights, October 15, 1992.

———. *Summary Injustice. Military Tribunals in Burma (Myanmar).* New York: Lawyers Committee for Human Rights, 1991.

Lehman, Frederick K., ed. *Military Rule in Burma Since 1962: A Kaleidoscope of Views.* Singapore: Maruzen Asia, Issued under the Auspices of the Institute of Southeast Asian Studies, 1981.

Lei Maung. *Myanma Naingnganyei Thamaing.* [History of Myanmar's Politics]. Yangon: Sarpay Beikman, 1974. 2 vols.

Lim, Joo-Jook and S. Vani, eds. *Armed Separatism in Southeast Asia.* Singapore: Regional Strategic Studies Programme, Institute of Southeast Asian Studies, 1984.

Ling, Trevor. *Buddhism, Imperialism and War. Burma and Thailand in Modern History.* London: George Allen and Unwin, 1979.

Lintner, Bertil. *Aung San Suu Kyi and Burma's Unfinished Renaissance.* Clayton, Australia: Center of Southeast Asian Studies, Monash University, 1990.

———. *Cross-Border Drug Trade in the Golden Triangle* (S.E.

Asia). Durham, England: Boundaries Research Press, for International Boundaries Research Unit, Department of Geography, University of Durham, 1991. (International Boundaries Research Unit, Territory Briefing, no. 1).

——. *Land of Jade: A Journey Through Insurgent Burma*. Edinburgh: Kiscadale Publications; Bangkok: White Lotus, 1990.

——. *Outrage: Burma's Struggle for Democracy*. London: White Lotus UK; Bangkok: White Lotus, 1990. rev. ed.

——. *The Rise and Fall of the Communist Party of Burma (CPB)*. Ithaca, New York: Southeast Asia Program, Cornell University, 1990. (Southeast Asia Program Series, no. 6).

——. "Heroin and Highland Insurgency in the Golden Triangle" in *War on Drugs. Studies in the Failure of U.S. Narcotics Policy*. Edited by Alfred W. McCoy and A. Alan Block. Boulder, San Francisco and Oxford: Westview, 1992, pp. 281–317.

——. "The Shans and the Shan States of Burma," *Contemporary Southeast Asia*, vol. 5, no. 4 (March 1984), pp. 403–50.

Lissak, Moshe. *Military Roles in Modernization: Civil-Military Relations in Thailand and Burma*. Beverly Hills, California; London: Sage, 1976.

McCoy, Alfred W. *The Politics of Heroin in Southeast Asia*. New York: London: Harper and Row, 1972.

Matthews, Bruce. "The Problem of Communalism in Contemporary Burma and Sri Lanka," *International Journal*, Toronto, vol. 34, no. 3 (Summer 1979), pp. 430–42.

Maung Maung. *Political Developments in Burma, 1962–1974*. Dissertation. Jawaharlal Nehru University, New Delhi, 1984.

Maung Maung Gyi. *Burmese Political Values: The Socio-Political Roots of Authoritarianism*. New York: Praeger, 1983.

Mehden, Fred R. von der. *Religion and Nationalism in Southeast Asia (Burma, Indonesia, The Philippines)*. Madison: University of Wisconsin Press, 1963.

———. "Politics and the Military in Burma" in *The Military and Politics in Five Developing Countries*. Edited by J. P. Lovell. Kensington, England: 1970, pp. 203–33.

Ministry of Defence, Union of Burma. *The National Ideology and the Role of Defence Services*. Yangon: Ministry of Defence, 1959.

Moksha Yitri. "The Crisis in Burma: Back from the Heart of Darkness?," *Asian Survey*, vol. 29, no. 6 (June 1989), pp. 543–58.

Mya Maung. "The Burma Road from the Union of Burma to Myanmar," *Asian Survey*, vol. 30, no. 6 (June 1990), pp. 602–24.

The Nine Months After Ten Years: The Caretaker Government, November 1958-July 1959. Yangon: Ministry of Information, 1959.

Nu, U. *Saturday's Son: Memoirs of the Former Prime Minister*. Translated by Law Yone. Edited by Kyaw Win. New Haven, Connecticut; London: Yale University Press, 1975.

Pye, Lucian W. *Asian Power and Politics: the Cultural Dimensions of Authority*. Cambridge, Massachusetts; London: Harvard University Press, 1985.

———. *Burma: Opening on the Left in the Military Manner*. Cambridge, Massachusetts: Massachusetts Institute of Technology, Center for International Studies, June 1963.

———. *Politics, Personality and Nation Building: Burma's Search for Identity*. New Haven, Connecticut: Yale University Press, 1962.

Reynolds, Frank E. and Regina T. Clifford. "Sangha, Society and the Struggle for National Interpretation: Burma and Thailand" in *Transitions and Transformations of the History of Religions. Essays in Honor of Joseph M. Kitagawa.* Edited by Frank E. Reynolds and Theodore M. Ludwig. Leiden: Brill, 1980, pp. 56–88.

Sarkisyanz, Emmanuel. *Buddhist Backgrounds of the Burmese Revolution.* The Hague: Martinus Nijhoff, 1965.

———. "Buddhist Backgrounds of Burmese Socialism" in *Religion and Legitimation of Power in Thailand, Laos and Burma.* Edited by Bardwell L. Smith. Chambersburg, Pennsylvania: Anima, 1978.

Saw Maung, General. *State Law and Order Restoration Council Chairman, Commander-in Chief of the Defence Services, Senior General Saw Maung's Addresses.* Yangon: Ministry of Information, 1990–1991. 3 vols.

Sein Win. *The Split Story: An Account of Recent Political Upheaval in Burma with Emphasis on AFPFL.* Yangon: The Guardian, 1959.

Selth, Andrew. *Death of a Hero: The U Thant Disturbances in Burma, December 1974.* Nathan, Australia: Centre for the Study of Australian-Asian Relations, Griffith University, 1989. Australia-Asia Papers no. 49.

Shwe Lu Maung. *Burma, Nationalism and Ideology: An Analysis of Society, Culture and Politics.* Dhaka, Bangladesh: [Dhaka] University Press, 1989.

Silverstein, Josef. *Burma: Military Rule and the Politics of Stagnation.* Ithaca, New York; London: Cornell University Press, 1977.

———. *Burmese Politics: The Dilemma of National Unity.* New Brunswick, New Jersey: Rutgers University Press, 1980.

——— ed. *The Future of Burma in Perspective: A Symposium.* Edited, with Introduction by Josef Silverstein. Athens, Ohio:

Ohio University Center for International Studies, Southeast Asia Program, 1974. (Papers in International Studies, Southeast Asia Series, no. 35).

———. ed. *Independent Burma at Forty Years: Six Assessments.* Ithaca, New York: Cornell University Southeast Asia Program, 1989.

———. "Civil War and Rebellion in Burma," *Journal of Southeast Asian Studies*, vol. 21, no. 1 (March 1990), pp. 114–34.

———. "Minority Problems in Burma Since 1962" in *Military Rule in Burma Since 1962. A Kaleidoscope of Views.* Edited by F. K. Lehman. Singapore: Maruzen Asia, Issued under the Auspices of the Institute of Southeast Asian Studies, 1981, pp. 29–51.

Sirisimpundh, Kasem. *Emergence of the Modern National State in Burma and Thailand.* Ph.D. Dissertation, The University of Wisconsin, 1962.

Sitte, Fritz. *Rebellenstaat im Burma-Dschungel.* Graz, Vienna, Cologne: Styria, 1979.

Smith, Bardwell L., ed. *Religion and Legitimation of Power in Thailand, Laos and Burma.* Chambersburg, Pennsylvania: Anima Books, 1978.

Smith, Charles B. *The Burmese Communist Party in the 1980s.* Singapore: Institute of Southeast Asian Studies, Regional Strategic Studies Programme, 1984.

Smith, Donald Eugene. *Religion and Politics in Burma.* Princeton, New Jersey: Princeton University Press, 1965.

Smith, Martin. *Burma: Insurgency and the Politics of Ethnicity.* London: Zed Books, 1991.

Steinberg, David I. *The Future of Burma: Crisis and Choice in Myanmar.* Lanham, Maryland; New York; London: University Press of America and the Asia Society, 1990. (Asian Agenda Report 14).

———. "Burma Under the Military: Towards a Chronology," *Contemporary Southeast Asia*, vol. 3, no. 3 (December 1981), pp. 244–85.

———. "Constitutional and Political Bases of Minority Insurrections in Burma" in *Armed Separatism in Southeast Asia*. Edited by Lim Joo-Jock and Vani Shanmugaratnam. Singapore: Institute of Southeast Asian Studies, 1984, pp. 49–80. (Issues in Southeast Asian Security).

Tatmadaw Researcher. *A Concise History of Myanmar and the Tatmadaw's Role, 1948–1988*. Yangon: News and Periodicals Enterprise, 1991.

Taylor, Robert H. *The State in Burma*. London: C. Hurst; Honolulu: University of Hawaii Press; Hyderabad, Pakistan: Orient Longman, 1987.

———. "Burma" in *Military-Civilian Relations in South-East Asia*. Edited by Zakaria Haji Ahmad and Harold Crouch. Singapore; Oxford; New York: Oxford University Press, 1985, pp. 13–49.

———. "Burma-Giving a Brief Introduction to Burmese Political History and Political Parties" in *Political Parties of Asia and the Pacific*. Edited by Haruhiro Fukui. Westport, Connecticut; London: Greenwood Press, 1985, pp. 99–154.

———. "Burma: Political Leadership, Security, Perceptions and Policies" in *Leadership Perceptions and National Security: the Southeast Asian Experience*. Edited by Mohammed Ayoob and Chai Samudavanija. Singapore: Regional Strategic Studies Programme, Institute of Southeast Asian Studies, 1989, pp. 205–23.

———. "Burma's Ambiguous Breakthrough," *Journal of Democracy*, vol. 1, no. 4 (Fall 1990), pp. 52–71.

———. "The Burmese Communist Movement and Its Indian Connection: Formation and Factionalism," *Journal of Southeast Asian Studies*, vol. 14, no. 1 (March 1983), pp. 95–108.

———. "The Burmese Concepts of Revolution" in *Context Meaning and Power in Southeast Asia*. Edited by Mark Hobart and Robert H. Taylor. Ithaca, New York: Cornell University Southeast Asia Program, 1986, pp. 79–92.

———. "The Evolution of Burmese Political Thought-1900s to 1940s" in *Proceedings Seventh IAHA Conference*, vol. 2 (22–26 August 1977), Bangkok: Chulalongkorn University, 1977, pp. 795–812.

———. "Government Responses to Armed Communist and Separatist Movements" in *Governments and Rebellions in Southeast Asia*. Edited by Chandran Jeshurun. Singapore: Institute of Southeast Asian Studies, 1984, pp. 103–25.

———. "Perceptions of Ethnicity in the Politics of Burma," *Southeast Asian Journal of Social Science*, vol. 10, no. 1 (1982), pp. 7–22.

———. "An Undeveloped State: The Study of Modern Burma's Politics" in *Sociology of "Developing Societies": Southeast Asia*. Edited by John G. Taylor and Andrew Turton. London: Macmillan, 1988, pp. 33–47.

Than Myint, U. "Prospects for Change in Burma," *Burma Review*, no. 20 (October 1990), pp. 26–7, 31.

Thomas, John Seabury. "Marxism in Burma" in *Marxism in Southeast Asia: A Study of Four Countries*. Edited by Frank N. Trager. Stanford, California: Stanford University Press; London: Oxford University Press, 1960, pp. 14–57.

Tin Maung Maung Than. "The Sangha and Sasana in Socialist Burma," *Sojourn, Social Issues in Southeast Asia*, vol. 3, no. 1 (February 1988), pp. 26–61.

Wiant, Jon A. "Insurgency in the Shan State" in *Armed Separatism in Southeast Asia.* Edited by Joo-Jock Lim and Vani Shanmugaratnam. Singapore: Institute of Southeast Asian Studies, 1984, pp. 81–107. (Issues in Southeast Asian Security).

——. "Tradition in the Service of Revolution: The Political Symbolism of *Taw-hlan-ye khit*" in *Military Rule in Burma Since 1962. A Kaleidoscope of Views.* Edited by F. K. Lehman. Singapore: Maruzen Asia, Issued under the Auspices of the Institute of Southeast Asian Studies, 1981, pp. 59–73.

Wiant, Jon A. and David I. Steinberg. "Burma: The Military and National Development" in *Soldiers and Stability in Southeast Asia.* Edited by J. Soedjati Djiwandono and Yong Mun Cheong. Singapore: Institute of Southeast Asian Studies, 1988, pp. 293–321.

Win, Kanbawza. *A Burmese Perspective Daw Aung San Suu Kyi, the Nobel Prize Laureate.* Bangkok: CPDSK Publications, 1992.

The Working People's Daily: Collected Articles. Yangon: Guardian Press, News and Periodicals Enterprise of Ministry of Information, 1988. 8 vols.

Yawnghwe, Tzang Chao (Thaik, Eugene). *The Shan of Burma: Memoirs of a Shan Exile.* Singapore: Institute of Southeast Asian Studies, 1987. (Local History and Memoirs, no. 6).

2. Foreign Relations

Bandyopadhyaya, Kalyani. *Burma and Indonesia: Comparative Political Economy and Foreign Policy.* New Delhi; Madras: South Asian Publishers, 1983.

Bečka, Jan. "Burma and the Non-Aligned: A Retrospect," *The Non-Aligned World* (New Delhi), no. 4 (1983), pp. 533–39.

Bert, Wayne. "Chinese Policy Toward Democratization Movements: Burma and the Philippines," *Asian Survey*, vol. 30, no. 11 (November 1990), pp. 1066–83.

Bingham, June. *U Thant of Burma: The Search for Peace*. London: Victor Gollancz, 1966; New York: A. Knopf, 1966.

Burma Socialist Programme Party. *Foreign Policy of the Revolutionary Government of the Union of Burma*. 2d ed. Yangon: Burma Socialist Programme Party, Central Committee Headquarters, 1973.

Desai, W. S. *India and Burma*. Bombay: Orient Longman, 1954.

Fleischmann, Klaus. *Arakan: Konfliktregion zwischen Birma und Bangladesh*. Hamburg: Institute für Asienkunde, 1981. (Mitteilungen des Instituts für Asienkunde, no. 121).

———. *Birma zwischen der Sowjetunion und der Volksrepublik China*. Cologne: Bundesinstitut für Ostwissenschaftliche und Internationale Studien, 1977.

Government of the Union of Burma. *Kuomintang Aggression against Burma*. Yangon: Ministry of Information, Government of the Union of Burma, 1953.

Johnstone, William Crane. *Burma's Foreign Policy: A Study in Neutralism*. Cambridge, Massachusetts: Harvard University Press, 1963.

———, comp. *A Chronology of Burma's International Relations 1945–1958*. Yangon: Rangoon-Hopkins Center for Southeast Asian Studies, Yangon University, 1959.

Kozicki, Richard Joseph. *India and Burma, 1937–1957: A Study in International Relations*. Ph.D. Dissertation, University of Pennsylvania, Philadelphia, 1959.

Liang, Chi Shad. *Burma's Foreign Relations: Neutralism in Theory and Practice*. New York: Praeger, 1990.

Maung Maung Gyi. "Foreign Policy of Burma Since 1962: Negative Neutralism for Group Survival" in *Military Rule in Burma Since 1962. A Kaleidoscope of Views*. Edited by F. K. Lehman. Singapore: Maruzen Asia, Issued under the Auspices of the Institute of Southeast Asian Studies, 1981, pp. 9–29.

Misra, K. P. "Burma's Farewell to the Nonaligned Movement," *Asian Affairs*, vol. 12, pt. 1 (February 1981), pp. 49–56.

Mookherji, Sudhansu Bimal. *Burma and the West*. Agra, India: Ranjan Prakashan, 1975.

Nassif, Ramses. *U Thant in New York 1961–1971: A Portrait of the Third UN Secretary-General*. London: C. Hurst, 1988.

Parker, Edward Harper. *Burma with Special Reference to Her Relations with China*. Yangon: Rangoon Gazette Press, 1893.

Pettman, Ralph. *China in Burma's Foreign Policy*. Canberra: Australian National University Press, 1973. (Contemporary China Papers, no. 7).

Singh, Uma Shankar. *Burma and India 1948–1962: A Study in the Foreign Policies of Burma and India and Burma's Policy Towards India*. New Delhi: Oxford and IBH, 1979.

———. "Burma's Foreign Policy in the Seventies," *India Quarterly*, vol. 34, no. 3 (July-September 1978), pp. 347–64.

Sola, Richard. "Le Non-Alignment Birman," *L'Afrique et l'Asie Modernes*, no. 153, (Éte 1987), pp. 68–84.

Taylor, Robert H. *Foreign and Domestic Consequences of the KMT Intervention in Burma*. Ithaca, New York: Cornell University Southeast Asia Program, 1973. (Cornell University Southeast Asia Program Data Papers, no. 93).

———. "Burma's Foreign Relations since the Third Indochina Conflict" in *Southeast Asian Affairs 1983*. Institute of Southeast Asian Studies. Aldershot, England: Gower, 1983, pp. 102–14.

Than Han, Daw. *Common Vision: Burma's Regional Outlook.* Washington, D.C.: Institute for the Study of Diplomacy, Georgetown University, 1988 (Occasional Paper, Georgetown University, Institute for the Study of Diplomacy, School of Foreign Service).

Tin Maung Maung Than. "Burma's National Security and Defence Posture," *Contemporary Southeast Asia*, vol. 11, no. 1 (June 1989), pp. 40–60.

Win, Kanbawza. "An Epilogue on Burma-American Relations: A Burmese Perspective," *Asian Perspective*, vol. 10, no. 2 (Fall-Winter 1986), pp. 311–31.

Yambem, Sanamani. *Indo-Burmese Relations up to the Emergence of Military Rule in Burma.* M. Phil. Dissertation, Jawaharlal Nehru University, School of International Studies, New Delhi, 1973.

Young, Kenneth Ray. *Nationalist Chinese Troops in Burma: Obstacles in Burma's Foreign Relations 1949–1961.* Ph.D. Dissertation: New York University, 1970.

VII. SCIENCE

1. Botany

Biswas, Kalipada and C. C. Calder. *Hand-Book of Common Water and Marsh Plants of India and Burma, 1936.* 2d ed. Dehra Dun, India: Bishen Singh Mahendra Pal Singh, 1984.

Collet, Henry and W. Botting Hemsley. *Collection of Plants from Upper Burma and the Shan States.* Dehra Dun, India: Bishen Singh Mahendra Pal Singh, 1979.

Davis, John Henry. *The Forests of Burma.* Bronx, New York: New York Botanical Gardens, 1964.

Desraj, V. *Some Common Burmese Timbers and Other Relevant Information.* Yangon: Student Press, 1961.

Grant, Bartle. *The Orchids of Burma (Including the Andaman Islands)*. Yangon: Hanthawaddy Press, 1895; Dehra Dun, India: Bishen Singh Mahendra Pal Singh, [1976].

Harbinson, Rod. "Burma's Forests Fall Victim to War," *The Ecologist*, vol. 22, no. 2 (1992), pp. 72–3.

Hundley, H. G. and Chit Ko Ko. *List of Trees, Shrubs, Herbs, and Principal Climbers, etc. Recorded from Burma: With Vernacular Names*. 3rd rev. ed. Yangon: Superintendent, Government Printing and Stationery, 1961.

Kingdon-Ward, Francis. *Plant Hunting on the Edge of the World: Travels of a Naturalist in Assam and Upper Burma*. London: Minerva, 1974.

Kurz, Sculpiz. *Forest Flora of British Burma*. Calcutta, India: Office of the Superintendent of Government Printing, 1877; Dehra Dun, India: Bishen Singh Mahendra Pal Singh and Periodical Experts, Delhi, 1974. 2 vols.

Morehead, Frederick Thomas. *The Forests of Burma*. London: Longmans, 1944.

Nath, Mohinder. "Botanical Survey of the Southern Shan States; with a Note on the Vegetation of the Inle Lake," Yangon: *Burma Research Society Fiftieth Anniversary Publications*, no. 1 (1961), pp. 157–418.

Perry, Lily M. *Medical Plants of East and Southeast Asia: Attributed Properties and Their Uses*. With the Assistance of Judith Metzger. Cambridge, Massachusetts; London: MIT Press, 1980.

Rhind, D. *The Grasses of Burma*. Calcutta, India: American Mission Press, 1945.

San Khin and Tha Myat, eds. *Some Medicinal and Useful Plants, Both Indigenous and Exotic, of Burma*. Yangon: Student Press, 1970.

Whitmore, T. C. *Tropical Rain Forests of the Far East*. 2d ed. Oxford: English Language Book Society/Oxford University Press, 1986.

2. Climate

Bennett, Don C. *Temperature Change with Elevation in Burma: A Study*. Bloomington, Indiana: Indiana University Foundation Research Division, 1962.

Huke, Robert H. *Rainfall in Burma*. Hanover, New Hampshire: Dartmouth College, 1966.

3. Geography and Geology

Ahmad, Nafis. *Economic Resources of the Union of Burma*. Natick, Massachusetts: Earth Sciences Laboratory, US Army Natick Laboratories, 1971. (Technical Report 71-61-ES, Series ES-70).

Bender, Friedrich. *Geology of Burma*. With Contributions by Dietrich Bannert, Jorn Brinckmann, Franz Graman, and Dietrich Helmcke. Berlin: Borntraeger, 1983. (Beiträge zur Regionalen Geologie der Erde, vol. 16).

Bradshaw, E. J. *Organizations and Functions of the Burma Geological Department*. Yangon: Superintendent, Government Printing and Stationery, 1948.

Burma, Earth Sciences Research Division. *Geological Map of the Socialist Republic of the Union of Burma*, 1977.

Burma, Survey Department Drawing Office. *The Socialist Republic of the Union of Burma*. 4th ed. [Yangon]: The Office, [1984]. 1 map, col., 10 x 102 x 55 cm.

Chhibber, Harbans Lal. *The Geology of Burma*. London: Macmillan, 1934.

——. *The Mineral Resources of Burma.* London: Macmillan, 1934.

——. *The Physiography of Burma.* London: Longmans, Green, 1933; New York: AMS Press, 1975.

Clegg, E. L. G. *The Mineral Deposits of Burma.* Bombay: Times of India Press, 1944.

Fell, R. T. *Early Maps of South-East Asia.* Singapore; Oxford; New York: Oxford University Press, 1988. (Images of Asia).

Fisher, Charles A. *South-East Asia: A Social, Economic and Political Geography.* 2d ed. London: Methuen, 1966.

Garson, Magnus S., B. J. Amos, and A. H. G. Mitchell. *The Geology of the Area Around Neyaungga and Yengan, Southern Shan States, Burma.* London: H. M. Stationery Office, 1976.

Krishnan, Maharajpuram Sittaram. *Geology of India and Burma.* 5th ed. Madras, India: Higginbothams, 1968.

Pascoe, Edwin Hall. *The Oil Fields of Burma.* Calcutta: Geological Survey of India; London: Kegan Paul Trench, Trübner, 1912. (Geological Survey of India, Memoirs, vol. 40, pt. 1).

Penzer, Norman Mosley. *The Mineral Resources of Burma.* London: George Routledge; New York: E. P. Dalton, 1922.

Tourist Map of Mandalay. Scale [ca 1:29,000]. Yangon: Tourist Burma, 1985.

Tourist Map of Rangoon. Scale [ca 1:29,000]. Yangon: Tourist Burma, 1985.

Ulack Richard and Gyula Pauer. *Atlas of Southeast Asia.* New York: Macmillan; London: Collier Macmillan, 1989.

United States Board on Geographic Names. *Burma: Official Standard Names Approved by the United States Board on Geo-*

graphic Names. Washington, D.C.: Department of the Interior, Office of Geography, 1966. (Gazetteer no. 96).

4. Zoology

Blanford, William Thomas, C. T. Bingham et al., ed. *The Fauna of British India, Including Ceylon and Burma*. London: Taylor and Francis, 1888-[1950]. Multi-vols.

Evans, Griffith H. *Elephants and Their Diseases: A Treatise on Elephants*. Reprint. Yangon: Superintendent, Government Printing and Stationery, 1961.

Jayaram, K. C. *The Freshwater Fishes of India, Pakistan, Bangladesh, Burma and Sri Lanka. Handbook*. Calcutta, India: Zoological Survey of India, 1981.

King, Ben and Edward C. Dickinson. *The Collins Field Guide to the Birds of South-East Asia*. Illustrated by Martin W. Woodcock. Lexington, Massachusetts: Stephen Greene Press, 1988.

Peacock, Edgar Henry. *A Game-Book for Burma and Adjoining Territories: The Types, Distribution and Habits of Large and Small Game, Together with Notes on Game Preservation, Photography, Tracking, Still-Hunting and the Care and Measurement of Trophies*. London: H. F. and G. Witherby, 1933; New Delhi: International Books and Periodicals Supply Service, 1985.

Pocock, Robine, Dorothy Silkstone Richards, Moira Swift, and Vic Watson. *The Burmese Cat*. London; Sydney: B. T. Batsford, 1975.

Smythies, Betram Evelyn. *The Birds of Burma*. Edinburgh; London: Oliver and Boyd, 1953; 2d ed. Dehradun, India: International Book Distributors, 1984.

Toke Gale. *Burmese Timber Elephant*. Yangon: Trade Corporation, 1974.

Tun Yin. *Wild Animals of Burma*. Yangon: Rangoon Gazette, 1967.

VIII. Society

1. Anthropology and Ethnology

Anderson, John. "The Selungs of the Mergui Archipelago" in *Contributions to the Fauna of Mergui and Its Archipelago*. Compiled by John Anderson. London: Taylor and Francis, 1889.

Bareigts, André. *Les lautu: contribution à l'étude de l'organisation sociale d'une ethnie chin de Haute-Birmanie*. Paris: SELAF, 1981. (Langues et Civilisations de l'Asie du Sud-Est et du Monde Insulindien, 11).

Barua, S. N. *Tribes of Indo-Burma Border. A Socio-Cultural History of the Inhabitants of the Patkai Range*. New Delhi: Mittal, 1992.

Baruah, Tapan Kumar M. *The Singhpos and Their Religion*. Shillong, India: Director of Information and Public Relations, Government of Arunachal Pradesh, 1977.

Bernard, Patrick and Michel Huteau. *Karennis: les combattants de la spirale d'or*. Paris: L'Harmattan, 1988.

Bunker, Alonzo. *Sketches from the Karen Hills*. New York; London: Fleming H. Revell, 1910.

Carey, Bertram Sausmarez and H. N. Tuck. *The Chin Hills: A History of the People, Our Dealings with Them, Their Customs and Manners, and a Gazetteer of Their Country*. Yangon: Superintendent, Government Printing, 1896; Delhi: Cultural Publication House, 1983. 2 vols.

Carrapiett, W. J. S. *The Kachin Tribes of Burma, for the Information of Officers of the Burma Frontier*. Yangon: Government Printing, 1929.

Chakravarti, Nalini Ranian. *The Indian Minority in Burma: The Rise and Decline of an Immigrant Community.* With a Foreword by Hugh Tinker. London: Oxford University Press, 1971.

Cochrane, Wilbur Willis. *The Shans.* Yangon: Superintendent, Government Printing, 1915; New York: AMS, 1981.

Colquhoun, Archibald Ross. *Amongst the Shans.* London: Field and Tuer; Simpkin, Marshall; New York: Scribner and Welford, 1885.

Cuming, E. D. *With the Jungle Folk. A Sketch of Burmese Village Life.* London: Osgood, McIvaine, 1897.

Desai, W. S. "The Karens of Burma," *Indian Quarterly*, vol. 6 (July-September 1950), pp. 276–82.

Enriquez, Colin Metcalf Dallas. *Races of Burma.* Calcutta, India: Government of India Central Publication Department, 1924; Delhi: Manager of Publications, 1933; New York: AMS Press, 1981.

Gilhodes, C. *The Kachins: Religion and Customs.* Calcutta, India: Catholic Orphan Press; London: Kegan Paul, Trench, Trübner, 1922.

Halliday, Robert. *The Talaings.* Yangon: Superintendent, Government Printing, 1917.

Hamilton, James W. *Pwo Karen: The Edge of Mountain and Plain.* St. Paul, Minnesota: West Publication Company, 1976.

Hanson, Ola. *The Kachins: Their Customs and Traditions.* Yangon: American Baptist Mission Press, 1913; New York: AMS, 1982.

Kammerer, Cornelia Ann. "Customs and Christian Conversion

Among Akha Highlanders of Burma and Thailand," *American Ethnologist*, vol. 17 (May 1990), pp. 227–91.

Kondapi, Chenchal. *Indians Overseas, 1938–1949*. New Delhi: Indian Council of World Affairs, 1951.

Koop, John Clement. *The Eurasian Population in Burma*. New Haven, Connecticut: Yale University Southeast Asia Studies, 1960.

Kunstadter, Peter, ed. *Southeast Asian Tribes, Minorities and Nations*. Princeton, New Jersey: Princeton University Press, 1967.

Lalthangliana, B. *History of Mizo in Burma*. Aizawl, Mizoram, India: Zawlbuk Agencies, 1980.

Leach, Edmund Ronald. *Political Systems of Highland Burma: A Study of Kachin Social Structure*. London: G. Bell, 1954; London: Athlone, 1981.

———. *Rethinking Anthropology*. London: University of London, Athlone, 1961.

Le Bar, Frank M., Gerald C. Hickey and John K. Musgrave. *Ethnic Groups of Mainland Southeast Asia*. New Haven, Connecticut: Human Relations Area Files, 1964.

Lehman, Frederick K. *The Structure of Chin Society: A Tribal People of Burma Adapted to a Non-Western Civilization*. Urbana, Illinois: University of Illinois Press, 1963. (Illinois Studies in Anthropology, no. 3)

———. "Internal Inflationary Pressures in the Prestige Economy of the Feast of Merit Complex: the Chin and Kachin Cases from Upper Burma" in *Ritual, Power and Economy: Upland-Lowland Contrasts in Mainland Southeast Asia*. Edited by Susan D. Russell. De Kalb, Illinois: Northern Illinois University, Center for Southeast Asian Studies, 1989, pp. 89–102.

Lewis, Paul. *Ethnographic Notes on the Akhas of Burma*. New Haven, Connecticut: Hraflex, 1969–70. 4 vols. (Descriptive Ethnography Series).

Lewis, Paul and Elaine Lewis. *Peoples of the Golden Triangle: Six Tribes in Thailand*. London: Thames and Hudson, 1984.

Lowis, Cecil Champain. *A Note on the Palaungs of Hsipaw and Tawngpeng*. Yangon: Superintendent, Government Printing, 1906.

———. *The Tribes of Burma*. Yangon: Superintendent, Government Printing, 1910; Government Printing, 1919. (Ethnographical Survey of India: Burma no. 4).

McMahon, Alexander Ruxton. *The Karens of the Golden Chersonese*. London: Harrison, 1876.

Mahajani, Usha. *The Role of Indian Minorities in Burma and Malaya*. Westport, Connecticut: Greenwood, 1973.

Marshall, Harry Ignatius. *The Karen People of Burma: A Study in Anthropology and Ethnology*. Columbus, Ohio: Ohio State University Press, 1922; New York: AMS, 1980.

Milne, M. L. (Mrs. Leslie Milne). *The Home of an Eastern Clan: A Study of the Palaung of the Shan States*. Oxford: Clarendon, 1924.

———. *Shans at Home: With Two Chapters on Shan History and Literature* by the Rev. Wilbur Willis Cochrane. London: John Murray, 1910; New York: Paragon, 1970.

Mya Tu, Ko Ko, Aung Than Batu, Kywe Thein. C. J. R. Francis and Than Tun Aung Hlaing. *The Tarons of Burma: The Results of a Scientific Expedition*. Yangon: Burma Medical Research Institute, 1966.

Pearn, B. R. *The Indian in Burma*. Ledbury, Herefordshire, England: Le Play House, 1946.

Purcell, Victor. *The Chinese in Southeast Asia*. 2d ed. London; Kuala Lumpur; Hong Kong: Oxford University Press, under the Auspices of the Royal Institute for International Affairs, 1965.

Saimong, Mangrai, trans. *The Padaeng Chronicle and the Jengtung State Chronicle Translated*. Ann Arbor, Michigan: University of Michigan, Center for South and Southeast Asian Studies, 1981.

———. "Cula Sakaraja and the Sixty Cyclical Year Names," *Journal of the Siam Society*, vol. 69, pts. 1–2 (1981), pp. 4–12.

San, Crombie Po. *Burma and the Karens*. London: Elliot Stock, 1928.

Scott, James George. *Burma and Beyond*. London: Grayson and Grayson, 1932.

Spiro, Melford E. *Anthropological Other or Burmese Brother? Studies in Cultural Analysis*. New Brunswick and London: Transaction, 1992.

Stevenson, Henry Noel Cochrane. *Economics of the Central Chin Tribes*. Foreword by Reginald Hugh Dorman-Smith, Governor of Burma. Bombay: Times of India Press, [1943]; Farnborough, England: Gregg, 1968.

———. *The Hill People of Burma*. London: Longmans, Green, 1944.

Thompson, Virginia and Richard Adloff. *Minority Problems in Southeast Asia*. Stanford, California: Stanford University Press, Issued under the Auspices of International Secretariat, Institute of Pacific Relations, 1955.

Vum Ko Hau. *Profile of Burma Frontier Man*. Foreword by Dr. Maung Maung. Bandung, Indonesia: Kilatmadju, 1963.

Vumson. *Zo History, with an Introduction to Zo Culture, Economy, Religion and Their Status as an Ethnic Minority in India, Burma and Bangladesh*. Aizawl, India: The Author, 1987.

Whitehead, John. *Far Frontiers: People and Events in North-Eastern India, 1857–1947*. London: BACSA, 1989.

Wijeyewardene, Gekan. "The Theravada Compact and the Karens," *Sojourn*, vol. 2, no. 1. (February 1987), pp. 31–54.

2. Demography

Gunasekharan, S. and Mya Than. "Population Change in Burma: A Comparison of the 1973 and 1983 Censuses," *Sojourn*, vol. 3, no. 2 (August 1988), pp. 171–86.

Ismael Khin Maung, M. *The Population of Burma, An Analysis of the 1973 Census*. Honolulu: East-West Center, 1986. (Paper of the East-West Population Institute, no. 97).

———. "Cultural Pluralism and Urban Fertility Differentials in Postwar Burma," *Asian Profile* (Hong Kong), vol. 6, no. 5 (October 1978), pp. 423–53.

———. "Population Trends in Burma," *Southeast Asian Affairs* (1979), pp. 85–102.

Lubeight, Guy. "The Village of the Irrawaddy Valley in Central Burma," *Etudes Rurales*, January-December 1974. Translated in *Contemporary Burma and Thailand: French Scholarship; 1974–1984*. Compiled by H. S. Vasudevan. Calcutta, India: Calcutta University, Centre for Southeast Asian Studies, 1986. (Occasional Paper).

Sundrum, R. M. *Census Data on the Labour Force and the Income Distribution in Burma, 1953–54*. Yangon: Department of Economics, Statistics and Commerce, University of Yangon, 1957.

3. Education

Ba, Vivian. "The Beginnings of Western Education in Burma:

The Catholic Effort," *Journal of the Burma Research Society*, vol. 47, pt. 2 (December 1964), pp. 287–324.

Bagshawe, L. E. *A Literature of School Books: A Study of the Burmese Books Approved for Use in Schools by the Education Department in 1885, and of Their Place in the Developing Educational System in British Burma.* M. Phil. Thesis, University of London, 1976.

Birkelund, Palle. *Report on the Development of Burmese University and Research Libraries.* Paris: UNESCO, 1969.

Furnivall, John Sydenham. *Educational Progress in Southeast Asia.* New York: Institute of Pacific Relations, International Secretariat, 1943. (IPR Inquiry Series).

Gamble, William Keith. *An Analysis of Agricultural Education, Training and Personnel Requirements as a Basis for National Development in Burma.* Ph.D. Dissertation: Cornell University, Ithaca, New York, 1961.

Gelfand, Moris Arthur. *Report of the Survey of the Libraries of the University of Rangoon.* Yangon: University of Yangon, 1959.

Kaung, U. "The Beginning of Christian Missionary Education in Burma, 1600–1824," *Journal of the Burma Research Society*, vol. 20, pt. 2 (December 1930), pp. 59–75.

———. "1824–1853: Roman Catholic and Baptist Mission Schools," *Journal of the Burma Research Society*, vol. 21, pt. 1 (June 1931), pp. 1–12.

———. "A Survey of the History of Education in Burma Before the British Conquest and After," *Journal of the Burma Research Society*, vol. 46, pt. 2 (December 1963), pp. 1–124.

Ling, Trevor. "Buddhism and Education in Burma and Thailand," *Religion*, vol. 14, no. 1 (1984), pp. 53–66.

Nyi Nyi. "The Development of University Education in Burma,"

Journal of the Burma Research Society, vol. 47, pt. 1 (June 1964), pp. 11–76.

———. "The University of Rangoon. A Factual Survey." Part I-IV. *New Burma Weekly* (Yangon), vol. I, no. 8–12 (July 19, 1958 to August 16, 1958).

Tissinger, Richard M., L. C. Hernandez and Francis T. Fairey. *Report of the Mission to Burma, May 1951*. Paris: UNESCO, 1952.

Tun Lwin. "The Burmese Experience in University Education by Correspondence," *Bulletin of the UNESCO Regional Office of Education in Asia and Oceania*, vol. 19 (June 1978), pp. 150–63.

Win, Kanbawza. "Education in the Socialist Republic of the Union of Burma," *Asian and Pacific Quarterly of Cultural and Social Affairs*, vol. 16, no. 1 (1984), pp. 52–9.

4. Health

Anderson, Roy K. *Drug Smuggling and Taking in India and Burma*. Calcutta, India: Thacker, Spink, 1922.

Brant, Charles S. *Tadagale: A Burmese Village in 1950*. New York: Cornell University, 1954.

Burma (Union), Directorate of Health Services. *Guide to Rural Health Centre Work in Burma*. Yangon: Superintendent, Government Printing and Stationery, 1962.

Central Committee for Drug Abuse Control, Union of Burma. *Narcotics Report 1988*. Yangon: CCDAC, Ministry of Home and Religious Affairs, 1989.

Khin Maung Lwin and Mya Tu. *Handbook of Biological Data on Burma*. Yangon: Burma Medical Research Institute, 1967. (Special Report Series, no. 3).

Khin Maung Naing, Cho Nwe Oo and Tin Tin Oo. "A Study on the Aetiology of Endemic Goitre in Lowland Burma," *European Journal of Clinic Nutrition*, vol. 43 (October 1989), pp. 693–98.

Khin Maung Win, ed. *Current Trends in Medical Practices*. Yangon: Department of Medical Education, Ministry of Health, [1975].

Khin Tint. "Herbs That Cure", (Traditional Medicine of Burma), *Hemisphere*, vol. 26, no. 24 (January-February 1982), pp. 228–31.

MacDonald, Keith Norman. *The Practice of Medicine among the Burmese. Translated from Original Manuscripts, with an Historical Sketch of the Progress of Medicine from the Earliest Times*. Edinburgh: MacLachlan and Stewart, 1879; New York: AMS, 1979.

Maule, Robert B. "The Opium Question in the Federated Shan States, 1931–36: British Policy Discussion and Scandal," *Journal of Southeast Asian Studies*, vol. 23, no. 1 (March 1992), pp. 14–36.

Mya Than. "A Burmese Village Revisited" in *Seven Probes in Rural Southeast Asia: Socio-Economic and Anthropological*. Edited by Jan Barend Terwiel. Gaya, India: Centre for South East Asian Studies, 1979, pp. 1–15.

———. "Little Change in Rural Burma: A Case Study of Burmese Village (1960–1980)," *Sojourn*, vol. 2, no. 1 (February 1987), pp. 55–88.

Sein Hla, Maung. *Let Us All Together Prevent the Heroin Danger*. Yangon: Information and Broadcasting Department, Ministry of Information, Socialist Republic of the Union of Burma, 1981.

Tin Aye, Daw, David A. Sack and I. Kaye Wachsmuth. "Neonatal Diarrhea at a Maternity Hospital in Rangoon," *American Journal of Public Health*, vol. 81 (April 1991), pp. 480–1.

World Health Organization. *Collaboration in Health Development in South East Asia 1948–1988*. New Delhi: World Health Organization, Regional Office for South-East Asia, 1988.

5. Urbanization

Kyaw, Maung. *Structure of Coastal (Maritime) Urbanization Based on the Conditions of Burma-Tenasserim Coastal Region*. Poznan, Poland: Panstwowe Wydawn, Naukove, 1976.

Maung Lwin, Maung. *Burmese Urbanization: An Overview*. Nagoya, Japan: Economic Research Center, Faculty of Economics, Nagoya University, [1983].

———. *A Preliminary Study on Urban Informal Sector of Myanmar: The Case of Capital City Yangon*. Chikusa-Ku, Nagoya, Japan: Economic Research Center, Faculty of Economics, Nagoya University, 1991.

Naing Oo. "Urbanization and Economic Development in Burma," *Sojourn*, vol. 4, no. 2 (August 1989), pp. 233–60.

6. Religion

Ba, Vivian. "The Early Catholic Missionaries in Burma: A Study of the Manuscripts and the First Casting and Printing of Burmese Alphabets, Outline Grammar, and Catechism in 1776, from Latin, Italian, Portuguese and French Sources," *The Guardian Monthly* (Yangon), vol. 9 (August 1962), pp. 17–20; (September 1962), pp. 17–20; (October 1962), pp. 21–24; (November 1962), pp. 29–32; (December 1962), pp. 20–24.

Ba Khin. *What Buddhism Is*. Yangon: Vipassana Research Association, 1961.

Ba Shin. "The Coming of Islam to Burma Down to 1700 AD,"

Bulletin of the Burma Historical Commission, vol. 3 (1963), pp. 1–19.

Beasley, Ina. *Pagodas and Prisons: The Life of Ann Hasseltine Judson (1789–1826)*. London: LLRS Publications, 1982.

Bechert, Heinz. *Buddhismus, Staat und Gesselschaft in den Ländern des Theravada Buddhismus. Band 2: Birma, Kambodscha, Laos, Thailand*. Wiesbaden: Otto Harrassowitz, 1967.

———. "The Recent Attempt at a Reform of the Buddhist Sangha in Burma and Its Implications," *Internationales Asienforum: International Quarterly for Asian Studies*, vol. 20 (1989), pp. 303–24.

Bechert, Heinz and Richard Gombrich, eds. *The World of Buddhism*. London: Thames and Hudson, 1984.

Bekker, Sarah M. "Transformation of the Nats: The Humanization Process in the Depiction of the Thirty-Seven Lords of Burma," *Crossroads: An Interdisciplinary Journal of Southeast Asian Studies, Special Burma Studies Issue*, vol. 4, no. 1 (Fall 1988), pp. 40–5.

Brohm, John F. *Burmese Religion and the Burmese Religious Revival*. Ph.D. Dissertation; Cornell University, Ithaca, New York, 1957.

———. *Religion, Education and Public Information in Burma*. A Study by Associates for International Research, Inc., Washington, D.C.: George Washington University, Human Resources Research Office Library, January 14, 1955.

———. "Buddhism and Animism in a Burmese Village," *Journal of Asian Studies*, vol. 22 (February 1963), pp. 155–67.

Byles, Beuzeville. *Journey into Burmese Silence*. London: George Allen and Unwin, 1962.

Edwardes, Michael, ed. *A Life of the Buddha from a Burmese Manuscript*. London: Folio Society, 1959.

Fergusson, John P. *The Symbolic Dimensions of the Burmese Sangha*. Ph.D. Dissertation, Cornell University, Ithaca, New York, 1976.

——. "The Great Goddess Today in Burma and Thailand: An Exploration of Her Symbolic Relevance to Monastic and Female Roles" in *Mother Worship: Theme and Variations*. Edited by J. James Breston. Chapel Hill, North Carolina: University of North Carolina Press, 1982, pp. 283–303.

——. "The Quest for Legitimation by Burmese Monks and Kings: The Case of the Shwegyin Sect (19th-20th Centuries)" in *Religion and Legitimation of Power in Thailand, Laos and Burma*. Edited by Bardwell L. Smith. Chambersburg, Pennsylvania: Anima, 1978, pp. 66–86.

Fergusson, John P. and E. Michael Mendelsohn. "Masters of the Buddhist Occult: The Burmese Weikzas" in *Essays on Burma*. Edited by John P. Fergusson. Leiden, The Netherlands: E. J. Brill, 1981, pp. 62–80.

Hall, Fielding Harold. *The Hearts of Men*. London: Hutchinson, 1934.

Herbert, Patricia. *The Life of the Buddha*. London: British Library, 1993.

Houtman, Gustaaf. *Traditions of Buddhist Practice in Burma*. Ph.D. Thesis, University of London, 1990.

——. "The Noviation Ceremonial in Theravada Buddhist Burma. A 'Received' and an 'Interpreted' Version," *Research*, vol. 4, no. 1 (May 1984), pp. 50–76.

Howard, Randolph L. *Baptists in Burma*. Philadelphia: Judson Press, 1931.

Htin Aung. *Folk Elements in Burmese Buddhism.* London; Bombay; New York: Oxford University Press, 1962; Yangon: Buddha Sasana Council Press, 1975; Westport, Connecticut: Greenwood, 1978.

Htun Hmat Win. *The Initiation of Novicehood and the Ordination of Monkhood in the Burmese Buddhist Culture.* Yangon: Department of Religious Affairs, 1986.

Kawl Thang Vuta. *A Brief History of the Planting and Growth of the Church in Burma.* D. Miss. Dissertation, Fuller Theological Seminar, 1983.

Khin Khin Su. *The Acculturation of the Burmese Muslims.* M.A. Thesis, Yangon, Yangon University, 1960.

King, Winston L. *A Thousand Lives Away: Buddhism in Contemporary Burma.* Cambridge, Massachusetts: Harvard University Press, 1964.

Kyaw Min. *Introducing Buddhist Abhidhamma Meditation and Concentration.* Yangon: Department of Religious Affairs, 1979.

Lehman, F. K. "On the Vocabulary and Semantics of 'Field' in Theravada Buddhist Society" in *Essays on Burma.* Edited by John P. Fergusson. Leiden, The Netherlands: E. J. Brill, 1981, pp. 101–11.

Ling, Trevor. "Buddhism and Modern Society: The Social Application of Buddhist Humanism in Burma," *Bulletin of the Ramakhrishna Mission Institute of Culture*, vol. 36, no. 8 (August 1985), pp. 171–6.

———. "Religious Minorities in Burma in the Contemporary Period" in *Ethnic Conflict in Buddhist Societies: Sri Lanka, Thailand and Burma.* Edited by K. M. de Silva, Pensri Duke, Ellen S. Goldberg, and Nathan Katz. London: Pintner; Boulder, Colorado: Westview, 1988, pp. 172–86.

Luce, Gordon H. "The Advent of Buddhism in Burma" in *Buddhist Studies in Honour of I. B. Horner*. Edited by L. Cousins, A. Kunst and K. R. Norman. Dordrecht, Holland; Boston, Massachusetts: D. Reidel Publishing, 1974, pp. 119–138.

Mahasi Sayadaw. *The Satipatthana Vipassana Meditation*. Yangon: Department of Religious Affairs, 1979.

Mendelsohn, E. Michael. *Sangha and State in Burma: A Study of Monastic Sectarianism and Leadership*. Edited by John P. Fergusson. Ithaca, New York; London: Cornell University Press, 1975.

———. "The King of the Weaving Mountain," *Journal of the Royal Central Asian Society*, vol. 48 (1961), pp. 229–37.

———. "A Messianistic Buddhist Association in Upper Burma," *Bulletin of the School of Oriental and African Studies*, vol. 24 (1961), pp. 560–80.

———. "Observations on a Tour in the Region of Mount Popa, Central Burma," *France-Asie*, vol. 179 (1963), pp. 786–807.

———. "The Uses of Religious Scepticism in Modern Burma," *Diogenes*, vol. 41 (1963), pp. 94–116.

Nash, June C. "Living with Nats: An Analysis of Animism in Burma" in *Anthropological Studies in Theravada Buddhism*. Nash, Manning, et al., comp. New Haven, Connecticut: Yale University Southeast Asia Studies, 1966, pp. 117–36. (Yale University Southeast Asia Studies, Cultural Report Series, no. 13).

Nash, Manning. "Ritual and Ceremonial Cycle in Upper Burma" in *Anthropological Studies in Theravada Buddhism*. Nash, Manning, et al., comp. New Haven, Connecticut: Yale University Southeast Asia Studies, 1966, pp. 97–116. (Yale University Southeast Asia Studies, Cultural Report Series, no. 13).

Nu, U. *The Buddha*. Calcutta, India: The University of Calcutta, 1961.

Pearn, Bertie Reginald. *Judson of Burma*. London: Edinburgh House, 1962.

Purser, William Charles Bertrand. *Christian Missions in Burma*. London: Society for the Propagation of the Gospel in Foreign Parts, 1911.

Ray, Niharranjan. *An Introduction to the Study of Theravada Buddhism in Burma: A Study in Indo-Burmese Historical and Cultural Relations from the Earliest Times to the British Conquest*. Calcutta, India: Calcutta University Press, 1946.

———. *Sanskrit Buddhism in Burma*. Calcutta, India: University of Calcutta, 1936; Yangon: Buddha Sasana Council Press, [1970].

Robinson, Virgil E. *The Judsons of Burma*. Washington, D.C.: Review and Herald Publishing Association, 1966.

Rodrigue, Yves. *Nat-Pwe. Burma's Supernatural Culture*. Translated from the French by Roser Flotats. Gartmore, Stirlingshire, Scotland: Kiscadale Publications, 1992.

Schober, Julianne Sybille. *Paths to Enlightenment: Theravada Buddhism in Upper Burma*. Ph.D. Dissertation, University of Illinois at Urbana-Champaign, 1989.

———. "The Path to Buddhahood: The Spiritual Mission and Social Organization of Mysticism in Contemporary Burma," *Crossroads: An Interdisciplinary Journal of Southeast Asian Studies, Special Burma Studies Issue*, vol. 4, no. 1 (Fall 1988), pp. 13–30.

Shamsuddin, Ahmed. *Glimpses into the History of the Burmese and Chinese Muslims*, 1936–1978. Chittagong, Bangladesh: Sakina Shamsuddin Ahmed, 1978.

Slater, Robert Lawson. *Paradox and Nirvana: A Study of Religious Ultimates with Special Reference to Burmese Buddhism.* Chicago, Illinois: University of Chicago Press, 1951.

Spiro, Melford E. *Buddhism and Society: A Great Tradition and Its Burmese Vicissitudes.* 2d ed. Berkeley, California; Los Angeles, California; London: University of California Press, 1980.

——. *Burmese Supernaturalism: A Study in the Explanation and Reduction of Suffering.* 2d ed. Philadelphia: Institute for the Study of Human Issues, 1978.

Swearer, Donald K. *Buddhism and Society in Southeast Asia.* Chambersburg, Pennsylvania: Anima Books, 1981.

Tegenfeldt, Herman G. *A Century of Growth: The Kachin Baptist Church of Burma.* South Pasadena, California: William Carey Library, 1974.

Temple, Richard Carnac. *The Thirty-Seven Nats: A Phase of Spirit Worship Prevailing in Burma.* London: W. Griggs, 1906. Facsimile Reprint, 1991.

——. "A Native Account of the Thirty-Seven Nats: Being a Translation of a Rare Burmese Manuscript," *Indian Antiquary,* vol. 35 (1906), pp. 217–27.

Than Tun. *Essays on the History of Buddhism of Burma.* Edited by Paul Strachan. Whiting Bay, Scotland: Kiscadale, 1988.

——. "History of Buddhism in Burma, AD 1000–1300," *Journal of the Burma Research Society,* vol. 6, pts. 1–2 (December 1978), pp. 1–265.

Tin Maung Maung Than. "Sangha Reforms and Renewal of *Sasana* in Myanmar: Historical Trends and Contemporary Practice" in *Buddhist Trends in Southeast Asia.* Edited by Trevor Ling. Singapore: Institute of Southeast Asian Studies, Social Issues in Southeast Asia (ISEAS), 1993, pp. 6–63.

Trager, Helen F. *Burma Through Alien Eyes: Missionary Views of the Burmese in the Nineteenth Century*. New York: Frederick A. Praeger, 1966.

Yegar, Moshe. *The Muslims of Burma: A Study of a Minority Group*. Wiesbaden: Otto Harrassowitz, 1972. (Schriftenreihe des Südasien-Instituts der Universität Heidelberg).

———. "The Muslims in Burma" in *The Crescent in the East: Islam in Asia Major*. Edited by Raphael Izraeli. London: Curzon, 1982, pp. 102–39.

Zwalf, Wladimir, ed. *Buddhism: Art and Faith*. London: British Museum Publications, 1985.

7. Sociology

Bekker, Sarah M. "The Concept of *Anade*: Personal, Social and Political Implications" in *Essays on Burma*. Edited by John P. Fergusson. Leiden, The Netherlands: E. J. Brill, 1981, pp. 19–37.

Children of Burma: IYC Special Issue, 1979. Yangon: UNICEF, 1979.

Coleman, Eli, Philip Colgan and Louis Gooren. "Male Cross-Gender Behavior in Myanmar (Burma): A Description of the Adult," *Archives of Sexual Behavior*, vol. 21 (June 1992), pp. 313–21.

Denis, R. B. *Games and Children's Play*. Yangon: Burma Research Society, 1952.

Friedman, Jonathan. *System, Structure and Contradiction in the Evolution of 'Asiatic' Social Formations*. Copenhagen: National Museum of Denmark, 1979.

Guillon, Claude Delachet. *Daw Sein: Les Dix Milles Vies d'Une Femme Birmane*. Paris: Editions du Seuil, 1978.

Herbert, Patricia M. "Burma" in *The Encyclopaedia of Asian Cooking*. Edited by Jeni Wright. London: Octopus Books, 1980.

Khin Maung Kyi, U et al. *Process of Communication in Modernization of Rural Society: A Survey Report on Two Burmese Villages*. Yangon: Department of Research, Institute of Economics, 1972.

Nash, Manning. *The Golden Road to Modernity: Village Life in Contemporary* Burma. New York; London: John Wiley, 1965; Chicago; London: University of Chicago Press, 1973.

———. *Unfinished Agenda: The Dynamics of Modernization in Developing Nations*. Boulder, Colorado; London: Westview, 1984.

Renard, Ronald D. "Minorities in Burmese History," *Sojourn*, vol. 2, no. 2 (August 1987), pp. 255–71.

Spiro, Melford E. *Kinship and Marriage in Burma: A Cultural and Psychodynamic Analysis*. Berkeley, California; Los Angeles, California; London: University of California Press, 1977.

ABOUT THE AUTHOR

JAN BEČKA (M.A., Ph.D., Charles University, Prague), has been a researcher of the Oriental Institute of the Czechoslovak (now Czech) Academy of Sciences in Prague since 1964 and is currently Senior Research Fellow and Head of the Department of South Asia there. He lived in Myanmar as a student of the University of Yangon (1958–1960) and has since visited the country several times. He specializes in Myanmar's modern history and contemporary affairs. He has researched and published on the independence movement in Myanmar during the late British colonial period and in World War II. Another area of his interest is the impact of Buddhism and Marxism on modern Myanmar's political thought. In addition to articles in various scholarly journals and other writings, he is the author of *The National Liberation Movement in Burma during the Japanese Occupation Period (1941–1945)* (Academia Publishing House, Prague, 1983). The present volume builds on and develops his previous study of Myanmar.